Foundations of Mathematical Analysis

TERTIARY EDUCATION TRUST FUND
Book Development Project

The Tertiary Education Trust Fund (TETFund) has the mandate to establish and nurture Higher Education Book Development Project in Nigeria. Book scarcity has reached a crisis proportion in the country as evident not only in the quantity of books available, but also in the quality of locally produced books. Given the seriousness of the paucity of reading and learning materials in Nigeria's higher educational institutions, TETFund Book Development Project is designed to reactivate and *nurture research* and the publication of academic books and journals in hard and e-forms in Nigerian higher educational institutions, thereby empowering tertiary institutions in Nigeria to benefit from and contribute to knowledge production nationally and globally. Advancement in science and technology, especially ICT and the influence of globalization have profoundly transformed the context, form and scope of knowledge production that Nigerian higher educational institutions should be assisted to fully participate in and contribute to the global system of generating and disseminating knowledge. The uniqueness of the present intervention lies in the fact that through it, TETFund will assist Nigerian higher educational institutions to restore and sustain the capacity for academic publishing. The promotion of indigenous authorship and the resuscitation of local publishing of books are critical instruments in addressing the dearth of textbooks, including basic texts and specialized textbooks in various disciplines in Nigeria's higher educational institutions. Restoring the culture of indigenous authorship and the production of indigenous books would ensure the availability of books that address local needs and reflect familiar realities and experiences. The *book production* component *is one* of the three areas of intervention of the TETFund Book Development Project. The others are the *revitalization of academic publishing* and the support of academic journals.

This first phase of the book production intervention is directed at the production of peer-reviewed basic textbooks written by Nigerian academics for universities, polytechnics and colleges of education and specialized books in various subject areas as well as the publication as books of high quality PhD theses from Nigerian universities that have successfully gone through a rigorous assessment process. This would contribute to solving the problem of paucity of books in Nigeria's higher educational institutions.

Tertiary Education Trust Fund,
6, Zambezi Crescent, Off Aguiyi Ironsi Street,
Maitama, Abuja, Nigeria.

Foundations of Mathematical Analysis

C. E. Chidume
African University of Science and Technology,
Abuja, Nigeria.

Chukwudi O. Chidume
Department of Mathematics and Statistics,
Auburn University, Auburn, Alabama, USA.

IBADAN UNIVERSITY PRESS

2013

Ibadan University Press
Publishing House
University of Ibadan
Ibadan, Nigeria.

© 2013 C.E. Chidume
      Chukwudi O. Chidume

First Published 2013

All Rights Reserved

ISBN: 978-978-8456-32-2

To Ifeoma, Ada, KK and Okey.

Preface

This book is intended as a serious introduction to the study of *mathematical analysis*. In contrast to calculus, mathematical analysis does not involve formula manipulation, memorizing integrals or applications to other fields of science. No. It involves geometric intuition and *proofs* of theorems. It is *pure* mathematics! Given the mathematical preparation and interest of our intended audience which, apart from mathematics majors, includes students of statistics, computer science, physics, students of mathematics education and students of engineering, we have not given the axiomatic development of the real number system. However, we assume that the reader is familiar with sets and functions. This book is divided into two parts. **Part I** covers elements of mathematical analysis which include: the real number system, bounded subsets of real numbers, sequences of real numbers, monotone sequences, Bolzano-Weierstrass theorem, Cauchy sequences and completeness of $\mathbb{R}$, continuity, intermediate value theorem, continuous maps on $[a, b]$, uniform continuity, closed sets, compact sets, differentiability, series of nonnegative real numbers, alternating series, absolute and conditional convergence; and re-arrangement of series. The contents of Part I are adequate for a semester course in mathematical analysis at the 200 level. **Part II** covers Riemann integrals. In particular, the Riemann integral, basic properties of Riemann integral, pointwise convergence of sequences of functions, uniform convergence of sequences of functions, series of real-valued functions: term by term differentiation and integration; power series: uniform convergence of power series; uniform convergence at end points; and equicontinuity are covered. Part II covers the standard syllabus for a semester mathematical analysis course at the 300 level. The topics covered in this book provide a reasonable preparation for any serious study of higher mathematics. But for one to really benefit from the book, one must spend a great deal of time on it, studying the contents very carefully and attempting *all* the exercises, especially the miscellaneous exercises at the end of the book. These exercises constitute an important integral part of the book.

Each chapter begins with clear statements of the most important theorems of the chapter. The proofs of these theorems generally contain fundamental ideas of mathematical analysis. Students are therefore encouraged to study them very carefully and to *discover* these ideas.

We wish to thank: Dr. Habtu Zegeye, Dr. Aniefiok Udomene, Dr Ngalla Djite, Dr. E.U. Ofoedu, Jerry Ezeora and Ma'aruf Minjibir for their invaluable assistance in typesetting this book, drawing the figures and for their numerous suggestions.

Finally, we wish to thank immensely the Tertiary Education Trust Fund Board (TETFB) of the Federal Republic of Nigeria for financing the publication of this book.

C. E. Chidume; C. O. Chidume
Abuja, 2012.

Contents

Part I

Classical Analysis

CHAPTER 1

The Real Number System

1.1 Set of Real Numbers

In this chapter, we shall introduce the basic properties of the set that, in High School, is generally called the *x-axis*. This set is denoted in mathematical analysis by the letter $\mathbb{R}$ and is called *the set of real numbers*. It is the basis for all our study in this book. Members of $\mathbb{R}$ are called *real numbers*. In what follows, we shall denote the set of *natural numbers* by $\mathbb{N} = \{1, 2, 3, ...\}$. We shall also denote the set of *all integers* by $\mathbb{Z} = \{..., -2, -1, 0, 1, 2, ...\}$; and the set of *rational numbers (or fractions)* by $\mathbb{Q} = \{\frac{p}{q} : p, q \in \mathbb{Z}, q \neq 0\}$.

1.2 The order relation

In this section, we define an **order relation** $(<)$ with the following order axioms.

Axiom 1 (Tricotomy Law). For all $x, y \in \mathbb{R}$, **exactly one**

3

of the following three relations must hold:

$$(i)\ x = y;\ (ii)\ x < y;\ (iii)\ y < x.$$

It is conventional to agree that $x < y$ means $y > x$. Also, we write $x \leq y$ for $x < y$ or $x = y$. Similarly, $y \geq x$ means $y > x$ or $y = x$. Numbers $x \in \mathbb{R}$ such that $x > 0$ are called **positive**, and numbers $y \in \mathbb{R}$ such that $y < 0$ are called **negative**. The tricotomy axiom asserts that every real number other than zero is either positive or negative but never both, and zero is neither positive nor negative. Furthermore, the tricotomy axiom says that no numbers are neglected by the order relation.

We now introduce two more order relations.
Axiom 2. For all $x, y, z \in \mathbb{R}$,

$$x < y \text{ if and only if } x + z < y + z.$$

Axiom 3. For all $x, y \in \mathbb{R}$, if $x > 0$ and $y > 0$, then,

$$x + y > 0;\ xy > 0.$$

With these order axioms, we prove the following proposition.

Proposition 1.2.1 *For all $x, y \in \mathbb{R}$,*

(i) $x < y$ if and only if $x - y < 0$ if and only if $y - x > 0$.

(ii) If $x < y$ and $y < z$, then $x < z$.

Proof. $x < y$ if and only if $x + (-y) < y + (-y)$, (by Axiom 2), i.e.,

$$x < y \text{ if and only if } x - y < 0.$$

Moreover,

$$x - y < 0 \text{ if and only if } x - y + (y - x) < 0 + (y - x),$$

i.e.,

$$x - y < 0$$

if and only if

$$x - y + y - x < y - x$$

if only if

$$0 < y - x.$$

From the above inequalities, we obtain that

$$x < y \text{ if and only if } x - y < 0 \text{ if and only if } y - x > 0,$$

establishing (i).

To prove (ii), we use Axiom 3 as follows: Assume $x < y$ and $y < z$. This is the same as

$$y - x > 0 \text{ and } z - y > 0.$$

By Axiom 3, the sum of these two positive numbers is positive. Hence,

$$(y - x) + (z - y) > 0, \ i.e., \ z - x > 0, \ i.e., \ x < z. \quad \square$$

With proposition 1.2.1 proved, we can now use obvious statements such as these:

For all $x, y, z \in \mathbb{R}$,

(a) $x < y$ and $y \le z \Rightarrow x < z$.

(b) $x \le y$ and $y \le z \Rightarrow x \le z$,

and so on.

We shall also need the notion of *absolute value* of a real number. If $a \in \mathbb{R}$, we define the *absolute value of a*, denoted by $|a|$, by

$$|a| = \begin{cases} a & \text{if } a > 0, \\ 0 & \text{if } a = 0, \\ -a & \text{if } a < 0. \end{cases}$$

For example, $|-3| = 3$; $\ |3| = 3$, and so on. Intuitively, the absolute value of a represents the distance from 0 to a.

Some basic properties of the absolute value are given in the following theorem.

Theorem 1.2.2   (i) $|a| \geq 0$ *for all* $a \in \mathbb{R}$; $|a| = 0$ *if and only if* $a = 0$.

(ii) $|a| \leq \epsilon$ *if and only if* $-\epsilon \leq a \leq \epsilon$.

(iii) $|ab| = |a||b|$ *for all* $a, b \in \mathbb{R}$;

(iv) $|a + b| \leq |a| + |b|$ *for all* $a, b \in \mathbb{R}$.

Proof. (i) There are two cases. If $a \geq 0$, then $|a| = a \geq 0$. On the other hand, if $a < 0$, then $|a| = -a > 0$. In both cases, $|a| \geq 0$.

(ii) Since $a = |a|$ or $a = -|a|$, it follows that $-|a| \leq a \leq |a|$. Now, if $|a| < \epsilon$, then we have $-\epsilon \leq -|a| \leq a \leq |a| \leq \epsilon$. Conversely, suppose $-\epsilon \leq a \leq \epsilon$. If $a \geq 0$, then $|a| = a \leq \epsilon$. And if $a < 0$, then $|a| = -a \leq \epsilon$. In both cases, $|a| \leq \epsilon$.

(iii) Consider FOUR cases when a and b are both positive, both negative, or have opposite signs.

From the inequalities $-|a| \leq a \leq |a|$ and $-|b| \leq b \leq |b|$, we obtain that

$$-(|a| + |b|) \leq a + b \leq |a| + |b|.$$

This implies that $|a + b| \leq |a| + |b|$. $\square$

Remark 1.2.3 Condition (iv) of Theorem 1.2.2 is often called the **triangle inequality**. It roughly says that the length of any side of a triangle is less than or equal to the sum of the lengths of the other two sides. A useful variant of the triangle inequality is

$$\big||a| - |b|\big| \leq |a - b| \text{ for all } a, b \in \mathbb{R}.$$

EXERCISES 1.1

1. Prove that if $\epsilon > 0$ and $a, x \in \mathbb{R}$, then $|a - x| < \epsilon$ if and only if $x - \epsilon < a < x + \epsilon$.

2. Find all $x \in \mathbb{R}$ that satisfy the following inequalities:
   (i) $|4x - 3| \leq 11$ (ii) $|x - 2| > |x + 1|$
   (iii) $|2 - 5x| \leq 7$ (iv) $|x^2 - 4| < 5$
   (v) $|x| + |x + 2| < 5$ (vi) $|x| + |x + 2| + |2 - x| \leq 8$.

3. Prove that for all $a, b \in \mathbb{R}$,
$$\Big| |a| - |b| \Big| \leq |a - b|.$$

4. Prove that if $b \neq 0$, then $\left| \frac{a}{b} \right| = \frac{|a|}{|b|}$. (Hint: For any $x \in \mathbb{R}$, (i) $x > 0$ if and only if $\frac{1}{x} > 0$. (ii) $\frac{x}{y} > 0$ if and only if x and y are both positive or are both negative).

5. Show that for $a, b \in \mathbb{R}$,
$$|a - b| \geq |a| - |b|.$$
   (Hint: Write $a = (a - b) + b$).

6. Prove that for all $a, b, c \in \mathbb{R}$,
$$|a + b + c| \geq |a| - |b| - |c|.$$

7. Show that for all $a, b \in \mathbb{R}$,
   (i) $ab \leq \frac{1}{2}(a^2 + b^2)$
   (ii) $\left(\frac{a+b}{2} \right)^2 \leq (a^2 + b^2)$.
   (iii) $\sqrt{ab} \leq \frac{1}{2}(a + b)$, for $a, b \geq 0$ such that a and b have square roots.

8. Show that for all $a, b, c, d \in \mathbb{R}$, with $a, b, c, d \geq 0$,
   (i) $\sqrt{ab}\sqrt{cd} \leq \frac{1}{4}(a^2 + b^2 + c^2 + d^2)$.
   (ii) $(abcd)^{\frac{1}{4}} \leq \frac{1}{4}(a + b + c + d)$.

9. Solve the inequality $|x - \frac{1}{2}| > 1$.

10. Solve the inequality $|3x - 8| < 0.1$.

1.3 The natural numbers, $\mathbb{N}$

While we do not wish to develop the real number system, we will examine here the important subset of the real numbers consisting of the **natural numbers**: $1, 2, 3, \ldots$ (note that we have not included 0 as a natural number) and prove some of their basic properties. This will enable us to introduce the important concept of *mathematical induction.*

Recall that the set of real numbers $\mathbb{R}$ (your usual "x-axis") has numerous subsets. For example, the set of rational numbers, Q, is a subset of $\mathbb{R}$; the set $\mathbb{Z}$ of all integers is a subset of $\mathbb{R}$; the set $\mathbb{N}$ of natural numbers is a subset of $\mathbb{R}$, and so on. However, the set $\mathbb{N}$ of **natural numbers** is **the smallest** subset of $\mathbb{R}$ with the following two properties:

$P1$: 1 is in the set.

$P2$: $n + 1$ is in the set whenever n is in the set.

The two properties $P1$ and $P2$ are called **inductive properties.**

Fact 1. Suppose A and B are two sets that have the inductive properties and let

$$S = A \cap B.$$

Then, S has the inductive properties (verify).

Fact 2. Suppose $A_i, i = 1, 2, 3, \ldots$ is a family of sets with inductive properties and let

$$S = \bigcap A_i, i = 1, 2, 3, \ldots.$$

Then, S is the **smallest** such set , i.e., $S = \mathbb{N}$ (since $\mathbb{N}$ is the **smallest** set with the inductive properties).

From Facts 1 and 2, it is clear that **the smallest** set with the inductive properties exists and this shows that the definition of $\mathbb{N}$ as that smallest subset of $\mathbb{R}$ with inductive properties makes sense.

Recall that $S = \{1, 2, 3, .., 9\}$ is a subset of $\mathbb{N}$. We can denote these numbers as follows:

$$1 = 1+0$$
$$2 = 1+1$$
$$3 = 2+1$$
$$4 = 3+1$$
$$5 = 4+1$$
$$6 = 5+1$$
$$7 = 6+1$$
$$8 = 7+1$$
$$9 = 8+1.$$

The numbers $0, 1, 2, 3, 4, 5, 6, 7, 8, 9$ are called **units**. We shall assume, as is well known, that

$$0 < 1 < 2 < 3 < 4 < 5 < 6 < 7 < 8 < 9.$$

Theorem 1.3.1 (Mathematical induction- *the basis for arithmetic).*
(i) If $P(n)$ denotes a proposition that depends on n;
(ii) $P(1)$ is true; and
(iii) $P(n+1)$ is true whenever $P(n)$ is true.
Then,
$P(k)$ is true for all $k \in \mathbb{N}$.

Let us take a particular example to illustrate the ideas of this theorem.

Example 1.3.2 . *Prove that*

$$1 + 2 + 3 + ... + n = \frac{1}{2}n(n + 1).$$

Comparing this with the theorem, we have the following:
(i) $P(n)$ is $1+2+3+...+n = \frac{1}{2}n(n+1)$, a proposition which depends on n.
(ii) $P(1)$ means replacing n by 1 in $P(n)$. For this,

$$LHS = 1, \ RHS = \frac{1}{2}.1(1 + 1) = 1.$$

Hence, $P(1)$ is true.

(iii) This statement says $P(n+1)$ is true whenever $P(n)$ is true. This means we must **assume** $P(n)$ is true and then check whether or not $P(n+1)$ is true. So, assume $P(n)$ is true, i.e., **assume**

$$1 + 2 + 3 + \ldots + n = \frac{1}{2}n(n+1)$$

is true. We now want to check if $P(n+1)$ is true. But this is the same as checking if

$$1 + 2 + 3 + \ldots + n + (n+1) = \frac{1}{2}(n+1)\Big((n+1)+1\Big)$$

is true. To do this, we start with the LHS and see if we can get the RHS. Now,

$$\begin{aligned}
LHS &= 1 + 2 + 3 + \ldots + n + (n+1) \\
&= \frac{1}{2}n(n+1) + (n+1), \\
&\quad \text{(using our assumption that } P(n) \text{ is true)} \\
&= \frac{1}{2}(n+1)[(n+1)+1] = RHS.
\end{aligned}$$

Hence, $P(n+1)$ is true whenever $P(n)$ is. By the induction theorem, $P(k)$ is true for all $k \in \mathbb{N}$.

We now use **mathematical induction** to prove a basic arithmetic fact about the natural numbers, $\mathbb{N}$.

Proposition 1.3.3 *Every element of* $\mathbb{N}$ *is positive.*

Proof. Let $n \in \mathbb{N}$ be arbitrary. We want to prove: $n > 0$ holds. We already know that $1 > 0$. If we identify, $P(n) = n > 0$, we then have that $P(1)$ is true. Assume now $P(n)$ is true, i.e., that $n > 0$. We want to show $P(n+1)$ is true. But

$$P(n+1) = n + 1 > 0 + 1 \ (\text{ by using } P(n) = n > 0) = 1 > 0,$$

and so $P(n+1) = n+1 > 0$ whenever $P(n) = n > 0$. Hence, $P(k) = k > 0$ for all $k \in \mathbb{N}$. So, every natural number is positive. $\square$

We give more examples of proofs by induction.

Example 1.3.4 *Prove, by induction or otherwise, that $11^n - 8^n$ is a multiple of 3 for all $n \in \mathbb{N}$.*

Solution. For $n = 1$, $11^n - 8^n = 11 - 8 = 3$, and so, the result holds for $n = 1$. Assume now it holds for n, i.e., that $11^n - 8^n = 3t$ for some $t \in \mathbb{R}$. We want to prove it holds for $n + 1$, i.e., that $11^{n+1} - 8^{n+1}$ is a multiple of 3. But,

$$
\begin{aligned}
11^{n+1} - 8^{n+1} &= 11.11^n - 8.8^n \\
&= 11.11^n - 11.8^n + 11.8^n - 8.8^n \\
&= 11(11^n - 8^n) + (8^n(11 - 8)) \\
&= 33k + 3.8^n = 3(11k + 8^n).
\end{aligned}
$$

Thus, $11^n - 8^n$ is a multiple of 3, and so the result holds for $n + 1$. Hence, by induction, we conclude that it holds for all $n \in \mathbb{N}$.

Example 1.3.5 *(The Binomial Theorem) For any two numbers a and b and for any $n \in \mathbb{N}$,*

$$
\begin{aligned}
(a + b)^n &= a^n + na^{n-1}b + \frac{n(n-1)}{2!}a^{n-2}b^2 + \cdots \\
&\quad + \frac{n!}{(n-k)!k!}a^{n-k}b^k + \cdots + b^n.
\end{aligned}
\qquad (1.3.1)
$$

Proof. Observe that equation (1.3.1) has $(n+1)$ terms and that the coefficient of $a^{(n-k)}b^k$ is $\frac{n!}{(n-k)!k!}$ for $k = 0, 1, ..., n$ where $n!$ (n factorial) is defined inductively by

$$
0! = 1, \quad 1! = 1, \quad (n+1)! = (n+1)n!.
$$

For $n = 1$, there are 2 terms $a + b$ in equation (1.3.1) and the coefficient formula gives 1 for $k = 0$ and 1 for $k = 1$, i.e.,

$$\frac{1!}{(1-0)!0!} = 1, \quad \frac{1!}{(1-1)!1!} = 1.$$

So, the formula holds for $n = 1$. Assume now that equation (1.3.1) holds for some $n \in \mathbb{N}$. We calculate the coefficient of $a^{n+1-k}b^k$ in $(a+b)^{n+1}$. Now, the two terms involving $a^{n+1-k}b^k$ arise as $a \times \frac{n!}{(n-k)!k!}a^{n-k}b^k$ and $b \times \frac{n!}{(n-(k-1))!(k-1)!}a^{n-(k-1)}b^{k-1}$. It is easy to show (see Exercises 1.2, Problem 3) that

$$\frac{n!}{(n-k)!k!} + \frac{n!}{(n-(k-1))!(k-1)!} = \frac{(n+1)!}{(n+1-k)!k!},$$

which is the coefficient of $a^{n+1-k}b^k$ in $(a+b)^{n+1}$ in equation (1.3.1). The result follows by induction.

EXERCISES 1.2

1. Show that if S is a subset of natural numbers containing some given number N_0, and $n + 1 \in S$ whenever $n \in S$, then S contains all natural numbers.
   (**Hint.** Consider the set B that consists of S together with all natural numbers less than N_0).

2. Consider the following statement: For all $n \in \mathbb{N}, n > n + 3$. Call this $P(n)$. We show that $P(n + 1)$ is true whenever $P(n)$ is true. So, assume $P(n)$ is true, i.e., assume $n > n+3$. Then, this implies, $n+1 > n+1+3$ which implies $P(n + 1)$ is true. Hence, by induction, $n > n + 3$ for all $n \in \mathbb{N}$.
   We know this conclusion is false. What is wrong with the argument?

3. Prove that
   $$\frac{n!}{(n-k)!k!} + \frac{n!}{(n-(k-1))!(k-1)!} = \frac{(n+1)!}{(n+1-k)!k!}.$$

4. Prove by induction that the following identities and inequalities hold for all natural numbers n.

(i) $1^2 + 2^2 + 3^2 + ... + n^2 = \frac{1}{6}n(n+1)(2n+1)$.

(ii) $1^3 + 2^3 + 3^3 + ... + n^3 = \frac{1}{4}n^2(n+1)^2$.

(iii) $1^3 + 2^3 + 3^3 + ... + n^3 = (1 + 2 + 3 + ... + n)^2$.

(iv) $1 + r + r^2 + ... + r^n = \frac{1-r^{n+1}}{1-r}$, $r \neq 1$.

(v) $1 = 1^2$
$1 + 3 = 2^2$
$1 + 3 + 5 = 3^2$
$1 + 3 + 5 + 7 = 4^2$
$\vdots$
$1 + 3 + 5 + 7 + ... + (2n - 1) = n^2$.

(vi) $(1 + p)^n \geq 1 + np$, $p \geq 0$.

(vii) $2^n \geq n^2$, $n \geq 4$.

$(viii)$ $n! \geq 2^{n-1} \; \forall \; n \in \mathbb{N}$.

5. Use induction to prove *Bernoulli's inequality*. If $1+x > 0$, then,

$$(1 + x)^n \geq 1 + nx \; \forall \; n \in \mathbb{N}.$$

6. In the following, say whether the statement made is true or false. If it is true, prove it. If it is false, give a counter-example.
(i) $3^{2n} - 4$ is a multiple of 5.
(ii) $7^{2n} - 9$ is a multiple of 2.

1.4   Countable and Uncountable Sets

Definition 1.4.1 . *Two sets R and S are said to have the same* **cardinality** *(roughly speaking, same size) if there is a one-to-one and onto correspondence between them.*

If the sets R and S have the same cardinality, we shall denote this by $\#(R) = \#(S)$. We also observe that **having the same cardinality** defines an equivalence relation between sets.

Definition 1.4.2 . *A set S is said to be* **infinite** *if there exists a one-to-one correspondence between S and at least one of its* **proper** *subsets, or if there exists a proper subset of S, say A , such that $\#(A) = \#(S)$.*

Example 1.4.3   (i) The set $\mathbb{Z}$ of all integers is infinite since there is a one-to-one correspondence between $\mathbb{Z}$ and its **proper** subset S given as follows:

$$\mathbb{Z} = \{..., -3, -2, -1,\ 0,\ 1,\ 2,\ 3, ...\}$$
$$\updownarrow\ \ \updownarrow\ \ \updownarrow\ \ \updownarrow\ \ \updownarrow\ \ \updownarrow\ \ \updownarrow$$
$$S = \{..., 7,\ \ 5,\ \ \ 3,\ \ \ 1,\ 2,\ 4,\ 6, ...\}.$$

This correspondence can be written compactly as follows:

$$f(n) = \begin{cases} 2n, & \text{if } n \text{ is positive,} \\ -2n + 1, & \text{if } n \text{ is nonpositive .} \end{cases}$$

(ii) The set $S = (-1, 1)$ is an infinite set. To see this, we have to produce at least one *proper* subset of S which can be put in one-to-one correspondence with S. Take $R = (0, 1)$ and define

$$f : (0, 1) \to (-1, 1) \ \text{ by } \ f(x) = 2x - 1 \ \ \forall\ x \in (0, 1).$$

Then $f^{-1} : (-1, 1) \to (0, 1)$ is given by

$$f^{-1}(y) = \frac{1}{2}(y + 1) \ \ \forall\ y \in (-1, 1). \ \ \square$$

Definition 1.4.4 *A set S is called* **countable** *if and only if there is a one-to-one correspondence between S and the set of natural numbers,* $\mathbb{N}$.

Example 1.4.5 (i) Every **finite** set is clearly countable. (ii) The set $\mathbb{Z}$ of all integers is countable, i.e. $\#(\mathbb{Z}) = \#(\mathbb{N})$. The natural way to 'count' $\mathbb{Z}$ is to write $\mathbb{Z} = \{0, 1, -1, 2, -2, \ldots\}$. More precisely, it is easy to check that $f : \mathbb{N} \to \mathbb{Z}$ defined by

$$f(n) = \begin{cases} \frac{n}{2}, & \text{if } n \text{ is even,} \\[2mm] \frac{1-n}{2}, & \text{if } n \text{ is odd }, \end{cases}$$

is one-to-one and onto.

Remark 1.4.6 Since the set $\mathbb{Z}$ of integers is infinite and countable , we then say that $\mathbb{Z}$ is **countably infinite**.

Proposition 1.4.7 *The union of two countable sets is countable.*

Proof. Let A and B be two countable sets. So, each can be put in a one-to-one correspondence with $\mathbb{N}$. Consequently, we can write A and B as follows:

$$A = \{a_{11},\ a_{12},\ a_{13},\ a_{14},\ \ldots\},$$

$$\downarrow\nearrow\downarrow\quad\nearrow\quad\downarrow\nearrow\downarrow$$

$$B = \{b_{21},\ b_{22},\ b_{23},\ b_{24},\ \ldots\}.$$

Then $A \cup B = \{\underbrace{a_{11}, b_{21}}, \underbrace{a_{12}, b_{22}}, \underbrace{a_{13}, b_{23}}, \underbrace{a_{14}, b_{24}}, \ldots\}.$ $\square$

Proposition 1.4.8 *Let $\{A_n\}$ be a countable collection of countable sets. Then $\displaystyle\bigcup_{n=1}^{\infty} A_n$ is countable.*

Proof. Since each A_n is countable we have the following display:

$A_1 = \{a_{11}, a_{12}, a_{13}, \cdots\}, \quad A_2 = \{a_{21}, a_{22}, a_{23}, \cdots\},$
$A_3 = \{a_{31}, a_{32}, a_{33}, \cdots\}, \cdots, \quad A_n = \{a_{n1}, a_{n2}, a_{n3}, \cdots\}, \cdots.$
Then,

$$\bigcup_{n=1}^{\infty} A_n = \left\{ a_{11}; \underbrace{a_{21}, a_{12}}_{m+n=3}; \underbrace{a_{31}, a_{22}, a_{13}}_{m+n=4}; \underbrace{a_{41}, a_{32}, a_{23}, a_{14}}_{m+n=5}; \cdots \right\}$$

which is certainly in one-to-one correspondence with $\mathbb{N}$. $\quad\square$

Remark 1.4.9 Observe that in Proposition 1.4.8, each term in $\bigcup_{n=1}^{\infty} A_n$ contains only the a_{mn}'s for which the sum $m+n$ is the same. We only omit repeated terms. Proposition 1.4.8 actually says that "a countable union of countable sets is countable".

Proposition 1.4.10 *The set S of* **all** *sequences with coordinates either zeros or ones is uncountable.*

Proof. Assume, for contradiction, that S is countable. Let $S = \{s_1, s_2, s_3, \cdots\}$ where the s_i's can be listed (for example) as follows:

$$
\begin{aligned}
s_1 &= \{0, 1, 0, 0, 1, 1, 0, ...\} \\
s_2 &= \{1, 0, 0, 1, 1, 1, 0, 1, 1, 0, ...\} \\
s_3 &= \{1, 1, 1, 1, 1, 0, 1, 1, ...\} \\
s_4 &= \{0, 0, 0, 1, 1, 0, 0, ...\}
\end{aligned}
$$

.

.

.

We can always construct a sequence s^* from members of S as follows: s^* differs from s_i in the ith coordinate, $i = 1, 2, 3, ...$. For example, with s_1 to s_4 as above, we construct

$s^* = \{1, 1, 0, 0, ...\}$. Clearly, $s^* \neq s_i$, $\forall\ i = 1, 2, 3, ...$ But s^* has coordinates either zeros or ones. Hence $s^* \in S$. This contradiction shows that S is uncountable. $\square$

Proposition 1.4.11 *The set of rationals, $\mathbb{Q}$, is countable.*

(Hint: You may use the following result. **Proposition*** Let S be a nonempty subset of $\mathbb{R}$. Then, the following are equivalent:

(a) S is countable.
(b) There exists an injection $f : S \to \mathbb{N}$.
(c) There exists an onto map $g : \mathbb{N} \to S$.

Now, let Q^+ and Q^- denote the set of positive rationals and negative rationals, respectively. First, show that Q^+ is countable. Recall that any member of Q^+ can be written *uniquely* as $\frac{m}{n}$, where $m, n \in \mathbb{N}, n \neq 0$, and m and n have no common prime divisors. Define $f : Q^+ \to \mathbb{N}$ by $f\left(\frac{m}{n}\right) = 2^m \times 3^n$. Now, use Proposition* to show that Q^+ is countable. Since $Q = Q^- \cup \{0\} \cup Q^+$, apply Proposition 1.15 (two times) to conclude that Q is countable).

CHAPTER 2

Bounded Subsets of Real Numbers

2.1 Introduction

In this chapter we introduce the notion of the **infimum** or **greatest lower bound** (*glb* for short; also denoted by "inf") and that of the **supremum** or **least upper bound** (*lub* for short; also denoted by "sup") of a subset S of the real numbers, $\mathbb{R}$. These two concepts are, perhaps, the most important among those that characterize modern analysis.

2.2 Bounded Sets

Definition 2.2.1 *A subset S of real numbers is said to be* **bounded from below** *(or simply* **bounded below***) if there exists $\alpha \in \mathbb{R}$ such that*

$$\alpha \leq x \quad \text{for all} \ \ x \in S.$$

19

The subset S is said to be **bounded from above** *(or simply* **bounded above***) if there exists $\beta \in \mathbb{R}$ such that*

$$x \leq \beta \quad \text{for all} \quad x \in S.$$

The subset S is said to be **bounded** *if it is* **bounded** *both from above and from below. In this case, it is customary to say that there exists a constant $M > 0$ such that $|x| \leq M$ for all $x \in S$. Recall that $|x| \leq M$, for all $x \in S$ if and only if $-M \leq x \leq M$, for all $x \in S$.*

Example 2.2.2 (i) Any *finite* subset of $\mathbb{R}$ is bounded. For example, $S = \{-1, 0, 4, 5\}$ is bounded. Here $-1 \leq x \leq 5 \; \forall \; x \in S$ and, of course, we can take $M = 5$ and write $|x| \leq 5 \; \forall \; x \in S$.

(ii) The set of natural numbers, $\mathbb{N} = \{1, 2, 3, ...\}$ is bounded from below, and is not bounded from above.

(iii) The set $S = \{\frac{n}{2n+1}, n = 1, 2, 3, ...\}$ is bounded from above (by $\frac{1}{2}$) and bounded from below (by $\frac{1}{3}$).

(iv) The set $\mathbb{Z} = \{..., -2, -1, 0, 1, 2, ...\}$ of all integers is neither bounded from below nor bounded from above.

(v) The interval $I = (0, 1)$ is bounded. In particular, $0 < x < 1 \; \forall \; x \in I$.

(vi) The interval $I^* = [0, 1]$ is bounded.

Remark 2.2.3 (a) A set which is bounded *below* by α, say, may not contain α. For example, the set $(-1, 1)$ is bounded below by -1 but does not contain -1. Also, the set $S = \{1, \frac{1}{2}, \frac{1}{3}, ..., \frac{1}{n}, ...\}$ is bounded below by 0 but does not contain 0, since there is no natural number n such that $\frac{1}{n} = 0$.

(b) The set $S = \{1, 2, 3, ...\}$ is bounded below by 1 and also contains 1. Similarly the set $I^* = [0, 1]$ is bounded below by 0 and contains 0.

(c) As in part (a) above, a set which is bounded *above* by β may or may not contain β. For example, the set $S = \{0, \frac{1}{2}, \frac{2}{3}, ..., \frac{n-1}{n}, ...\}$ is bounded above by 1 (since $\frac{n-1}{n} < 1$ for all positive integers n) but does not contain 1 since there is no integer n for which $\frac{n-1}{n} = 1$. Also, the set $(-1, 1)$ is bounded above by 1 but does not contain 1, whereas the set $[-1, 1]$ is bounded above by 1 and contains 1.

2.3   Infimum of a Subset of $\mathbb{R}$

Definition 2.3.1 *If a subset S of real numbers is bounded below by α, say, then α is called a* **lower bound for S** *and if S is bounded above by β, then β is called an* **upper bound for S**.

Remark 2.3.2 If α is a lower bound for a subset S of the real numbers, any number less than α is also a lower bound for S. So, if a set has one lower bound, it has infinitely many. Similarly, if a set has an upper bound β, any number greater than β is another upper bound. Again, a set with one upper bound has infinitely many upper bounds. These discussions bring us to the following definitions.

Definition 2.3.3 *Let S be a subset of the real numbers which is bounded from below. The* **greatest lower bound for S** *(glb for short), or the* **infimum of** *S (denoted by $\inf S$) α_0 (say) is a real number satisfying the following* **two** *conditions:*

$$(A1): \quad \alpha_0 \leq s \; \forall \; s \in S;$$
$$(A2): \quad if \; \alpha \leq s \; \forall \; s \in S \quad then \quad \alpha \leq \alpha_0.$$

Remark 2.3.4 The two conditions given in Definition 2.3.3 can be formulated in another form to give an equivalent definition for $\inf S$.

Let S be a subset of the real numbers which is bounded from below. Then

$$\alpha_0 = \inf S$$

if and only if the following two conditions are satisfied:

$(B1):$ α_0 is a lower bound for S;

$(B2):$ $\forall\, \epsilon > 0,$ the number $\alpha_0 + \epsilon$ is **not** a lower bound for S.

We have yet another equivalent definition given as follows:

$$\alpha_0 = \inf S$$

if and only if the following two conditions are satisfied:

$(C1):$ α_0 is a lower bound for S;

$(C2):$ $\forall\, \epsilon > 0,$ there exists $s_\epsilon \in S$ such that $\alpha_0 \leq s_\epsilon < \alpha_0 + \epsilon.$

Remark 2.3.5 First observe where the signs "$\leq$" and "$<$" are used in $(C2)$. We illustrate conditions $(B1), (B2)$ and $(C1), (C2)$ with pictures. Consider the set S shown below in Fig. 2.1.

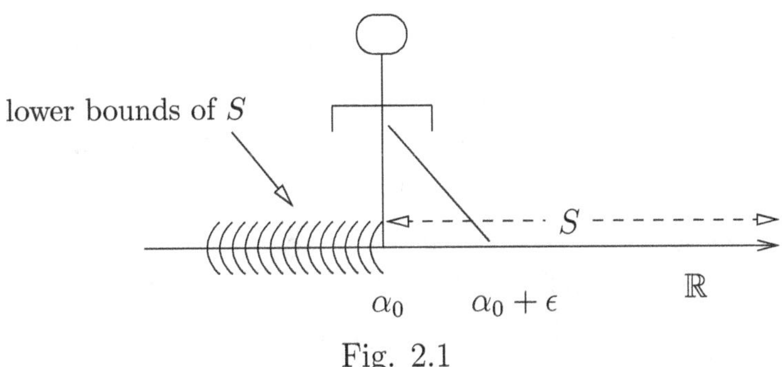

Fig. 2.1

Let α_0 denote the *greatest* lower bound of S, i.e., $\alpha_0 = \inf S$. Condition $(B2)$ says that if α_0 is the **greatest** of the lower bounds, any number greater than α_0 (even by a tiny bit, $\epsilon > 0$) cannot be a lower bound for S. Condition $(C2)$ says even more. It says that if $\alpha_0 = \inf S$, and if someone stands on α_0 and steps into the set S by a little bit ($\epsilon > 0$), no matter how small, the person must "trap" **at least one member of** S between α_0 and $\alpha_0 + \epsilon$. This condition is very useful in solving problems involving "inf".

2.4 Supremum of a Subset of $\mathbb{R}$

We now introduce the notion of **least upper bound** or **supremum** (denoted by "sup" for short) of a set S that is bounded above.

Definition 2.4.1 *Let S be a subset of the real numbers which is bounded from above. The* **least upper bound for S** *(lub for short) or the* **supremum of** *S (denoted by $\sup S$), β_0 (say) is a real number satisfying the following* **two** *conditions:*

$$(A1'): \quad s \leq \beta_0 \; \forall \; s \in S;$$
$$(A2'): \quad if \; s \leq \beta \; \forall \; s \in S \;\; then \;\; \beta_0 \leq \beta.$$

These conditions can be formulated in the following two equivalent forms:

$$\beta_0 = \sup S$$

if and only if the following two conditions are satisfied:

$(B1'): \quad \beta_0$ is an upper bound for S;
$(B2'): \quad \forall \; \epsilon > 0$, the number $\beta_0 - \epsilon$ is **not** an upper bound for S.

Equivalently, $\beta_0 = \sup S$ if and only if the following two conditions are satisfied:

$(C1'): \quad \beta_0$ is an upper bound for S;
$(C2'): \quad \forall \; \epsilon > 0$, there exists $s_\epsilon \in S$ such that
$$\beta_0 - \epsilon < s_\epsilon \leq \beta_0.$$

Again, note where the signs " $\leq$ " and " $<$ " are used in $(C2')$. To fix ideas, the reader may draw a "picture" as in Remark 2.3.5.

Remark 2.4.2 The **existence** of the " inf " and the " sup " is an axiom of the real number system. It is not necessarily true that in any number system, a set that is bounded above has the least upper bound. For example, in the system of **rational numbers** Q, the subset $S = \{x \in Q : x^2 \le 2\}$ is bounded above by $\sqrt{2}$ which is the least upper bound for S but $\sqrt{2}$ is not in Q. Hence, in the set of rational numbers, the set S is bounded above but has no least upper bound. If a subset S of real numbers is **not** bounded from below, we define inf $S = -\infty$ and if it is **not** bounded from above, we define sup $S = \infty$.

We now give more examples.

Example 2.4.3   (i) Prove that $\sup\{\frac{n}{2n+1}, n = 1, 2, 3, ...\} = \frac{1}{2}$.

Solution: It suffices to verify conditions $(C1')$ and $(C2')$. Clearly,

$$\frac{n}{2n+1} < \frac{n}{2n} = \frac{1}{2}, \ \forall \ \text{integers} \ \ n \ge 1,$$

so $\frac{1}{2}$ is an upper bound, verifying $(C1')$. To verify condition $(C2')$, let $\epsilon > 0$ be arbitrary. Recall that here, our set S is given by

$$S = \left\{\frac{n}{2n+1}, n = 1, 2, 3, ...\right\}.$$

So, we try to find $s_\epsilon \in S$ such that $\frac{1}{2} - \epsilon < s_\epsilon \le \frac{1}{2}$. But $s_\epsilon \in S$ must be of the form $\frac{n_\epsilon}{2n_\epsilon+1}$ for *some* positive integer n_ϵ. So, we must find some positive integer n_ϵ such that

$$\frac{1}{2} - \epsilon < \frac{n_\epsilon}{2n_\epsilon + 1} \le \frac{1}{2}.$$

But $\frac{n_\epsilon}{2n_\epsilon+1} \le \frac{1}{2}$ holds always for *all* integers $n_\epsilon \ge 1$. Also, $\frac{1}{2} - \epsilon < \frac{n_\epsilon}{2n_\epsilon+1}$ holds for all positive integers n_ϵ

such that $n_\epsilon > \frac{1-2\epsilon}{4\epsilon}$. Hence,

$$\sup\left\{\frac{n}{2n+1}, n = 1, 2, 3, ...\right\} = \frac{1}{2}.$$

(ii) Prove that $\inf\{\frac{n}{2n+1}, n = 1, 2, 3, ...\} = \frac{1}{3}$.

Solution: Let $a_n = \frac{n}{2n+1}$. Then

$$a_{n+1} - a_n = \frac{1}{(2n+3)(2n+1)} \geq 0,$$

so that $a_{n+1} \geq a_n$ for all integers $n = 1, 2, ...$. Hence $a_n \geq a_1 = \frac{1}{3}$. So, $\frac{1}{3}$ is a lower bound for $S = \{\frac{n}{2n+1}, n = 1, 2, 3, ...\}$, verifying condition $(C1)$. We now verify condition $(C2)$. Let $\epsilon > 0$ be arbitrary. We want to find $s_0 \in S$ such that

$$\frac{1}{3} \leq s_0 < \frac{1}{3} + \epsilon.$$

Again, s_0 must be of the form $\frac{n_0}{2n_0+1}$ for some positive integer n_0. So, we try to find at least one integer n_0 satisfying the following inequalities,

$$\frac{1}{3} \leq \frac{n_0}{2n_0 + 1} < \frac{1}{3} + \epsilon.$$

In particular, $n_0 = 1$ satisfies them. Hence $\inf S = \frac{1}{3}$.

Remark 2.4.4 *We note here that , by definition, if $\emptyset$ denotes the empty set, then*

$$\sup \emptyset = -\infty.$$

$$\inf \emptyset = +\infty.$$

These definitions are reasonable because, every real number, no matter how negative, is an upper bound for $\emptyset$ (See, Fig. 2.2), and the least upper bound should be as far leftward as possible, i.e., $-\infty$.

Similarly, (See, Fig. 2.3) any real number, no matter how positive, is a lower bound for the $\emptyset$ and the greatest of the lower bounds must be as far to the right as possible, i.e., $+\infty$. Hence, $\inf \emptyset = +\infty$.

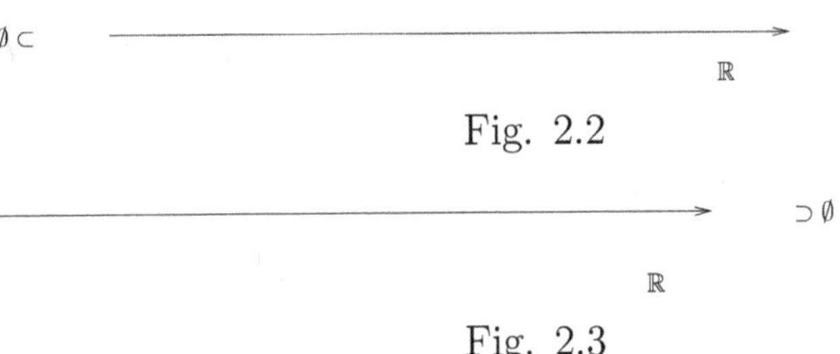

Fig. 2.2

Fig. 2.3

2.5   Basic Properties

Proposition 2.5.1 *Let $\{a_i\}$ and $\{b_i\}$, $i = 1, 2, 3, \ldots$ be bounded subsets of real numbers. Then:*

$$(a) \quad \sup_{i \geq 1}\{a_i + b_i\} \leq \sup_{i \geq 1} a_i + \sup_{i \geq 1} b_i;$$

$$(b) \quad \inf_{i \geq 1}\{a_i + b_i\} \geq \inf_{i \geq 1} a_i + \inf_{i \geq 1} b_i.$$

Proof. (a) Let $\beta = \sup_{i \geq 1}\{a_i\}$, $\gamma = \sup_{i \geq 1}\{b_i\}$. But from the definitions, we obtain that

$$a_i \leq \beta, \ b_i \leq \gamma, \ \forall \, i \geq 1,$$

so that adding, we obtain that $a_i + b_i \leq \beta + \gamma$, $\forall \, i = 1, 2, \ldots$. Hence $\beta + \gamma$ is an upper bound for the numbers $\{a_i + b_i\}$. But since **every** upper bound is greater than or equal to the **least** upper bound (i.e., the 'sup'), we have

$$\beta + \gamma \geq \sup\{a_i + b_i\},$$

i.e.,

$$\sup_{i \geq 1}\{a_i\} + \sup_{i \geq 1}\{b_i\} \geq \sup_{i \geq 1}\{a_i + b_i\},$$

completing the proof of (a).

(b) The proof is similar to that of part (a) and is left as an easy exercise. $\square$

Proposition 2.5.2 *Let S be a subset of real numbers which is bounded. Then the following equation holds:*

$$\sup(-S) = -\inf S \ (equivalently, \ \inf(-S) = -\sup S).$$

Proof. To prove that $\sup(-S) = -\inf S$, it suffices to prove that

$$\inf S = -\sup(-S).$$

Let $\alpha = \inf S$. Then,

$$(i) \ \alpha \leq s \ \forall \ s \in S, \qquad (ii) \ \forall \ \epsilon > 0, \ \exists \ s_0 \in S : \alpha \leq s_0 < \alpha + \epsilon.$$

Conditions (i) and (i) imply

$$(i^*) - s \leq -\alpha \ \forall - s \in -S,$$
$$(ii^*) \ \forall \ \epsilon > 0, \exists - s_0 \in -S : (-\alpha) - \epsilon < -s_0 \leq -\alpha.$$

Conditions (i^*) and (ii^*) imply

$$-\alpha = sup \ (-S), \quad i.e., -inf \ S = sup(-S),$$

completing the proof. $\square$

Now,

$$A \subseteq B, \Rightarrow \ \inf B \leq \inf A; \quad \sup A \leq supB.$$

This is best illustrated in Figure 2.4.

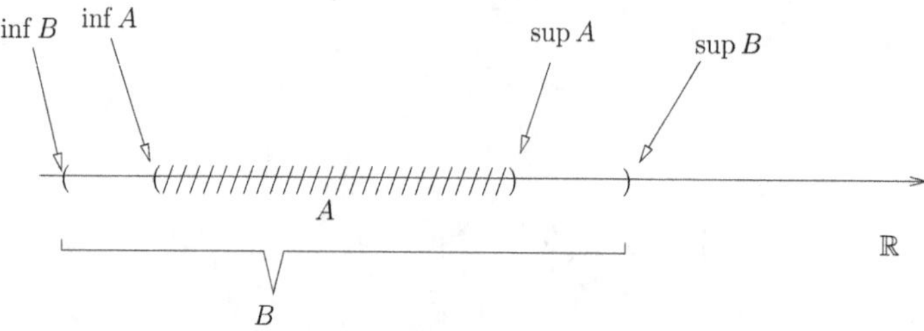

Fig. 2.4

We now prove this fact formally.

Proposition 2.5.3 *Let A and B be bounded subsets of real numbers such that $A \subseteq B$. Then*

$$\inf B \le \inf A \le \sup A \le \sup B.$$

Proof. Let $\alpha = \inf B$. Then, $\alpha \le x \; \forall \; x \in B$. This implies, in particular, $\alpha \le x \; \forall \; x \in A$. Hence α is a lower bound for A so that $\alpha \le \inf A$. But $\alpha = \inf B$. Hence,

$$\inf B \le \inf A.$$

Clearly, for the set A, $\inf A \le x \le \sup A \; \forall \; x \in A$. It now remains to prove that $\sup A \le \sup B$. Let $\beta = \sup B$. Then $x \le \beta \; \forall \; x \in B$. But then this implies, in particular, $x \le \beta \; \forall \; x \in A$ (since $A \subseteq B$) so that β is an upper bound for A. Hence $\sup A \le \beta$, i.e., $\sup A \le \sup B$. The proof is complete. $\square$

Proposition 2.5.4 *Let S be a subset of the real numbers which is bounded from below such that $\inf S > 0$. Let $\frac{1}{S}$ denote the subset of the real numbers defined as follows: $\frac{1}{S} = \{\frac{1}{x} : x \in S\}$. Then,*

$$\sup \left(\frac{1}{S}\right) = \frac{1}{\inf S}.$$

Proof. Let $\alpha = \inf S$. Then α satisfies the following two conditions:

(i) $0 < \alpha \le x \; \forall \; x \in S$;

(ii) $\forall \; \bar{\epsilon} > 0$, there exists $s_0 \in S$ such that $\alpha \le s_0 < \alpha + \bar{\epsilon}$.

From these two conditions we obtain the following inequalities:

(1) $\frac{1}{x} \le \frac{1}{\alpha} \; \forall \; \frac{1}{x} \in \frac{1}{S}$;

(2) $\forall \; \bar{\epsilon} > 0$, there exists $\frac{1}{s_0} \in \frac{1}{S}$ such that $\frac{1}{\alpha + \bar{\epsilon}} < \frac{1}{s_0} \le \frac{1}{\alpha}$.

Now, we have from (1) that $\frac{1}{S}$ is bounded above by $\frac{1}{\alpha}$. So, $\sup\left(\frac{1}{S}\right)$ exists. Suppose for contradiction that $\frac{1}{\alpha} \neq \sup\left(\frac{1}{S}\right)$. Let $\gamma = \sup\left(\frac{1}{S}\right)$. Then $\gamma \neq \frac{1}{\alpha}$. So $\gamma < \frac{1}{\alpha}$. This implies that $\frac{1}{x} \leq \gamma < \frac{1}{\alpha}$, $\forall \frac{1}{x} \in \frac{1}{S}$; or equivalently, $\alpha < \frac{1}{\gamma} \leq x$, $\forall x \in S$. Thus $\frac{1}{\gamma}$ is a lower bound of S and is strictly greater than α. This implies that $\alpha \neq \inf(S)$, a contradiction. This completes the proof. $\square$

The following is an application of the definition of the "sup".

Example 2.5.5 Verify that $\displaystyle\bigcup_{n=1}^{\infty}\left(0, \frac{n}{2n+1}\right) = \left(0, \frac{1}{2}\right)$.

Solution: Clearly, $(0, \frac{n}{2n+1}) \subset (0, \frac{1}{2})$ $\forall$ integers $n \geq 1$. So, it suffices to prove $(0, \frac{1}{2}) \subset \displaystyle\bigcup_{n=1}^{\infty}\left(0, \frac{n}{2n+1}\right)$. We have proved in Example 2.4.3(i) that $\sup\{\frac{n}{2n+1}, n = 1, 2, ...\} = \frac{1}{2}$. Then $\forall \epsilon \in (0, \frac{1}{2})$, $\exists n_\epsilon \in \mathbb{N}$ such that

$$0 < \frac{1}{2} - \epsilon < \frac{n_\epsilon}{2n_\epsilon + 1}.$$

Observe that , $\forall x \in (0, \frac{1}{2})$, $\frac{1}{2} - x > 0$, and so, for $\epsilon_x = \frac{1}{2} - x > 0, \exists n_x$ such that $0 < x < \frac{n_x}{2n_x+1}$. Hence,

$$x \in \left(0, \frac{n_x}{2n_x + 1}\right) \subset \bigcup_{n=1}^{\infty}\left(0, \frac{n}{2n + 1}\right)$$

so that

$$\left(0, \frac{1}{2}\right) \subset \bigcup_{n=1}^{\infty}\left(0, \frac{n}{2n + 1}\right).$$

The verification is complete.

Example 2.5.6 *inf* $(a, b) = a$.

Solution: Set $S = (a, b)$. Then,

(i) $a < x \ \forall x \in S$.

(ii) Let $\epsilon > 0$ be given. We want to find $s_\epsilon \in S$ such that $a \leq s_\epsilon < a + \epsilon$. We may choose

$$s_\epsilon = \begin{cases} a + \frac{\epsilon}{2}, & \text{if } \epsilon \leq b - a \\ \text{any fixed } x_0 \in S, & \text{otherwise.} \end{cases}$$

Example 2.5.7 *Let S be a bounded subset of $\mathbb{R}$. For $\lambda \in \mathbb{R}$, let*

$$S + \lambda = \{s + \lambda : s \in S\}.$$

Prove:

$$\sup (S + \lambda) = \lambda + \sup S.$$

Solution: Write $S = (S + \lambda) - \lambda, \ \lambda \in \mathbb{R}$. Then,

$$\sup S \leq \sup (S + \lambda) + \sup(-\lambda) = \sup (S + \lambda) - \lambda,$$

so that
$$\lambda + \sup S \leq \sup (S + \lambda). \qquad (i)$$

By Proposition 2.5.1, we have,

$$\sup (S + \lambda) \leq \lambda + \sup S. \qquad (ii)$$

From (i) and (ii), we obtain

$$\sup(S + \lambda) = \lambda + \sup S,$$

as required.

EXERCISES 2.1

1. Verify directly that s_0 defined in Example 2.5.6 actually satisfies $(*)$.

2. Apply Example 2.5.6 to show the following:
   (a) $\inf(-2, 0) = -2$;   (b) $\inf(-3, -1) = -3$;   (c) $\inf[0, 1] = 0$;
   (d) $\inf(-0.1, -0.01) = -0.1$;   (e) $\inf(0.01, 0.02) = 0.01$.

3. Derive an expression for s_0 as in Example 2.5.6 which can be used to prove that $\sup(a, b) = b$ for all $a, b \in \mathbb{R}$, $a < b$. Use your expression to show the following:

   (a) $\sup(0, 1) = 1$;   (b) $\sup(-0.1, -0.01) = -0.01$;

   (c) $\sup(-3, -1) = -1$;   (d) $\sup(0.01, 0.02) = 0.02$.

   In each case, verify that your s_0 satisfies

   $$b - \epsilon < s_0 \leq b.$$

4. Let A and B be any two bounded nonempty subsets of real numbers and let $A + B = \{a + b : a \in A;\ b \in B\}$. Show that $\sup(A + B) = \sup A + \sup B$.

   Observe that if $A = \{a_n\}$, $B = \{b_n\}$, then, $A + B = \{a_n + b_n\}$, and in this case, show that necessarily,

   $$\sup_{n \geq 1}\{a_n + b_n\} \neq \sup_{n \geq 1} a_n + \sup_{n \geq 1} b_n.$$

   To see this, take $\{a_n\} = \{(-1)^n\}$, $\{b_n\} = \{\frac{1}{n}\}$.

5. Give an example to show that Proposition 2.5.4 is false if the condition $\inf S > 0$ is dropped.

6. Let S be a subset of the real numbers bounded from above and let $R \subseteq S$ satisfy the following condition:

$$\forall\, x \in S, \exists\, r \in R \ \text{ such that } \ x \leq r.$$

Prove that $\sup S = \sup R$.

7. (a) Let S be a subset of the real numbers bounded from below and let $R \subseteq S$ satisfy the following condition: $\forall\, x \in S, \exists\, r \in R$ such that $r \leq x$. Prove that $\inf S = \inf R$.

(b) Give examples of S and R such that condition of part (a) is satisfied.

(c) Give examples of S and R such that condition of part (a) fails to hold.

8. Let S be a bounded subset of $\mathbb{R}$. For any $\lambda \in \mathbb{R}$, let

$$S + \lambda = \{s + \lambda : s \in S\}, \quad \text{and} \quad S_\lambda = \{\lambda x : x \in S\}.$$

Prove the following assertions.

(a) Prove part (b) of Proposition 2.5.1; Prove $\inf(S + \lambda) = \lambda + \inf S$;

(b) $\sup S_\lambda = \lambda \sup S$, and $\inf S_\lambda = \lambda \inf S$, if $\lambda > 0$;

(c) $\sup S_\lambda = \lambda \inf S$, and $\inf S_\lambda = \lambda \sup S$, if $\lambda < 0$.

CHAPTER **3**

Sequences of Real Numbers

3.1 Introduction

With the foundations laid in the previous chapters, we now pursue questions of more analytic nature. We start with the study of **real sequences**.

In the next three chapters, we study sequences of real numbers. We begin in this chapter with the definition of a sequence and also define **convergent** sequences. We give some examples and prove *one* basic property of *convergent sequences*, i.e., **that every convergent sequence is bounded.**

3.2 Definition, Example and a Basic Property

A **sequence** in a set X is **a function on an infinite subset of** $\mathbb{N} = \{1, 2, 3, ...\}$ of natural numbers **whose range is**

33

contained in the set X. Here we will be concerned with **sequences in** $\mathbb{R}$, also called **real sequences**.

Definition 3.2.1 *A sequence* $\{a_n\}_{n=1}^{\infty}$ *of real numbers is a function* $a :$
$D(a) \subset \mathbb{N} \to \mathbb{R}$ *of an infinite subset* $D(a)$ *of the natural numbers* $\mathbb{N}$ *into the real numbers* $\mathbb{R}$ *defined by*

$$a(n) = a_n \in \mathbb{R} \quad \forall \quad n \in \mathbb{N}.$$

The function a *is generally denoted by* $\{a_n\}_{n=1}^{\infty}$ *or* $\{a_n\}_{n=p}^{\infty}$ *for some integer* $p \in \mathbb{N}$. *The notation* a_n *is not crucial. The function* a *can also be denoted by any other letter, e.g.,* $b_n, c_n, d_n, \ldots$.

Example 3.2.2 Let $f : \mathbb{N} \to \mathbb{R}$ be defined by

$$f(n) = a_n = \frac{n}{n+1} \quad \forall \quad n \in \mathbb{N}.$$

Let us examine the sequence $\{a_n\}_{n=1}^{\infty} \equiv \{\frac{n}{n+1}\}_{n=1}^{\infty}$ more closely. We construct the following table of values of a_n for some n's in $\mathbb{N}$.

n	1	2	3	$\cdots$	10	$\cdots$	100	$\cdots$	1000	$\cdots$
$a_n = \frac{n}{n+1}$	$\frac{1}{2}$	$\frac{2}{3}$	$\frac{3}{4}$	$\cdots$	$\frac{10}{11}$	$\cdots$	$\frac{100}{101}$	$\cdots$	$\frac{1000}{1001}$	$\cdots$

Table 3.1

It is clear from *Table 3.1* that as the value of n increases, the value of $a_n = \frac{n}{n+1}$ approaches the value 1. We write this in mathematical language in any of the following three ways:

(i)　　$\lim\limits_{n \to \infty} a_n = 1;$

(ii)　　$\lim a_n = 1;$

(iii)　　$a_n \to 1$ as $n \to \infty,$

and say that "the limit of a_n as n goes to infinity is 1" or that "a_n converges to 1", or a_n approaches 1 as n approaches infinity.

Remark 3.2.3 It is generally not necessary to make a table in order to find what a given convergent sequence approaches.

Before we give more examples of convergent sequences, we first give the following formal definition.

Definition 3.2.4 (Convergent sequences) *A sequence $\{a_n\}_{n=1}^{\infty}$ of real numbers is said to* **converge** *to a real number a^* if and only if for each $\epsilon > 0$, there exists a natural number $\bar{n}(\epsilon)$ such that*

$$|a_n - a^*| < \epsilon \quad \forall \quad n \geq \bar{n}(\epsilon).$$

In this case we write:

$$\lim_{n \to \infty} a_n = a^* \text{ or } \lim a_n = a^* \text{ or } a_n \to a^* \text{ as } n \to \infty.$$

The number a^* is called the **limit** of a_n. The notation $\bar{n}(\epsilon)$ indicates that the natural number $\bar{n}(\epsilon)$ depends on the $\epsilon > 0$ given. A sequence which does not converge to some real number is said to **diverge**. Recall that $|a_n - a^*| < \epsilon$ can be re-written as

$$a^* - \epsilon < a_n < a^* + \epsilon.$$

Furthermore, from the definition, we see that the values of a_n for all $n < n(\epsilon)$ do not affect the condition $|a_n - a^*| < \epsilon$. Hence, ignoring a *finite* number of terms of a sequence does not affect the convergence or divergence of the sequence.

We define **the greatest integer function**, denoted by $[x]$ as **the greatest integer less than or equal to** x, i.e.,

$$[x] = n \in \mathbb{Z} : n \leq x.$$

For example, $[2.3] = 2$, $[5.9] = 5, ...$, and so on.

Example 3.2.5 $\quad(i)$ The sequence $\{a_n\}_{n=1}^{\infty}$ where $a_n = \frac{1}{n}$ is the infinite sequence $\{1, \frac{1}{2}, \frac{1}{3}, ..., \frac{1}{n}, ...\}$. Formally, of course, this is the function with domain $\mathbb{N}$, whose value at each n is $\frac{1}{n}$. The set of values is $\{1, \frac{1}{2}, \frac{1}{3}, ...\}$.

(ii) Consider the sequence given by $\{b_n\}_{n=1}^{\infty} = \{(-1)^n\}_{n=1}^{\infty}$. This is also the infinite sequence $\{-1, 1, -1, 1, ...\}$. This sequence represents a function whose domain is $\mathbb{N}$ and it's set of values is $\{-1, 1\}$. This is an **alternating sequence** (a sequence in which the consecutive terms have opposite signs).

(iii) The sequence $\{a_n\}_{n=1}^{\infty} = \{3\}_{n=1}^{\infty}$ is the constant sequence $\{3, 3, 3, ...\}$ whose set of values is the singleton $\{3\}$.

(iv) Consider the sequence $\left\{ \cos \frac{n\pi}{3} \right\}$, $n \in \mathbb{N}$. The first term of this sequence is $\cos \frac{\pi}{3} = \cos 60^o = \frac{1}{2}$ and the sequence is given by

$$\left\{ \frac{1}{2}, \frac{-1}{2}, -1, \frac{-1}{2}, \frac{1}{2}, 1, \frac{1}{2}, \frac{-1}{2}, -1, \frac{-1}{2}, \frac{1}{2}, ... \right\}.$$

The set of values is

$$\left\{ \cos\left(\frac{n\pi}{3}\right) : n \in \mathbb{N} \right\} = \left\{ \frac{1}{2}, \frac{-1}{2}, -1, 1 \right\}.$$

(v) If $\{c_n\}_{n=1}^{\infty} = \{n^{1/n}, n \in \mathbb{N}\}$, the sequence is

$$(1, \sqrt{2}, \sqrt[3]{3}, \sqrt[4]{4}, ...).$$

If we approximate values to four decimal places, the sequence is given by

$$\{1, 1.4142, 1.4422, 1.4142, 1.3797, 1.3480, ...\}.$$

It turns out that c_{100} is approximately 1.0471 and that c_{1000} is approximately 1.0069. This sequence actually converges to 1. We shall prove this later (Example 4.5.4 (iii)).

(vi) Prove that $\displaystyle\lim_{n\to\infty} \frac{n}{n+1} = 1$

(in order words, that the sequence $\{a_n\}_{n=1}^{\infty} \equiv \left\{\dfrac{n}{n+1}\right\}_{n=1}^{\infty}$ converges to 1).

Solution: Let $\epsilon > 0$ be given. We need to produce an integer $\bar{n}(\epsilon) > 0$ such that

$$\left|\frac{n}{n+1} - 1\right| < \epsilon \quad \forall \quad n \geq \bar{n}(\epsilon).$$

We compute as follows: $\left|\frac{n}{n+1} - 1\right| = \left|\frac{-1}{n+1}\right| = \frac{1}{n+1} < \frac{1}{n}$.
We can now set $\frac{1}{n} < \epsilon$ to get $n > \frac{1}{\epsilon}$. Take $\bar{n}(\epsilon) = [\frac{1}{\epsilon}+1]$.
Then, we have $\left|\frac{n}{n+1} - 1\right| < \epsilon$, $\forall\, n \geq \bar{n}(\epsilon)$. $\square$

(vii) Prove that $\displaystyle\lim_{n\to\infty} \frac{1}{n^2} = 0$.

Solution: Let $\epsilon > 0$ be given. Then, $\left|\frac{1}{n^2} - 0\right| = \frac{1}{n^2} \leq \frac{1}{n}$. Now set $\frac{1}{n} < \epsilon$ to get $n > \frac{1}{\epsilon}$. We then take $\bar{n}(\epsilon) = \left[\frac{1}{\epsilon} + 1\right]$. So,

$$\left|\frac{1}{n^2} - 0\right| < \epsilon \quad \forall \quad n \geq \bar{n}(\epsilon) = \left[\frac{1}{\epsilon} + 1\right].$$

($viii$) Prove that $\displaystyle\lim_{n\to\infty} \frac{3n+1}{7n-4} = \frac{3}{7}$.

Solution: For each $\epsilon > 0$, we need $\bar{n}(\epsilon) \in \mathbb{N}$ such that

$$\left|\frac{3n+1}{7n-4} - \frac{3}{7}\right| < \epsilon \quad \forall \quad n \geq \bar{n}(\epsilon).$$

So, we estimate as follows:

$$\left|\frac{3n+1}{7n-4} - \frac{3}{7}\right| = \frac{19}{7(7n-4)}$$

$$(\text{since} \quad |7n-4| = 7n-4 \quad \forall \quad n \in \mathbb{N})$$

$$< \frac{19}{7(7n - \frac{7n}{2})},$$

$$\left(\text{where} \quad \frac{7n}{2} > 4, \ i.e., \ n > \frac{8}{7}\right)$$

$$= \frac{19}{7(\frac{7n}{2})} = \frac{38}{49n}.$$

Hence, for all $n \geq \frac{8}{7}$, $\left|\frac{3n+1}{7n-4} - \frac{3}{7}\right| < \frac{38}{49n}$. Now set $\frac{38}{49n} < \epsilon$ to get $n > \frac{38}{49\epsilon}$. But from $\frac{7n}{2} > 4$ we have $n > \frac{8}{7}$. Therefore, we can choose $\overline{n}(\epsilon) = \max\{[\frac{8}{7}+1], [\frac{38}{49\epsilon}+1]\}$.

(ix) Prove that $\displaystyle\lim_{n\to\infty} \frac{3n+1}{7n-45} = \frac{3}{7}$.

Solution: For each $\epsilon > 0$, we need $\overline{n}(\epsilon) \in \mathbb{N}$ such that

$$\left|\frac{3n+1}{7n-45} - \frac{3}{7}\right| < \epsilon \quad \forall \quad n \geq \overline{n}(\epsilon).$$

So, we estimate as follows:

$$\left|\frac{3n+1}{7n-45} - \frac{3}{7}\right| = \left|\frac{142}{7(7n-45)}\right|$$

$$= \frac{142}{7} \frac{1}{|7n-45|}$$

$$< \frac{142}{7} \frac{1}{(7n - \frac{7n}{2})},$$

$$\text{provided} \quad \frac{7n}{2} > 45 \ \left(\ i.e., \ n > \frac{90}{7}\right)$$

$$= \frac{284}{49n}.$$

From the above, we get that

$$\frac{284}{49n} < \epsilon \Longrightarrow n > \frac{284}{49\epsilon}.$$

But $n > \frac{90}{7}$. Therefore, we take $\overline{n}(\epsilon) = \max\left\{\left[\frac{90}{7} + 1\right], \left[\frac{284}{49\epsilon} + 1\right]\right\}$.

(x) Prove that $\lim_{n\to\infty} \dfrac{4n^3 + 3n}{n^3 - 6} = 4$.

Solution: For each $\epsilon > 0$, we need $\overline{n}(\epsilon) \in \mathbb{N}$ such that

$$\left|\frac{4n^3 + 3n}{n^3 - 6} - 4\right| < \epsilon.$$

So we estimate as follows:

$$\left|\frac{4n^3 + 3n}{n^3 - 6} - 4\right| = \frac{3n + 24}{|n^3 - 6|} \leq \frac{3n + 24n}{|n^3 - 6|} < \frac{27n}{n^3 - \frac{n^3}{2}} = \frac{54}{n^2},$$

(provided $\frac{n^3}{2} > 6$). Now, set $\frac{54}{n^2} < \epsilon$ to get $n > \sqrt{\frac{54}{\epsilon}}$. But from $\frac{n^3}{2} > 6$ we have $n > (12)^{\frac{1}{3}}$. So, we can choose,

$$\overline{n}(\epsilon) = \max\left\{\left[(12)^{\frac{1}{3}} + 1\right], \left[\sqrt{\frac{54}{\epsilon}} + 1\right]\right\}. \quad \square$$

We now prove the following basic property of convergent sequences.

Theorem 3.2.6 *Every convergent sequence is bounded.*

Proof. Let $\{a_n\}$ be a convergent sequence. Let a^* be its limit. Then, given any $\epsilon > 0$, there exists an integer $\overline{n}(\epsilon) > 0$ such that

$$|a_n - a^*| < \epsilon \ \forall \ n \geq \overline{n}(\epsilon).$$

For simplicity, we shall write $\overline{n}(\epsilon)$ simply as N_0. In particular, let $\epsilon = 1$. Then,

$$|a_n - a^*| < 1 \ \forall \ n \geq N_0.$$

Hence we obtain the estimates:

$$|a_n| - |a^*| \leq \big||a_n| - |a^*|\big| \leq |a_n - a^*| < 1 \quad \forall \quad n \geq N_0.$$

This implies that

$$|a_n| \leq 1 + |a^*| \quad \forall \quad n \geq N_0. \qquad (3.2.1)$$

Thus, we have shown that $|a_n| \leq 1 + |a^*|$ if $n = N_0, N_0 + 1, \dots$.

But, to conclude that $\{a_n\}_{n=1}^{\infty}$ is bounded, we must prove that

$$|a_n| \leq M \quad \text{(for some constant } M > 0) \textbf{ for all } n \in \mathbb{N}.$$

So, it remains to show that $|a_n|$, $n = 1, 2, \dots, N_0 - 1$ is bounded. But there is only a **finite number** of these. Let $m^* = \max\{|a_n|, n = 1, 2, \dots, N_0 - 1\}$. Then for these,

$$|a_n| \leq m^*, \quad \text{for} \quad n = 1, 2, \dots, N_0 - 1. \qquad (3.2.2)$$

So, from inequalities (3.2.1) and (3.2.2), we have that $|a_n| \leq 1 + |a^*| + m^*$ for *all* integers $n \geq 1$. So we have $|a_n| \leq M$ for all integers $n \geq 1$, where $M = 1 + |a^*| + m^*$. Hence, $\{a_n\}_{n=1}^{\infty}$ is bounded. This completes the proof. $\square$

Remark 3.2.7 The converse of Theorem 3.2.6 is false. A bounded sequence need not be convergent. To see this, we consider the sequence $\{(-1)^n\}_{n=1}^{\infty} = \{-1, 1, -1, 1, \dots\}$. Clearly, this sequence whose set of values is $\{-1, 1\}$ is bounded since

$$|a_n| = |(-1)^n| = 1 \quad \forall \text{ integers } n \geq 1.$$

However, $\{(-1)^n\}_{n=1}^{\infty}$ is **not** convergent. To show this, we assume it is convergent and establish a contradiction. Now, suppose

$$\lim_{n \to \infty} (-1)^n = a^*.$$

Then, for $\epsilon = \frac{1}{2}$ (say), there exists an integer $N_0 \geq 0$ such that

$$|(-1)^n - a^*| < \frac{1}{2} \quad \forall \quad n \geq N_0.$$

In particular,

$$|(-1)^{N_0+1} - a^*| < \frac{1}{2} \quad \text{and} \quad |(-1)^{N_0+2} - a^*| < \frac{1}{2}.$$

Observe that $|(-1)^{N_0+1} - (-1)^{N_0+2}| = 2$ (justify). Hence,

$$
\begin{aligned}
2 &= |(-1)^{N_0+1} - (-1)^{N_0+2}| \\
&= |(-1)^{N_0+1} - a^* + a^* - (-1)^{N_0+2}| \\
&\leq |(-1)^{N_0+1} - a^*| + |a^* - (-1)^{N_0+2}| \\
&< \frac{1}{2} + \frac{1}{2} = 1,
\end{aligned}
$$

a contradiction. Hence, we conclude that the bounded sequence $\{(-1)^n\}_{n=1}^{\infty}$ does not converge.

3.3   Limits and Order Relation

A useful fact is that the order relation " $\leq$ " is preserved when taking limits.

Theorem 3.3.1 *Suppose $\{a_n\}$ and $\{b_n\}$ are convergent sequences and that $\lim a_n = a^*$, $\lim b_n = b^*$. If*

$$a_n \leq b_n \quad \forall n \in \mathbb{N},$$

then $a^* \leq b^*$.

Proof. Assume for contradiction, that $a^* > b^*$. Take $\epsilon = \frac{(a^* - b^*)}{2} > 0$. Since $\lim a_n = a^*$, there exists $N_1 \in \mathbb{N}$ such that $a^* - \epsilon < a_n < a^* + \epsilon$ $\forall n \geq N_1$. Similarly, $\lim b_n = b^*$ implies that there exists $N_2 \in \mathbb{N}$ such that $b^* - \epsilon < b_n < b^* + \epsilon$ $\forall n \geq N_2$. Let $N = \max\{N_1, N_2\}$. Then, for all $n \geq N$, $b_n < b^* + \epsilon = b^* + \frac{a^* - b^*}{2} = a^* - \epsilon < a_n$, which contradicts the assumption that $a_n \leq b_n$ for all n. Hence $a^* \leq b^*$. $\square$

Corollary 3.3.2   (a) If $\{a_n\}$ converges to a^* and $a_n \geq 0$ for all $n \in \mathbb{N}$, then $a^* \geq 0$.
(b) If $a \leq a_n \leq b$ for all n, and $\lim a_n = a^*$, then $a \leq a^* \leq b$.

3.4   More Example

Example 3.4.1 *Prove that the sequence $\{n!\}$ is not convergent.*

Solution: We proceed by contradiction. Assume that it converges to a. Take $\epsilon = \frac{1}{2}$. Then, there exists an integer $N_0 \geq 1$ such that

$$|n! - a| < \frac{1}{2} \ \forall \ n \geq N_0.$$

In particular, take $n = N_0 + 1$. Then,

$$|(N_0 + 1)! - a| < \frac{1}{2}.$$

Take $n = N_0 + 2$. Then,

$$|(N_0 + 2)! - a| < \frac{1}{2}.$$

Observe that

$$|(N_0 + 1)! - (N_0 + 2)!| = (N_0 + 1)(N_0 + 1)!.$$

Hence,

$$(N_0+1)(N_0+1)! \leq |(N_0+1)!-a+a-(N_0+2)!| < \frac{1}{2}+\frac{1}{2} = 1.$$

Since $N_0 > 1$, this is a contradiction. Hence $\{n!\}$ does not converge.

Example 3.4.2 *Prove that the sequence $\{73+(-1)^n\}$ is not convergent.*

Solution. We proceed by contradiction. Assume that it converges to a. Take $\epsilon = \frac{1}{2}$. Then, there exists an integer $N_0 > 0$ such that

$$|73 + (-1)^n - a| < \frac{1}{2} \ \forall \ n \geq N_0.$$

In particular, take $n = N_0 + 1$. Then,

$$|73 + (-1)^{N_0+1} - a| < \frac{1}{2}.$$

Take $n = N_0 + 2$. Then,

$$|73 + (-1)^{N_0+2} - a| < \frac{1}{2}.$$

Observe that

$$2 = \left|73 + (-1)^{N_0+2} - 73 + (-1)^{N_0+1}\right|.$$

Hence,

$$2 = \left|73 + (-1)^{N_0+2} - a + a - 73 + (-1)^{N_0+1}\right| \le \frac{1}{2} + \frac{1}{2} = 1,$$

a contradiction. Hence, the sequence $\{73 + (-1)^n\}$ is not convergent.

Example 3.4.3 *Prove that the sequence $\{n\}$ is not convergent.*

Solution. We proceed by contradiction. Assume that it converges to a. Take $\epsilon = \frac{1}{3}$. Then, there exists an integer $N_0 \ge 1$ such that

$$|n - a| < \frac{1}{3} \ \forall \ n \ge N_0.$$

In particular,

$$|N_0 + 1 - a| < \frac{1}{3}.$$

$$|N_0 + 2 - a| < \frac{1}{3}.$$

Observe that

$$1 = |N_0 + 2 - (N_0 + 1)|$$

Hence,

$$1 = |N_0 + 2 - a + a - (N_0 + 1)| \le \frac{1}{3} + \frac{1}{3} = \frac{2}{3},$$

a contradiction. Hence, the sequence $\{n\}$ is not convergent.

EXERCISES 3.1

1. For each of the sequences below determine whether it converges and, if it converges, guess its limit and prove your guess using the $\epsilon - N$ argument.

   (a) $\{\sqrt{n^2 + 1} - n\}$

   (b) $\{\sqrt{4n^2 + n} - 2n\}$.

2. Prove the following:

   (a) $\lim\limits_{n \to \infty} \dfrac{(-1)^n}{n} = 0$

   (b) $\lim\limits_{n \to \infty} \dfrac{1}{\sqrt[3]{n}} = 0$

   (c) $\lim\limits_{n \to \infty} \dfrac{2n - 1}{3n + 2} = \dfrac{2}{3}$

   (d) $\lim\limits_{n \to \infty} \dfrac{n + b}{n^2 - 6} = 0, b \in \mathbb{R}$

   (e) $\lim\limits_{n \to \infty} \left(\sqrt{n^2 + 1} - n\right) = 0$

   (f) $\lim\limits_{n \to \infty} \left(\sqrt{n^2 + n} - n\right) = \dfrac{1}{2}$

   (g) $\lim\limits_{n \to \infty} \left(\dfrac{\sqrt{n}}{\sqrt{n + 1} + \sqrt{n}}\right) = \dfrac{1}{2}$.

3. Guess the limits of the following convergent sequences and then prove your guesses:

   $(i)\{\, a_n\} = \left\{\dfrac{n}{n^2 + 1}\right\}$ $(ii)\ \{b_n\} = \left\{\dfrac{7n - 19}{3n + 7}\right\}$

   $(iii)\ \{c_n\} = \left\{\dfrac{4n + 3}{7n - 5}\right\}$.

4. Show that the following sequences do not converge:

   (a) $\{\cos \frac{n\pi}{3}\}$ (b) $\{(-1)^n n\}$ (c) $\{\sin \frac{n\pi}{3}\}$.

5. Find the *supremium* and *infimum* of the following sequences.

$$(a) \ \left\{ \frac{n-1}{2n} \right\} \qquad (b) \ \left\{ \frac{(-1)^n n}{2n+1} \right\} \qquad (c) \ \left\{ \frac{1+(-1)^n}{3} \right\}.$$

6. (a) Give an example where strict inequality holds in Proposition 3.3.6(a), i.e., an example where

$$\sup_{i\geq 1}(a_i + b_i) < \sup_{i\geq 1} a_i + \sup_{i\geq 1} b_i$$

holds.

CHAPTER 4

Monotone Sequences

4.1   Introduction

For any given sequence, one question that is always of interest is whether or not the sequence is convergent. This question may sometimes be difficult to answer. But there is a class of sequences for which the situation is rather easy to handle. This is the class of *monotone* sequences. The following are two most important theorems concerning convergence of *bounded monotone* sequences and they are among the most important theorems of this chapter.

(a)   A monotone non-decreasing sequence of real numbers which is bounded above converges.
(b)   A monotone non-increasing sequence of real numbers which is bounded below converges.

Also, in this chapter, we shall establish the following limits which are important in their own right in mathematical analysis. The reader is advised to study their proofs care-

47

fully. We summarize them in the following box.

---

1. $\lim\limits_{n\to\infty} \left(1 + \frac{1}{n}\right)^n = \lim\limits_{n\to\infty} \left(1 + \frac{1}{n}\right)^{n+1} = e.$

2. If $|a| < 1$, then $\lim a^n = 0$.

3. If $|a| < 1$, then $\lim na^n = 0$.

4. $\lim\limits_{n\to\infty} n^{\frac{1}{n}} = 1.$

5. $\lim\limits_{n\to\infty} a^{\frac{1}{n}} = 1, a > 0.$

4.2   Definition, Example and Basic Properties

Definition 4.2.1 *A sequence $\{a_n\}$ of real numbers is called:*

(a) **monotone non-decreasing** *if $a_{n+1} \geq a_n \ \forall \ n \in \mathbb{N}$;*

(b) **strictly monotone increasing** *if $a_{n+1} > a_n \ \forall \ n \in \mathbb{N}$;*

(c) **monotone non-increasing** *if $a_{n+1} \leq a_n \ \forall \ n \in \mathbb{N}$;*

(d) **strictly monotone decreasing** *if $a_{n+1} < a_n \ \forall \ n \in \mathbb{N}$.*

Remark 4.2.2 In order to verify that a given sequence $\{a_n\}$ is monotone, one may use any of the following **four** methods.

Method 1. Examine the difference: $a_{n+1} - a_n$. If $a_{n+1} - a_n \geq 0$ then the sequence is monotone non-decreasing. If $a_{n+1} - a_n \leq 0$ then the sequence is monotone non-increasing.

Method 2. Examine the quotient: $\frac{a_{n+1}}{a_n}$ (provided $a_n > 0 \ \forall \ n \in \mathbb{N}$). If $\frac{a_{n+1}}{a_n} \geq 1$, then the sequence is monotone non-decreasing. If $\frac{a_{n+1}}{a_n} \leq 1$, then the sequence is monotone non-increasing.

Method 3. Use Calculus: Rewrite the sequence as a function f of x; $x \geq 1$. Differentiate f and examine $f'(x)$, where $x \geq 1$. If $f'(x) \geq 0$ then the sequence is monotone non-decreasing. If $f'(x) \leq 0$, the sequence is monotone non-increasing.

Method 4. Use **Induction.**

The inequalities for testing strictly increasing or decreasing sequences are obvious.

Example 4.2.3 Verify if the sequences defined by
(i) $\{a_n\} = \{1 - \frac{1}{n}\}$ (ii) $\{b_n\} = \{n^3\}$
(iii) $\{c_n\} = \{(-1)^n\}$ (iv) $\{d_n\} = \{\frac{1}{n^2}\}, n \geq 1,$
are monotone non-decreasing, monotone non-increasing or not monotone.

Solution:

(i) Here,

$$a_{n+1} - a_n = \left(1 - \frac{1}{n+1}\right) - \left(1 - \frac{1}{n}\right)$$

$$= \frac{1}{n^2 + n} > 0 \ \forall \ n \in \mathbb{N}.$$

Hence, the sequence defined by $\{a_n\} = \{1 - \frac{1}{n}\}$ is strictly monotone increasing.

Alternatively, consider the function $f(x) = 1 - \frac{1}{x}, \ x \geq 1$. Then, $f'(x) = \frac{1}{x^2} > 0$. Hence, f is strictly monotone increasing and so, $\{a_n\} = \left\{1 - \frac{1}{n}\right\}$ is strictly monotone increasing.

(ii) Clearly,

$$
\begin{aligned}
b_{n+1} - b_n &= (n+1)^3 - n^3 \\
&= 3n^2 + 3n + 1 > 0 \ \forall \ n \in \mathbb{N}.
\end{aligned}
$$

Hence, the sequence defined by $\{b_n\} = \{n^3\}$ is strictly monotone increasing.

(iii) We observe that,

$$
c_{n+1} - c_n = (-1)^{n+1} - (-1)^n = \begin{cases} 2 > 1, & \text{if } n \text{ is odd}, \\ -2 < 1, & \text{if } n \text{ is even}. \end{cases}
$$

Hence, the sequence defined by $\{c_n\} = \{(-1)^n\}$ is not monotone.

(iv) In this case,

$$
\begin{aligned}
d_{n+1} - d_n &= \frac{1}{(n+1)^2} - \frac{1}{n^2} \\
&= \frac{-2n - 1}{\left(n(n+1)\right)^2} < 0 \ \forall \ n \in \mathbb{N}.
\end{aligned}
$$

Hence, the sequence defined by $\{d_n\} = \{\frac{1}{n^2}\}$ is strictly monotone decreasing.

4.3   A Fundamental Theorem

If a sequence of real numbers is bounded above, we know that the "sup" exists. Call this β. If the sequence is, in addition, monotone non-decreasing, then eventually all its elements will come "very close" to β but will never exceed β. As n increases further the elements of the sequence will "pile up" under β. This suggests that the sequence converges to β. This is, in fact, true, i.e., a **monotone non-decreasing** sequence of real numbers **which is bounded above** converges to its "sup". Similarly, **a monotone non-increasing** sequence of real numbers **which is bounded**

below converges to its "inf". These facts are the contents of the following important theorem.

Theorem 4.3.1   (a) *A monotone non-decreasing sequence of real numbers which is bounded above converges.*

(b) *A monotone non-increasing sequence of real numbers which is bounded below converges.*

Proof. (see Fig. 4.1(a)).

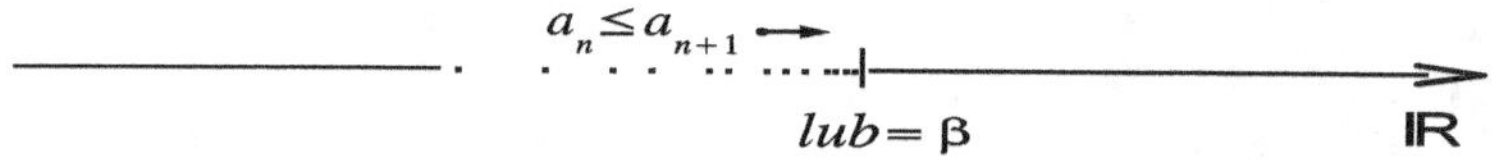

Fig. 4.1(a)

(a) Let $\{a_n\}_{n=1}^{\infty}$ denote the sequence. Since $\{a_n\}$ is bounded above, $\sup\{a_n\}$ exists. Let $\beta = \sup\limits_{n \geq 1} a_n$. From the definition of "sup", we obtain that:

(i) $a_n \leq \beta \ \forall n \geq 1;$

(ii) $\forall\, \epsilon > 0,\ \exists\, n_\epsilon \in \mathbb{N}$ such that $\beta - \epsilon < a_{n_\epsilon} \leq \beta.$

Since $\{a_n\}_{n=1}^{\infty}$ is monotone non-decreasing, we obtain that

$$\forall\, n \geq n_\epsilon, \quad a_n \geq a_{n_\epsilon}. \tag{4.3.1}$$

From condition (ii), inequality (4.3.1), and condition (i) we obtain that

$$\beta - \epsilon < a_{n_\epsilon} \leq a_n \leq \beta < \beta + \epsilon \ \forall\, n \geq n_\epsilon.$$

This gives that

$$\beta - \epsilon < a_n < \beta + \epsilon \quad \forall \quad n \geq n_\epsilon,$$

i.e.,

$$|a_n - \beta| < \epsilon \quad \forall \quad n \geq n_0.$$

This means, $\{a_n\}_{n=1}^{\infty}$ converges to β, proving part (a).

(b)(see Fig. 4.1(b)).

Fig. 4.1(b)

$\{a_n\}_{n=1}^{\infty}$ bounded below $\implies \inf\limits_{n \geq 1} a_n$ exists. Let $\alpha = \inf\limits_{n \geq 1} a_n$. Then,

$$(i) \quad \alpha \leq a_n \ \forall n \in \mathbb{N};$$
$$(ii) \quad \forall \ \epsilon > 0, \ \exists \ n_\epsilon \in \mathbb{N} \text{ such that}$$
$$\alpha \leq a_{n_\epsilon} < \alpha + \epsilon. \tag{4.3.2}$$

Since $\{a_n\}_{n=1}^{\infty}$ is monotone non-increasing, we obtain that

$$\forall \ n \geq n_\epsilon, \ a_n \leq a_{n_\epsilon}. \tag{4.3.3}$$

From (4.3.2) and (4.3.3), we obtain, using the fact that $\alpha \leq a_n \ \forall \ n$,

$$\alpha - \epsilon < \alpha \leq a_n \leq a_{n_\epsilon} < \alpha + \epsilon, \ \forall \ n \geq n_\epsilon,$$

so that

$$\alpha - \epsilon < a_n < \alpha + \epsilon \ \forall \ n \geq n_\epsilon.$$

i.e.,

$$|a_n - \alpha| < \epsilon \ \forall \ n \geq n_\epsilon, \ \text{ proving part (b)} . \ \square$$

4.3.1 The Euler Number, e

We shall give some important applications of Theorem 4.3.1. The first of such applications we shall give here will enable us prove that

$$\lim_{n\to\infty} \left(1 + \frac{1}{n}\right)^n = \lim_{n\to\infty} \left(1 + \frac{1}{n}\right)^{n+1} = e.$$

We now begin by first proving the following important and useful inequality. (This is basically Exercises 1.2, Problem 5).

Lemma 4.3.2 (Bernoulli's inequality) *Let $p > -1$, $p \neq 0$. Then for every integer $n \geq 2$, we have*

$$(1 + p)^n > 1 + np.$$

Proof. (see Fig. 4.2).

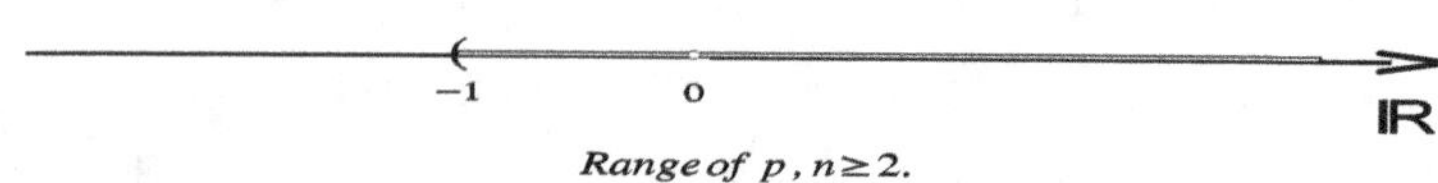

Fig. 4.2 (Condition for Bernoulli inequality)

The proof is by induction. For $n = 2$, the lemma is clearly true. In fact,

$$(1 + p)^2 = 1 + 2p + p^2 > 1 + 2p.$$

Assume now the inequality holds for k, i.e., $(1 + p)^k > 1 + kp$ for $k \in \mathbb{N}$. We prove it holds for $n = k + 1$. Now,

$$\begin{aligned}
(1 + p)^{k+1} &= (1 + p)^k (1 + p) \\
&> (1 + kp)(1 + p) \quad \text{(by our assumption)} \\
&= 1 + (k + 1)p + kp^2 > 1 + (k + 1)p.
\end{aligned}$$

Hence, by induction, the inequality is true for all integers $n \geq 2$. The proof is complete. $\square$ We present next an application of Lemma 4.3.2 which will be used later in some interesting examples.

Lemma 4.3.3 *Let*

$$a_n = \left(1 + \tfrac{1}{n}\right)^n \ \forall \ \text{integers } n \geq 1;$$
$$b_n = \left(1 + \tfrac{1}{n}\right)^{n+1} \ \forall \ \text{integers } n \geq 1.$$

Then

(a) $a_n \leq b_n$ *for all integers* $n \geq 1$;

(b) $\{a_n\}$ *is a monotone increasing sequence;*

(c) $\{b_n\}$ *is a monotone decreasing sequence;*

(d) $\{a_n\}$ *is bounded above and* $\{b_n\}$ *is bounded below.*

(Consequently, $\{a_n\}$ converges and $\{b_n\}$ converges. Actually, both sequences converge to the same limit).

Proof. (see Fig. 4.3).
(a)

$$b_n = \left(1 + \frac{1}{n}\right)^{n+1} = \left(1 + \frac{1}{n}\right)^n \left(1 + \frac{1}{n}\right)$$
$$= a_n\left(1 + \frac{1}{n}\right) > a_n \ \forall \ \text{integers } n \geq 1.$$

(b)   We compute as follows:

$$\frac{a_n}{a_{n-1}} = \left(\frac{n^2 - 1}{n^2}\right)^n \left(\frac{n}{n-1}\right) = \left(1 - \frac{1}{n^2}\right)^n \left(\frac{n}{n-1}\right), \ n \geq 2$$
$$> \left(1 - \frac{1}{n}\right)\left(\frac{n}{n-1}\right), \quad \text{(by Bernoulli inequality),}$$
$$= 1.$$

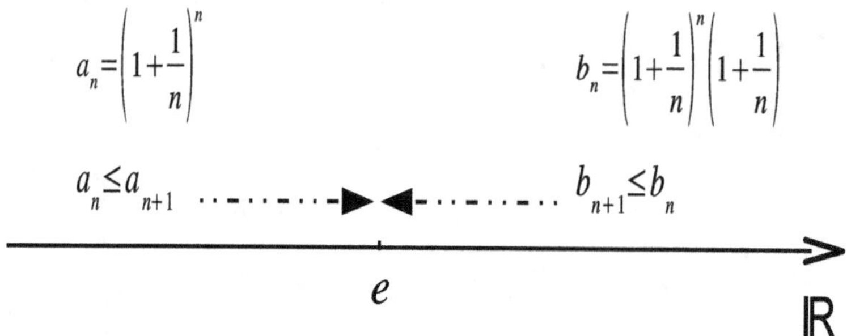

Fig. 4.3

Hence, $a_n > a_{n-1}$ for all integers $n \ge 2$, and so $\{a_n\}$ is monotone increasing.

(c) We compute

$$\begin{aligned}
\frac{b_{n-1}}{b_n} &= \left(1 + \frac{1}{(n-1)(n+1)}\right)^n \left(\frac{n}{n+1}\right) \\
&> \left(1 + \frac{n}{(n-1)(n+1)}\right)\left(\frac{n}{n+1}\right), \\
&\quad \text{(by Bernoulli inequality),} \\
&= \frac{n}{n+1} + \frac{n^2}{(n^2-1)(n+1)} > \frac{n}{n+1} + \frac{1}{n+1}, \quad n \ge 2, \\
&= 1.
\end{aligned}$$

Hence, $b_{n-1} \ge b_n \; \forall$ integers $n \ge 2$, and so, (b_n) is monotone decreasing.

(d) Since $\{b_n\}$ is decreasing, it follows that $b_n \le b_1 \; \forall \, n \ge 1$. But, from (a), $a_n \le b_n \; \forall$ integers $n \ge 1$. Hence $a_1 \le a_n \le$

$b_n \leq b_1 \; \forall$ integers $n \geq 1$, (since $\{a_n\}$ is monotone increasing by part (b)). $\quad \square$

Example 4.3.4 Let $a_n = \left(1 + \frac{1}{n}\right)^n$ and

$b_n = \left(1 + \frac{1}{n}\right)^{n+1}$.

Prove that:

(i) $\{a_n\}$ converges; $\{b_n\}$ converges.

(ii) $\{a_n\}$ and $\{b_n\}$ converge to the same limit.

Solution: (i) By Lemma 4.3.3, $\{a_n\}$ is a monotone increasing sequence which is bounded above. By Theorem 4.3.1, it converges. Similarly, $\{b_n\}$ is a monotone decreasing sequence which is bounded below, so it converges.

(ii) We know, $a_n \leq b_n$ for all integers $n \geq 1$. So

$$0 \leq b_n - a_n = \left(1 + \frac{1}{n}\right)^{n+1} - \left(1 + \frac{1}{n}\right)^n = \frac{\left(1 + \frac{1}{n}\right)^n}{n} \leq \frac{3}{n},$$

(see Exercise 4.1, Problem 5), i.e.,

$$0 \leq b_n - a_n \leq \frac{3}{n}.$$

We know $\{b_n\}$ converges, $\{a_n\}$ converges and $\left\{\frac{3}{n}\right\}$ converges. So, we can take limits of all sides of the last inequality to get (using Theorem 3.3.1 and Corollary 3.3.2):

$$\lim_{n \to \infty} 0 \leq \lim_{n \to \infty} b_n - \lim_{n \to \infty} a_n \leq \lim_{n \to \infty} \frac{3}{n}$$

which gives

$$0 \leq \lim_{n \to \infty} b_n - \lim_{n \to \infty} a_n \leq 0,$$

so that $\lim_{n \to \infty} b_n = \lim_{n \to \infty} a_n$, as required.

Remark 4.3.5 We have used the following facts: For any two convergent sequences $\{a_n\}$ and $\{b_n\}$, $\lim(a_n + b_n) = \lim a_n + \lim b_n$. For a proof of this, see Theorem 4.7.1 below. See also Theorem 4.5.1 below (sandwich theorem) which has also been used here.

Definition 4.3.6 The **Euler number e** is defined as the limit of $\left(1 + \frac{1}{n}\right)^n$, i.e.,

$$\boxed{\mathbf{e} = \lim_{n \to \infty} \left(1 + \frac{1}{n}\right)^n.}$$

Remark 4.3.7 If the number e is given as in the above definition, one must first show that it is well-defined, i.e., one must show that this limit actually exists. The way to do this is to set $a_n = \left(1 + \frac{1}{n}\right)^n$ and to show that $\{a_n\}$ is a monotone increasing sequence of real numbers which is bounded above and therefore converges, i.e., its limit exists. We have already proved this in Lemma 4.3.3. Note that in order to establish that $\{a_n\}$ is bounded above, we used the sequence $\{b_n\}$ to obtain that $a_n \leq b_1 \ \forall \ n \geq 1$. We note that the value of the **Euler number** is approximately $2.718281828459045\cdots$, and e is the base of the natural logarithm. This number e and the number π are, perhaps, the two most important numbers in mathematics.

Example 4.3.8   (i) The sequence $\{n\} = \{1, 2, 3, \ldots\}$ is monotone increasing (since $a_{n+1} - a_n = n + 1 - n = 1 > 0$) but is not bounded above. We saw in Example 3.3.5 that it is not convergent. This example shows that *monotonicity alone* is *not sufficient* to guarantee the convergence of a sequence.

(ii) For $a \in \mathbb{R}$, $n \in \mathbb{N}$, the sequence $\{a^n\}$ converges if and only if $|a| < 1$ or $a = 1$. In fact,

$$\lim_{n \to \infty} a^n = \begin{cases} 0, & \text{if} \quad |a| < 1, \\ 1, & \text{if} \quad a = 1. \end{cases}$$

We shall prove this later (Example 4.5.4 below).

Note that for $a > 1$, the sequence is monotone increasing but is not bounded above, hence it does not converge. In particular, if $a = 2$, $\{a^n\} = \{2^n\} = \{2, 2^2, 2^3, ...\}$ which does not converge. Also, if $a = -1$, $\{a^n\} = \{(-1)^n\} = \{-1, 1, -1, 1, ...\}$ is bounded but is not convergent (Remark 3.2.7). Hence, this example shows that *boundedness alone* is *not sufficient* to guarantee the convergence of a sequence.

(iii) The sequence $\left\{\frac{1}{n}\right\} = \left\{1, \frac{1}{2}, \frac{1}{3}, ...\right\}$ is monotone decreasing and is bounded below. So, by Theorem 4.3.5(b), it converges to its **infimum** which is 0.

(iv) Prove that $\left\{\frac{1}{\sqrt{n}}\right\}$ converges and find its limit.

Solution: Observe that

$$\frac{a_{n+1}}{a_n} = \sqrt{\frac{n}{n+1}} < 1 \ \forall \ n \geq 1,$$

i.e., $a_n \geq a_{n+1} \ \forall \ n \geq 1$. So, $\left\{\frac{1}{\sqrt{n}}\right\}$ is a monotone decreasing sequence bounded below by 0. Hence $\lim\limits_{n\to\infty} \dfrac{1}{\sqrt{n}}$ exists.

Claim. $\lim\limits_{n\to\infty} \dfrac{1}{\sqrt{n}} = 0$. For, $\left|\frac{1}{\sqrt{n}} - 0\right| = \frac{1}{\sqrt{n}} < \epsilon$ if $n > \frac{1}{\epsilon^2}$.

So, given $\epsilon > 0$, choose $n(\epsilon) = \left[\frac{1}{\epsilon^2} + 1\right]$.

(v) Let $\{a_n\}$ be a convergent sequence. Prove that $\lim a_{n+1} = \lim a_n$ (Exercises 4.1, Problem 1(a)).

4.4   Sequences Defined by Recurrence Relations

Problems on convergence or divergence of sequences defined by recurrence relations are generally solved

by applying Theorem 4.3.1 and using Example 4.3.8(v).

Example 4.4.1 Let $b_1 = 1$ and $b_{n+1} = \sqrt{2 + b_n}$. Show that $\{b_n\}$ is convergent and find the limit.

Solution: From $b_1 = 1$, we obtain

$$b_2 = \sqrt{2 + b_1} = \sqrt{3}, \; b_3 = \sqrt{2 + b_2} = \sqrt{2 + \sqrt{3}} \approx \sqrt{2 + 1.732},$$

and so on. Hence, we **suspect** that the sequence is monotone increasing and try to prove this **by induction**.

Claim 1. $b_n \leq b_{n+1}$ for all $n \geq 1$.
Clearly the claim holds for $n = 1$ (since $b_1 = 1 < \sqrt{3} = b_2$).
Assume it holds for $n = k$ (i.e., that $b_k \leq b_{k+1}$). Then,

$$b_{k+2} = \sqrt{2 + b_{k+1}} \geq \sqrt{2 + b_k} = b_{k+1}.$$

Hence, by induction, $\{b_n\}$ is monotone increasing.

Claim 2. $b_n \leq 2$ for all $n \geq 1$.
The proof of this claim is also by induction. For $n = 1$, $b_1 = 1 < 2$. Assume $b_k \leq 2$ for some integer $k > 0$. Then $b_{k+1} = \sqrt{2 + b_k} \leq \sqrt{4} = 2$. Hence, by induction $\{b_n\}$ is bounded above. By Theorem 4.3.1(a), $\{b_n\}$ converges.
Let $\lim b_n = x$. Then, since $\lim b_n = \lim b_{n+1}$, we have $x = \sqrt{2 + x}$ which yields $x^2 - x - 2 = 0$. Hence $x = 2$ or $x = -1$. Since $b_1 = 1$ and $\{b_n\}$ is monotone increasing, $\lim b_n = 2$.

EXERCISES 4.1

1. (a) Let $\{a_n\}$ be a convergent sequence. Prove that $\lim a_{n+1} = \lim a_n$.

   (b) Let $a_1 > 1$ and $a_{n+1} = 2 - \frac{1}{a_n}$ for $n \geq 1$. Show that $\{a_n\}$ is bounded and monotone. Find the limit of $\{a_n\}$.

2. Establish the convergence or the divergence of the sequence $\{b_n\}$ where $b_n = \frac{1}{n+1} + \frac{1}{n+2} + \cdots + \frac{1}{2n}$ for $n \in \mathbb{N}$.

3. Let $a_n = \frac{1}{1^2} + \frac{1}{2^2} + \cdots + \frac{1}{n^2}$ for each $n \in \mathbb{N}$. Prove that $\{a_n\}$ is increasing and bounded, and hence converges.

   (**Hint**: Note that if $k \geq 2$, then $\frac{1}{k^2} \leq \frac{1}{k(k-1)} = \frac{1}{k-1} - \frac{1}{k}$.)

4. Establish the convergence and find the limits of the following sequences:

   (a) $\{(1 + \frac{1}{n})^{n+1}\}$ (b) $\{(1 + \frac{1}{n})^{2n}\}$

   (c) $\{(1 + \frac{1}{n+1})^{n}\}$ (d) $\{(1 - \frac{1}{n})^{n}\}$.

5. Verify the fact used in Example 4.3.4(*ii*) that
   $$\left(1 + \frac{1}{n}\right)^n \leq 3 \text{ for all integers } n > 1.$$
   Hint: Use binomial expansion.

4.5   Sandwich Theorem and Some Applications

If we cannot compute a limit directly (when it exists), we may be able to find it indirectly by means of a theorem called the *Sandwich Theorem*. This theorem refers to a sequence $\{b_n\}$ whose n^{th} term is sandwiched between the nth terms of two other *convergent* sequences $\{a_n\}$ and $\{c_n\}$. If $\{a_n\}$ and $\{c_n\}$ have *the same limit* as $n \to \infty$, then $\{b_n\}$ has this limit also. We now prove a special case of the Sandwich Theorem in which $\{a_n\}$ is the constant sequence $a_n = l \ \forall \ n$. The proof of the general case is left as an easy exercise (Exercises 4.2, Problem 9).

Theorem 4.5.1 (Sandwich Theorem) *Suppose $\{a_n\}$ and $\{b_n\}$ are sequences of real numbers such that for some integer*

$N_0 \geq 1$, *we have*

$$l \leq b_n \leq a_n \ \forall \ n \geq N_0.$$

If $\{a_n\}$ converges to l, then $\{b_n\}$ also converges to l.

Proof. By definition, $a_n \to l$ means given any $\epsilon > 0$, there exists an integer $\overline{n} > 0$ such that $|a_n - l| < \epsilon$ for all $n > \overline{n}$. Observe that $0 \leq b_n - l$, so that since $b_n \leq a_n$ we have $0 \leq |b_n - l| \leq |a_n - l|$. So, for the given $\epsilon > 0$, and all $n > \max(\overline{n}, N_0)$, we have

$$|b_n - l| \leq |a_n - l| < \epsilon.$$

Hence, $b_n \to l$ as $n \to \infty$. $\square$

Definition 4.5.2 (a) If a sequence $\{a_n\}$ of real numbers converges to 0, it is called a **null sequence**.

(b) If a sequence does not have a limit, it is also called an **oscillating sequence**. If the sequence is also bounded, then it is called a **finite oscillating sequence**. If it is not bounded, it is called an **infinite oscillating sequence**.

Example 4.5.3
The sequence $\{(-1)^n\}$ is a *finite oscillating* sequence, whereas $\{(-1)^n n\}$ is an *infinite oscillating* sequence.

4.5.1 Some Applications of Sandwich Theorem

One very important application of the Sandwich Theorem is in the proof of one of the fundamental theorems of mathematical analysis- the Bolzano-Weierstrass Theorem which we shall prove in the next chapter. Meanwhile we give other applications.

In Section 4.3, we proved that

$$\lim_{n\to\infty}\left(1+\frac{1}{n}\right)^n = \lim_{n\to\infty}\left(1+\frac{1}{n}\right)^{n+1} = e.$$

This is the first result in the box at the beginning of this chapter. In this section, we compute the remaining four limits. The *Sandwich Theorem, Bernoulli's inequality and the Binomial Theorem* are the tools necessary for the computations. We present the computations as an example.

Example 4.5.4

Prove the following statements.

(*i*) $\displaystyle\lim_{n\to\infty}\frac{1}{n^p} = 0$ for $p > 0$;

(*ii*) If $|a| < 1$, then $\{a^n\}$ and $\{na^n\}$ are null sequences.

(*iii*) $\displaystyle\lim_{n\to\infty}\sqrt[n]{n} = 1$;   (*iv*) $\displaystyle\lim_{n\to\infty}\sqrt[n]{a} = 1$ for $a > 0$.

Proof:

(i) Let $\epsilon > 0$ be given. We show that there exists $N(\epsilon) \in \mathbb{N}$ such that

$$\left|\frac{1}{n^p} - 0\right| < \epsilon \ \forall \ n \geq N(\epsilon),$$

i.e., we want to show there exists $N(\epsilon) \in \mathbb{N}$ such that $\forall \ n \geq N(\epsilon)$,

$$\frac{1}{n^p} < \epsilon \text{ i.e., } n > \frac{1}{\sqrt[p]{\epsilon}}.$$

Choose $N(\epsilon) = \left[\frac{1}{\sqrt[p]{\epsilon}} + 1\right]$ and this completes the proof.

(ii) If $a = 0$, then we are done. So assume that $a \neq 0$. Since $|a| < 1$ then $\frac{1}{|a|} > 1$. Let $\frac{1}{|a|} = 1 + p$, $p > 0$. Then, using Bernoulli's inequality, (Lemma 4.3.2),

$$\frac{1}{|a|^n} = (1 + p)^n > 1 + np > np \quad \text{for} \quad n > 1, \ (\text{or } n \geq 2).$$

i.e., $0 \leq np|a|^n < 1$ for all integers $n > 1$, so that

$$0 \leq |a|^n < \frac{1}{np}, \quad n > 1, \ a \neq 0.$$

Since $\frac{1}{np} \to 0$ as $n \to \infty$, by the sandwich theorem, $|a|^n \to 0$ as $n \to \infty$. So, $\{a^n\} \to 0$ as $n \to \infty$, as required, establishing No. 2 in the box.

In the same manner, using the same notations and Binomial Theorem,

$$
\begin{aligned}
0 \leq |na^n - 0| &= n|a|^n \\
&= \frac{n}{(1 + p)^n} = \frac{n}{1 + \binom{n}{1}p + \binom{n}{2}p^2 + \cdots + p^n} \\
&< \frac{n}{\binom{n}{2}p^2} \quad \text{(since all terms are positive).}
\end{aligned}
$$

This gives,

$$0 \leq |na^n - 0| < \frac{2}{(n-1)p^2}$$

and since $\frac{2}{(n-1)p^2} \to 0$ as $n \to \infty$, it follows from the sandwich theorem that $\{na^n\}$ is a null sequence if $|a| < 1$, establishing No. 3 in the box.

(iii) Let $a_n = n^{1/n} - 1$ and note that $a_n \geq 0$ for all n. We then need to show that $\lim_{n\to\infty} a_n = 0$. Since $1 + a_n =$

$n^{1/n}$, we have $n = (1 + a_n)^n$. For $n \geq 2$, we use the *binomial expansion* of $(1 + a_n)^n$ to conclude that

$$n = (1+a_n)^n \geq 1 + na_n + \frac{n(n-1)}{2}a_n{}^2 > \frac{n(n-1)}{2}a_n{}^2.$$

Thus $n > \frac{n(n-1)}{2}a_n{}^2$ and so $a_n{}^2 < \frac{2}{n-1}$. Consequently we have $a_n < \sqrt{\frac{2}{n-1}}$ for $n \geq 2$. So, $0 \leq a_n \leq \sqrt{\frac{2}{n-1}}$ for $n \geq 2$, and by the sandwich theorem, $\lim\limits_{n\to\infty} a_n = 0$, establishing No. 4 in the box.

(iv) First, suppose $a \geq 1$. Then for $n \geq a$, we have $1 \leq a^{1/n} \leq n^{1/n}$. Since $\lim n^{1/n} = 1$, it follows that $\lim\limits_{n\to\infty} a^{1/n} = 1$. Now suppose that $0 < a < 1$. Then $\frac{1}{a} > 1$ and so $\lim\limits_{n\to\infty} \sqrt[n]{\frac{1}{a}} = 1$. Hence $\lim\limits_{n\to\infty} a^{1/n} = 1$, establishing No. 5 in the box.

Example 4.5.5 Prove the following statements.

(i) The sequence $\{a_n\}$ defined by $a_n = \frac{n+3}{n^2-1}$ is a null sequence.

(ii) The sequence $\{a_n\}$ defined by $a_n = \frac{2n^2+3}{n^2-5}$ converges to 2.

(iii) $\lim\limits_{n\to\infty} \dfrac{2n^3 - 3n + 1}{n^3 + 7} - 2.$

(iv) $\{(-\frac{2}{3})^n\}$ converges to 0.

Solution: (i) Clearly $a_n \geq 0$ for $n > 1$. Then

$$0 \leq a_n = \frac{n+3}{n^2-1} < \frac{2n}{n^2-1} \quad \text{for} \quad n > 3$$

$$< \frac{2n}{n^2 - \frac{n^2}{2}} = \frac{2n}{\frac{n^2}{2}} = \frac{4}{n}, \text{ since } n > 3.$$

By the sandwich theorem, the result follows.

(ii)   Here,

$$|a_n - 2| = \frac{13}{|n^2 - 5|} < \frac{13}{n^2 - \frac{n^2}{2}} = \frac{26}{n^2} \quad \text{for} \quad \frac{n^2}{2} > 5 \quad \text{or} \quad n > \sqrt{10}.$$

Hence,

$$0 \leq |a_n - 2| < \frac{26}{n^2}.$$

The result follows by sandwich theorem.

(iii)   For this,

$$0 \leq \left| \frac{2n^3 - 3n + 1}{n^3 + 7} - 2 \right| = \frac{3n + 13}{n^3 + 7} < \frac{3n + 13}{n^3}$$

$$\leq \frac{4n}{n^3} = \frac{4}{n^2} \quad \text{for} \quad n \geq 13.$$

By sandwich theorem, the result follows.

(iv)   Take $a = \frac{-2}{3}$. Then $|a| = \frac{2}{3} < 1$. By part (ii) of Example 4.5.4, $\{(\frac{-2}{3})^n\}$ converges to 0.

Remark 4.5.6 The reader is advised to note the tricks employed in taking estimates for the cases when the 'denominator' involves a negative constant and when it involves a positive constant as illustrated in (i), (ii) and (iii), respectively.

Next we prove the following "Ratio Test" for sequences of positive terms that can be used to show that certain sequences converge to zero. (**This theorem can be handy in proving "convergence to zero" and should be remembered**).

Theorem 4.5.7 *Suppose that $\{a_n\}$ is a sequence of positive terms and that the limit*

$$L = \lim_{n \to \infty} \frac{a_{n+1}}{a_n} \ \text{exists} .$$

If $L < 1$, then $\lim_{n \to \infty} a_n = 0$.

Proof. Since $L < 1$, there exists $r \in \mathbb{R}$ such that $L < r < 1$. Let $\epsilon_0 = r - L > 0$. Then, there exists an integer N_0 such that for all $n > N_0$,

$$\left| \frac{a_{n+1}}{a_n} - L \right| < \epsilon_0.$$

Fix $k = N_0 + 1$. Then, $\forall\, n > k$ we have $n - 1 > N_0$, so that

$$\frac{a_n}{a_{n-1}} < L + \epsilon_0 = L + (r - L) = r.$$

It follows that for all $n > k$,

$$0 < a_n < r a_{n-1} < r^2 a_{n-2} < \cdots < r^{n-k} a_k.$$

Let $M = \frac{a_k}{r^k}$. Then $0 < a_n < M r^n$ for all $n > k$. Since $0 < r < 1$, we have $\lim_{n \to \infty} r^n = 0$. Thus, by sandwich theorem, $\lim_{n \to \infty} a_n = 0$. $\square$

EXERCISES 4.2

1. Find $n_0 \in \mathbb{N}$ such that $\left| \frac{3n}{n+2} - 3 \right| < \frac{1}{7}$ for all $n > n_0$.

2. Prove that the sequence $\{a_n\}$ is null when a_n is given by

$$(a)\ \frac{3n + 2}{n^2 + 1} \quad (b)\ \frac{n^2 + 4}{n^3 - 12} \quad (c)\ \frac{(-1)^n}{\sqrt{n}} \quad (d)\ \frac{n^3 + 2n^2 - 1}{n^4 - n^2 + 2}.$$

3. Prove that the following sequences converge:

   (a) $\left\{\frac{n-1}{n+1}\right\}$ (b) $\left\{\frac{3n^3+3n^2-n-1}{n^3+n^2-2}\right\}$ $(n \geq 2)$

   (c) $\left\{\frac{2n^2+1}{n^2+3n}\right\}$ (d) $\left\{\frac{3n^2-1}{n^2-5n}\right\}$ $(n \geq 6)$

   (e) $\{\sqrt{n}(\sqrt{n+1}-\sqrt{n})\}$ (f) $\left\{\frac{5n-3}{8n+11}\right\}$.

4. Find the **supremum** and **infimum** of each of the following sequences:

   (a) $\left\{\frac{n-1}{2n}\right\}$ (b) $\left\{\frac{(-1)^n n}{2n+1}\right\}$

   (c) $\left\{\frac{1+(-1)^n}{3}\right\}$ (d) $\left\{\sin\frac{n\pi}{2}\right\}$

   (e) $\left\{\frac{1}{n} - \sin\frac{n\pi}{2}\right\}$ (f) $\left\{\left(1+\frac{1}{2n}\right)\cos\frac{n\pi}{3}\right\}$.

5. Show that

   (a) $\{(a^{1/n} - 1)\}$, $a > 0$, is a null sequence;   (b) $\left\{\frac{3n}{n+2}\right\}$ converges to 3.

   (Note that (a) is the 5th limit in the box at the begining of this chapter. We already established it in Example 4.5.4(iv). Here, you are required to use a particular method. Hint: Examine the cases $a = 1$, $a \in (0, 1)$, $a \geq 1$).

6. Let $a_1 = \frac{2}{1} \cdot \frac{1}{1^2}$, $a_2 = \frac{2 \cdot 4}{1 \cdot 3} \cdot \frac{1}{2^2}$, $a_3 = \frac{2 \cdot 4 \cdot 6}{1 \cdot 3 \cdot 5} \cdot \frac{1}{3^2}$, ... Write down the general expression for a_n and show that $a_n < \frac{2}{n}$. Discuss the convergence or divergence of $\{a_n\}$.

7. Determine which of the following sequences are monotone. Then guess their limits (where applicable) and prove that your guess is correct.

(a) $\left\{\frac{3n+2}{2n-5}\right\}$ (b) $\left\{\frac{n^2+1}{n}\right\}$

(c) $\left\{\frac{2n^2-1}{2n^2+1}\right\}$ (d) $\left\{1+\frac{1}{n^2}\right\}$

(e) $\left\{\frac{(n-1)(n+2)}{(n+1)(n-3)}\right\}$ (f) $\left\{1+\frac{(-1)^n}{n}\right\}$

(g) $\{n+(-1)^n\}$ (h) $\{2n+(-1)^n\}$

(i) $\left\{\frac{10^n}{n!}\right\}.$

8. For the following sequences, show that they are monotone and bounded. Prove that they converge to the
   indicated limits as $n \to \infty$.

   (a) $a_1 = 1,\ a_{n+1} = \sqrt{a_n + 1},\ n = 1, 2, 3, \ldots$ $\left(a_n \to \frac{1+\sqrt{5}}{2}\right).$

   (b) $a_{n+1} = a_n^2 + \frac{1}{4},\ n = 1, 2, 3, \ldots$ and $a_1 = a.$
   $\left(a_n \to \frac{1}{2}\ \text{if}\ 0 < a \leq \frac{1}{2}\ \text{and}\ a_n \to \infty\ \text{if}\ a > \frac{1}{2}\right).$

9. Suppose that $\{a_n\}$, $\{b_n\}$ and $\{c_n\}$ are sequences such
   that $a_n \leq b_n \leq c_n$ for all $n \in \mathbb{N}$ and such that $\lim a_n =
   \lim c_n = a^*.$ Prove that $\lim b_n = a^*.$ (This is the
   general form of the Sandwich Theorem).

4.6 Uniqueness of Limit

Having studied convergent sequences, the question before us
now is: can a convergent sequence converge to more than
one limit? In this section, we answer this question as well
as study some algebraic operations enjoyed by convergent
sequences.

Theorem 4.6.1 *If a sequence $\{a_n\}$ converges to a limit,
then the limit is unique.*

Proof. Suppose, for contradiction, that the sequence $\{a_n\}$ converges to two limits a and b, $a \neq b$. Then given any $\epsilon > 0$ there exists $N(\epsilon) \in \mathbb{N}$ such that

$$|a_n - a| < \frac{\epsilon}{2} \ \forall \ n \geq N(\epsilon).$$

Also, there exists $\overline{N}(\epsilon) \in \mathbb{N}$ such that

$$|a_n - b| < \frac{\epsilon}{2} \ \forall \ n \geq \overline{N}(\epsilon).$$

Hence, for all $n \geq \max\{N(\epsilon), \overline{N}(\epsilon)\}$, both inequalities $|a_n - a| < \frac{\epsilon}{2}$ and $|a_n - b| < \frac{\epsilon}{2}$ hold. Then

$$
\begin{aligned}
|a - b| &= |a - a_n + a_n - b| \\
&< |a - a_n| + |a_n - b| \\
&< \epsilon \ \text{for all} \ n \geq \max\{N(\epsilon), \overline{N}(\epsilon)\}.
\end{aligned}
$$

This implies that $a = b$. Contradiction. Hence the theorem is proved. $\square$

Remark 4.6.2 By Theorem 4.6.1, we are then justified to use the definite article before "limit" of **a convergent sequence**. Note that we **cannot** associate the word **limit** with any sequence until we have shown that the sequence is convergent.

4.7   Limit Theorems

Given one or more sequences, one can form new sequences in a natural way. For instance, we define the sum of $\{a_n\}$ and $\{b_n\}$ as $\{s_n\}$ where

$$s_n = a_n + b_n, \ \text{for all} \ n = 1, 2, 3, \ldots.$$

In a similar manner, one defines the difference of $\{a_n\}$ and $\{b_n\}$ as $v_n = a_n - b_n$ and $w_n = b_n - a_n$. Note that $\{v_n\} =$

$\{-w_n\}$. The product of $\{a_n\}$ and $\{b_n\}$ is $\{a_n b_n\}$ while their quotient is $\{\frac{a_n}{b_n}\}$ provided $0 \notin \{b_n\}$.

Having seen how to form "new" sequences from "old" ones, the question now is: Suppose the "old" sequences converge, what happens to the "new" ones? For this, we have the following theorem.

Theorem 4.7.1 *Let $\{a_n\}$, $\{b_n\}$ be sequences of real numbers and let*
$a_n \to a$, $b_n \to b$. Then

(a) $a_n + b_n \to a + b$;

(b) $a_n b_n \to ab$;

(c) $k + a_n \to k + a$, $\quad k a_n \to ka \quad (k \in \mathbb{R})$;

(d) $\frac{a_n}{b_n} \to \frac{a}{b}$ provided $b_n \neq 0$, $n = 1, 2, 3, ...$, and $b \neq 0$.

Proof.

(a) To prove that the sum $\{a_n + b_n\}$ of the sequences $\{a_n\}$ and $\{b_n\}$ has the limit $a + b$ as $n \to \infty$, we must show that for any $\epsilon > 0$ there exists $N(\epsilon) \in \mathbb{N}$ such that

$$|(a_n + b_n) - (a + b)| < \epsilon \; \forall \, n \geq N(\epsilon). \qquad (4.7.1)$$

If $\epsilon > 0$, then so is $\frac{\epsilon}{2}$, and because $\lim_{n \to \infty} a_n = a$ we know that there exists $N_1(\epsilon) \in \mathbb{N}$ such that

$$|a_n - a| < \frac{\epsilon}{2} \; \forall \, n \geq N_1(\epsilon). \qquad (4.7.2)$$

Similarly, there exists $N_2(\epsilon) \in \mathbb{N}$ such that

$$|b_n - b| < \frac{\epsilon}{2} \; \forall \, n \geq N_2(\epsilon). \qquad (4.7.3)$$

Now let $N(\epsilon) = \max\{N_1(\epsilon),\ N_2(\epsilon)\}$. Then the inequalities (4.7.2) and (4.7.3) hold for all $n \geq N(\epsilon)$. Thus,

$$
\begin{aligned}
|(a_n + b_n) - (a + b)| &= |(a_n - a) + (b_n - b)| \\
&< |a_n - a| + |b_n - b| \\
&< \frac{\epsilon}{2} + \frac{\epsilon}{2} = \epsilon.
\end{aligned}
$$

This establishes (4.7.1) and proves part (a) of the theorem.

(b) Since every convergent sequence is bounded (Theorem 3.2.6), there exists $M > 0$ such that $|a_n| \leq M$, $|b_n| \leq M$, $|b| \leq M$, $\forall$ integers $n \geq 1$. Since $b_n \to b$ and $a_n \to a$, given any $\epsilon > 0$, there exists an integer $n(\epsilon) > 0$ such that $|b_n - b| < \frac{\epsilon}{2(M+1)}$, $|a_n - a| < \frac{\epsilon}{2(M+1)}$ $\forall$ integers $n \geq n(\epsilon)$. These inequalities imply that for $n \geq n(\epsilon)$ we have that

$$
\begin{aligned}
|a_n b_n - ab| &= |a_n b_n - a_n b + a_n b - ab| \\
&= |a_n(b_n - b) + b(a_n - a)| \\
&< |a_n|.|b_n - b| + |b|.|a_n - a| \\
&< M\frac{\epsilon}{2(M+1)} + M\frac{\epsilon}{2(M+1)} < \epsilon.
\end{aligned}
$$

Thus $a_n b_n \to ab$.

(c) $|k + a_n - (k + a)| = |a_n - a| \to 0$ as $n \to \infty$, completing the proof of the first part of (c). The second part is also trivial and is left for the reader.

(d) It suffices to prove that $\frac{1}{b_n} \to \frac{1}{b}$ and then the result follows from part (b). Now, $b_n \to b$ implies given $\epsilon^* = \frac{1}{2}|b| > 0$ (since $b \neq 0$), there exists an integer $n(\epsilon^*) > 0$ such that $|b_n - b| < \epsilon^*$ for all integers $n \geq n(\epsilon^*)$. Moreover, $\Big||b_n| - |b|\Big| \leq |b_n - b| < \epsilon^*$ so that $|b_n| > |b| - \epsilon^* = \frac{|b|}{2}$ for all integers $n \geq n(\epsilon^*)$. Now, let $\epsilon > 0$

be arbitrary. There exists an integer $n(\epsilon)$ such that for all integers $n \geq n(\epsilon)$, $|b_n - b| < \frac{\epsilon}{2}|b|^2$. Choose $N = \max\{n(\epsilon^*), n(\epsilon)\}$. Then, for all integers $n \geq N$,

$$\left|\frac{1}{b_n} - \frac{1}{b}\right| = \frac{|b_n - b|}{|b_n|.|b|} = |b_n - b|\frac{1}{|b_n|}\frac{1}{|b|} < \frac{\epsilon}{2}|b|^2.\frac{2}{|b|}\frac{1}{|b|} = \epsilon$$

and so $\frac{1}{b_n} \to \frac{1}{b}$ as $n \to \infty$. By part (b), $\frac{a_n}{b_n} \to \frac{a}{b}$ as $n \to \infty$. $\square$

EXERCISES 4.3

1. A sequence $\{a_n\}$ is defined by $a_1 = 1$ and $a_{n+1} = \frac{1}{1+a_n}$ for all $n \geq 1$. Assuming that $\{a_n\}$ is convergent, find its limit.

2. Find the limit of the sequence defined by

$$\left\{\sqrt{3}, \sqrt{3\sqrt{3}}, \sqrt{3\sqrt{3\sqrt{3}}}, ...\right\}.$$

3. A sequence $\{a_n\}$ is given by $a_1 = \sqrt{3}$, $a_{n+1} = \sqrt{3 + a_n}$. Show that the sequence $\{a_n\}$ is convergent and find its limit.

4. Show that the sequence $\{a_n\}$ defined by $a_1 = 2$, $a_{n+1} = \frac{1}{3-a_n}$ is convergent and find its limit.

5. Prove that each of the following sequences converges and find its limit.

(a) $a_1 = 1$ and $a_{n+1} = \frac{1}{3}(2a_n + 3)$ $\forall\, n \geq 1$.

(b) $a_1 = 2$ and $a_{n+1} = \sqrt{2a_n + 1}$ $\forall\, n \geq 1$.

(c) $a_1 = 3$ and $a_{n+1} = \sqrt{10a_n - 17}$ $\forall\, n \geq 1$.

6. Suppose that $\lim a_n = a^*$, and $a^* > 0$. Prove that there exists $N_0 \in \mathbb{N}$ such that $a_n > 0$ for all $n > N_0$.

7. Suppose that $\lim a_n = 0$ and $\{b_n\}$ is a sequence in $\mathbb{R}$.
   (i) Is $\lim a_n b_n = 0$? If your answer is yes, prove it. If it is no, give a counter example.
   (ii) If you have produced a counter example to (i), give a sufficient condition on $\{b_n\}$ which will guarantee that $\lim a_n b_n = 0$. Prove that your condition is sufficient.

8. Prove that each of the following sequences is divergent.
   (a) $a_n = 3n$ (b) $a_n = (-2)^n$.

9. In the following, say whether the statement made is true or false. If it is true, prove it. If it is false, give a counter example.
   (a) If $\{a_n\}$ converges to a^*, then $\{|a_n|\}$ converges to $|a^*|$.
   (b) If $\{|a_n|\}$ converges, then $\{a_n\}$ converges.
   (c) $\lim a_n = 0$ if and only if $\lim |a_n| = 0$.

10. Given a sequence $\{a_n\}$ and given $k \in \mathbb{N}$, let $\{b_n\}$ be the sequence defined by $b_n = a_{n+k}$, i.e., the terms in $\{b_n\}$ are the same terms in $\{a_n\}$ after the first k terms of $\{a_n\}$ have been dropped. Prove that $\{a_n\}$ converges if and only if $\{b_n\}$ converges. Show that if they converge, then $\lim a_n = \lim b_n$.

    Remark: This exercise shows that the convergence of a sequence is not affected by omitting or changing a *finite* number of terms.

11. If $a_n = ns^n$ and $0 < s < 1$, prove $\lim\limits_{n \to \infty} a_n = 0$.

12. For what values of s is the sequence $\{ns^n\}$ convergent?

13. The set $N(a, \epsilon) = \{x \in \mathbb{R} : |x - a| < \epsilon\}$ is called a neighbourhood of a with radius $\epsilon > 0$. Prove the

following assertions.

(a) $a_n \to a$ if and only if $\forall\, \epsilon > 0, \exists\, N_0 \in \mathbb{N}$ such that $a_n \in N(a, \epsilon)\ \forall\, n \geq N_0$.

(b) $a_n \to a$ if and only if $\forall\, \epsilon > 0$, all but finitely many a_n are in $N(a, \epsilon)$.

4.8   Sequences Diverging to $+\infty$ and $-\infty$

Definition 4.8.1 A sequence $\{a_n\}$ is said to *diverge to* $+\infty$, and we write $\lim\limits_{n \to \infty} a_n = +\infty$, if:

For any given $M \in \mathbb{R}, \exists\, n_M \in \mathbb{N}$ such that $n \geq n_M \Rightarrow a_n > M$.

(See Fig. 4.4).

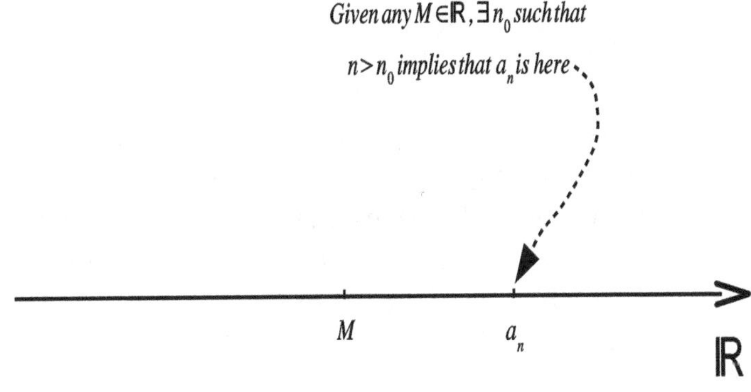

Fig 4.4

Similarly, a sequence $\{a_n\}$ is said to *diverge to* $-\infty$, and we write $\lim\limits_{n \to \infty} a_n = -\infty$, if:

For any given $M \in \mathbb{R}, \exists\, n_0 \in \mathbb{N}$ such that $n > n_0 \Rightarrow a_n < M$.

(See Fig. 4.5).

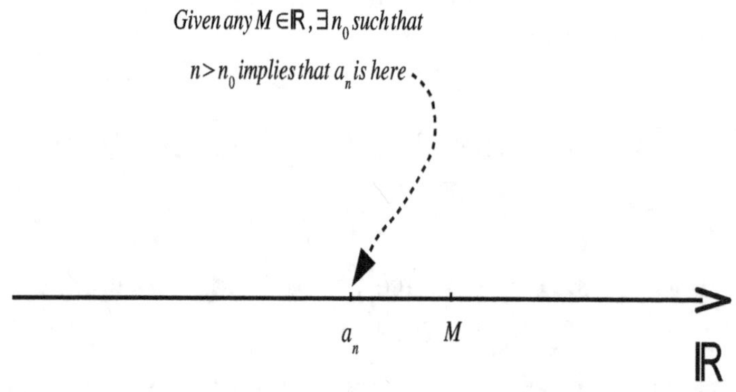

Fig 4.5

Remark 4.8.2 Note that the symbols $+\infty$ and $-\infty$ do not represent real numbers. When $\lim a_n = +\infty$ or $-\infty$, we say the limit exists, but this does not mean the sequence converges. Truly, a sequence in $\mathbb{R}$ converges if and only if the limit exists **and is a real number**.

Example 4.8.3

$$\lim_{n\to\infty} \frac{3n^2 - 4}{n + 1} = +\infty.$$

Solution: Let $a_n = \frac{3n^2-4}{n+1}$.
The trick is to get a *lower* bound for $\{a_n\}$. So, we proceed as follows:

$$3n^2 - 4 \;\geq\; 3n^2 - n^2, \quad \text{when } n > 2$$
$$= 2n^2.$$

Furthermore, we have

$$n+1 \;\le\; n+n, \quad \text{for } n > 1$$
$$= \; 2n.$$

So for $n > 2$, we obtain,

$$\frac{3n^2 - 4}{n+1} \ge \frac{2n^2}{2n} = n.$$

Hence $a_n \ge n \;\forall\; n \ge 2$. But recall, we already imposed the conditions $n > 1$ and $n > 2$, ($n > 2$ covers both). So, given any $M \in \mathbb{R}$, take $n_M = \max\{2, M\} + 1$. Then for $n \ge n_M$, we have, $a_n \ge n \ge n_M = \max\{2, M\} + 1 > M$. This completes the solution.

We prove the following theorem.

Theorem 4.8.4 *Suppose that $\{a_n\}$ and $\{b_n\}$ are sequences such that $a_n \le b_n \;\forall\; n \in \mathbb{N}$. (See Fig. 4.6).*

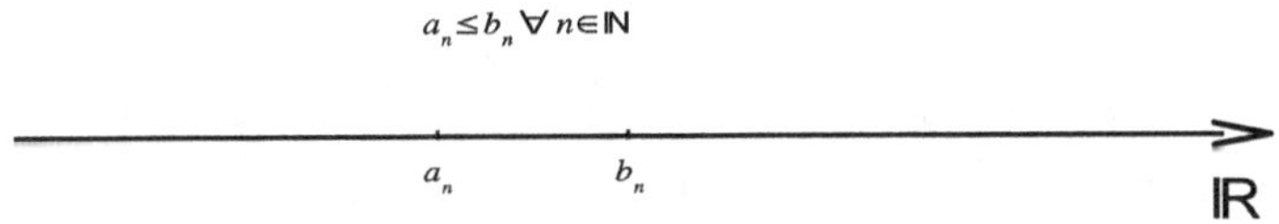

Fig 4.6

(a)   *If* $\lim a_n = +\infty$, *then* $\lim b_n = +\infty$.

(b)   *If* $\lim b_n = -\infty$, *then* $\lim a_n = -\infty$.

Proof. (a) Let $M \in \mathbb{R}$ be given. Since $\lim a_n = +\infty$, $\exists\, n_M \in \mathbb{N}$ such that $n \geq n_M \Rightarrow a_n > M$. But $b_n \geq a_n$. Hence, $n \geq n_M \Rightarrow b_n \geq a_n > M$ so that $\lim b_n = +\infty$.

(b) Proof is similar. $\square$

We conclude this section with the following theorem.

Theorem 4.8.5 *Let $\{a_n\}$ be a sequence of positive numbers. Then,*

$$\lim a_n = +\infty \iff \lim_{n \to \infty} \frac{1}{a_n} = 0.$$

Proof.   Exercise (See Exercises 4.4, Problem 8).

EXERCISES 4.4

1. Show that (i) $\{2^n\}$ diverges; (ii) $\{\sqrt{n} - 7\}$ diverges.

2. Complete the second part of the proof of Theorem 4.8.4.

3. (a) Give an example of a *convergent* sequence $\{a_n\}$ of positive numbers such that $\lim \frac{a_{n+1}}{a_n} = 1$.
   (b) Give an example of a *divergent* sequence $\{b_n\}$ of positive numbers such that $\lim \frac{b_{n+1}}{b_n} = 1$.

4. Let $\{a_n\}$ be a sequence of positive terms such that $L = \lim \frac{a_{n+1}}{a_n}$ exists. Prove that if $L > 1$, then $\lim a_n = +\infty$.

5. (a) Show that $\lim_{n \to \infty} \frac{r^n}{n!} = 0$ for all $r \in \mathbb{R}$.
   (Hint: Think of a test in this chapter for convergence of a *sequence* to zero and use it).

6. Suppose that $\{a_n\}$ is a convergent sequence with $a \leq a_n \leq b$ for all $n \geq 1$. Prove that

$$a \leq \lim a_n \leq b.$$

7. Prove the following assertions.

   (a)   If $\lim a_n = +\infty$ and $\alpha > 0$, then $\lim \alpha a_n = +\infty$.

   (b)   If $\lim a_n = +\infty$ and $\alpha < 0$, then $\lim \alpha a_n = -\infty$.

   (c) $\lim a_n = +\infty$ if and only if $\lim(-a_n) = -\infty$.

   (d)   If $\lim a_n = +\infty$ and $\{b_n\}$ is a bounded sequence, then

$$\lim(a_n + b_n) = +\infty.$$

8. Prove Theorem 4.8.5.

CHAPTER 5

Bolzano-Weierstrass Theorem; Cauchy Sequences and Completeness of $\mathbb{R}$

5.1 Introduction

In Chapter 3, we introduced sequences of real numbers. In this chapter, we first introduce **subsequences** of sequences of real numbers. We prove *two* very important theorems concerning subsequences.

Theorem 5.2.3 *A sequence $\{a_n\}$ is convergent to the limit a^* if and only if all of its subsequences converge to a^*.*

Theorem 5.3.1 (The Bolzano-Weierstrass Theorem) *Every bounded sequence in $\mathbb{R}$ has a convergent subsequence.*

Then we study the important notions of *upper and lower limits of a sequence.* We also introduce the notion of a *Cauchy sequence* and the related notion of *completeness.* We conclude the chapter with the following theorem.

Theorem 5.7.6 *A sequence $\{a_n\}$ in $\mathbb{R}$ is Cauchy if and only if it is convergent.*

79

5.2   Subsequences

Definition 5.2.1 Let $f : \mathbb{N} \to X$ be a sequence of elements of a set X denoted by $\{a_n\}_{n=1}^{\infty}$. Let

$$n : \mathbb{N} \to \mathbb{N}$$

be an increasing one-to-one function (or equivalently, a *strictly increasing function*) which is defined by

$$n(k) = n_k \in \mathbb{N} \; \forall \; k \in \mathbb{N}.$$

By a **subsequence** $\{a_{n_k}\}_{k=1}^{\infty}$ of $\{a_n\}_{n=1}^{\infty}$, we mean the **composition map**

$$a \circ n : \mathbb{N} \xrightarrow{\; n \;} \mathbb{N} \xrightarrow{\; a \;} X.$$

Clearly, $(a \circ n)(k) = a_{n_k}, \; k \in \mathbb{N}.$

Notation: A subsequence $\{a_{n_j}\}$ has its terms numbered by j as follows:

$$\{a_{n_1}, a_{n_2}, a_{n_3}, ...\}.$$

Thus, $\{a_{n_j}\} = \{a_{n_j}\}_{j=1}^{\infty}.$

If we delete a finite number of the terms of a sequence and re-number the remaining terms *in the same order*, we obtain a subsequence. In fact, we may delete *infinitely many* terms from the original sequence as long as there are still infinitely many terms left. Thus, the sequence

$$\{a_n\} = \{1, 2, 3, ...\}$$

has, for example, $\{1, 3, 5, ...\}$ and $\{2, 4, 6, ...\}$ as subsequences. It is clear that $\{a_n\}$ may have other subsequences, for example, $\{a_n\}$ *itself*. We note, however, that $\{3, 1, 4, 5, ...\}$ is *not* a subsequence of $\{a_n\}$ (Why?).

The following proposition is very important for subsequences.

Proposition 5.2.2. *Let $\{n_k\}_{k=1}^{\infty}$ be a sequence of natural numbers such that $n_k < n_{k+1}$ for all $k \in \mathbb{N}$. Then,*

$$n_k \geq k \ \forall \ k \in \mathbb{N}.$$

Proof. Since $n_1 \in \mathbb{N}$, it follows that $n_1 \geq 1$. So, statement is true for $k = 1$. Now, suppose $n_k \geq k$ for some $k \in \mathbb{N}$. Then, by hypothesis,

$$n_{k+1} > n_k$$

and by induction hypothesis, $n_k \geq k$. Hence,

$$n_{k+1} > n_k \geq k, \ i.e., \ n_{k+1} > k,$$

and this implies (since $k \in \mathbb{N}$) that $n_{k+1} \geq k+1$, completing the induction and completing the proof. $\quad \square$

Definition 5.2.1 can be re-written informally as follows:

Definition 5.2.1*. Let $\{a_n\}$ be a sequence in X and let $\{n_k\}$ be *any* sequence of *natural numbers* such that $n_1 < n_2 < n_3 < \dots$ The sequence $\{a_{n_k}\}_{k=1}^{\infty}$ is called a subsequence of $\{a_n\}$.

We now prove the following very important theorem for subsequences.

Theorem 5.2.3 *A sequence $\{a_n\}_{n=1}^{\infty}$ is convergent to the limit a^* if and only if all of its subsequences converge to the same limit.*

Proof. ($\Longrightarrow$) Let $\{a_n\}$ be a convergent sequence and suppose it converges to a^*. Let $\{a_{n_k}\}_{k=1}^{\infty}$ be an arbitrary subsequence of $\{a_n\}_{n=1}^{\infty}$. We prove $\{a_{n_k}\}_{k=1}^{\infty}$ also converges to a^*. But from the definition of $a^*(= \lim\limits_{n \to \infty} a_n)$ we have that $\forall \ \epsilon > 0, \exists$

an integer $n(\epsilon) > 0$ such that

$$|a_n - a^*| < \epsilon \ \forall \ n \geq n(\epsilon).$$

Then, for any $k > n(\epsilon)$, by Proposition 5.2.2, $n_k \geq k > n(\epsilon)$ so that, replacing n by n_k, we obtain that $\forall \ k \geq n(\epsilon)$,

$$|a_{n_k} - a^*| < \epsilon.$$

This implies, $a_{n_k} \to a^*$ as $k \to \infty$.

($\Longleftarrow$) Suppose **every** subsequence of $\{a_n\}_{n=1}^\infty$ converges to a^*. We want to prove $\{a_n\}_{n=1}^\infty$ converges to a^*. But $\{a_n\}_{n=1}^\infty$ is a subsequence of itself. The result follows. The proof is complete. $\square$

Remark 5.2.4 Theorem 5.2.3 is very useful in showing that a sequence is **not** convergent. By the theorem, it suffices to produce two *subsequences* of the given sequence which converge to different limits. For example, if

$$\{a_n\}_{n=1}^\infty = \{(-1)^n\}_{n=1}^\infty$$

, then the subsequence $\{1, 1, 1, ...\}$ converges to 1 and the subsequence $\{-1, -1, -1, ...\}$ converges to -1. Hence,

$$\{(-1)^n\}_{n=1}^\infty$$

is **not** convergent (by Theorem 5.2.3).   (Compare with Remark 3.2.7).

5.3   The Bolzano-Weierstrass Theorem

We now also prove the following extremely important classical theorem.

Theorem 5.3.1 (The Bolzano-Weierstrass Theorem)
Every bounded sequence in $\mathbb{R}$ has a convergent subsequence.

Plan of the proof.
Let $\{x_n\}$ be a bounded sequence. Let a_0 be a lower bound
and b_0 be an upper bound for $\{x_n\}$. The plan of the proof is
as follows: we will define inductively two sequences, $\{a_n\}$ and
$\{b_n\}$ such that each interval $[a_{n+1}, b_{n+1}]$ is a half of the previous interval $[a_n, b_n]$ and each $[a_n, b_n]$ contains infinitely many
terms of $\{x_n\}$. The a_n's and b_n's will "squeeze" towards a
limit, l. Since each interval $[a_j, b_j]$ contains infinitely many
terms of x_n, we can choose a subsequence $\{x_{n_j}\}$ such that
each $x_{n_j} \in [a_j, b_j]$, and hence $x_{n_j} \to \ell$. We proceed to do
this. The sequences $\{a_n\}$, $\{b_n\}$ are defined as follows.

Proof. We know that $a_0 \leq x_n \leq b_0$ for all $n \geq 1$. Let
$m_0 = \frac{1}{2}(a_0 + b_0)$, the mid point of $[a_0, b_0]$. If there are infinitely many indices j such that $a_0 \leq x_j \leq m_0$, then let
$[a_1, b_1] = [a_0, m_0]$, i.e., let $[a_1, b_1]$ be the left half of $[a_0, b_0]$.
Otherwise there must be infinitely many indices j such that

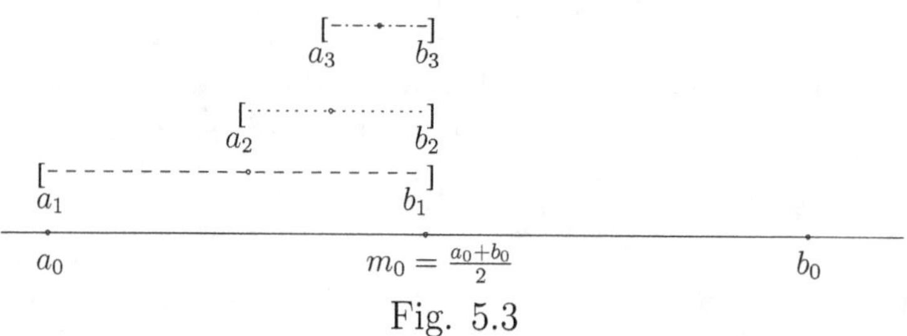

Fig. 5.3

x_j lies in the right half of $[a_0, b_0]$ and , in this case, we take
$[a_1, b_1] = [m_0, b_0]$ where $[a_1, b_1]$ contains points x_j for infinitely many j (See Fig. 5.3). Without loss of generality, let
us assume $[a_1, b_1] = [a_0, m_0]$.

The next step is to let $[a_2, b_2]$ be a half of $[a_1, b_1]$ containing infinitely many terms x_j. Continuing inductively, we let

$[a_{n+1}, b_{n+1}]$ be a half of $[a_n, b_n]$ containing infinitely many terms x_j. It is clear that $\{a_n\}$ is a non-decreasing sequence bounded above by b_0, and b_n is a non-increasing sequence bounded below by a_0. Hence $\{a_n\}$ and $\{b_n\}$ converge. Furthermore, since

$$0 \leq b_n - a_n = \frac{(b_0 - a_0)}{2^n},$$

it follows, by the sandwich theorem, that $\quad \lim a_n = \lim b_n$. Let

$$\lim a_n = \lim b_n = \ell.$$

To define a **subsequence** that converges to ℓ, let $x_{n_1} \in [a_1, b_1]$. Pick $n_2 > n_1$ such that $x_{n_2} \in [a_2, b_2]$. This is possible since $[a_2, b_2]$ contains x_j for infinitely many j, and so there is such a j larger than n_1. Inductively, pick $n_{k+1} > n_k$ such that $x_{n_{k+1}} \in [a_{k+1}, b_{k+1}]$. Again this is possible because $[a_{k+1}, b_{k+1}]$ has infinitely many terms of the sequence. Since $a_k \leq x_{n_k} \leq b_k$ for all k, and $a_k \to \ell, b_k \to \ell$, we have (by the sandwich theorem) that $x_{n_k} \to \ell$. The proof is complete. $\quad\square$

Remark 5.3.2 We remark on the technique used to find a limit of a subsequence in the proof of Bolzano-Weierstrass theorem. The entire sequence is located in an initial interval $[a_0, b_0]$, and in a half of this interval $[a_1, b_1]$ containing infinitely many terms of a_n, and so on. The intervals "squeezed" to **a single point** (since $\lim a_n = \lim b_n = l$) which serves as a limit of some subsequence. The essence of this argument is contained in the next important theorem.

(**The Nested Interval Theorem**) *Let $\{[a_n, b_n]\}$ be any sequence of nested intervals, i.e.,*

$$[a_1, b_1] \supset [a_2, b_2] \supset [a_3, b_3] \supset \cdots.$$

If $b_n - a_n \to 0$ as $n \to \infty$, then the intersection

$$\bigcap_{n=1}^{\infty} [a_n, b_n]$$

contains only one point.

EXERCISES 5.1

1. Convince yourself that the assertion in the proof of Bolzano-Weierstrass theorem that $b_n - a_n = \frac{b_0 - a_0}{2^n}$ for all integers $n \geq 1$ is correct.

2. Show that **every** sequence has a nondecreasing subsequence or a non-increasing subsequence.
   Hint. Assume $\{a_n\}$ has no non-decreasing subsequence, and show it has a non-increasing subsequence as follows. Since there is no non-decreasing subsequence, there exists n_1 such that $a_{n_1} > a_k \ \forall \ k > n_1$. Also the tail sequence $\{a_j\}_{j=n_1+1}^{\infty}$ has no non-decreasing subsequence, so there exists $n_2 > n_1$ such that $a_{n_1} > a_{n_2}$, and so on.

3. Use Problem 2 to prove the Bolzano-Weierstrass theorem.

5.4   Limit Superior and Limit Inferior

5.4.1   The Limit Superior

Definition 5.4.1 Let $\{a_n\}_{n=1}^{\infty}$ be a **bounded sequence** of real numbers.
Consider the **numbers** M_n defined as follows:

$$M_n = \sup_{n}\{a_n, a_{n+1}, a_{n+2}, ...\} = \sup_{j \geq n} a_j$$

so that

$$M_{n+1} = \sup_{n}\{a_{n+1}, a_{n+2}, a_{n+3}, ...\} = \sup_{j \geq n+1} a_j.$$

Observe that

$$A = \{a_{n+1}, a_{n+2}, a_{n+3}, ...\} \subset B = \{a_n, a_{n+1}, a_{n+2}, ...\},$$

so that $supA \leq supB$ and so , it follows from these definitions that $M_{n+1} \leq M_n$ for all integers n. Hence $\{M_n\}_{n=1}^{\infty}$ is a monotone non-increasing sequence of real numbers which is bounded below (since $\{a_n\}_{n=1}^{\infty}$ is bounded). Hence, $\{M_n\}_{n=1}^{\infty}$ converges to $\inf_n M_n$. Denote this $\inf_n M_n$ by β, i.e.,

$$\beta = \lim_{n\to\infty} M_n = \inf_{n\geq 1} M_n = \inf_{n\geq 1} \left(\sup_{i\geq n} a_i \right).$$

The number β is called the **upper limit** or **limit superior**, (or simply, $\lim_{n\to\infty} \sup$) of the bounded sequence $\{a_n\}_{n=1}^{\infty}$. In the sequel, we shall always use the notation:

$$\boxed{\beta = \limsup_{n\to\infty} a_n = \inf_{n\geq 1} \left(\sup_{i\geq n} a_i \right).}$$

Notation:

$\limsup_{n\to\infty} a_n$ is also sometimes denoted by $\overline{\lim}_{n\to\infty} a_n$.

We now give some consequences of the definition of the $\lim_{n\to\infty} \sup$ of a bounded sequence $\{a_n\}_{n=1}^{\infty}$. Let $\beta = \limsup_{n\to\infty} a_n$. This means that

$$\lim_{n\to\infty} M_n = \beta.$$

This implies, given $\epsilon > 0$, $\exists$ an integer $n(\epsilon) > 0$ such that

$$|M_n - \beta| < \epsilon \; \forall \; n \geq n(\epsilon).$$

This implies that

$$\beta - \epsilon < M_n < \beta + \epsilon \; \forall \; n \geq n(\epsilon).$$

But

$$M_n = \sup_{j \geq n} a_j$$

so that we obtain

$$(*) \qquad \beta - \epsilon < \sup_{j \geq n} a_j < \beta + \epsilon \ \forall \ n \geq n(\epsilon).$$

The right-hand inequality implies that

$$a_n \leq \sup_{j \geq n} a_j < \beta + \epsilon \ \forall \ n \geq n(\epsilon).$$

This gives us our first consequence (illustrated in Fig. 5.2) as follows:

$$\mathbf{C_1} \quad \boxed{\ \lim_{n \to \infty} \sup a_n = \beta \implies \begin{cases} \text{given } \epsilon > 0, \ \exists \ n(\epsilon) > 0 : \\ \forall \ n \geq n(\epsilon), \ a_n < \beta + \epsilon. \end{cases}}$$

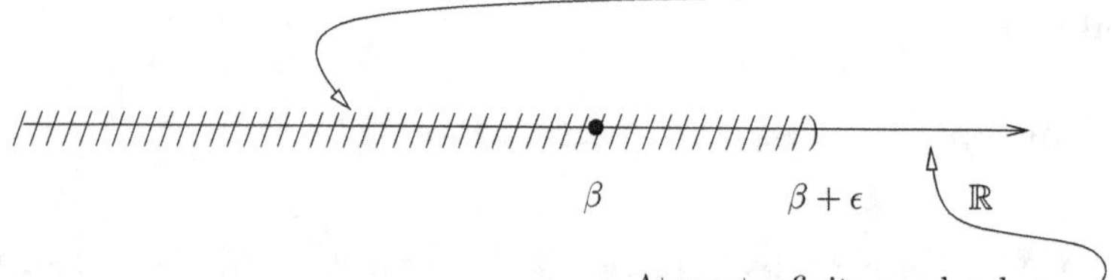

Fig. 5.2

To obtain our second consequence, recall that

$$M_n = \sup_{j \geq n} a_j, \ \ \beta = \inf_{n \geq 1} M_n, \ \ \lim_{n \to \infty} M_n = \beta.$$

Using our characterization of *sup* and *inf*, we obtain our second consequence as follows.

$$\mathbf{C_2} \quad \boxed{\ \lim_{n \to \infty} \sup a_n = \beta \implies \begin{cases} \exists \ \{a_{n_j}\}_{j=1}^{\infty} \subseteq \{a_n\}_{n=1}^{\infty} : \\ a_{n_j} \to \beta \ \text{ as } \ j \to \infty. \end{cases}}$$

We now prove the following proposition which gives our third consequence of the definition of $\limsup_{n\to\infty}$ of a bounded sequence of real numbers.

Proposition 5.4.2 *Let $\{a_n\}_{n=1}^{\infty}$ be a bounded sequence of real numbers and let*

$$\beta = \limsup_{n\to\infty} a_n \ \left(= \inf_{n\geq 1}\left(\sup_{i\geq n} a_i\right)\right).$$

Then, for any given $\epsilon > 0$, the set

$$\{i : a_i \geq \beta + \epsilon\}$$

*is a **finite** set (see Fig. 5.2).*

The proposition asserts that if β is the lim sup of a_n, then for **any** $\epsilon > 0$ given, the number of elements of the sequence on the **right** of $\beta + \epsilon$ (the unshaded part) is finite (see Fig. 5.2).

We now give a proof of the proposition.

Proof. The proof is by contradiction. Suppose there are infinitely many terms of the sequence greater than or equal to $\beta + \epsilon$. These terms constitute a **subsequence** $\{a_{n_k}\}$ of $\{a_n\}_{n=1}^{\infty}$ with the property that

$$a_{n_k} \geq \beta + \epsilon.$$

Thus,

$$M_{n_k} = \sup_{i\geq n_k} a_i \geq a_{n_k} \geq \beta + \epsilon.$$

But

$$\beta = \lim_{n\to\infty} M_n = \lim_{k\to\infty} M_{n_k} \geq \beta + \epsilon,$$

a contradiction. Hence, the set $\{i : a_i > \beta + \epsilon\}$ is finite. $\square$

5.4.2   The Limit Inferior

Definition 5.4.3 Let $\{a_n\}_{n=1}^{\infty}$ be a bounded sequence of real numbers.

Consider the **numbers** m_n defined as follows:

$$m_n = \inf\{a_n, a_{n+1}, a_{n+2}, ...\} = \inf_{j \geq n} a_j$$

so that

$$m_{n+1} = \inf\{a_{n+1}, a_{n+2}, a_{n+3}, ...\} = \inf_{j \geq n+1} a_j.$$

It follows that $\{m_n\}_{n=1}^{\infty}$ is a monotone non-decreasing sequence which is bounded above (since $\{a_n\}_{n=1}^{\infty}$ is bounded) and so converges to $\sup_{n \geq 1} m_n$. Denote this $\sup_{n \geq 1} m_n$ by α, i.e.,

$$\alpha = \lim_{n \to \infty} m_n = \sup_n m_n = \sup_n \left(\inf_{j \geq n} a_j \right).$$

The number α is called the **lower limit** or **limit inferior**, (or simply, $\liminf_{n \to \infty}$) of the bounded sequence $\{a_n\}_{n=1}^{\infty}$. In the sequel, we shall always use the notation:

$$\boxed{\alpha = \liminf_{n \to \infty} a_n = \sup_{n \geq 1} \left(\inf_{i \geq n} a_i \right)}$$

Notation:

$$\liminf_{n \to \infty} a_n \text{ is also denoted by } \varliminf_{n \to \infty} a_n.$$

Following the method similar to that used for $\limsup_{n \to \infty} a_n$, we obtain the following consequences of the definition of $\liminf_{n \to \infty} a_n$ for a bounded sequence $\{a_n\}_{n=1}^{\infty}$ of real numbers (See Exercises 5.2, Problem 5).

$$\boxed{\mathbf{C_1} \quad \liminf_{n \to \infty} a_n = \beta \implies \begin{cases} \text{given } \epsilon > 0, \ \exists \, n(\epsilon) > 0 : \\ \forall \, n \geq n(\epsilon), \ a_n > \beta - \epsilon. \end{cases}}$$

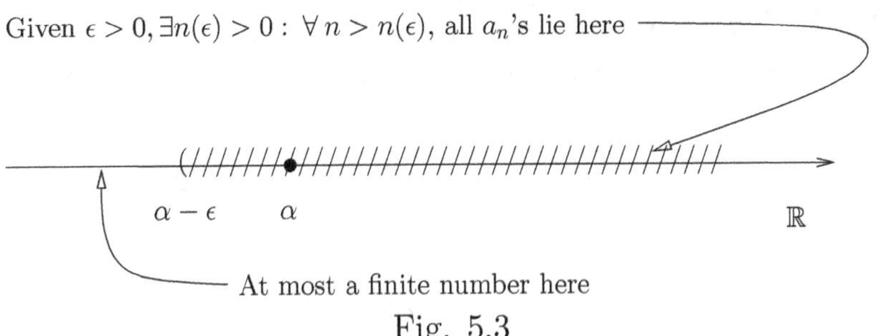

Fig. 5.3

$$\boxed{\mathbf{C_2} \quad \liminf_{n\to\infty} a_n = \alpha \implies \begin{cases} \exists \{a_{n_j}\}_{j=1}^{\infty} \subseteq \{a_n\}_{n=1}^{\infty} : \\ a_{n_j} \to \alpha \ \text{ as } \ j \to \infty. \end{cases}}$$

We also have the following consequence of the definition of lim inf of a bounded sequence.

Proposition 5.4.4 *Let* $\{a_n\}_{n=1}^{\infty}$ *be a bounded sequence of real numbers and let*

$$\alpha = \liminf_{n\to\infty} a_n \quad \left(= \sup_{n\geq 1} \left(\inf_{j\geq n} a_j \right) \right).$$

Then, for any given $\epsilon > 0$, *the set*

$$\{i : a_i \leq \alpha - \epsilon\}$$

is a **finite** *set (see Fig. 5.3)..*

5.5 Convergent Sequences Re-visited

We now prove the following important proposition.

Proposition 5.5.1 *A bounded sequence* $\{a_n\}_{n=1}^{\infty}$ *of real numbers is convergent to* $a^* \in \mathbb{R}$ *if and only if*

$$\liminf_{n\to\infty} a_n = a^* = \limsup_{n\to\infty} a_n.$$

Proof. ($\Longrightarrow$) Let the sequence $\{a_n\}_{n=1}^{\infty}$ converge to $a^* \in \mathbb{R}$. Then, $\{a_n\}$ is bounded. Moreover, $\forall\, \epsilon > 0,\ \exists\, n(\epsilon) \in \mathbb{N}$ such that

$$a^* - \epsilon < a_n < a^* + \epsilon \ \forall\, n \geq n(\epsilon).$$

This yields

$$(i)\ a^* - \epsilon - \liminf_{n\to\infty} a_n < 0.$$

$$(ii)\ \limsup_{n\to\infty} a_n - a^* - \epsilon < 0.$$

From (i) and (ii), we obtain

$$0 < \limsup_{n\to\infty} a_n - \liminf_{n\to\infty} a_n < 2\epsilon.$$

Since ϵ is arbitrary, we have

$$\limsup_{n\to\infty} a_n = \liminf_{n\to\infty} a_n,$$

completing proof of this direction.

($\Longleftarrow$) Let

$$\liminf_{n\to\infty} a_n = a^* = \limsup_{n\to\infty} a_n.$$

But $\limsup_{n\to\infty} a_n = a^* \Rightarrow$ given $\epsilon > 0, \exists N_1(\epsilon) \in \mathbb{N}$ such that

$$a_n < a^* + \epsilon \ \forall\, n \geq N_1(\epsilon).$$

Also, $\exists N_2(\epsilon) \in \mathbb{N}$ such that

$$a^* - \epsilon < a_n \ \forall\, n \geq N_2(\epsilon).$$

Let $N(\epsilon) = \max\{N_1(\epsilon), N_2(\epsilon)\}$. Then, for $\epsilon > 0$,

$$a^* - \epsilon < a_n < a^* + \epsilon \ \forall\, n \geq N(\epsilon).$$

Hence,

$$|a_n - a^*| < \epsilon \ \forall\, n \geq N(\epsilon),$$

and so, $a_n \to a^*\ (n \to \infty)$. $\square$

From Proposition 5.4.2 and Proposition 5.4.4 we obtain immediately the following proposition.

Proposition 5.5.2 *Let $\{a_n\}_{n=1}^{\infty}$ be a bounded sequence of real numbers. Let*

$$\alpha = \liminf_{n\to\infty} a_n,$$

$$\beta = \limsup_{n\to\infty} a_n.$$

*Then, for every $\epsilon > 0$, there are at most a finite number of terms of the sequence which are **outside** the interval:*

$$(\alpha - \epsilon, \ \beta + \epsilon).$$

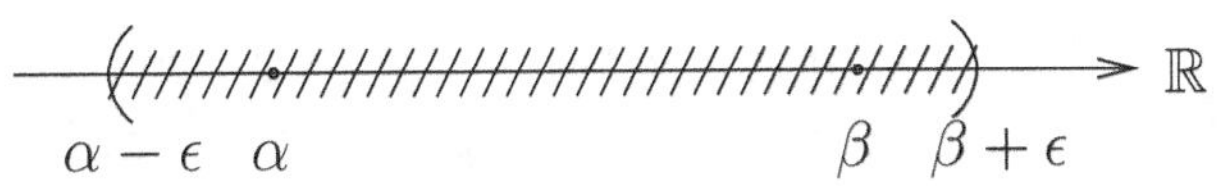

Fig. 5.4

(See Fig. 5.4 in which the interval is shaded; at most a finite number of terms of the sequence lies **outside** the interval).

We conclude this section with the following corollary.

Corollary 5.5.3 *Let $\{a_n\}_{n=1}^{\infty}$ be a **convergent** sequence and let*

$$a^* = \lim_{n\to\infty} a_n.$$

*Then, for each $\epsilon > 0$, there are at most a finite number of terms of the sequence **outside** the interval $(a^* - \epsilon, a^* + \epsilon)$.*

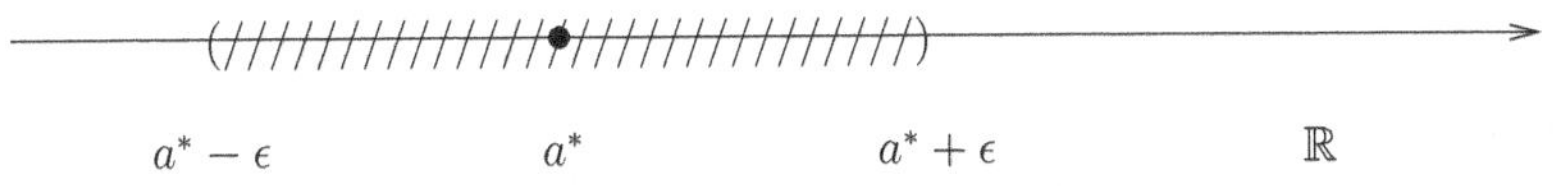

Fig. 5.5

Proof. Since the sequence converges, we must have

$$\beta = \limsup_{n\to\infty} a_n = a^* = \liminf_{n\to\infty} a_n = \alpha.$$

The result follows by setting $\alpha = \beta = a^*$ in Proposition 5.5.2 (see Fig. 5.5). $\square$

Remark 5.5.4 The interval $(a^* - \epsilon, a^* + \epsilon)$ in the above corollary is generally called a **neighbourhood of** a^*. Because of this, if a sequence $\{a_n\}_{n=1}^{\infty}$ converges to a^*, say, Corollary 5.5.3 is usually interpreted as follows: Any neighbourhood of a^* contains **all** elements of the sequence $\{a_n\}_{n=1}^{\infty}$ except possibly a finite number. More professionally, the statement is as follows: Any neighbourhood of a^* contains **all but** a finite number of terms of the sequence.

Notation: Neighbourhood is generally abbreviated *nbd*.

Remarks. (i) For any sequence $\{a_n\}$, $\lim \sup a_n$ always exists. It is either a real number or $+\infty$ or $-\infty$.

(ii) If $\beta = \lim \sup a_n$, then, for $a \in \mathbb{R}$, writing $\beta > a$ means β is a real number greater than a or $\beta = +\infty$. Similarly, $\beta < a$ means β is a real number less than a or $\beta = -\infty$.

(iii) **Notation.** Sometimes we write

$$a < \lim \sup a_n < +\infty$$

to rule out the possibility that $\lim \sup a_n = +\infty$.

5.6   Alternate Definition

Definition 5.6.1 Let $\{a_n\}$ be a bounded sequence. A **subsequential limit** of $\{a_n\}$ is any real number that is the limit of some subsequence of $\{a_n\}$. Let

$$S = \{a^* : a^* \text{ is the limit of some subsequence of } \{a_n\}\},$$

i.e., S is the set of all subsequential limits of $\{a_n\}$. Then, we define

$$\lim_{n} \sup a_n = \sup S.$$
$$\lim_{n} \inf a_n = \inf S.$$

Remark 5.6.2 In Definition 5.6.1, the sequence $\{a_n\}$ is required to be bounded. Hence, by the Bolzano-Weierstrass theorem, $\{a_n\}$ has at least one convergent subsequence. Hence $S \neq \emptyset$. Furthermore, the set S is bounded (since $\{a_n\}$ is bounded). Hence $\sup S$ and $\inf S$ exist. If $\{a_n\}$ is not bounded above it is conventional to take $\limsup a_n = \infty$, and if $\{a_n\}$ is not bounded below, we define $\liminf a_n = -\infty$.

Example 5.6.3

(a) Let $\{a_n\} = \{(-1)^n + \frac{1}{n}\}$. Then, $|a_n| = |(-1)^n + \frac{1}{n}| \leq 2$ for all integers $n \geq 1$. Hence $\{a_n\}$ is bounded. The first few terms are $\{0, \frac{3}{2}, \frac{-2}{3}, \frac{5}{4}, \frac{-4}{5}, ...\}$. The subsequence $\{a_{2n}\}$ converges to 1 and the subsequence $\{a_{2n-1}\}$ converges to -1. Hence, $S = \{-1, 1\}$ so that $\liminf a_n = -1$; $\limsup a_n = 1$.

(b) Let $a_n = n \sin^2(\frac{\pi n}{2})$, $n = 1, 2, ...$. The first few terms are $1, 0, 3, 0, 5, 0, ...$, so that $S = \{0, \infty\}$. Hence $\liminf a_n = 0$ and $\limsup a_n = +\infty$.

(c) Let $\{a_n\} = \{\frac{1}{2}, \frac{1}{5}, \frac{1}{6}, \frac{1}{9}, \frac{1}{10}, \frac{1}{13}, ...\}$. Then $\{a_{2n}\}$ converges to 0 and $\{a_{2n-1}\}$ converges to 0. Hence, by Exercise 5.3(12), $a_n \to 0$ as $n \to \infty$. Here, $\liminf a_n = \limsup a_n = \lim a_n = 0$.

We conclude this chapter with the following important theorem.

Theorem 5.6.4 *Suppose $\lim a_n = a > 0$ and $\{b_n\}$ is a bounded sequence. Then, $\limsup a_n b_n = a \limsup b_n$.*

Proof. Let $b = \limsup b_n$ and $\beta = \limsup a_n b_n$. So, it suffices to prove $\beta = ab$. Clearly, there exists a subsequence $\{b_{n_j}\}$ of $\{b_n\}$ such that $b_{n_j} \to b$. Now, $\lim a_{n_j} = a$. So, $\lim a_{n_j} b_{n_j} = ab$. Thus, $ab \leq \limsup a_n b_n = \beta$. Similarly, let $\{a_{n_j} b_{n_j}\}$ be a subsequence of $\{a_n b_n\}$ that converges to β. Then, since $a > 0$, $\lim b_{n_j} = \lim_{j \to \infty} \frac{a_{n_j} b_{n_j}}{a_{n_j}} = \frac{\beta}{a}$, so, that $\frac{\beta}{a} \leq b$, (why?) i.e., $\beta \leq ab$. Hence $\beta = ab$ (why?). $\square$

EXERCISES 5.2

1. For each of the following sequences $\{a_n\}$, find $\liminf\limits_{n\to\infty} a_n$ and $\limsup\limits_{n\to\infty} a_n$, state whether the sequence converges or diverges, and find the limit if it converges.

 (a) $\left\{\frac{n+1}{n}\right\}$ (b) $\{1, 1, 2, 1, 2, 3, 1, 2, 3, 4, ...\}$

 (c) $\{(-1)^n\}$ (d) $\{0, -1, 0, -2, 0, -3, ...\}$

 (e) $\left\{\frac{n^2+1}{n^3}\right\}$ (f) $\{n^2(-1 + (-1)^n)\}$

 (g) $\{n(n-1)\}$ (h) $\{2, 0, -2, 0, 2, 0, -2, 0, ...\}$

 (i) $\{n\sin(\frac{\pi n}{2})\}$ (j) $\{(-1)^n n\}$

 (k) $\{\frac{(-1)^n}{n}\}$ (l) $\{1, -1, \frac{1}{2}, -2, \frac{1}{3}, -3, ...\}$.

2. Prove that if $\{a_n\}$ has a subsequence which is bounded below by α then $\limsup\limits_{n\to\infty} a_n \geq \alpha$, while if $\{a_n\}$ has no subsequence which is bounded below, then $\limsup\limits_{n\to\infty} a_n = -\infty$. State and prove a similar result for $\liminf\limits_{n\to\infty} a_n$.

3. Let $\{a_n\}$ and $\{b_n\}$ be bounded sequences of real numbers.

(a) Prove:
 (i) $\limsup\limits_{n\to\infty}(a_n + b_n) \leq \limsup\limits_{n\to\infty} a_n + \limsup\limits_{n\to\infty} b_n$.
 (ii) $\liminf\limits_{n\to\infty}(a_n + b_n) \geq \liminf\limits_{n\to\infty} a_n + \liminf\limits_{n\to\infty} b_n$.

(b) Find examples to show that equality may not hold in (i) and (ii).

4. Assume now that $\{a_n\}$ and $\{b_n\}$ are bounded and $\{b_n\}$ or $\{a_n\}$ converges, prove that equality holds in 3(a)(i) and 3(a)(ii), i.e.,

(iii) $\lim\sup_{n\to\infty}(a_n + b_n) = \lim\sup_{n\to\infty} a_n + \lim\sup_{n\to\infty} b_n$ and

(iv) $\lim\inf_{n\to\infty}(a_n + b_n) = \lim\inf_{n\to\infty} a_n + \lim\inf_{n\to\infty} b_n$.

5. Derive conditions c_1 and c_2 for limit inferior.

6. Prove Proposition 5.4.4.

5.7   Cauchy Sequences

Definition 5.7.1 *A sequence $\{a_n\}_{n=1}^{\infty}$ of real numbers is called a **Cauchy sequence** (or a **fundamental sequence**) if it satisfies the following condition: $\forall\, \epsilon > 0, \exists\, n(\epsilon) \in \mathbb{N}$ such that*

$$|a_n - a_m| < \epsilon \;\; \forall\, n, m \geq n(\epsilon),$$

i.e., (equivalently),

$$|a_n - a_m| \to 0 \;\; as\; n, m \to \infty.$$

Theorem 5.7.2 *Every convergent sequence is a Cauchy sequence.*

Proof. Let $\{a_n\}_{n=1}^{\infty}$ be a convergent sequence and let its limit be a^*. We show that $\{a_n\}_{n=1}^{\infty}$ is a Cauchy sequence. So, let $\epsilon > 0$ be given. From the definition of convergence,

$$\exists\, n(\epsilon) \in \mathbb{N} \text{ such that } |a_n - a^*| < \frac{\epsilon}{2} \;\; \forall\, n \geq n(\epsilon)$$

and

$$|a_m - a^*| < \frac{\epsilon}{2} \;\; \forall\, m \geq n(\epsilon).$$

Hence,

$$|a_n - a_m| \leq |a_n - a^*| + |a^* - a_m| < \frac{\epsilon}{2} + \frac{\epsilon}{2} = \epsilon \;\; \forall\, n, m \geq n(\epsilon).$$

This implies $\{a_n\}_{n=1}^{\infty}$ is a Cauchy sequence. $\square$

We also have the following theorem.

Theorem 5.7.3 *Every Cauchy sequence in $\mathbb{R}$ is bounded.*

Proof. Exercise.

5.7.1 Completeness of the Real Number System

Definition 5.7.4 *A set S is called* **complete** *if every Cauchy sequence in S converges to an element of S.*

Remark 5.7.5 The set $\mathbb{Q}$ of rational numbers is **not** complete.

To justify this, it suffices to produce just one Cauchy sequence in $\mathbb{Q}$ which converges to an element **not** in $\mathbb{Q}$. For this, we consider the sequence $\{a_n\}_{n=1}^{\infty}$ defined by $\{a_n\}_{n=1}^{\infty} = \left\{\left(1+\frac{1}{n}\right)^n\right\}_{n=1}^{\infty}$. This sequence is Cauchy (verify). We have already seen that its limit is e. But then e is **not** a rational number. (Justify).

We conclude this chapter with the following important theorem.

Theorem 5.7.6 (Cauchy Convergence Criterion) *A sequence of real numbers is convergent if any only if it is a Cauchy sequence.*

Proof. ($\Rightarrow$) Let $\{a_n\}$ be a sequence of real numbers which is convergent. We want to prove that it is Cauchy. We have already proved this (Theorem 5.7.2).
($\Leftarrow$) Let $\{a_n\}$ be a Cauchy sequence of real numbers. We want to prove $\{a_n\}$ converges.

The proof is based on the following two steps.

Step 1. By Theorem 5.7.3, every Cauchy sequence is bounded. So, by the Bolzano-Weierstrass theorem, every Cauchy sequence has a subsequence which converges.

Step 2. If a Cauchy sequence has a subsequence that converges, then the Cauchy sequence converges.

We now proceed to prove the sufficiency part of Theorem 5.7.6. Let $\{a_n\}$ be a Cauchy sequence. Given $\epsilon^* = 1$, there exists $N_0 \in \mathbb{N}$ such that $|a_n - a_m| < 1 \;\; \forall n \geq N_0$ and $m \geq N_0$.

In particular, $|a_n - a_{N_0}| < 1 \;\forall n \geq N_0$, and so $a_{N_0} - 1 < a_n < a_{N_0} + 1 \;\forall n \geq N_0$, i.e., $a_n \in (a_{N_0} - 1, a_{N_0} + 1)$, for $n = N_0, N_0 + 1, N_0 + 2, \ldots$. The remaining $(N_0 - 1)$ terms of the sequence, $a_1, a_2, a_3, \ldots, a_{N_0-1}$ have a largest number b (say) and a smallest number a (say). Let $\alpha = \min\{a, a_{N_0} - 1\}$ and $\beta = \max\{b, a_{N_0} + 1\}$. Then $\alpha < a_n < \beta$ for **all** integers $n \geq 1$. Since $\{a_n\}$ is bounded, by the Bolzano-Weierstrass Theorem, $\{a_n\}$ has a convergent subsequence $\{a_{n_k}\}$. Let $a_{n_k} \to a^*$ as $k \to \infty$.

Claim. $a_n \to a^*$ as $n \to \infty$. Let $\epsilon > 0$ be given. Then, there exists $K \in \mathbb{N}$ such that $|a_{n_k} - a^*| < \frac{\epsilon}{2}$ if $k \geq K$. Since $\{a_n\}$ is Cauchy, there exists $N^* \in \mathbb{N}$ such that $|a_n - a_m| \leq \frac{\epsilon}{2}$ if $n, m \geq N^*$. We can take $N^* > K$, so that $n_{N^*} \geq N^* \geq K$ and $|a_{n_{N^*}} - a^*| < \frac{\epsilon}{2}$. If $n \geq N^*$, then $|a_n - a^*| \leq |a_n - a_{n_{N^*}}| + |a_{n_{N^*}} - a^*| < \frac{\epsilon}{2} + \frac{\epsilon}{2} = \epsilon$. The proof is complete. $\square$

EXERCISES 5.3

1. Check which of these sequences in $\mathbb{R}$ is a Cauchy sequence. Hence establish their convergence or divergence in $\mathbb{R}$.

     1. $\left\{\frac{1}{n}\right\}$ 2. $\left\{\frac{n^2+1}{n}\right\}$

     3. $\{a^n\}, a \geq 1$.   4. $\{a^n\}, 0 \leq a < 1$.

     5. $\{a_n\}$, where $a_1 = 1, a_2 = 2$, and $a_n = \frac{1}{2}(a_{n-1} + a_{n-2})$ for all $n > 2$.

     6. $\{a_n\}$, where $a_n = \displaystyle\sum_{k=1}^{n} \frac{1}{k}$ for all $n \in \mathbb{N}$.

7.   If $\{a_n\}$ is a subsequence of $\{b_n\}$ and $\{b_n\}$ is a subsequence of $\{a_n\}$, can we conclude that $\{a_n\} = \{b_n\}$? Justify your answer.

8. Apply Theorem 5.2.3 to find the limit of the following convergent sequence $\{s_n\}$ defined by $s_n = a^{\frac{1}{n}}, 0 < a < 1$.

(a) Show that $\{s_n\}$ is a monotone increasing sequence bounded above, and hence is convergent. Let the limit be s.

(b) Show that for each $n \in \mathbb{N}, s_{2n} = \sqrt{s_n}$. Apply Theorem 5.2.3 to get that $\lim s_{2n} = \lim s_n$ so that

$$s = \lim s_n = \lim s_{2n} = \lim \sqrt{s_n} = \sqrt{\lim s_n} = \sqrt{s}.$$

Hence, $s = 0$ or 1.

(c) Observe that $s_1 = a > 0$, and conclude $s = 1$ (Why?).

(Note: This exercise is a special case of Example 4.5.4, part (iv) . See also Exercises 4.2, Problem 5(a). The purpose of repeating it here is to show an application of Theorem 5.2.3).

9.   We note that if a sequence is divergent, the behaviour of its subsequences can be varied. For example, we have seen that the divergent sequence $\{(-1)^n\}_{n=1}^{\infty}$ has two subsequences converging to different numbers. Give an example of a divergent sequence for which *none* of its subsequences converges (remember the Bolzano-Weierstrass Theorem).

10.   Prove the following important result.

Theorem. Every *unbounded sequence* $\{a_n\}$ in $\mathbb{R}$ contains a monotone subsequence that has either $+\infty$ or $-\infty$ as a limit.

Proof. Suppose that $\{a_n\}$ is not bounded above. We shall construct a subsequence of $\{a_n\}$ which is increasing and unbounded. Now, given $M \in \mathbb{R}$, since $\{a_n\}$ is unbounded, there exist infinitely many terms of $\{a_n\}$ larger than M. In particular, there exists $n_1 \in \mathbb{N}$ such that $a_{n_1} > 1$. Then, there exists $n_2 > n_1$ such that $a_{n_2} > \max\{2, a_{n_1}\}$. In general, given $n_1, n_2, ..., n_k$, there exists $n_{k+1} > n_k$ such that $a_{n_{k+1}} > \max\{k, a_{n_k}\}$. It follows that the subsequence $\{a_{n_k}\}$ is unbounded and increasing.

Now, if $\{a_n\}$ is not bounded below, use a similar argument to produce an unbounded decreasing subsequence having limit $-\infty$. (Note: This is Problem 2 of Exercises 5.1).

11. Prove that every Cauchy sequence is bounded (theorem 5.7.3).

12*. (a) Show that if $\lim a_{2n} = L$ and $\lim a_{2n+1} = L$, then $\{a_n\}$ is convergent and $\lim a_n = L$.

(b) Let a sequence $\{a_n\}$ be such that $a_1 = 1$ and $a_{n+1} = 1 + \frac{1}{1+a_n}$. Find the first 10 terms of the sequence. Then, use part (a) to show that $\lim a_n = \sqrt{2}$.

Remark . Part (a) of this exercise is important. It says that if the sequence of *even terms* of a given sequence converges to L and the sequence of *odd terms* converges to L, then the given sequence also converges to L. Part (b) gives us the *continued function* expansion $\sqrt{2} = 1 + \frac{1}{2 + \frac{1}{2 + \cdots}}$.

CHAPTER **6**

Continuity

6.1   Introduction

In this chapter, we introduce the fundamental and very important notion of *continuous maps*. In the next chapter we shall prove two fundamental theorems of mathematical analysis concerning continuous maps defined on subsets of $\mathbb{R}$.

We begin here with the concept of *limits of functions*.

6.2   Limits of Functions

6.2.1   The Slope of a Function at a Point

The reader is certainly familiar with the notion of *the slope of a line*. The aim of this section is to extend that notion to *arbitrary functions*. We would recognize those real-valued functions f for which a sensible meaning can be given to the phrase **the slope of a function at a point** $\left(x_0, f(x_0)\right)$, $x_0 \in \mathcal{D}(f)$, where $\mathcal{D}(f)$, as usual, denotes the domain of f.

101

Suppose that f is a real-valued function and P_0 is the point $(x_0, f(x_0))$ on its graph (see Fig.6.1). If $P(x, f(x))$ is any

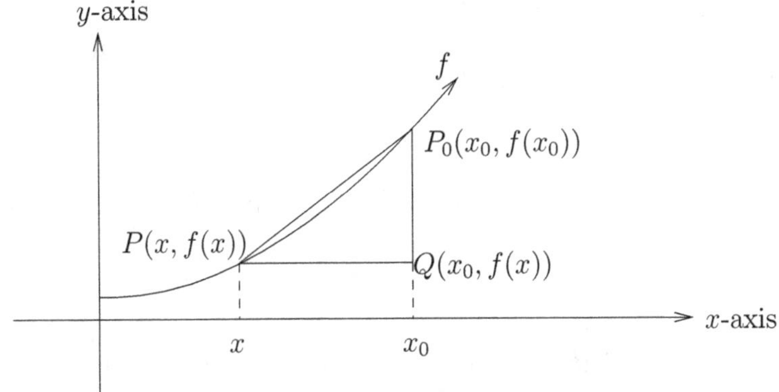

Figure 6.1:

other point on the graph of f and Q is the point $(x_0, f(x))$, then the slope of the line PP_0, denoted by $\mathcal{M}_{PP_0}$ is given by

$$\mathcal{M}_{PP_0} = \frac{f(x_0) - f(x)}{x_0 - x} \left(= \frac{f(x) - f(x_0)}{x - x_0} \right). \qquad (6.2.1)$$

Remark 6.2.1 We immediately make the following very important observation: The slope $\mathcal{M}_{PP_0}$ **is undefined if** $x = x_0$. Now, the problem of defining the **slope of the function** f **at** $(x_0, f(x_0))$ on its graph becomes that of giving a useful meaning to $\mathcal{M}_{PP_0}$.

An intuitive idea of the **slope of a function** f at $(x_0, f(x_0))$ leads us to think that if there exists a number, let us denote it by $f'(x_0)$, such that the **slope of** PP_0 approaches $f'(x_0)$ as P approaches P_0, then we should define **the slope of** f **at** P_0 to be that number, $f'(x_0)$. The number $f'(x_0)$ will be called **the derivative of** f **at** x_0, and will be defined as the limit of the slopes of the line segments $P_0(x_0, f(x_0))$ to nearby points $P(x, f(x))$ as $x \to x_0$. This means we will need a meaning for the following:

$$\lim_{x \to x_0} \frac{f(x) - f(x_0)}{x - x_0}. \qquad (6.2.2)$$

6.2.2   Limits of Real-valued Functions

We have already discussed (Chapter 3) limits of **convergent** sequences of real numbers. Here, we do not have sequences of real numbers explicitly appearing in the expression (6.2.2). So, we shall introduce here a kind of "limit" for functions that makes sense out of expression (6.2.2).

Definition 6.2.2 *For a real-valued function f, we say that*

$$\lim_{x \to a} f(x) = \ell$$

if and only if the following two conditions are satisfied:

*(a) f is defined on some **deleted interval** around a, D_a, where D_a is defined by*

$$D_a = \{x : 0 < |x - a| < \delta\}.$$

(See Fig. 6.2)

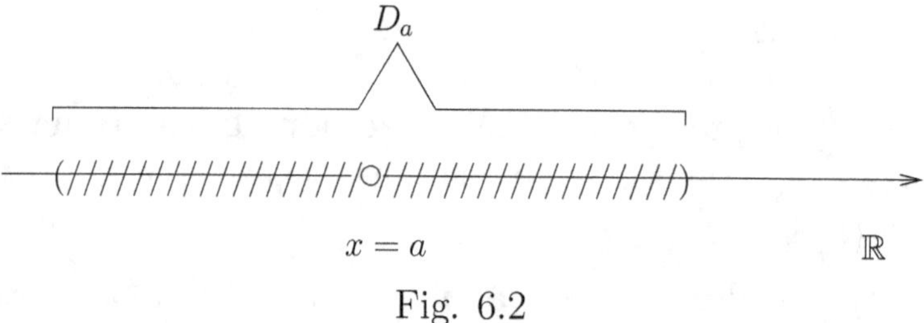

Fig. 6.2

(b) For every sequence $\{x_n\}$ in D_a such that $x_n \to a$, we have $\lim_{n \to \infty} f(x_n) = \ell$.

Remark 6.2.3 (i) Observe that the condition $0 < |x - a|$ implies $x \neq a$ and this is necessary in view of Remark 6.2.1. $\lim_{x \to a} f(x) = \ell$ is sometimes written as $f(x) \to \ell$ as $x \to a$ and read "$f(x)$ approaches ℓ as x approaches a". Observe that $\{f(x_n)\}$ is a sequence of real numbers.

(ii) The function f need not be defined at $x = a$. But if it is defined at $x = a$, *its value there has no influence on whether or not the limit exists.*

(iii) It is clear that limits are unique whenever they exist. Consequently, instead of always writing "$f(x) \to \ell$ as $x \to a$", we shall simply write, in place of this, the following expression:

$$\lim_{x \to a} f(x) = \ell.$$

6.2.3   One-sided Limits

In some situations, it will be convenient to use the notion of limits as x approaches a from one side only. So, we introduce the following definition.

Definition 6.2.4   *(a)* $\lim\limits_{x \to a^+} f(x) = c$ *if the following two conditions are satisfied: (See Fig. 6.3)*

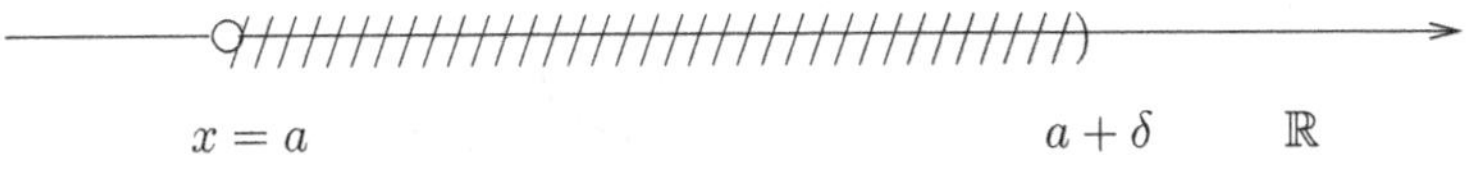

Fig. 6.3

(i) *f is defined on some interval $(a, a + \delta)$, $\delta > 0$;*

(ii) *If $\{x_n\}$ is an arbitrary sequence in $(a, a + \delta)$ such that $x_n \to a$, then $f(x_n) \to c$ as $n \to \infty$.*

(b) $\lim\limits_{x \to a^-} f(x) = c$ *is defined similarly. (See Fig. 6.4).*

For arbitrary $\{x_n\}$ in $(a, a - \delta)$ with $x_n \to a$ we have $f(x_n) \to l$.

Fig. 6.4

Proposition 6.2.5 *Let* $f : D(f) \subset \mathbb{R} \to \mathbb{R}$ *be any map. Then,*

$$\lim_{x \to a} f(x) = c \text{ if and only if } \lim_{x \to a^+} f(x) = \lim_{x \to a^-} f(x) = c.$$

Proof. ($\Rightarrow$) $\lim_{x \to a} f(x) = c \implies$ (i) f is defined on $D_a = \{x : 0 < |x - a| < \delta,$ for some $\delta > 0\}$, and (ii) for all sequences $\{x_n\}_{n=1}^{\infty}$ in D_a such that $x_n \to a$, we have $f(x_n) \to c$. We observe that since $(a, a + \delta) \subset D_a$, we have immediately that:

$(i)^*$ f is defined on $(a, a + \delta)$; and that:

$(ii)^*$ $\forall$ sequence $\{x_n\}_{n=1}^{\infty}$ in $(a, a + \delta)$ such such $x_n \to a$ we have $f(x_n) \to c$.

Hence $\lim_{x \to a^+} f(x) = c$. Similarly, $\lim_{x \to a^-} f(x) = c$. This completes the proof of this direction.

($\Leftarrow$) $\lim_{x \to a^+} f(x) = \lim_{x \to a^-} f(x) = c \implies$ f is defined on $(a-\delta, a) \cup (a, a+\delta)$ and this is exactly $D_a = \{x : 0 < |x-a| < \delta\}$. Hence f is defined on D_a. Furthermore, let $\{x_n\}_{n=1}^{\infty}$ be a sequence in D_a such that $x_n \to a$. For all integers $i > 0$ such that $x_i \in (a - \delta, a)$, since every subsequence of $\{x_n\}$ converges to a, we have
$\exists$ an integer $N_1 > 0$ such that for any given $\epsilon > 0$,

$$|f(x_i) - c| < \epsilon \; \forall \; i \geq N_1.$$

Similarly, for all integers $j > 0$ such that $x_j \in (a, a + \delta)$, $\exists$ an integer $N_2 > 0$ such that

$$|f(x_j) - c| < \epsilon \; \forall \; j \geq N_2.$$

But $\{n\} = \{i\} \cup \{j\}$. Let $N = \max\{N_1, N_2\}$. Then for all integers $n \geq N$,

$$|f(x_n) - c| < \epsilon,$$

so that $f(x_n) \to c$ as $n \to \infty$. The proof is complete. $\square$

6.2.4   Limit Theorems

Theorem 6.2.6 *Suppose $f(x) \to k$ as $x \to a$, and $g(x) \to \ell$ as $x \to a$. Then,*

(i) $f(x) + g(x) \to k + \ell$ *as $x \to a$;*

(ii) $f(x) - g(x) \to k - \ell$ *as $x \to a$;*

(iii) $f(x)g(x) \to k\ell$ *as $x \to a$;*

(iv) $\frac{f(x)}{g(x)} \to \frac{k}{\ell}$ *provided $g(x) \neq 0$ $\forall x$, as $x \to a$, if $\ell \neq 0$.*

Proof. Exercise.

6.3   Topological Notions

A **continuous curve** can be seen as one which can be drawn without taking the pen off the paper. Before we give a formal definition, we first introduce the following **two** important notions that will be connected with a formal definition of *continuity*:

(i) An **open ball** in $\mathbb{R}$;

(ii) An **open set** in $\mathbb{R}$;

To introduce these notions, we shall assume that for arbitrary $x, y \in \mathbb{R}$, the **distance** between x and y, denoted by $d(x, y)$ is given by the absolute value of the difference between x and y, i.e., $d(x, y) = |x - y| \ \forall \ x, y \in \mathbb{R}$. (There are other ways to denote the distance between arbitrary x and y in $\mathbb{R}$ but we do not discuss these here). With this notation, we introduce the following definitions.

Definition 6.3.1 *By an **interval** of $\mathbb{R}$ we mean any set of the form of any of the following nine sets. For $a < b$; a, $b \in \mathbb{R}$,*

Bounded Intervals	Unbounded Intervals
(a, b)	(a, ∞)
$[a, b]$	$[a, \infty)$
$[a, b)$	$(-\infty, b]$
$(a, b]$	$(-\infty, b)$
	$(-\infty, \infty) = \mathbb{R}$

Definition 6.3.2 For any fixed $x_0 \in \mathbb{R}$, the **open ball** centered at x_0 with radius $r > 0$, denoted by $B_r(x_0)$ or $B(x_0, r)$ is defined as follows:

$$B_r(x_0) = \{x \in \mathbb{R} : d(x, x_0) < r\} = \{x \in \mathbb{R} : |x - x_0| < r\}.$$

Example 6.3.3 Compute (i) $B_{\frac{1}{2}}(-2)$, (ii) $B_2(4)$.

Solution: (i) (See Fig. 6.5).

$$
\begin{aligned}
B_{\frac{1}{2}}(-2) &= \{x \in \mathbb{R} : |x - (-2)| < \tfrac{1}{2}\} \\
&= \{x \in \mathbb{R} : |x + 2| < \tfrac{1}{2}\} \\
&= \{x \in \mathbb{R} : \tfrac{-5}{2} < x < \tfrac{-3}{2}\}.
\end{aligned}
$$

Fig. 6.5

(ii) $B_2(4)$ is sketched in Fig. 6.6.

$$B_2(4) = \{x \in \mathbb{R} : |x - 4| < 2\} = \{x \in \mathbb{R} : 2 < x < 6\}.$$

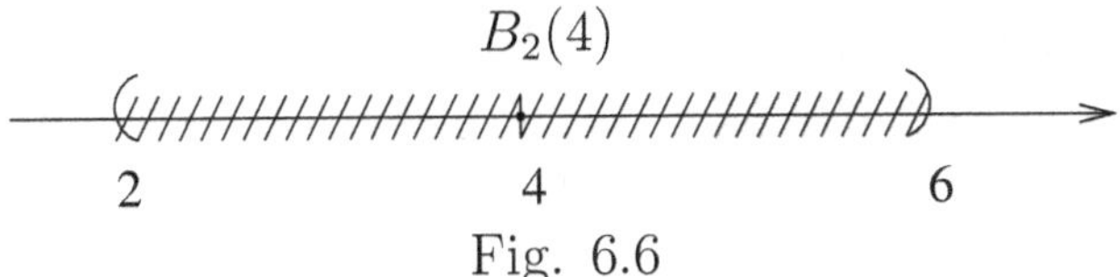

$$B_2(4)$$

Fig. 6.6

Remark 6.3.4 With the notion of distance d between two elements of $\mathbb{R}$ assumed above, it is easy to see that **all open balls** are **open and bounded intervals.** It is also true that **every** open and bounded interval is an open ball. In fact, (a, b) is the open ball centered at $\frac{a+b}{2}$ with radius $\frac{b-a}{2}$. For example, $(-2, 2) = B_2(0)$; $(0, 1) = B_{\frac{1}{2}}(\frac{1}{2})$; $(-2, 11) = B_{\frac{13}{2}}(\frac{9}{2})$. Compute $B_2(0)$, $B_{\frac{1}{2}}(\frac{1}{2})$ and $B_{\frac{13}{2}}(\frac{9}{2})$ to confirm these assertions.

We next introduce the notion of an **open set** in $\mathbb{R}$.

Definition 6.3.5 *A subset U of $\mathbb{R}$ is called an* **open set** *in $\mathbb{R}$ if for arbitrary $u_0 \in U$, there exists an open ball (an open and bounded interval) with center u_0 which is contained in U.*

Remark 6.3.6 An *open ball* must have *a center* and *a radius*. An *open set* need not have either. In fact, an open set is defined in terms of open balls.

Example 6.3.7
(a) Let $U = (-3, 4)$, a subset of $\mathbb{R}$. Then U is an open set **in** $\mathbb{R}$. To see this, let $u_0 \in U$ be arbitrary, (see Figure 6.7*).*

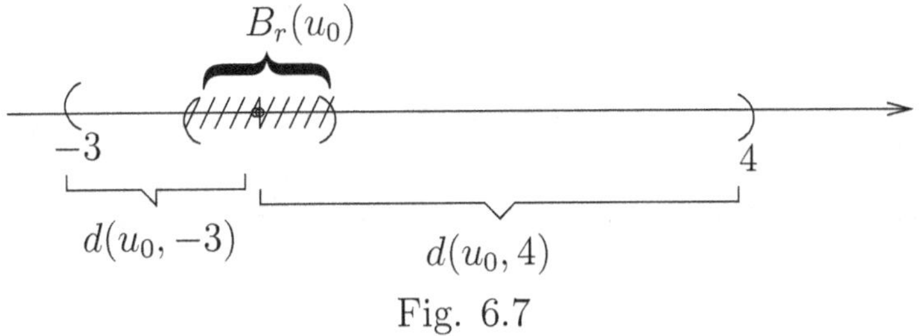

Fig. 6.7

To find an open ball (open and bounded interval) with centre u_0 which will be contained in the interval $(-3, 4)$, the radius of that ball must be less than the minimum of the distance of u_0 from -3 and its distance from 4. That is, r must be less than

$$\min\{d(u_0, -3), d(u_0, 4)\} = \min\{|u_0 - (-3)|, |u_0 - 4|\}$$
$$= \min\{|u_0 + 3|, |u_0 - 4|\}.$$

*So, we can choose $r = \frac{1}{2}\min\{|u_0 + 3|, |u_0 - 4|\}$. Then $B_r(u_0) = (u_0 - r, u_0 + r)$ is clearly contained in $(-3, 4)$. Since u_0 is arbitrary, $(-3, 4)$ is an open set **in** $\mathbb{R}$.*

*(b) Following the method of part (a), it is easy to show that every open ball in $\mathbb{R}$ (an open and bounded interval) is an open set. We note that the converse statement is not true. There are open sets which are **not** open balls. For example, $U = (-1, 0) \cup (4, 5)$ (see Figure 6.8) is an open set but **not** an open ball. Also the open intervals $(0, \infty)$, $(-\infty, 2)$, $(-\infty, \infty)$*

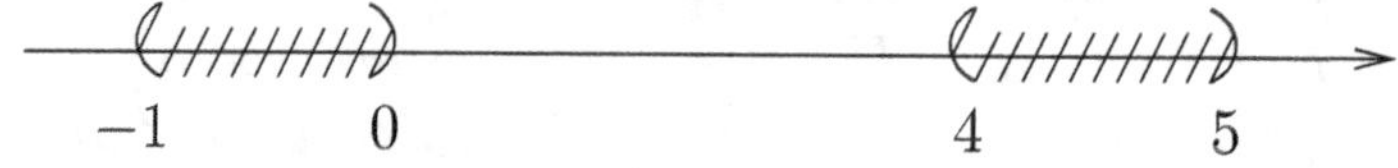

−1   0   4   5

Fig. 6.8

*are examples of open sets which are **not** open balls.*

*(c) The set $S = [0, 1)$ is not an open set **in** $\mathbb{R}$. To establish this, it suffices to produce at least one point u_0 in S such that **no open ball** centred at u_0 is contained in S. Let $u_0 = 0$. Then **any** open ball centered at 0 with radius $r > 0$ is of the form $(-r, r)$ and certainly contains negative numbers which are not in S. So, S is **not** open in $\mathbb{R}$. Observe that for **any other** point s_0, say in $[0, 1)$ we can always find an open ball V_{s_0} centered at s_0 such that $V_{s_0} \subset S$.*

(d) Any set of the form $S = \{x \in \mathbb{R} : |x - x_0| < r\}$ is an open ball in $\mathbb{R}$. It is easy to check that $S = B_r(x_0)$. For example, in particular, $S = \{x \in \mathbb{R} : |x - \frac{1}{2}| < 3\} = B_3(\frac{1}{2})$ and $S = \{x \in \mathbb{R} : |x + 5| < \frac{1}{3}\} = B_{\frac{1}{3}}(-5)$, and so on.

6.4 Continuity

We are now ready to give the definition of a continuous map.

Definition 6.4.1 *Let* $f : \mathcal{D}(f) \subseteq \mathbb{R} \to \mathbb{R}$ *be a map with domain* $\mathcal{D}(f)$ *in* $\mathbb{R}$. *Then* f *is said to be* **continuous at** $x_0 \in \mathcal{D}(f)$ *if given any* $\epsilon > 0$, *there exists a* $\delta = \delta(\epsilon) > 0$ *such that*

$$|f(x) - f(x_0)| < \epsilon \ \ whenever \ \ |x - x_0| < \delta.$$

Remark 6.4.2 We explain Definition 6.4.1 a little more (see Figure 6.9). We shall regard the range of f as the y-axis and $\mathcal{D}(f)$ as a subset of the x-axis. Suppose we want to find out if a function f is continuous at $x = 3 \in \mathcal{D}(f)$. **We start on**

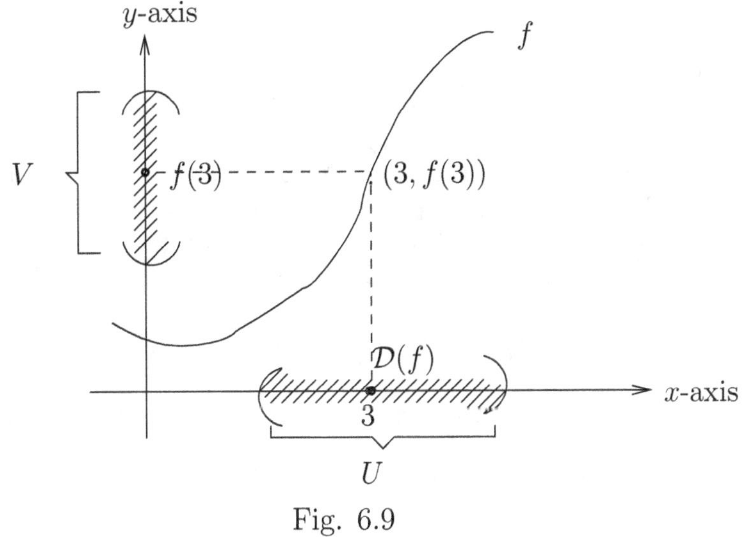

Fig. 6.9

the y-axis at $f(3)$. Then for any open ball V on the y-axis, **containing** $f(3)$, we want to find an open ball U on x-axis, **containing 3**, such that f maps U into V.

Recall that $\delta = \delta(\epsilon)$, simply means that δ depends on $\epsilon > 0$ given. We now give some examples.

Example 6.4.3 (a) Prove that $f : \mathbb{R} \to \mathbb{R}$ defined by $f(x) = 3x^2 - 2x + 1$ is continuous at $x = 5$.

Solution: Let $\epsilon > 0$ be given. We want to find a $\delta = \delta(\epsilon) > 0$ such that if $|x - 5| < \delta$ then $|f(x) - f(5)| < \epsilon$.

Note: The trick in finding a $\delta > 0$ lies in the use of the given condition that $|x - 5| < \delta$, and in the method of evaluation of $|f(x) - f(5)|$. Now,

$$
\begin{aligned}
|f(x) - f(5)| &= |3x^2 - 2x + 1 - [3(5)^2 - 2(5) + 1]| \\
&= |3(x^2 - 5^2) - 2(x - 5)|.
\end{aligned}
$$

Observe that we did not use the numerical value of $f(5) = 3(5^2) - 2(5) + 1 = 66$. This is because we would like to get a factor of $|x - 5|$ in our estimate of $|f(x) - f(5)|$. This will enable us to use the condition that $|x - 5| < \delta$. So, continuing we have that

$$
\begin{aligned}
|f(x) - f(5)| &\leq 3|x - 5| \cdot |x + 5| + 2|x - 5| \\
&\leq 3\delta|x + 5| + 2\delta = (3|x + 5| + 2)\delta.
\end{aligned}
$$

Once we have factored out one δ from $|f(x) - f(5)|$, we would like to estimate any factor associated with this δ by an integer. We always use the given condition $|x - 5| < \delta$ to do this. Now, from $|x - 5| < \delta$ we have

$$
|x| = |x - 5 + 5| \leq |x - 5| + 5 < \delta + 5.
$$

Here **we can assume** $\delta < 1$ so that $|x| < 6$. With this,

$$
3|x + 5| + 2 < 3(|x| + 5) + 2 < 3(6 + 5) + 2 = 35.
$$

Hence,

$$
|f(x) - f(5)| \leq (3|x + 5| + 2)\delta < 35\delta = \epsilon \text{ if } \delta = \frac{\epsilon}{35}.
$$

Recall that we already made the restriction that $\delta < 1$. So, given $\epsilon > 0$, we choose $\delta = \min\{1, \frac{\epsilon}{35}\}$. Then,

$$
|f(x) - f(5)| < \epsilon \text{ whenever } |x - 5| < \delta,
$$

so that f is continuous at 5.

(b)   Prove that $f : \mathbb{R} \to \mathbb{R}$ defined by $f(x) = 3 + 2x^3$ is continuous at $x = -4$.

Solution: Let $\epsilon > 0$ be given. We want to find a $\delta = \delta(\epsilon) > 0$ such that if $|x - (-4)| < \delta$ (i.e., $|x + 4| < \delta$) then $|f(x) - f(-4)| < \epsilon$. Now,

$$\begin{aligned}
|f(x) - f(-4)| &= |3 + 2x^3 - (3 + 2(-4)^3)| \\
&= 2|x^3 - (-4)^3| = 2|x^3 + 4^3| \\
&= 2|x + 4|.|x^2 - 4x + 4^2| \\
&\leq 2|x^2 - 4x + 4^2|\delta.
\end{aligned}$$

But $|x + 4| < \delta$ implies

$$|x| = |x + 4 - 4| \leq |x + 4| + 4 < \delta + 4 < 5 \;\boxed{if\ \delta < 1}.$$

So,

$$2|x^2 - 4x + 4^2| \leq 2|x|^2 + 8|x| + 32 < 50 + 40 + 32 = 122.$$

Hence, $|f(x) - f(-4)| \leq 2|x^2 - 4x + 4^2|\delta < 122\delta = \epsilon$ if $\delta = \frac{\epsilon}{122}$. Hence, given $\epsilon > 0$, choose $\delta = \min\{1, \frac{\epsilon}{122}\}$. Then, $|f(x) - f(-4)| < \epsilon$, whenever $|x - (-4)| < \delta$, so that f is continuous at $x = -4$.

(c)   Define the function $f : \mathbb{R} \to \mathbb{R}$ by

$$f(x) = \begin{cases} x\sin(1/x), & x \neq 0, \\ 0, & x = 0. \end{cases}$$

Then f is continuous at $x = 0$.

Solution: We observe that, for $x \neq 0$,

$$|f(x) - f(0)| = |x\sin(1/x)| \leq |x|. \qquad (*)$$

Given $\epsilon > 0$, we want to find a

$\delta = \delta(\epsilon) > 0$ such that $|x - 0| < \delta \implies |f(x) - f(0)| < \epsilon$.

But $|x - 0| = |x| < \delta \implies$ using $(*)$, that

$$|f(x) - f(0)| \leq |x| < \delta,$$

so that we can choose $\delta = \epsilon$. Then
$|x - 0| < \delta \implies |f(x) - f(0)| < \epsilon$. Hence f is continuous at
$x = 0$. $\quad\square$

We now give another definition of continuity which is very
convenient in applications.

Definition 6.4.4 *A function* $f : \mathcal{D}(f) \subseteq \mathbb{R} \to \mathbb{R}$ *is* **continuous at** $x_0 \in \mathcal{D}(f)$ *if for any sequence* $\{x_n\}_{n=1}^{\infty}$ *in* $\mathcal{D}(f)$
such that $x_n \to x_0$, *then* $f(x_n) \to f(x_0)$.

This definition of continuity is used most frequently in applications.

Definition 6.4.5 *Let* $x_0 \in \mathcal{D}(f)$. *Then* f *is said to be* **discontinuous at** x_0 *if* f *is not continuous at* x_0.

As a consequence of Definition 6.4.4, a function f is **discontinuous at** $x_0 \in \mathcal{D}(f)$ if there exists a sequence $\{x_n\}_{n=1}^{\infty}$ in
$\mathcal{D}(f)$ such that $x_n \to x_0$ but $f(x_n) \nrightarrow f(x_0)$.

We give some more examples.

Example 6.4.6
Let $f : \mathbb{R} \to \mathbb{R}$ be defined by

$$f(x) = \mathrm{sgn}\, x = \begin{cases} 1, & \text{if } x > 0 \\ 0, & \text{if } x = 0 \\ -1, & \text{if } x < 0. \end{cases}$$

Then f is discontinuous at $x = 0$. (See Figure 6.10).

Solution: We give two methods.

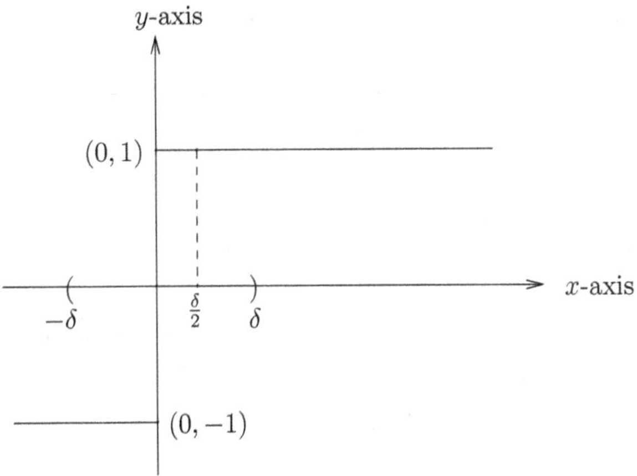

Fig. 6.10

(i) We produce a sequence $\{x_n\}_{n=1}^{\infty}$ in $\mathbb{R}$ such that $x_n \to 0$
     but
     $f(x_n) \not\to f(0)$. Consider the sequence $\{1/n\}_{n=1}^{\infty}$. Clearly
     $1/n \to 0$. But since $1/n > 0$ for all n, we have
     $f(1/n) = 1 \not\to 0$. Hence f is not continuous at 0.

(ii) We show that there exists some $\epsilon > 0$ such that there
     is no $\delta > 0$ such that $|x - 0| < \delta \implies |f(x) - f(0)| < \epsilon$.
     Take $\epsilon = 1/4$ (any $\epsilon \in (0, 1)$ will do). Suppose there
     exists $\delta > 0$ such that
     $|x - 0| < \delta \implies |f(x) - f(0)| < 1/4$. Now, $|x - 0| <$
     $\delta \implies -\delta < x < \delta$. Choose $x_0 = \delta/2 > 0$. Then,
     x_0 lies in the interval $-\delta < x < \delta$. (See Figure 6.10).
     But $|f(x_0) - f(0)| = |1 - 0| = 1 > 1/4$, contradiction.
     Hence, f is not continuous at $x = 0$. $\square$

EXERCISES 6.1

1. Use the $\epsilon - \delta$ definition of continuity to prove that the functions are continuous at the points indicated:

    (a) x^2 at $x = 2$ (b) $|x|$ at $x = 1$

    (c) x^4 at $x = x_0$ (d) x^{-2} at $x = 1$

    (e) $\sqrt{x}$ at $x = 2$ (f) $\frac{x^2-4}{x-1}$ at $x = 0$ and $x = 2$.

2. For what values of x in its domain of definition is each of the functions in (g) to (j) continuous? Prove that your answer is correct.

    (g) $\frac{x^2}{x-2}, x \in \mathbb{R}$ (h) $[x] - [-x], x \in \mathbb{R}$

    (i) $\sqrt{(x-a)(b-x)}, b > a$ (j) $\sqrt{\frac{x-a}{b-a}}, b > a.$

3. (a) Prove that if f is continuous at $x = a$ and $f(a) > 0$, then there is a $\delta > 0$ such that $f(x) > 0$ for $a - \delta < x < a + \delta$.

    (b)   Prove that if f is continuous at $x = a$ and $f(a) < 0$, then there is a $\delta > 0$ such that $f(x) < 0$ for $a - \delta < x < a + \delta$.

4. Prove that if f is continuous at $x = a$, then **there is** a $\delta > 0$ such that f is **bounded** in $a - \delta < x < a + \delta$.

5. Show that, in $[0, 1]$, the function

$$f(x) = \begin{cases} x, & \text{when } x \text{ is rational,} \\ 1 - x, & \text{when } x \text{ is irrational,} \end{cases}$$

is continuous only at $x = 1/2$.

6. Given $f(x) = \begin{cases} 1/q, & \text{when } x = p/q, \\ 0, & \text{when } x \text{ is irrational,} \end{cases}$

show that f is continuous at each irrational value of x in $(0, 1)$.

7. Is the function $f(x) = \begin{cases} x^2, & \text{if } x \neq 1, \\ 0, & \text{if } x = 1, \end{cases}$ continuous at $x = 1$? Justify your answer.

8. Given $f(x) = \begin{cases} sin\frac{1}{x}, & \text{when } x \neq 0, \\ 0, & \text{when } x = 0, \end{cases}$
   is f is continuous at $x = 0$? Justify your answer.

   (Hint: Use the remark following Definition 6.4.5, i.e., construct a sequence $\{a_n\}$ in $\mathbb{R}$ such that $a_n \to 0$ but $f(a_n)$ does not converge to 0. Take $a_n = \frac{2}{\pi n} \; \forall \, n \geq 1$).

9. Given $f(x) = \begin{cases} x^2 sin\frac{1}{x}, & \text{when } x \neq 0, \\ 0, & \text{when } x = 0, \end{cases}$
   is f is continuous at $x = 0$? Justify your answer.

10. Given $f(x) = \begin{cases} cos\frac{1}{x}, & \text{when } x \neq 0, \\ 1, & \text{when } x = 0, \end{cases}$
    is f is continuous at $x = 0$? Justify your answer.

11. Let $f : \mathbb{R} \to \mathbb{R}$ be defined by $f(x) = \frac{x^2+1}{x-2}$. Prove that f is not continuous at $x = 2$.

6.5 One-sided Continuity

From the definition of continuity, it is possible that we could have a "one-sided continuous function". Thus, we have the following definitions:

Definition 6.5.1 *(a) A function $f : \mathcal{D}(f) \subseteq \mathbb{R} \to \mathbb{R}$ is said to be*
continuous on the right at $x = x_0$ if :

(i) $x_0 \in \mathcal{D}(f)$; and

(ii) for every $\epsilon > 0$, $\exists \, \delta > 0$ such that if $x \in \mathcal{D}(f)$ satisfies

$$\boxed{x_0 \leq x < x_0 + \delta} \; then \; |f(x) - f(x_0)| < \epsilon.$$

(b) A function $f : \mathcal{D}(f) \subseteq \mathbb{R} \to \mathbb{R}$ is said to be
continuous on the left at $x = x_0$ if :

(i) $x_0 \in \mathcal{D}(f)$*; and*

(ii) for every $\epsilon > 0$*,* $\exists\ \delta > 0$ *such that if* $x \in \mathcal{D}(f)$ *satisfies*

$$\boxed{x_0 - \delta < x \leq x_0}\ \textit{then}\ |f(x) - f(x_0)| < \epsilon.$$

Remark 6.5.2 f is continuous at $x = x_0$ if and only if f is continuous to the left and to the right at $x = x_0$.

Example 6.5.3

(1)   Consider the real-valued function

$$f(x) = \begin{cases} 2, & \text{if } x > 3, \\ 1, & \text{if } x \leq 3. \end{cases}$$

Then

(a) f is continuous to the left at $x = 3$,

(b) f is discontinuous to the right at $x = 3$.

Hence, f is discontinuous at $x = 3$.

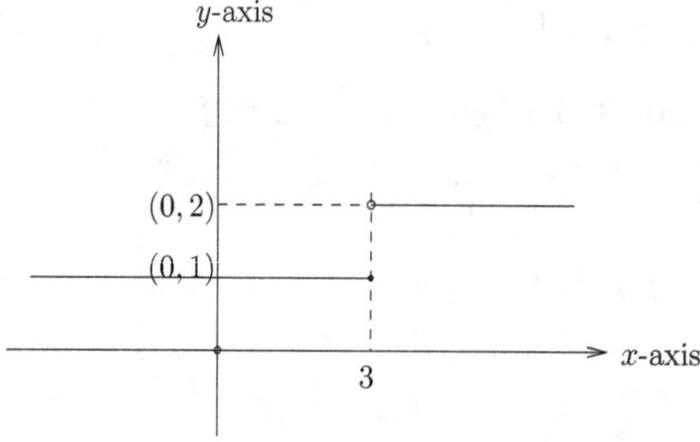

Fig. 6.11

Solution: (See Figure 6.11).

(a) Let $\epsilon > 0$ be given. We want to find a $\delta > 0$ such that if $3 - \delta < x \leq 3$ then $|f(x) - f(3)| < \epsilon$. But $3 - \delta < x \leq 3 \implies$ (in particular), $x \leq 3$ and so (from the definition of f), $f(x) = 1$. Observe also that $f(3) = 1$. Hence, for $3 - \delta < x \leq 3$, we have

$$|f(x) - f(3)| = |1 - 1| = 0 < \epsilon \text{ for any } \epsilon > 0.$$

So, given $\epsilon > 0$, **any** $\delta > 0$ can be chosen. Then $3 - \delta < x \leq 3 \implies |f(x) - f(3)| < \epsilon$. Hence f is continuous to the left at $x = 3$.

(b) It suffices to show that there is some $\epsilon > 0$ such that there is no $\delta > 0$ such that

$$3 \leq x < 3 + \delta \implies |f(x) - f(3)| < \epsilon.$$

Assume that such a $\delta > 0$ exists. Take $\epsilon = 1/2$. Now, since $3 \leq x < 3 + \delta$, it follows that for this interval, $f(x) = 2$. Again, from the definition of f, $f(3) = 1$. Hence, for $3 \leq x < 3 + \delta$ we have

$$|f(x) - f(3)| = |2 - 1| = 1 > \frac{1}{2} = \epsilon.$$

Contradiction. Hence f is discontinuous to the right at $x = 3$.

(2)   Consider the real-valued function

$$f(x) = \begin{cases} x^2, & \text{if } x \geq 3, \\ x - 1, & \text{if } x < 3. \end{cases}$$

Prove that f is continuous to the right at $x = 3$.

Solution: (See Figure 6.12). Let $\epsilon > 0$ be given. We want to find a $\delta > 0$ such that if $3 \leq x < 3 + \delta$ then

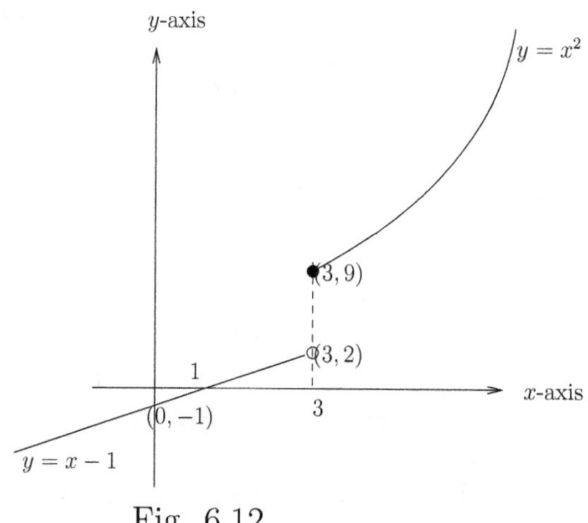

Fig. 6.12

$|f(x) - f(3)| < \epsilon$. First observe that $f(3) = 9$. Further, since $3 \le x < 3 + \delta$, we have that $f(x) = x^2$ (since $x \ge 3$). Now, for $3 \le x < 3 + \delta$,

$$|f(x) - f(3)| = |x^2 - 9| = |x - 3| \cdot |x + 3|.$$

But $3 \le x < 3 + \delta \implies x - 3 < \delta$. So we have:

$$|f(x) - f(3)| < |x + 3|\delta.$$

Furthermore,

$$x - 3 < \delta \implies x < 3 + \delta < 4 \text{ if } \boxed{\delta < 1}.$$

Hence $x + 3 < 4 + 3 = 7$. Using this estimate, we obtain that

$$|f(x) - f(3)| < 7\delta = \epsilon \text{ if } \boxed{\delta = \frac{\epsilon}{7}}.$$

Hence, given $\epsilon > 0$, choose $\delta = \min\{1, \epsilon/7\}$. Then,

$$3 \le x < 3 + \delta \implies |f(x) - f(3)| < \epsilon.$$

So, f is continuous to the right at $x = 3$. $\quad\square$

(3) Prove that $f : [0, \infty) \to \mathbb{R}$ defined by $f(x) = \sqrt{x}$ is continuous at 0.

Solution: The domain of f is $[0, \infty)$ and we want to prove that f is continuous at 0. Hence, we can only talk of *continuity to the right.* Let $\epsilon > 0$ be given. We estimate as follows:

$$|f(x) - f(0)| = |\sqrt{x} - 0| = \sqrt{x} \leq \sqrt{|x|} < \sqrt{\delta} = \epsilon \text{ if } \delta = \epsilon^2.$$

Hence f is continuous at 0.

We now have the following characterization of continuity of a real-valued function in terms of limit of the function.

Theorem 6.5.4 *Let f be a real-valued function defined on some interval around $x_0 \in \mathcal{D}(f)$. Then f is continuous at x_0 if and only if*

$$\lim_{x \to x_0} f(x) = f(x_0).$$

Proof. This is an immediate corollary of Proposition 6.2.5.

Remark 6.5.5 Theorem 6.5.4 gives us a method of establishing that a given function is **not** continuous at x_0. We first observe that the theorem demands that $\lim_{x \to a} f(x)$ **exists.** But by Proposition 6.2.5, this limit exists when $\lim_{x \to a^+} f(x) = \lim_{x \to a^-} f(x)$. Thus, combining this with Theorem 6.5.4, we obtain that f is continuous at a if and only if $\lim_{x \to a^+} f(x) = \lim_{x \to a^-} f(x) = f(a)$.

For example, for the function f whose graph is sketched in Figure 6.13, $\lim_{x \to 2} f(x)$ does not exist. It is clear that $\lim_{x \to 2^-} f(x) = 1$, $\lim_{x \to 2^+} f(x) = 3$, but $\lim_{x \to 2} f(x)$ does not exist because $\lim_{x \to 2^+} f(x) \neq \lim_{x \to 2^-} f(x)$. In Figure 6.14, $\lim_{x \to 2^-} f(x) =$

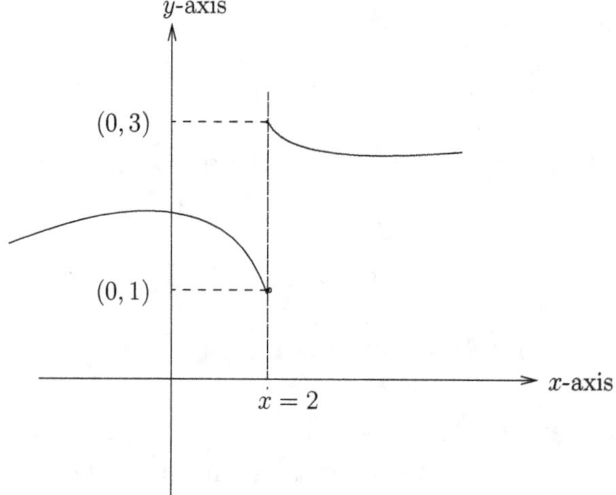

Fig. 6.13

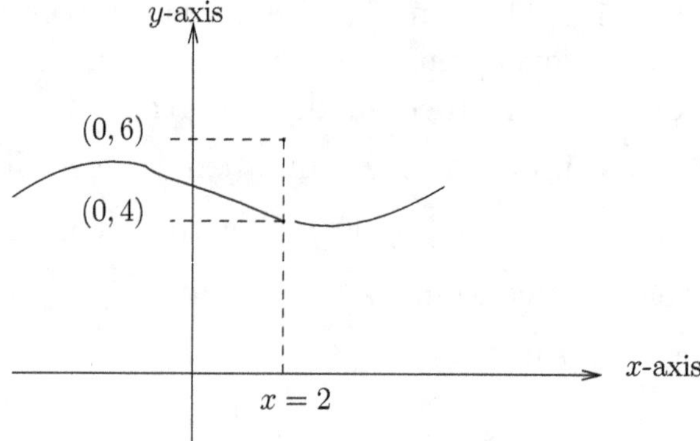

Fig. 6.14

$\lim_{x \to 2^+} f(x) = 4$. *Hence* $\lim_{x \to 2} f(x)$ *exists. Moreover,* $\lim_{x \to 2} f(x) = 4$. *However, the value of* f *at* $x = 2$ *is 6. Hence,* $\lim_{x \to 2} f(x) \neq f(2)$, *and so, by Theorem 6.5.4,* f *is not continuous at* $x = 2$.

6.6 Continuity Theorems

In this section, we consider theorems concerning the sums, differences, products and quotients of continuous functions at points in the domain on which the combinations are defined.

Theorem 6.6.1 *Let* f *and* g *be continuous at a point* $x_0 \in \mathcal{D}(f) \cap \mathcal{D}(g)$ *and let* $\alpha \in \mathbb{R}$. *Then*

(i) αf *is continuous at* x_0;

(ii) $f + g$ *is continuous at* x_0;

(iii) $f - g$ *is continuous at* x_0;

(iv) fg *is continuous at* x_0, *where* $(fg)(x) = f(x)g(x) \; \forall \; x \in \mathcal{D}(f) \cap \mathcal{D}(g)$.

Proof.

(i) We first note that if $\alpha = 0$, then the result holds trivially. For, $|(\alpha f)(x) - (\alpha f)(x_0)| = 0 < \epsilon$ for any $\epsilon > 0$, and $\forall \; x \in \mathcal{D}(f)$. So, we shall assume $\alpha \neq 0$. By the continuity of the function f at the point x_0, for any given $\epsilon > 0$ there exists a $\delta > 0$ such that, for all x with $|x - x_0| < \delta$, we have,

$$|f(x) - f(x_0)| < \frac{\epsilon}{1 + |\alpha|}.$$

Hence, for all x such that $|x - x_0| < \delta$, we have,

$$
\begin{aligned}
|(\alpha f)(x) - (\alpha f)(x_0)| &= |\alpha| \cdot |f(x) - f(x_0)| \\
&< |\alpha| \cdot \frac{\epsilon}{1 + |\alpha|} < \epsilon,
\end{aligned}
$$

so that (αf) is continuous at x_0.

(ii) Since the functions f and g are continuous at the point x_0, $\exists\ \delta_1 > 0, \delta_2 > 0$ such that

$$|f(x) - f(x_0)| < \frac{\epsilon}{2}\ \forall\ x \text{ such that } |x - x_0| < \delta_1,$$

and

$$|g(x) - g(x_0)| < \frac{\epsilon}{2}\ \forall\ x \text{ such that } |x - x_0| < \delta_2.$$

Take $\delta = \min\{\delta_1, \delta_2\}$. Then, for all x such that $|x - x_0| < \delta$ we have,

$$
\begin{aligned}
|(f + g)(x) - (f + g)(x_0)| &= |f(x) - f(x_0) + \\
&\quad g(x) - g(x_0)| \\
&< |f(x) - f(x_0)| \\
&\quad + |g(x) - g(x_0)| \\
&< \frac{\epsilon}{2} + \frac{\epsilon}{2} = \epsilon,
\end{aligned}
$$

and so $f + g$ is continuous at x_0.

(iii) The proof that $f - g$ is continuous at x_0 if f and g are continuous at the point $x_0 \in \mathcal{D}(f) \cap \mathcal{D}(g)$ can be deduced easily from parts (i) and (ii) by observing that $f - g = f + (-1)g$. By part (i), the function $(-1)g$ is continuous at x_0 if the function g is continuous at the same point. Therefore, by part (ii), we conclude that the function $f - g = f + (-1)g$ is continuous at the point x_0 since the functions f and $(-1)g$ are continuous at the same point.

(iv) To prove that fg is continuous at x_0 if f and g are continuous at the point $x_0 \in \mathcal{D}(f) \cap \mathcal{D}(g)$, we must show that given any $\epsilon > 0$ there exists a $\delta > 0$ such that

$$|(fg)(x) - (fg)(x_0)| < \epsilon\ \forall\ x \text{ such that } |x - x_0| < \delta.$$

But f continuous at $x_0 \Rightarrow \forall\, \epsilon > 0,\ \exists\, \delta_1 > 0$ such that

$$|f(x) - f(x_0)| < \epsilon, \qquad\qquad (*)$$

for all x such that $|x - x_0| < \delta_1$. Also, g continuous at $x_0 \Rightarrow \forall\, \epsilon > 0,\ \exists\, \delta_2 > 0$ such that

$$|f(x) - f(x_0)| < \epsilon, \qquad\qquad (**)$$

for all x such that $|x - x_0| < \delta_2$. Now,

$$
\begin{aligned}
|(fg)(x) - (fg)(x_0)| \;&\leq\; |g(x)[f(x) - f(x_0)]| \\
&\quad + |[g(x) - g(x_0)]f(x_0)| \\
&\leq\; |g(x)|.|f(x) - f(x_0)| \\
&\quad + |f(x_0)|.|g(x) - g(x_0)|
\end{aligned}
$$

From the nature of the last inequality, we modify $(*)$ and $(**)$ as follows:

$$|f(x) - f(x_0)| < \frac{\epsilon}{2(|g(x_0)| + \epsilon + 1)} \ \forall\, x : |x - x_0| < \delta_1.$$

$$|g(x) - g(x_0)| < \frac{\epsilon}{2(|f(x_0)| + \epsilon + 1)} \ \forall\, x : |x - x_0| < \delta_1.$$

We also observe that the continuity of g implies that g is bounded on $\{x : |x - x_0| < \delta_2\}$ (Verify this, or see Theorem 7.4.3 in the next chapter). Thus, on this interval, there exists $M > 0$ such that $|g(x)| \leq M$. Let $\delta = min\{\delta_1, \delta_2\}$. Then, for all x such that $|x - x_0| < \delta$, we have,

$$
\begin{aligned}
|(fg)(x) - (fg)(x_0)| \;\leq\; & M.\frac{\epsilon}{2(|g(x_0)| + \epsilon + 1)} \\
& + |f(x_0)|.\frac{\epsilon}{2(|f(x_0)| + \epsilon + 1)} < \epsilon.
\end{aligned}
$$

Hence, fg is continuous at x_0.

Theorem 6.6.2 *Let f and g be continuous at the point $x_0 \in \mathcal{D}(f) \cap \mathcal{D}(g)$ and suppose that $g(x_0) \neq 0$. Then $\frac{f}{g}$ is continuous at x_0.*

Proof. $g(x_0) \neq 0 \implies |g(x_0)| > 0$. Let $\epsilon_1 = \frac{|g(x_0)|}{2}$. Since g is continuous at $x_0, \exists\, \delta_1 > 0$ such that $|x - x_0| < \delta_1 \implies |g(x) - g(x_0)| < \frac{1}{2}|g(x_0)|$. This implies that

$$|g(x_0)| - |g(x)| \leq \big||g(x_0)| - |g(x)|\big| \leq |g(x) - g(x_0)| < \frac{1}{2}|g(x_0)|,$$

so that for all x such that $|x - x_0| < \delta_1$,

$$|g(x)| \geq |g(x_0)| - \frac{1}{2}|g(x_0)| = \frac{1}{2}|g(x_0)|.$$

Now, let $\epsilon > 0$ be given. Since g is continuous at $x_0, \exists\, \delta_2 > 0$ such that $\forall\, x$ such that $|x - x_0| < \delta_2$,

$$|g(x) - g(x_0)| < \frac{\epsilon}{2}|g(x_0)|^2.$$

Let $\delta = \min\{\delta_1, \delta_2\}$. Then, for all x such that $|x - x_0| < \delta$, we have,

$$
\begin{aligned}
\left|\frac{1}{g(x)} - \frac{1}{g(x_0)}\right| &= \left|\frac{g(x_0) - g(x)}{g(x_0)g(x)}\right| = \frac{|g(x_0) - g(x)|}{|g(x_0)| \cdot |g(x)|} \\
&\leq \frac{2|g(x_0) - g(x)|}{|g(x_0)|^2} < \epsilon.
\end{aligned}
$$

Hence, $\frac{1}{g}$ is continuous at the point x_0. Using the fact that $\frac{f}{g} = f\frac{1}{g}$ and applying Theorem 6.6.1(iv) to the functions f and $\frac{1}{g}$, one then concludes the proof of the theorem. $\square$

Proposition 6.6.3 *For any real-valued function f, $\lim\limits_{x \to a} f(x) = \ell$ if and only if for every $\epsilon > 0$, $\exists\, \delta > 0$ such that f is defined on $D_a = \{x \in D(f) : 0 < |x - a| < \delta\}$ and $|f(x) - \ell| < \epsilon$ whenever $0 < |x - a| < \delta$.*

Proof. ($\Leftarrow$) Assume the $\epsilon - \delta$ condition holds. For $\epsilon_0 = 1$, there exists some $\delta^* > 0$ such that, in particular, $f(x)$ is defined for $0 < |x - a| < \delta^*$. Recall that this condition is part of the requirement for $\lim_{x \to a} f(x)$ to make sense. Now, let $\{x_n\}$ be any sequence in $D_a = \{x : 0 < |x - a| < \delta^*\}$ with $x_n \to a$. To prove $f(x_n) \to \ell$, we let $\epsilon > 0$ and let $\delta > 0$ be corresponding numbers from the $\epsilon - \delta$ condition, so that $|f(x_n) - \ell| < \epsilon$ whenever $0 < |x_n - a| < \delta$. There exists an integer $N > 0$ such that $|x_n - a| < \delta$ if $n \geq N$ (since $x_n \to a$), and $0 < |x_n - a| \; \forall$ integers $n \geq 1$ (by assumption)). Hence, $|f(x_n) - \ell| < \epsilon$ if $n \geq N$ and so $f(x_n) \to \ell$. This completes the proof that the $\epsilon - \delta$ condition is sufficient for $\lim_{x \to a} f(x) = \ell$.

($\Longrightarrow$) Now, assume $f(x) \to \ell$ as $x \to a$. Then there exists a $\delta^* > 0$ such that $f(x)$ is defined on $\{x : 0 < |x - a| < \delta^*\}$. Let $\epsilon > 0$ be given. Assume that the $\epsilon - \delta$ condition is not true, i.e., assume that there is no $\delta > 0$ for this ϵ such that $|f(x) - \ell| < \epsilon$ if $0 < |x - a| < \delta$. For each $\delta = \frac{1}{n}$, we can pick x_n with $0 < |x_n - a| < \frac{1}{n}$ such that $|f(x_n) - \ell| \geq \epsilon$. Clearly, $x_n \to a$ but $f(x_n) \not\to \ell$, which contradicts our assumption. Hence, $f(x_n) \to \ell$ as $x_n \to a \Longrightarrow$ the $\epsilon - \delta$ condition. $\quad \square$

EXERCISES 6.2

1. Show that the function $f(x) = |x|$ is continuous at 0.

2. State and prove a theorem on the continuity of a composite function.

   Recall: The composite function is defined as follows. Let f be defined on $\mathcal{D}(f)$ and g be defined on $\mathcal{D}(g)$. The *composite function* h is defined on the set $\{x : x \in \mathcal{D}(g) \text{ and } g(x) \in \mathcal{D}(f)\}$. For any point in this set, $h(x) = f(g(x))$.

3. If in question 3, $\mathcal{D}(g)$ is a bounded interval with center a and $\mathcal{D}(f)$ is a bounded interval with center $b = g(a)$,

what can be said about the set on which h is defined? What are the simple choices for f and g if $h(x) = \sqrt{\sin x}$, $h(x) = \sin \sqrt{x}$, or $h(x) = (x-1)^6$?

4. Let $f(x) = [x]$ and $g(x) = x - [x]$. Determine the points at which f and g are continuous.

5. For $x \neq -1$ show that the following limit exists:

$$f(x) = \lim_{n \to \infty} \left(\frac{x^n - 1}{x^n + 1} \right)^2.$$

(a)   What is $\lim_{x \to 1} f(x)$?

(b)   What is $\lim_{x \to -1} f(x)$?

(c)   For which values of $x \neq -1$ is f continuous? Is it possible to define $f(-1)$ in such a way that f is continuous at -1?

128

CHAPTER 7

Intermediate Value Theorem; Continuous maps on $[a, b]$

In this chapter we prove the two fundamental theorems of mathematical analysis promised at the beginning of the last chapter. More precisely, we prove the following theorems.

Theorem 7.2.3 (The Intermediate Value Theorem) *If f is continuous on an interval I, then $f(I)$ is an interval.*

In order words, if f is continuous on an interval I, and $\alpha, \beta \in I$ with $\alpha < \beta$ (say) and if y is an intermediate point between $f(\alpha)$ and $f(\beta)$, i.e., $f(\alpha) < y < f(\beta)$, then $\exists\, c \in [\alpha, \beta]$ such that $f(c) = y$.

Theorem 7.4.4 *Let $f : [a, b] \to \mathbb{R}$ be continuous. Then,*

    (i) f is bounded on $[a, b]$.

    (ii) There exists a point $c \in [a, b]$ at which f attains a maximum value, i.e., there exists $c \in [a, b]$ such that $f(c) = max_{x \in [a,b]} f(x)$.

129

(iii) There exists a point $c^* \in [a,b]$ at which f attains a minimum value, i.e., there exists $c^* \in [a,b]$ such that $f(c^*) = \min_{x \in [a,b]} f(x)$.

(iv) $f([a,b]) = [f(c^*), f(c)]$.

*(v) f is **uniformly** continuous.*

We shall prove *(v)* in the next chapter after we would have introduced the concept of *uniform* continuity. We prove *(i)* to *(iv)* here. In order to give the proofs, we begin with the following observations.

7.1 Special Property of $[a,b]$

The interval $[a,b]$ has the following important property: If any sequence $\{a_n\}$ in $[a,b]$ converges, its limit is always in $[a,b]$. To see this, let $\{a_n\}$ be an arbitrary sequence in $[a,b]$ and let $a_n \to a^*$. Clearly, $a \leq a_n \leq b$ for all integers $n \geq 0$. By Theorem 3.3.1, $a \leq a^* \leq b$. So, $a^* \in [a,b]$. Observe that this property does not necessarily hold in (a,b). It suffices to note that $\frac{1}{n} \in (0,1), \frac{1}{n} \to 0$, but $0 \notin (0,1)$.

Recall (Bolzano-Weierstrass theorem) that any bounded sequence in $\mathbb{R}$ has a convergent subsequence. This property holds, of course, in (a,b) and in $[a,b]$. So, it is not actually a special property of $[a,b]$. However, we include it in the two properties of $[a,b]$ which we want to highlight. We now isolate these two very important properties of $[a,b]$ as follows:

P1. **Any sequence in $[a,b]$ has a convergent subsequence.**

P2. **Any convergent sequence in $[a,b]$ has its limit in $[a,b]$.**

These two properties will be central in the proofs of the two most important theorems of this chapter (Theorem 7.2.3 and Theorem 7.4.4).

7.2   The Intermediate Value Theorem

We begin with the following remarkable property of a continuous function defined on $[a, b]$.

Lemma 7.2.1 *Let $f : [a, b] \to \mathbb{R}$ be a continuous map. Suppose that:*

> *(i) $f(a) > 0$ and $f(b) < 0$, (see fig. 7.1) then $\exists\ x_0 \in [a, b]$ such that $f(x_0) = 0$; or equivalently,*

> *(ii) $f(a) < 0$ and $f(b) > 0$, then $\exists\ x_0 \in [a, b]$ such that $f(x_0) = 0$.*

Proof. We prove (i) only since the proof of (ii) is similar. Let $\epsilon > 0$ be given such that $f(a) - \epsilon > 0$. (This is possible since $f(a) > 0$). Since f is continuous on $[a, b]$, it is continuous to the right at a. So, with this $\epsilon > 0$ given, *by the continuity to the right at a*, there exists a $\delta > 0$ such that

$$|f(x) - f(a)| < \epsilon \ \forall\ x \text{ such that } a \leq x < a + \delta. \quad (*)$$

Thus, from $(*)$, $f(x) > f(a) - \epsilon \ \forall\ x \in [a, a + \delta)$. But $f(a) - \epsilon > 0$. Hence $f(x) > 0 \ \forall x \in [a, a + \delta)$. So, there exists an interval $[a, u]$ on which f is positive (see Figure 7.1).

Let $\mathcal{U} = \{u \in [a, b] : f(x) > 0 \text{ in } a \leq x < u\}$. Clearly, $\mathcal{U}$ is bounded above by b and so has a "supremum". Let $\sup \mathcal{U} = x_0$. Then, $x_0 \leq b$. In fact, $x_0 < b$. To see this, *we use the continuity to the left at b* and the fact that $f(b) < 0$, i.e., given $\epsilon > 0$ such that $f(b) + \epsilon < 0$, $\exists\ \delta > 0$ such that

$$|f(x) - f(b)| < \epsilon \ \forall\ x \text{ such that } b - \delta < x \leq b.$$

In particular, $f(x) < f(b) + \epsilon \ \forall\ x$ such that $b - \delta < x \leq b$. Since $f(b) < 0$, this implies that $f(x) \leq 0$ in some interval $(b - \delta, b]$, (see Figure 7.1). Now, the fact that $f(x) \leq 0$ on $(b - \delta, b] \implies \sup \mathcal{U} \neq b$. So $x_0 < b$.

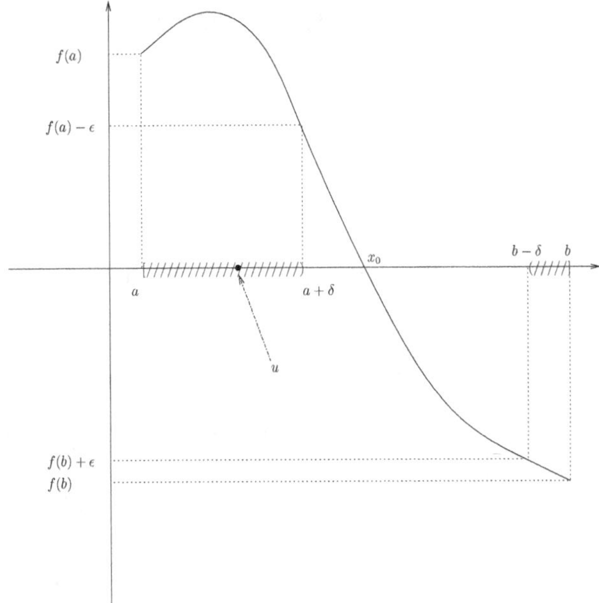

Fig. 7.1

(*i*) **Claim 1.** $f(x_0) \not> 0$.

Suppose $f(x_0) > 0$. Then, by the continuity of f at x_0, there exists an interval $[a, u]$ with $x_0 < u$ on which $f(x) > 0$ (Exercises 7.1, Problem 10(a) (See Fig. 7.2)). This contradicts the fact that $x_0 = \sup \mathcal{U}$. So, Claim 1 is proved.

(*ii* **Claim 2.** $f(x_0) \not< 0$.

For, if $f(x_0) < 0$, then, by the continuity of f at x_0, there exists an interval $[a, v]$, $v < x_0$ such that $f(x) < 0$ on $[a, v]$ (see Figure 7.2). This contradicts the fact that $f(x) > 0$ on $[a, x_0]$. Hence Claim 2 holds.

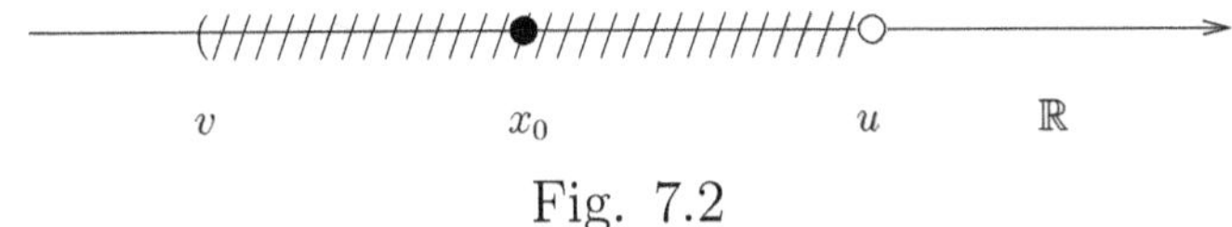

Fig. 7.2

From Claim 1 and Claim 2, we obtain that $f(x_0) = 0$. □

We now give a characterization of intervals which will be useful in our next theorem.

Proposition 7.2.2 *I is an interval if and only if $I \neq \emptyset$ and if x, y, z are such that $x \in I, z \in I$ and $x < y < z$, then $y \in I$.*

Theorem 7.2.3 (The Intermediate Value Theorem) *If f is continuous on an interval I, then $f(I)$ is an interval.*

In order words, *if f is continuous on an interval I, and $\alpha, \beta \in I$ with $\alpha < \beta$ (say) and if y is an intermediate point between $f(\alpha)$ and $f(\beta)$, i.e., $f(\alpha) < y < f(\beta)$, or $f(\beta) < y < f(\alpha)$, then $\exists\, c \in [\alpha, \beta]$ such that $f(c) = y$ (see Figure 7.3).*

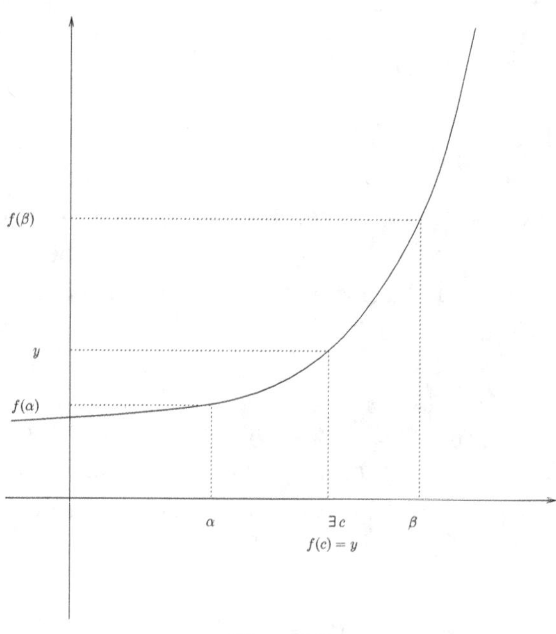

Fig. 7.3

We now give a proof of the Intermediate Value Theorem.

Proof. We shall use the characterization of intervals given in

Proposition 7.2.2. We consider any two points $f(\alpha)$ and $f(\beta)$ in $f(I)$, and without loss of generality, with $f(\alpha) < f(\beta)$. Then either $\alpha < \beta$ or $\alpha > \beta$ but $\alpha \neq \beta$. We assume, without loss of generality, $\alpha < \beta$ and prove that if $f(\alpha) < y < f(\beta)$ then $y \in f(I)$, i.e., we must show that there exists $c \in I$ such that $f(c) = y$.

For this, consider the function g defined on $[\alpha, \beta]$ by

$$g(x) = f(x) - y.$$

Clearly, g is continuous on $[\alpha, \beta]$ and $g(\alpha) < 0$, $g(\beta) > 0$. Hence by Lemma 7.2.1, there exists a point $c \in (\alpha, \beta)$ such that $g(c) = 0$. $\square$

Theorem 7.2.4 *If f is a continuous real-valued function whose domain $\mathcal{D}(f)$ is an interval, then*

$$\left(\inf_{x \in \mathcal{D}(f)} f(x), \; \sup_{x \in \mathcal{D}(f)} f(x) \right) \subseteq \mathcal{R}(f), \qquad (7.2.1)$$

where $\mathcal{R}(f)$ denotes the range of f.

Proof. If $f(x)$ is not bounded above, we take $\displaystyle\sup_{x \in \mathcal{D}(f)} f(x) = \infty$, and if $f(x)$ is not bounded below, we take $\displaystyle\inf_{x \in \mathcal{D}(f)} f(x) = -\infty$.

We now prove the inclusion (7.2.1). Let x^* be an element of

$$\left(\inf_{x \in \mathcal{D}(f)} f(x), \; \sup_{x \in \mathcal{D}(f)} f(x) \right).$$

This implies,

$$(i) \quad x^* < \sup_{x \in \mathcal{D}(f)} f(x); \qquad (ii) \quad \inf_{x \in \mathcal{D}(f)} f(x) < x^*.$$

By (i), there exists $b \in \mathcal{D}(f)$ such that $x^* < f(b)$. By (ii), there exists $a \in \mathcal{D}(f)$ such that $\inf f(x) < f(a) < x^*$. Hence, $f(a) < x^* < f(b)$, i.e., $x^* \in (f(a), f(b)) \subset [f(a), f(b)]$. But by Theorem 7.2.3, $[f(a), f(b)] \subseteq f([a, b]) \subset \mathcal{R}(f)$. Hence, $x^* \in \mathcal{R}(f)$. This verifies the inclusion (7.2.1) and completes the proof. $\square$

Remark 7.2.5 Theorem 7.2.4 is very useful in identifying the ranges of various continuous real-valued functions. The **range** of a continuous function *whose domain is an interval* must have **lower end point** as $\inf\limits_{x\in\mathcal{D}(f)} f(x)$ and **upper end point** as $\sup\limits_{x\in\mathcal{D}(f)} f(x)$. *Then, to decide which end point is in* $\left[\inf\limits_{x\in\mathcal{D}(f)} f(x),\ \sup\limits_{x\in\mathcal{D}(f)} f(x)\right]$ *or is* $-\infty$ *or* $+\infty$ *depends on whether or not the* " $\inf\limits_{x\in\mathcal{D}(f)} f(x)$ " *or* " $\sup\limits_{x\in\mathcal{D}(f)} f(x)$ " *is in the range of* f. We illustrate with the following examples.

Example 7.2.6
Find the range of each of the following real-valued functions:

(i) $f(x) = \dfrac{3}{x^2+1}$.

(ii) $f : (2,3] \to \mathbb{R}$ defined by $f(x) = \dfrac{1}{x-2}$.

(iii) $f : (-2,2) \to \mathbb{R}$ defined by $f(x) = \dfrac{2x}{4+x^2}$.

(iv) $f : (-2,2) \to \mathbb{R}$ defined by $f(x) = \dfrac{1}{x-2}$.

(v) $f : [-2,2] \to \mathbb{R}$ defined by $f(x) = \dfrac{2x}{4+x^2}$.

Solution: (i)

$$\inf_{x\in\mathcal{D}(f)} f(x) = \inf_{x\in\mathbb{R}} f(x) = \inf_{x\in\mathbb{R}} \left(\frac{3}{x^2+1}\right) = 0.$$

$$\sup_{x\in\mathcal{D}(f)} f(x) = \sup_{x\in\mathbb{R}} f(x) = \sup_{x\in\mathbb{R}} \left(\frac{3}{x^2+1}\right) = 3.$$

Since the domain of f is $\mathbb{R}$ (an interval), the range of f must be an interval (by Theorem 7.2.3), with lower end point 0 and upper end point 3. We now check if any of 0 or 3 is in the range of f.

For 0, we check if $f(x) = 0$ for any $x \in D(f)$. But $f(x) = 0 \Rightarrow \frac{3}{x^2+1} = 0$ and this is impossible for any $x \in \mathbb{R}$. So, the lower end point 0 is **not** in the range of f.

For 3, we check if $f(x) = 3$ for any $x \in \mathbb{R}$. But $f(x) = 3 \Rightarrow \frac{3}{x^2+1} = 3 \Rightarrow x^2 + 1 = 1 \Rightarrow x^2 = 0$ and clearly $x = 0 \in \mathbb{R}$. Hence, $3 \in \mathcal{R}(f)$. Hence, the range of f here is $(0, 3]$.

(ii) Observe first that f is continuous on $(2, 3]$. Now,

$$\inf_{x \in \mathcal{D}(f)} f(x) = \inf_{x \in (2,3]} f(x) = \inf_{x \in (2,3]} \left(\frac{1}{x-2} \right) = \frac{1}{3-2} = 1.$$

$$\sup_{x \in \mathcal{D}(f)} f(x) = \sup_{x \in (2,3]} f(x) = \sup_{x \in (2,3]} \left(\frac{1}{x-2} \right) = +\infty$$

(since as $x \to 2^+$, $\frac{1}{x-2} \to \infty$).

We now check if 1 is in the range of f (i.e., is there an $x \in (2, 3]$ such that $f(x) = 1$ i.e., $\frac{1}{x-2} = 1$?). This would imply $x - 2 = 1$ or $x = 3 \in (2, 3]$. Hence, range of $f = [1, \infty)$.

(iii) f is continuous on $(-2, 2)$.

$$\inf_{x \in \mathcal{D}(f)} f(x) = \inf_{x \in (-2,2)} f(x) = \inf_{x \in (-2,2)} \left(\frac{2x}{4+x^2} \right) = \frac{-1}{2}.$$

$$\sup_{x \in \mathcal{D}(f)} f(x) = \sup_{x \in (-2,2)} f(x) = \sup_{x \in (-2,2)} \left(\frac{2x}{4+x^2} \right) = \frac{1}{2}.$$

We now check if $\exists\ x \in (-2, 2)$ such that $\frac{2x}{4+x^2} = \frac{-1}{2}$. This holds if $-4 - x^2 = 4x$ or $x^2 + 4x + 4 = 0$, i.e., $(x+2)^2 = 0$ or $x = -2$ (twice). But $-2 \notin (-2, 2)$. So $\frac{-1}{2}$ is not in the range of f. Also, we check if $\exists\ x \in (-2, 2)$ such that $\frac{2x}{4+x^2} = \frac{1}{2}$. This holds if $x^2 + 4 = 4x$ or $(x - 2)^2 = 0$ i.e., $x = 2$ (twice). Again, $+2 \notin (-2, 2)$. Hence, $\frac{1}{2}$ is not in the range of f. Hence, range of $f = (\frac{-1}{2}, \frac{1}{2})$.

(iv) f is continuous on $(-2, 2)$.

$$\inf_{x \in \mathcal{D}(f)} f(x) = \inf_{x \in (-2,2)} f(x) = \inf_{x \in (-2,2)} \left(\frac{1}{x-2} \right) = -\infty$$

(since as $x \to 2^-$, $\frac{1}{x-2} \to -\infty$).

$$\sup_{x \in \mathcal{D}(f)} f(x) = \sup_{x \in (-2,2)} f(x) = \sup_{x \in (-2,2)} \left(\frac{1}{x-2} \right) = \frac{-1}{4}.$$

We check if $\exists\ x \in (-2, 2)$ such that $\frac{1}{x-2} = \frac{-1}{4}$. This would give $-x + 2 = 4$ or $x = -2 \notin (-2, 2)$. So, $\frac{-1}{4}$ is not in the range of f. Hence, the range of f is $(-\infty, \frac{-1}{4})$.

(v) f is continuous on $[-2, 2]$.

$$\inf_{x \in \mathcal{D}(f)} f(x) = \inf_{x \in [-2,2]} f(x) = \inf_{x \in [-2,2]} \left(\frac{2x}{4 + x^2} \right) = \frac{-1}{2}.$$

$$\sup_{x \in \mathcal{D}(f)} f(x) = \sup_{x \in [-2,2]} f(x) = \sup_{x \in [-2,2]} \left(\frac{2x}{4 + x^2} \right) = \frac{1}{2}.$$

Note that if $f(x) = \frac{-1}{2}$ then $\frac{2x}{4+x^2} = \frac{-1}{2}$ and this gives $x^2 + 4 = -4x$ or $(x + 2)^2 = 0$ which gives $x = -2$ (twice), and clearly $-2 \in [-2, 2]$. So, $\frac{-1}{2}$ is in the range of f. Similarly, $\frac{1}{2}$ is in the range of f. Hence, the range of f is $[\frac{-1}{2}, \frac{1}{2}]$.

7.3   Boundedness of Real Functions

In this section we study a property of continuous functions that is very useful in various applications. We begin with the following definition.

Definition 7.3.1 *Let $f : \mathbb{R} \to \mathbb{R}$ be any function and let S be a subset of $\mathbb{R}$, let $\mathcal{R}_S(f)$ denote the range of f on S. Then, the function f is said to be:*

(i) **bounded above on** S *if $\mathcal{R}_S(f)$ is bounded above;*

(ii) **bounded below on** S *if* $\mathcal{R}_S(f)$ *is bounded below;*

(iii) **bounded on** S *if* $\mathcal{R}_S(f)$ *is bounded above and below;*

(iv) **bounded** *if* $\mathcal{R}_D(f)$ *is bounded above and below, where* $\mathcal{R}_D(f)$ *denotes the range of* f *on its domain* D.

Example 7.3.2

(i) In Example 7.2.6(*i*), $S = \mathbb{R}$ and $R_S(f) = (0, 3]$ and so $f(x) = \frac{3}{x^2+1}$ is bounded on $\mathbb{R}$. Since the domain of f is $\mathbb{R}$, this function is bounded.

(ii) In Example 7.2.6(*ii*), $S = (2, 3]$ and $R_S(f) = [-1, \infty)$. Hence, the function f is bounded below on $(2, 3]$ and is not bounded above.

(iii) In Example 7.2.6(*iii*), $S = (-2, 2)$, $f(x) = \frac{2x}{4+x^2}$ and $R_S(f) = (\frac{-1}{2}, \frac{1}{2})$. So, f is bounded on $(-2, 2)$.

(iv) In Example 7.2.6(*iv*), $S = (-2, 2)$, $f(x) = \frac{1}{x-2}$ and $R_S(f) = (-\infty, \frac{-1}{4})$. So, f is bounded above on $(-2, 2)$ and is not bounded below.

(v) In Example 7.2.6(*v*), $S = [-2, 2]$, $f(x) = \frac{2x}{4+x^2}$ and $R_S(f) = [\frac{-1}{2}, \frac{1}{2}]$. Hence, f is bounded on $[-2, 2]$.

7.4 Continuous maps on $[a, b]$

We remark in passing that in Example 7.3.2(*v*), $S = [-2, 2]$, a **closed and bounded** interval, the function $f(x) = \frac{2x}{4+x^2}$ is continuous on $[-2, 2]$ and $R_S(f) = [\frac{-1}{2}, \frac{1}{2}]$, a **closed and bounded** interval.

Lesson 7.4.1 The main lesson of the last section can be summarized as follows:

(a) If a real-valued function f is defined and is continuous on a **bounded** interval, the range of that interval under f **may be a bounded interval** (as in Example 7.2.6(iii)) or **may be an unbounded interval** (as in Example 7.2.6(iv)).

(b) Lesson (a) says that a **continuous real-valued function** defined on a **bounded interval** may be bounded or unbounded.

(c) It turns out that if a continuous real-valued function f is defined on a **closed and bounded** interval $[a, b]$, say, , then the function **must be bounded**. In fact, the range of f is the **closed and bounded interval** given by

$$\left[\inf_{x \in [a,b]} f(x), \ \sup_{x \in [a,b]} f(x) \right],$$

and therefore f is bounded on $[a, b]$.

We shall give a proof of (c) as part of Theorem 7.4.4 below.

Remark 7.4.2 *While Lessons 7.4.1(a) and 7.4.1(b) emphasize, in particular, that a continuous function defined on (a, b) may or may not be bounded, our next theorem shows that* **for a continuous function on any domain in $\mathbb{R}$,** *there exists always an open interval centred at x_0 in the domain of f on which f is bounded. We prove this now.*

Theorem 7.4.3 *If f is a real-valued function which is continuous at $x_0 \in \mathcal{D}(f)$, then* **there exists** *an open interval centred at x_0 on which f is bounded.*

Proof. Since f is continuous at $x_0 \in \mathcal{D}(f) \subseteq \mathbb{R}$, given $\epsilon > 0$, there exists $\delta = \delta(\epsilon) > 0$, such that $|f(x) - f(x_0)| < \epsilon \ \forall \ |x -$

$x_0| < \delta$. Take $\epsilon = 1$. Then,

$$
\begin{aligned}
|f(x)| &= |f(x) - f(x_0) + f(x_0)| \le |f(x) - f(x_0)| + |f(x_0)| \\
&< 1 + |f(x_0)| \; \forall \; x \in (x_0 - \delta, x_0 + \delta).
\end{aligned}
$$

Hence, f is bounded on the open interval $(x_0 - \delta, x_0 + \delta)$. $\square$

Theorem 7.4.4 *Let $f : [a, b] \to \mathbb{R}$ be continuous. Then,*

(i) f is bounded, i.e., $\exists M \in \mathbb{R}$ such that $|f(x)| \le M \; \forall \; x \in [a, b]$.

(ii) There exists a point $c_1 \in [a, b]$ such that

$$
f(c_1) = \min_{x \in [a,b]} f(x).
$$

(iii) There exists a point $c_2 \in [a, b]$ such that

$$
f(c_2) = \max_{x \in [a,b]} f(x).
$$

(iv) $f([a, b]) = [f(c_1), f(c_2)]$.

Proof. (i) First we prove that f is bounded above. Suppose, on the contrary, that f is not bounded above. Then for each positive integer n, there exists $x_n \in [a, b]$ such that $f(x_n) > n$. (This is the negation of the statement that f is bounded above). Since $x_n \in [a, b]$ for every $n \ge 1$, $\{x_n\}$ is bounded. So, by $P1$, it has a convergent subsequence. Let $\{x_{n_j}\}$ be that subsequence and let $x_{n_j} \to x^*$ as $j \to \infty$. By $P2$, $x^* \in [a, b]$. Moreover, $f(x_{n_j}) \ge n_j \ge j$ for all $j \in \mathbb{N}$. Since f is continuous at x^*, (if $x^* \notin [a, b]$, we cannot assume f is continuous at x^*), $f(x_{n_j}) \to f(x^*)$. The convergent sequence $\{f(x_{n_j})\}$ is bounded, but that contradicts $f(x_{n_j}) \ge j$ for all j. Thus, f is bounded above. The proof that f is bounded below is similar. Hence f is bounded. This completes the proof of part (i).

For (ii), since f is bounded below on $[a, b]$, let $m^* = \inf\{f(x) : x \in [a, b]\}$. We prove $m^* = f(c_1)$ for *some* $c_1 \in [a, b]$. For each positive integer n, take $\epsilon_n = \frac{1}{n} > 0$. Then, there exists $u_n \in [a, b]$ with

$$m^* \le f(u_n) < m^* + \frac{1}{n}. \tag{7.4.1}$$

By the Bolzano-Weierstrass theorem, there exists a subsequence $\{u_{n_j}\}$ of $\{u_n\}$ such that $u_{n_j} \to x^*$. By P_2, $x^* \in [a, b]$. Then by the continuity of f, $f(u_{n_j}) \to f(x^*)$, and from (7.4.1), $f(u_{n_j}) \to m^*$. By the uniqueness of the limits, $f(x^*) = m^* = \inf\{f(x), x \in [a, b]\}$. Set $c_1 = x^*$ and we are done.

The existence of $c_2 \in [a, b]$ such that (iii) holds is proved similarly.

(iv) Since $f([a, b])$ is an interval, it must be the interval $[m^*, M^*]$. $\square$

EXERCISES 7.1

Note: A function f defined on $[a, b]$ is said to satisfy the **intermediate value property** on $[a, b]$ if for every $x_1, x_2 \in [a, b]$ with $x_1 < x_2$ and for every k between $f(x_1)$ and $f(x_2)$ there is a $c \in (x_1, x_2)$ with $f(c) = k$.

1. Show that the function $f(x) = x + 1$ on $(0, 1]$, $f(0) = 0$ does not satisfy the conclusion of the intermediate value theorem.

2. Suppose that f is continuous on $\mathbb{R}$, $\lim\limits_{x \to -\infty} f(x) = -3$ and $\lim\limits_{x \to \infty} f(x) = 17$. Show that there is at least one real number x such that $f(x) = 0$.

3. Find $M = \sup\limits_{x \in A} f(x)$ and $m = \inf\limits_{x \in A} f(x)$ for the following functions f defined on the indicated domain A and

then find points $x_1, x_2 \in A$ (if they exist) such that $f(x_1) = M$ and $f(x_2) = m$.

(a) $f(x) = 3 + 2x - x^2$ on $[0, 4]$
(b) $f(x) = 2 - |x - 1|$ on $[-2, 2)$
(c) $f(x) = e^{-\frac{1}{x}}$ on $(0, \infty)$
(d) $f(x) = 1 - x^2$ on $(-2, 1)$.

4. Verify whether or not the function defined by

$$f(x) = \begin{cases} sin\frac{1}{x}, & \text{when } x \neq 0, \\ 0, & \text{when } x = 0, \end{cases}$$

satisfies the **intermediate value property** on $[-1, 1]$.

5. Let $f : D \subset \mathbb{R} \to \mathbb{R}$ and $g : G \subset \mathbb{R} \to \mathbb{R}$ be continuous functions such that $f(D) \subseteq G$. If f is continuous at $x_0 \in D$ and g is continuous at $f(x_0)$, prove that $g \circ f : D \to \mathbb{R}$ is continuous at x_0.

6. Let f and g be functions from $D \subseteq \mathbb{R}$ to $\mathbb{R}$. Define the functions $\min(f, g)$ and $\max(f, g)$ from D to $\mathbb{R}$ by

$$\min(f, g)(x) = \min\{f(x), g(x)\},$$

$$\max(f, g)(x) = \max\{f(x), g(x)\}.$$

Show that

$$\min(f, g) = \frac{1}{2}(f + g) - \frac{1}{2}|f - g|,$$

and $\qquad \max(f, g) = \frac{1}{2}(f+g)+\frac{1}{2}|f-g|.$

Hint: Show that for all $a, b \in \mathbb{R}$, $\max(a, b) = \frac{1}{2}(a + b) + \frac{1}{2}|a - b|$. Do this by considering the two cases $b \geq a$ and $b < a$.

7. Prove that if f is continuous, then $|f|$ is also continuous. What can you say about the continuity of $\min(f, g)$ and $\max(f, g)$ if f and g are continuous?

8. Define $f : \mathbb{R} \to \mathbb{R}$ by

$$f(x) = \begin{cases} 1, & \text{if } x \text{ is rational,} \\ 0, & \text{if } x \text{ is irrational .} \end{cases}$$

Prove that f is *discontinuous* at every real number.

Hint: If $x_0 \in \mathbb{R}$, every neighbourhood of x_0 contains rational points (at which $f(x) = 1$) and contains irrational points (at which $f(x) = 0$). Can $\lim\limits_{x \to x_0} f(x)$ exist?

9. Prove part (iii) of Theorem 7.4.4 i.e., if $f : [a, b] \to \mathbb{R}$ is continuous, then, there exists $x^* \in [a, b]$ such that $f(x^*) = \max f(x), x \in [a, b]$.

(Hint: $f(x)$ is bounded, so $f(x^*) = \max \{f(x), x \in [a, b]\}$ exists. For each positive integer n, let $\epsilon_n = \frac{1}{n} > 0$. Use the definition of sup; then Bolzano-Wierstrass Theorem; then continuity of f; then uniqueness of limits).

10. (a) Justify the claim made in **Claim 1** in the proof of Lemma 7.2.1 that by the continuity of f at x_0, there exists an interval $[a, u]$ with $x_0 < u$ on which $f(x) > 0$.

(b) Justify the statement made in **Claim 2** in the proof of Lemma 7.2.1 that by the continuity of f at x_0, there exists an interval $[a, v]$, $v < x_0$ such that $f(x) < 0$ on $[a, v]$.

(Hint: Parts (a) and (b) follow from Exercises 6.1, Problem 3).

144

CHAPTER 8

Uniform Continuity

8.1 Introduction

In this chapter, we introduce a subclass of the class of continuous functions studied in the last chapter. This subclass is called the class of *uniformly continuous* maps. We begin by a motivation and the definition of uniform continuity. Then we prove the following important theorem which is the main result of this chapter.

Theorem 8.3.1 *Let $f : [a, b] \to \mathbb{R}$ be continuous. Then f is uniformly continuous on $[a, b]$.*

8.2 Motivation and Definition

Recall that a real-valued function f is said to be continuous at $x_0 \in \mathcal{D}(f)$ if and only if for any given $\epsilon > 0$, $\exists$ a $\delta = \delta(\epsilon) > 0$ such that if $x \in \mathcal{D}(f)$ and $|x - x_0| < \delta$ then $|f(x) - f(x_0)| < \epsilon$.

145

It is clear from this definition that if an $\epsilon > 0$ is given and a $\delta = \delta(\epsilon) > 0$ has been found such that

$$\text{for } x \in \mathcal{D}(f), \ |x - x_0| < \delta \Rightarrow |f(x) - f(x_0)| < \epsilon, \qquad (*)$$

then any other δ, say δ^*, such that $0 < \delta^* < \delta$ will also satisfy $(*)$. This says that for any $\delta > 0$ that works, any other smaller positive δ will also work for the same $\epsilon > 0$. However, the set of all δ's that work for fixed $\epsilon > 0$ and fixed $x_0 \in \mathcal{D}(f)$ may depend only on the given $\epsilon > 0$ or may depend on both the given $\epsilon > 0$ **as well as on the given** x_0. We illustrate.

Example 8.2.1 Let $f(x) = x$. Prove that f is continuous at $x = x_0$.

Solution: Let $\epsilon > 0$ be given. We want to find a $\delta = \delta(\epsilon) > 0$ such that if $x \in \mathcal{D}(f)$, $|x - x_0| < \delta$ then $|f(x) - f(x_0)| < \epsilon$. Now, $|f(x) - f(x_0)| = |x - x_0|$. Choose $\delta(\epsilon) = \frac{\epsilon}{2}$. Then $|x - x_0| < \delta$ implies that $|f(x) - f(x_0)| = |x - x_0| < \delta = \frac{\epsilon}{2} < \epsilon$.

Example 8.2.2 Prove that the function $f(x) = \frac{1}{x}$ is continuous at any $x_0 \in (0, \infty)$.

Solution: Let $x_0 \in (0, \infty)$ be arbitrary. Clearly $x_0 \neq 0$. We prove f is continuous at x_0. So let $\epsilon > 0$ be given. We want to find a $\delta > 0$ such that $\forall\, x \in (0, \infty)$, $|x - x_0| < \delta \Rightarrow |f(x) - f(x_0)| < \epsilon$. So,

$$|f(x) - f(x_0)| = \left| \frac{1}{x} - \frac{1}{x_0} \right| = \frac{|x - x_0|}{|x| \cdot |x_0|} < \frac{\delta}{|x| \cdot |x_0|}.$$

But $\big||x_0| - |x|\big| \leq |x_0 - x| < \delta$ so that if we choose

$$\boxed{\delta < \frac{1}{2}|x_0|\,,}$$

then
$|x| > \frac{1}{2}|x_0|$ so that $\frac{1}{|x|} < \frac{2}{|x_0|}$. Hence,

$$|f(x) - f(x_0)| \; < \; \frac{\delta}{|x| \cdot |x_0|}$$

$$< \; \frac{2\delta}{|x_0|^2} = \epsilon \text{ if } \delta = \frac{\epsilon|x_0|^2}{2}. \qquad (8.2.1)$$

Hence, given $\epsilon > 0$, choose $\delta = \min\left\{\frac{1}{2}|x_0|, \frac{\epsilon|x_0|^2}{2}\right\}$. Then $|x - x_0| < \delta \Rightarrow |f(x) - f(x_0)| < \epsilon$, and so f is continuous at arbitrary $x_0 \in (0, \infty)$.

(Observe that in this case, the δ we have found depends on **both** the given ϵ and the point x_0 at which f is continuous. It is not possible, in this case, to find a δ that depends only on $\epsilon > 0$).

Remark 8.2.3 In Example 8.2.2, the δ we found depends on **both** the given $\epsilon > 0$ and on the $x_0 \in \mathcal{D}(f)$ considered. In example 8.2.1, the δ we found depends only on the given ϵ. In this case, f is said to be **uniformly continuous** on $\mathcal{D}(f)$. Motivated by this kind of behaviour, we have the following definition.

Definition 8.2.4 *A real-valued function f is said to be* **uniformly continuous** *on a set S if*

(i) $S \subset \mathcal{D}(f)$; and,

(ii) $\forall \epsilon > 0, \exists \delta = \delta(\epsilon) > 0$ such that, $\forall x_1, x_2 \in S, |x_1 - x_2| < \delta \Rightarrow |f(x_1) - f(x_2)| < \epsilon$.

Remark 8.2.5 Clearly, if f is **uniformly continuous** on S, then f is uniformly continuous on any subset of S. Furthermore, f is continuous at each point of S.

Remark 8.2.6 Geometrically, given $\epsilon > 0$, the **steeper** the curve of a function is at x_0 the **smaller** $\delta > 0$ will have to be for any given $\epsilon > 0$. If the steepness is limited, the greater the chance that the function will be **uniformly** continuous. For example, the function $f(x) = \frac{1}{x}$ on $[3, \infty)$ has limited steepness at **any** $x_0 \in [3, \infty)$. This is because

$$f'(x) = -\frac{1}{x^2} \text{ and } |f'(x)| = \frac{1}{x^2} < \frac{1}{9} \ \forall \ x \in [3, \infty).$$

However, if we consider the same function $f(x) = \frac{1}{x}$ on $(0, \infty)$ then $|f'(x)| = \frac{1}{x^2} \to \infty$ as $x \to 0$, indicating that the steepness near $x = 0$ in $\mathcal{D}(f)$ is unlimited (cf. Example 8.2.2).

Example 8.2.7 Show that $f(x) = \frac{1}{x}$ is **not** uniformly continuous on $(0, \infty)$.

Solution. Let $\epsilon = \frac{1}{2}$ and suppose that $\delta > 0$ is arbitrary. Choose $n \in \mathbb{N}$ such that $\frac{1}{n} < \delta$ and let $x_1 = \frac{1}{n}$ and $x_2 = \frac{1}{n+1}$. Clearly,

$$x_1, x_2 \in (0, \infty), \quad \text{and} \quad |x_1 - x_2| = \frac{1}{n} - \frac{1}{n+1} < \frac{1}{n} < \delta.$$

On the other hand,

$$|f(x_1) - f(x_2)| = \left| \frac{1}{x_1} - \frac{1}{x_2} \right| = |n - (n+1)| = 1 > \frac{1}{2} = \epsilon.$$

Hence for $\epsilon = \frac{1}{2}$ there is no $\delta > 0$ which satisfies Definition 8.2.4. Therefore $f(x) = \frac{1}{x}$ is not uniformly continuous on $(0, \infty)$.

Example 8.2.8 (a) Define $f : (0, 1) \to \mathbb{R}$ by $f(x) = \frac{1}{x}$. Then f is continuous on $(0, 1)$. However, f is not uniformly continuous on $(0, 1)$. To see this, let $\epsilon = \frac{1}{2}$. Let $n \in \mathbb{N}$ be such that $\frac{1}{n} < \delta$. Take $x_1 = \frac{1}{n}, x_2 = \frac{1}{n+1} \in (0, 1)$. Then, $|x_1 - x_2| = \frac{1}{n(n+1)} < \frac{1}{n} < \delta$. But $|f(x_1) - f(x_2)| = |n - (n+1)| = 1 \not< \epsilon$.

(b)　Define $g : (0, 1) \to \mathbb{R}$ by $g(x) = x^2$. Clearly, g is continuous on $(0, 1)$. In fact, g is uniformly continuous on $(0, 1)$. (It is not difficult to see that g is **not** uniformly continuous on $(0, \infty)$ (See Exercises 8.1 Problem 2(ii))). To see this, let $\epsilon > 0$ be given. For arbitrary $x_1, x_2 \in (0, 1)$, let $|x_1 - x_2| < \delta$. Then, $|g(x_1) - g(x_2)| \leq (|x_1| + |x_2|)|x_1 - x_2| \leq 2|x_1 - x_2| < 2\delta = \epsilon$ if $\delta = \frac{\epsilon}{2}$. Hence, g is uniformly continuous on $(0, 1)$.

Remark 8.2.9 Example 8.2.8 *tells us that a continuous function on an* **open interval** *may fail to be uniformly continuous on that interval. We will see in Problem 7 of Exercises 8.1 a result which gives necessary and sufficient conditions under which a continuous function on a bounded, open interval will be* **uniformly continuous**. *Also, Exercises 8.1, Problems 8 to 10, give sufficient conditions for a continuous function on an* **unbounded interval** *to be uniformly continuous.*

However, any continuous map on the **closed and bounded interval** $[a, b]$ *is always uniformly continuous. We prove this in the next section.*

8.3　Uniform Continuity Theorems

We now prove the following result concerning continuous real-valued functions on $[a, b]$.

Theorem 8.3.1 *Let $f : [a, b] \to \mathbb{R}$ be continuous. Then f is uniformly continuous.*

Proof. The proof is by contradiction. Recall that f is uniformly continuous if for each $\epsilon > 0$, there exists $\delta > 0$ such that

$$\forall \; x_1, x_2, \in [a, b] \text{ with } |x_1 - x_2| < \delta \Rightarrow |f(x_1) - f(x_2)| < \epsilon.$$

Assume that f is continuous but is not uniformly continuous on $[a, b]$. Then, there exist some $\epsilon > 0$ such that for **all**

$\delta > 0$, there exist $x_1, x_2 \in [a, b]$ with $|x_1 - x_2| < \delta$ such that $|f(x_1) - f(x_2)| \geq \epsilon$. Hence for each $\delta_n = \frac{1}{n}$, choose x_n, x_n^* with $|x_n - x_n^*| < \frac{1}{n}$ and $|f(x_n) - f(x_n^*)| \geq \epsilon$.

Now, $\{x_n\}_{n=1}^{\infty}$ is in $[a, b]$, so it is a bounded sequence. By the Bolzano-Weierstrass theorem, $\{x_n\}$ has a convergence subsequence. Call it $\{x_{n_j}\}_{j=1}^{\infty}$ and let $x_{n_j} \to x_0 \in [a, b]$. From the condition $|x_n - x_n^*| < \frac{1}{n}$, we obtain that $x_{n_j}^* \to x_0$. Since f is continuous at x_0, $\exists\, \delta > 0$ corresponding to x_0 and $\frac{\epsilon}{2}$ such that $|x - x_0| < \delta \implies |f(x) - f(x_0)| < \frac{\epsilon}{2}$. There is an integer N such that $|x_{n_j} - x_0| < \delta$ and also $|x_{n_j}^* - x_0| < \delta$ if $j \geq N$. Then, for all $j \geq N$,

$$
\begin{aligned}
|f(x_{n_j}) - f(x_{n_j}^*)| &\leq |f(x_{n_j}) - f(x_0)| + |f(x_0) - f(x_{n_j}^*)| \\
&< \frac{\epsilon}{2} + \frac{\epsilon}{2},
\end{aligned}
$$

contradicting $|f(x_{n_j}) - f(x_{n_j}^*)| \geq \epsilon$ for all j. Thus, f is uniformly continuous on $[a, b]$. $\square$

Proposition 8.3.2 *If f is uniformly continuous on a bounded set, then f is bounded.* (**This is not true if f is only continuous**).

Proof. Let S denote the bounded set. Let $\epsilon = 1$ and let $\delta > 0$ be such that $x_1, x_2 \in S$ and $|x_1 - x_2| < \delta \Rightarrow |f(x_1) - f(x_2)| < 1$. Since S is bounded, there exist I_n such that $S \subseteq \bigcup_{n=1}^{k} I_n$, $n = 1, 2, ..., k$, where I_n is an interval with length less than δ. i.e., S is covered by a finite number of intervals with lengths less than δ. From each such interval that intersects S, pick one point of S, and let $\{x_1, x_2, ..., x_k\}$ be the resulting finite set, a subset of S.

Now for arbitrary $s \in S$, $|s - x_i| < \delta$ for **some** $i = 1, 2, ..., k$. So, for arbitrary $s \in S$,

$$
|f(s) - f(x_i)| < \epsilon = 1, \quad i = 1, 2, ..., k.
$$

This implies that $\forall\, s \in S$,

$$|f(s)| \leq |f(s) - f(x_i)| + |f(x_i)| \leq 1 + |f(x_i)|, \;\; i = 1, 2, ..., k.$$

This implies, $|f(s)| \leq 1 + \max\limits_{1 \leq i \leq k} |f(x_i)| \;\forall\, s \in S$, or

$$|f(s)| \leq M \;\forall\, s \in S, \;\; \text{where } M = 1 + \max\limits_{1 \leq i \leq k} |f(x_i)|.$$

Thus, f is bounded. $\square$

Remark 8.3.3 Compare Theorem 8.3.1 and Proposition 8.3.2 with Lesson 7.4.1 to see the "strength" of uniform continuous functions over continuous functions. (For an example to show that Proposition 8.3.2 is not necessarily true if f is merely continuous, consider the map $f : (0,1) \to \mathbb{R}$ defined by $f(x) = \frac{1}{x} \;\forall\, x \in (0,1)$).

Proposition 8.3.4 *If f is uniformly continuous on a set S into a set Y, and $\{x_n\}$ is a Cauchy sequence in S, then $\{f(x_n)\}_{n=1}^{\infty}$ is also a Cauchy sequence in Y.* (**This is not true if f is only continuous**).

Proof. We want to prove $\{f(x_n)\}_{n=1}^{\infty}$ is a Cauchy sequence in Y. So, let $\epsilon > 0$ be given. For this ϵ, pick a corresponding $\delta > 0$ from the assumption that f is uniformly continuous. Since $\{x_n\}$ is Cauchy, there exists an integer $N > 0$ such that $|x_n - x_m| < \delta$, whenever $n, m \geq N$. Therefore, by the uniform continuity of f, $|f(x_n) - f(x_m)| < \epsilon$ whenever $n, m \geq N$. But this implies $\{f(x_n)\}_{n=1}^{\infty}$ is a Cauchy sequence in Y. $\square$ Using Theorem 8.3.1, we are able to derive a useful test to determine when a continuous function defined on the *open* and bounded interval (a, b) is *uniformly* continuous. For this, we need the following terminology.

Let $D \subseteq X \subseteq \mathbb{R}$ and let $f : D \to \mathbb{R}$ be a function. We say that $F : X \to \mathbb{R}$ is an *extension of f* if $F(x) = f(x) \;\forall\, x \in D$. (See Figure 8.1).

We now prove the following theorem.

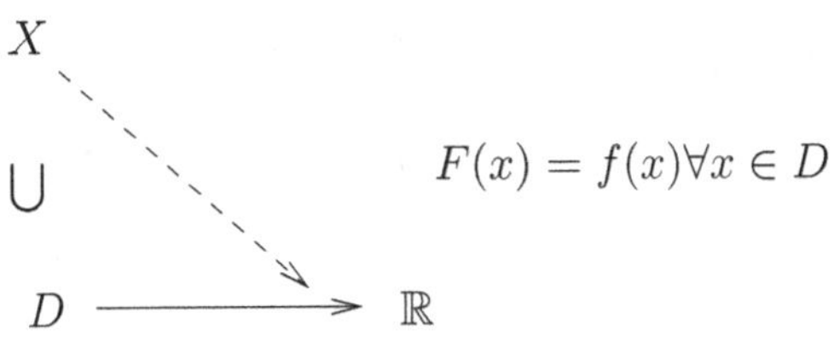

Figure 8.1:

Theorem 8.3.5 *Let $f : (a, b) \to \mathbb{R}$ be continuous. Then, f is uniformly continuous if and only if f has a unique extension $F : [a, b] \to \mathbb{R}$ of f which is continuous.*

Proof. ($\Leftarrow$) Suppose there exists an extension $F : [a, b] \to \mathbb{R}$ of f which is continuous. By Theorem 8.3.1, F is *uniformly* continuous on $[a, b]$. Hence F is uniformly continuous on any subset of $[a, b]$. In particular, F is uniformly continuous on (a, b). But $F(x) = f(x) \; \forall \; x \in (a, b)$. Hence f is uniformly continuous on (a, b).

$\implies$) Suppose f is uniformly continuous on (a, b). We want to prove that f can be extended uniquely to $F : [a, b] \to \mathbb{R}$ and F is continuous.

Claim $\lim\limits_{x \to a^+} f(x)$ exists and $\lim\limits_{x \to b^-} f(x)$ exists.

To see this, let $\{x_n\}, \{u_n\}$ be sequences in (a, b) such that $x_n \to a$ and $u_n \to a$ as $n \to \infty$. Then $\{x_n\}$ and $\{u_n\}$ are Cauchy. By the uniform continuity of f, $\{f(x_n)\}$ and $\{f(u_n)\}$ are Cauchy in $\mathbb{R}$. Since $\mathbb{R}$ is complete, $\{f(x_n)\}$ and $\{f(u_n)\}$ converge in $\mathbb{R}$. The sequence $\{x_n - u_n\}$ converges to 0 since $\{x_n\}$ and $\{u_n\}$ converge to the same real number a. So using uniform continuity, we have $f(x_n) - f(u_n) \to 0$. Hence $\lim\limits_{n \to \infty} f(x_n) = \lim\limits_{n \to \infty} f(u_n)$. Therefore for any sequence $\{x_n\}$ in (a, b) which converges to a, $\{f(x_n)\}$ converges to the same real number. Call this ℓ. From Definition 6.2.4, this implies $\lim\limits_{x \to a} f(x) = \ell$. Similarly, we obtain $\lim\limits_{x \to b} f(x) = k$, for some $k \in \mathbb{R}$.

If we now define $F : [a, b] \to \mathbb{R}$ by

$$F(x) = \begin{cases} f(x), & \text{if } a < x < b, \\ \ell, & \text{if } x = a, \\ k, & \text{if } x = b, \end{cases}$$

then F is a continuous extension of f. Since f is continuous on (a, b), so is F. But F is also continuous at a and b (by Theorem 6.5.4, since $\lim_{x \to a} F(x) = \ell = F(a)$ and $\lim_{x \to b} F(x) = k = F(b)$). Hence F is continuous on $[a, b]$. For uniqueness, suppose there exists another continuous extension $G : [a, b] \to \mathbb{R}$ of f. We show that $G = F$, i.e., $F(x) = G(x)$, $\forall\, x \in [a, b]$. Since F and G are both extensions of f, $F(x) = f(x) = G(x)$ for all $x \in (a, b)$. So we need only show that $F(a) = G(a)$ and $F(b) = G(b)$. Now let $\{x_n\}$ and $\{y_n\}$ be sequences in (a, b) which converge to a and b, respectively. Then by continuity of F and G, we have

$$\lim_{n \to \infty} F(x_n) = F(a), \quad \lim_{n \to \infty} F(y_n) = F(b)$$

and

$$\lim_{n \to \infty} G(x_n) = G(a), \quad \lim_{n \to \infty} G(y_n) = G(b).$$

Since $F(x_n) = f(x_n) = G(x_n)$ for each $n \in \mathbb{N}$, we must have $\lim_{n \to \infty} F(x_n) = \lim_{n \to \infty} G(x_n)$, that is, $F(a) = G(a)$. Similarly, $F(b) = G(b)$. Hence $F = G$. The proof is complete. $\square$

Example 8.3.6 The function $f(x) = \sin(\frac{1}{x})$ is continuous on $(0, \frac{1}{\pi})$ but is not uniformly continuous on this interval. This is because $\lim_{x \to 0} f(x)$ does not exist. (Verify). Hence f cannot be extended to a continuous function on $[0, \frac{1}{\pi}]$.

EXERCISES 8.1

1. Prove that the given functions are uniformly continuous in the given intervals.

153

$$(i) \quad f(x) = x^2, 0 \le x \le 2$$
$$(ii) \quad f(x) = \sqrt{x}, 1 \le x \le 2$$
$$(iii) \quad f(x) = \sqrt{x}, 0 \le x \le 1$$
$$(iv) \quad f(x) = \tfrac{1}{x}, x \ge 1$$
$$(v) \quad f(x) = x^3, 0 \le x \le 1$$
$$(vi) \quad f(x) = \cos x, -\infty < x < \infty$$
$$(vii) \quad f(x) = \sin x, -\infty < x < \infty$$
$$(viii) \quad f(x) = \tfrac{x}{1+x^2}, -\infty < x < \infty.$$

2. Determine which of the given functions are uniformly continuous in the indicated intervals, where $\mathbb{R}^+ = \{x \in \mathbb{R} : x > 0\}$.

$$(i)\ f(x) = x^3 - 3x^2 + 2x - 1, 0 < x < 3$$
$$(ii)\ f(x) = x^2, x \in \mathbb{R}^+$$
$$(iii)\ f(x) = x \sin \tfrac{1}{x}, 0 < x < \infty$$
$$(iv)\ f(x) = \tfrac{1}{x-1}, 0 < x < 1$$
$$(v)\ f(x) = \sin \tfrac{1}{x}, 0 < x < 1$$
$$(vi)\ f(x) = e^x, -1 < x < 2$$
$$(vii)\ f(x) = \tan^{-1} x, x \in \mathbb{R}$$
$$(viii)\ f(x) = x^3, x \in \mathbb{R}^+$$
$$(ix)\ f(x) = x \sin x, x \in \mathbb{R}$$
$$(x)\ f(x) = \tfrac{\sin x}{x}, x \in \mathbb{R}^+.$$

3. Prove that if f is uniformly continuous on I then f is continuous on I.

4. Prove or give a counter example: If $f(x)$ is continuous and bounded on $\mathbb{R}$ then f is uniformly continuous on $\mathbb{R}$.

5. Prove that if f and g are each uniformly continuous on I and $k \in \mathbb{R}$ then the sum $f + g$ and the scalar product $k \cdot f$ are uniformly continuous on I.

6. Show by example that if f and g are each uniformly continuous on I then the product $f \cdot g$ may fail to be uniformly continuous on I.

7. Prove that if f is continuous on (a, b), then f is uniformly continuous on (a, b) if and only if $\lim_{x \to a^+} f(x)$ and $\lim_{x \to b^-} f(x)$ both exist.

8. Prove that if f is continuous on $[a, \infty)$ and if $\lim_{x \to \infty} f(x)$ exists then f is uniformly continuous on $[a, \infty)$.

9. Prove that if f is continuous on $(-\infty, b]$ and if $\lim_{x \to -\infty} f(x)$ exists then f is uniformly continuous on $(-\infty, b]$.

10. Prove that if f is continuous on $\mathbb{R}$ and, if $\lim_{x \to -\infty} f(x)$ and $\lim_{x \to \infty} f(x)$ both exist then f is uniformly continuous on $\mathbb{R}$.

11. (a) Let $f : (0, 1) \to \mathbb{R}$ be defined by $f(x) = \frac{1}{x} \ \forall \ x \in (0, 1)$. Show that f is continuous on $(0, 1)$ but is not bounded.

    (b) If $\{x_n\}$ is a Cauchy sequence in $(1, 0)$, is $\{f(x_n)\}$ a Cauchy sequence in $\mathbb{R}$? Justify your answer.

156

CHAPTER 9

Closed Sets, Compact Sets

9.1   Introduction

Recall that in Chapter 7, Section 7.1 we observed that the interval $[a, b]$ has the following two properties:

$P1.$ Every sequence in $[a, b]$ has a convergent subsequence.

$P2.$ Every convergent sequence in $[a, b]$ has its limit in $[a, b]$.

It turns out that these two properties are also possessed by several other sets more general than $[a, b]$. In this chapter, we give a special name to sets that have these two properties and study some of their other special characteristics. The main results of this chapter are the following.

Theorem 9.3.4 *Let $K \subseteq \mathbb{R}$ be compact and $f : K \to \mathbb{R}$ be continuous. Then*
(i) f is bounded.

(ii) f attains its maximum value at some point of K.

(iii) f attains its minimum value at some point of K.

157

(iv) $f[K]$ is a compact set in $\mathbb{R}$, i.e., (the continuous image of a compact set is compact).

(v) f is uniformly continuous on K.

Proposition 9.3.5 *A subset S of $\mathbb{R}$ is compact if and only if every sequence in S has a subsequence that converges to a point of S.*

Proposition 9.4.2 (The Heine-Borel Theorem) *A subset K of $\mathbb{R}$ is compact if and only if every open cover of K is reducible to a finite subcover.*

We begin in the next section with the concept of *closed sets*.

9.2   Closed Sets; Bounded Sets

Definition 9.2.1 A set $F \subseteq \mathbb{R}$ is called *closed* if it contains the limits of all of its *convergent* sequences (this is analogous to property $P2$).

Remark 9.2.2 If a set $S \subseteq \mathbb{R}$ is *bounded,* then clearly any sequence in it is bounded. Hence, by the Bolzano-Weierstrass theorem, such a sequence has a convergent subsequence (this is analogous to property $P1$).

Example 9.2.3 The interval $[a, b]$ is closed and bounded and consequently has properties $P1$ and $P2$. The interval (a, b) is bounded (and so has property $P1$). Observe that the convergent sequence $\{\frac{1}{n}\}$ is in $(0, 1)$, but its limit $0 \notin (0, 1)$. Hence $(0, 1)$ is not closed and so does not have property $P2$.

Remark 9.2.4 Recall that a set $U \subseteq \mathbb{R}$ is said to be *open* if for arbitrary $x \in U$, there exists $\delta > 0$ such that $B_\delta(x) \equiv (x - \delta, x + \delta) \subseteq U$.

Notation For a set $A \subseteq \mathbb{R}$, we shall denote the complement of A by A^c, where $A^c = \mathbb{R} \backslash A$.

We now prove the following characterization of *closed (open)* sets.

Proposition 9.2.5 *A set $F \subseteq \mathbb{R}$ is closed if and only if its complement F^c is open in $\mathbb{R}$.*

Proof. ($\Rightarrow$) Let F be closed. We want to prove F^c is open. So, let $x_0 \in F^c$ be arbitrary. Assume F^c is not open. Then, for each $\delta = \frac{1}{n} > 0$,

$$\left(x_0 - \frac{1}{n}, x_0 + \frac{1}{n}\right) \cap F \neq \emptyset.$$

Let $x_n \in (x_0 - \frac{1}{n}, x_0 + \frac{1}{n}) \cap F$. Then, $|x_n - x_0| < \frac{1}{n} \to 0$ as $n \to \infty$. Hence $x_n \to x_0$ as $n \to \infty$. But $\{x_n\}$ is in F and F is closed. Hence, $x_0 \in F$. Contradiction. Hence F^c is open.

($\Leftarrow$) Let F^c be open. We want to prove F is closed. So, let $\{x_n\}$ be an arbitrary convergent sequence in F such that $x_n \to x^*$. We want to prove $x^* \in F$. Assume $x^* \notin F$. Then $x^* \in F^c$. Since F^c is open, there exists $\delta > 0$ such that $B_\delta(x^*) \equiv (x^* - \delta, x^* + \delta) \subset F^c$. This implies $B_\delta(x^*) \equiv (x^* - \delta, x^* + \delta) \cap F = \emptyset$. This contradicts the fact that only a finite number of elements of $\{x_n\}$ should be outside $B_\delta(x^*)$, but $x_n \in F$. $\square$

Example 9.2.6 It is now easy to see (by Proposition 9.2.5), for example, that the following sets are *closed*: $(-\infty, a]$, $[a, \infty)$. Furthermore, the empty set, $\emptyset$, is closed because there is no convergent sequence in $\emptyset$ which does not have its limit in $\emptyset$. Clearly, $\mathbb{R}$ is closed since every convergent sequence in $\mathbb{R}$ has its limit in $\mathbb{R}$. Hence, its complement, $\emptyset$, is open. So, we have that $\emptyset$ is both open and closed. Now, since $\emptyset$ is closed, its complement $\mathbb{R}$ is open. Hence, $\mathbb{R}$ is also both open and closed. Thus the empty set and the set $\mathbb{R}$ are two sets that are both open and closed.

We warn that there are several sets $S \subseteq \mathbb{R}$ that are neither open nor closed (see Exercises 9.1, Problem 1).

Proposition 9.2.7 (a) Arbitrary intersection of closed sets is closed.

(b) A finite union of closed sets is closed.

Proof.   (a) Let $\{F_\alpha\}_{\alpha \in \Delta}$ be an arbitrary family of closed sets, and let

$$F = \bigcap_{\alpha \in \Delta} F_\alpha.$$

We want to prove that F is closed. So, let $\{x_n\}$ be a convergent sequence in F and let $x_n \to x^*$. We shall prove $x^* \in F$. But $\{x_n\}$ in $F \Rightarrow \{x_n\} \in F_\alpha \ \forall \alpha \in \Delta$. But F_α is closed $\Rightarrow x^* \in F_\alpha$ for each $\alpha \in \Delta$. Hence $x^* \in \bigcap_{\alpha \in \Delta} F_\alpha = F$.

(b) Let $\{F_j\}_{j=1}^k$ be closed sets and let

$$U = \bigcup_{j=1}^k F_j.$$

We want to prove that U is closed. So, let $\{x_n\}$ be a convergent sequence in U and let $x_n \to x^*$. We need to show $x^* \in U$. But $x_n \in U \Rightarrow$ there must be an infinite number of indices n such that $x_n \in F_{j_0}$ for some $j_0 \in \{1, 2, ..., k\}$. This means that there is a subsequence $\{x_{n_k}\}$ of $\{x_n\}$ in F_{j_0}. Since $x_n \to x^*$, it follows that $x_{n_k} \to x^*$. But F_{j_0} is closed. Hence $x^* \in F_{j_0} \subset \bigcup_{j=1}^k F_j = U$. Hence U is closed.

Remark 9.2.8 An *infinite union* of closed sets need not be closed (see Exercises 9.1, Problem 2).

Corollary 9.2.9 (a) Arbitrary union of open sets is open.

(b) A finite intersection of open sets is open.

Proof.   Exercise (see Exercises 9.1, Problem 3).

9.3 Compact Sets and Continuous Maps

We recall that if a set $S \subseteq \mathbb{R}$ is bounded then every sequence in it has a convergent subsequence (Bolzano-Weierstrass Theorem). Thus, all bounded sets have property $P1$. With this in mind, we make the following definition.

Definition 9.3.1 A set $S \subseteq \mathbb{R}$ is said to be *compact* if and only if it is closed and bounded.

Example 9.3.2 The set $[a, b]$ is compact and the set (a, b) is not. The sets $(-\infty, a]$, $[a, \infty)$ are not compact. Any finite set is compact. Let $\{x_n\}$ be a convergent sequence and let $x_n \to x^*$. Then $S = \{x_n\}_{n=1}^{\infty} \cup \{x^*\}$ is compact.

Remark 9.3.3 If $S \subseteq \mathbb{R}$ is compact, then the following statements are immediate:
$PK1$: Any sequence in S has a convergent subsequence.
$PK2$: Any convergent sequence in S has its limit in S.

With this in mind, we now prove the following extremely important theorem which considers the behavior of *continuous maps defined on compact subsets of* $\mathbb{R}$.

Theorem 9.3.4 *Let $K \subseteq \mathbb{R}$ be compact and $f : K \to \mathbb{R}$ be continuous. Then*
(i) f is bounded.

(ii) f attains its maximum value at some point of K.

(iii) f attains its minimum value at some point of K.

(iv) $f[K]$ is a compact set in $\mathbb{R}$, i.e., (the continuous image of a compact set is compact).

(v) f is uniformly continuous on K.

Proof. **For** (i) We begin by first showing that f is bounded above. We prove by contradiction. So, assume f is *not* bounded above. Then, for each positive integer n, there exists $x_n \in K$ such that $f(x_n) \geq n$. (This is the negation of boundedness above of f). By condition $PK1$, $\{x_n\}$ has a convergent subsequence, $\{x_{n_j}\}$, say. Let $x_{n_j} \to x^*$ as $j \to \infty$. By $PK2$, $x^* \in K$. Moreover, $f(x_{n_j}) \geq n_j \geq j$ for all j, since $\{n_j\}$ is a strictly increasing sequence (why?). Now, since f is continuous at x^*, $f(x_{n_j}) \to f(x^*)$ as $j \to \infty$. But then, the sequence $\{f(x_{n_j})\}$ being convergent must be bounded, contradicting $f(x_{n_j}) \geq j$ for all j. Thus, f is bounded above. The proof that f is bounded below is similar. Hence, f is bounded. This completes the proof of part (i).

For (ii) As in the first part in the proof of (i), f is bounded above. Hence, $\sup\{f(x) : x \in K\}$ exists. Let $\beta = \sup\{f(x) : x \in K\}$. We show there exists $x^* \in K$ such that $f(x^*) = \beta$. Now, from the definition of β, given $\epsilon = \frac{1}{n} > 0$, for each integer $n > 0$, there exists $x_n \in K$ such that $\beta - \frac{1}{n} < f(x_n) \leq \beta$. By $PK1$, there exists a subsequence $\{x_{n_j}\}$ of $\{x_n\}$ such that $x_{n_j} \to x^*$ as $j \to \infty$, for some x^* and by $PK2$ we have $x^* \in K$. By the continuity of f, $f(x_{n_j}) \to f(x^*)$ as $j \to \infty$. But from the relation, $\beta - \frac{1}{n} < f(x_n) \leq \beta$ we obtain that $f(x_{n_j}) \to \beta$. By the uniqueness of limit, $f(x^*) = \beta$. This completes proof of part (ii).

For Part (iii) This follows as in the proof of part (ii) and is left as an exercise (Exercises 9.1, Problem 5).

For Part (iv) We want to prove $f[K]$ is compact. So, we must prove:
(a) $f[K]$ is bounded;
(b) $f[K]$ is closed.
Part (a) has been proved in part (i). It now remains to prove (b). For this, let $\{y_n\}$ be an arbitrary convergent sequence in $f[K]$ and let $y_n \to y^*$. We need to show $y^* \in f[K]$. But for

each $y_n \in f[K]$, there exists $x_n \in K$ such that $f(x_n) = y_n$.

By $PK1$, there exists a subsequence $\{x_{n_k}\}$ of $\{x_n\}$ such that $x_{n_k} \to x^*$. By $PK2$, $x^* \in K$.

Since f is continuous, $f(x_{n_k}) \to f(x^*)$. But $f(x_n) = y_n$. Hence, $y_{n_k} \to f(x^*)$. But $y_n \to y^*$ (and so, $y_{n_k} \to y^*$). By the uniqueness of limit, $f(x^*) = y^*$. This implies, $y^* \in f[K]$. The proof of part (iv) is complete.

For Part (v) The proof is by contradiction. So, assume f is *not* uniformly continuous on K. Then, there exists some ϵ_0 such that no matter how small $\delta > 0$ is, there exist points $x, y \in K$ with $|x - y| < \delta$ and $|f(x) - f(y)| > \epsilon_0$. For each $\delta = \frac{1}{n}$, let $x_n \in K, y_n \in K$ be such that $|x_n - y_n| < \frac{1}{n}$ and $|f(x_n) - f(y_n)| \geq \epsilon_0$. By PK1, there exists a subsequence $\{x_{n_k}\}$ of $\{x_n\}$ such that $x_{n_k} \to x^*$. By $PK2$, $x^* \in K$. Then, clearly, also there exists y_{n_k} such that $y_{n_k} \to x^*$ (since $|x_n - y_n| < \frac{1}{n}$). Since f is continuous at x^*, $\exists\, \delta > 0$ such that

$$|x - x^*| < \delta \implies |f(x) - f(x^*)| < \frac{\epsilon_0}{2}.$$

There exists N_0 such that $|x_{n_k} - x^*| < \delta$ if $k \geq N_0$, and $|y_{n_k} - x^*| < \delta$ if $k \geq N_0$. Then, it follows that if $k \geq N_0$,

$$\begin{aligned}
|f(x_{n_k}) - f(y_{n_k})| &\leq |f(x_{n_k}) - f(x^*)| + |f(x^*) - f(y_{n_k})| \\
&< \frac{\epsilon_0}{2} + \frac{\epsilon_0}{2} = \epsilon_0.
\end{aligned}$$

But $|f(x_{n_k}) - f(y_{n_k})| \geq \epsilon_0$ for all k, a contradiction. Hence, f is uniformly continuous. The proof of the theorem is complete.

$\square$

Next, we give a characterization of compactness which is useful even in spaces more general than $\mathbb{R}$.

Proposition 9.3.5 *A set S is compact if and only if every sequence in S has a subsequence that converges to a point of S.*

Proof. ($\Rightarrow$) Let S be compact and let $\{x_n\}$ be an arbitrary sequence in S. By $PK1$, $\{x_n\}$ has a convergent subsequence. Let $x_{n_k} \to x^*$. By $PK2$, $x^* \in S$. This completes the proof of necessity.

($\Leftarrow$) *Sufficiency.* Assume that *every* sequence in S has a subsequence that converges to a point of S. We want to prove that S is compact, i.e., S is closed and bounded. We first show S is closed. So, let $\{x_n\}$ be a convergent sequence in S and let $x_n \to x^*$. By hypothesis $\{x_n\}$ has a convergent subsequence $\{x_{n_k}\}$ which converges to a point of S. Since $x_n \to x^*$, all its subsequences must converge to x^*. Hence $x_{n_k} \to x^*$. By hypothesis, $x^* \in S$. Hence S is closed. We now show that S is bounded. We do this by contradiction. Suppose S is not bounded. Then, for each integer n, there exists $x_n \in S$ such that $|x_n| \geq n$. This sequence in S has no convergent subsequence. Contradiction. Hence S is bounded, and so is compact (since it is also closed). $\quad\square$

We prove another useful result about continuous maps defined on compact subsets of $\mathbb{R}$.

Proposition 9.3.6 *Let $K \subseteq \mathbb{R}$ be compact and $f : K \to \mathbb{R}$ be continuous. Assume f is $1 - 1$ and onto $f[K]$. Then, $f^{-1} : f[K] \to K$ is continuous.*

Proof. The proof is by contradiction. So, we assume there is at least one point y_0 (say) in $f[K]$ at which f^{-1} is *not* continuous. This implies (negating the statement of continuity), there exists some $\epsilon_0 > 0$ such that for every $\delta > 0$, there is a point $y \in f[K]$ with $|y - y_0| < \delta$ and $|f^{-1}(y) - f^{-1}(y_0)| \geq \epsilon_0$. For each $\delta = \frac{1}{n}$ we choose $y_n \in f[K]$ with $|y_n - y_0| < \frac{1}{n}$ and $|f^{-1}(y_n) - f^{-1}(y_0)| \geq \epsilon_0$. But $y_n \in f[K] \implies \exists\, x_n \in K$ such that $f(x_n) = y_n$.

By $PK1$, $\exists\, \{x_{n_j}\}$, subsequence of $\{x_n\}$, such that $x_{n_j} \to x^* \in K$ (by $PK2$). Continuity of f at x^* implies $f(x_{n_j}) \to f(x^*)$. But $f(x_{n_j}) = y_{n_j}$ and $|y_{n_k} - y_0| < \frac{1}{n_k}$ implies $y_{n_k} \to y_0$. By the uniqueness of limit, $f(x^*) = y_0$, i.e., $f^{-1}(y_0) = x^*$.

Now, we have

$$|f^{-1}(y_{n_k}) - f^{-1}(y_0)| \geq \epsilon_0 \ \forall \ k,$$

which is the same as $|x_{n_k} - x^*| \geq \epsilon_0 \ \forall \ k$, contradicting $x_{n_k} \to x^*$. $\square$

9.4   Compactness in terms of Open Covers

We shall end this chapter with yet another very important characterization of compact sets in $\mathbb{R}$. This characterization has actually become the definition of compact sets in spaces much more general than $\mathbb{R}$. To state this characterization, we need the following definitions.

Definition 9.4.1 A family $U = \{U_\alpha\}_{\alpha \in \Delta}$, (where Δ is an arbitrary index set) of open sets is called an *open cover* or an *open covering* of a set S if and only if $S \subseteq \bigcup_{\alpha \in \Delta} U_\alpha$. If some *finite* number, $U_{\alpha_1}, U_{\alpha_2}, \cdots, U_{\alpha_n}$ of members of $\{U_\alpha\}_{\alpha \in \Delta}$ is a cover for S $\left(\text{i.e., } S \subset \bigcup_{i=1}^{n} U_{\alpha_i}\right)$ then S is said to have a *finite subcover* of members of U.

We now state the following characterization of compact sets.

Proposition 9.4.2 (The Heine-Borel Theorem) *A subset K of $\mathbb{R}$ is compact if and only if every open cover of K is reducible to a finite subcover.*

Proof. $(\Rightarrow)$ Let K be compact and let $U = \{U_\alpha\}_{\alpha \in \Delta}$ be an arbitrary open cover for K, i.e., $K \subseteq \bigcup_{\alpha \in \Delta} U_\alpha$. We want to show there exists $n \in \mathbb{N}$ such that $K \subseteq \bigcup_{i=1}^{n} U_{\alpha_i}$. We establish this by contradiction. So, we assume that no finite number of members of $\{U_\alpha\}_{\alpha \in \Delta}$ is a cover for K. Since K is compact, it is bounded. So, we may assume $K \subset [a,b]$ for some $a, b \in \mathbb{R}$. Let $m = \frac{a+b}{2}$ (the midpoint of $[a,b]$). Consider the two halves: $[a,m]$ and $[m,b]$. (Figure 9.1). If part of K in

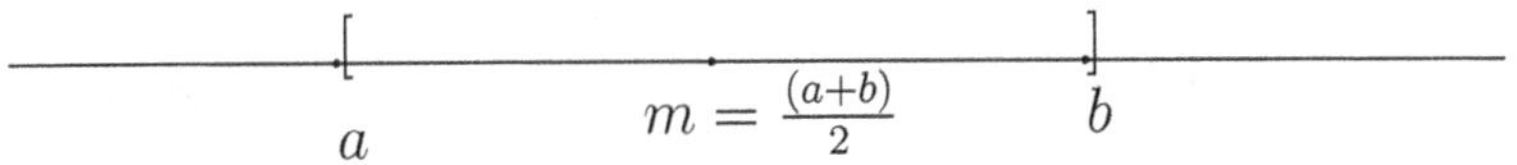

Figure 9.1:

$[a,m]$ is covered by a finite number of members of U and part of K in $[m,b]$ is also covered by a finite number of members of U, then K would be covered by a finite number of members of U, contrary to our assumption that K is not covered by a finite number of members of U. Hence, either the portion of K in $[a,m]$ has no finite subcover or the portion of K in $[m,b]$ has no finite subcover.

Without loss of generality, let $[a,m]$ be such that $[a,m] \cap K$ has no finite subcover. Denote $[a,m] \equiv [a_1, b_1]$. Then, $[a_1, b_1] \cap K$ has no finite subcover by members of U. Let $m_1 = \frac{a_1 + b_1}{2}$ and as above, we obtain $[a_2, b_2]$ such that $[a_2, b_2] \cap K$ has no finite subcover by members of U. Continuing, we obtain a sequence $\{[a_n, b_n]\}$ of such intervals such that $[a_n, b_n] \cap K$ has no finite subcover by members of U. Clearly $\{a_n\}$ is monotone increasing and bounded above by b and so converges. Similarly, $\{b_n\}$ is monotone decreasing and bounded below by a and so converges. Moreover,

$$0 \leq b_n - a_n = \frac{b-a}{2^n} \to 0 \text{ as } n \to \infty.$$

Hence $\lim b_n = \lim a_n = a^*$ (say), and so the intervals $[a_n, b_n]$ "shrink" to a single point a^*. Pick $x_{n_1} \in [a_1, b_1] \cap K, x_{n_2} \in [a_2, b_2] \cap K, ..., x_{n_j} \in [a_j, b_j] \cap K$. Hence, each $[a_j, b_j]$ clearly contains a point $x_{n_j} \in K$ and $x_{n_j} \to a^*$. Since K is closed, $a^* \in K$. Now, $a^* \in K \subset \bigcup_{\alpha \in \Delta} U_\alpha$ so that $a^* \in U_{\alpha^*}$ for some $\alpha^* \in \Delta$. But U_{α^*} is open. Hence $\exists\, \delta > 0$ such that $B_\delta(a^*) \equiv (a^* - \delta, a^* + \delta) \subset U_{\alpha^*}$. Since $[a_{n_j}, b_{n_j}] \to a^*$ as $j \to \infty$, $\exists N \in \mathbb{N}$ such that $[a_N, b_N] \subset (a^* - \delta, a^* + \delta) \subset U_{\alpha^*}$. This implies (intersecting with K) that

$$[a_N, b_N] \cap K \subset U_{\alpha^*} \cap K \subset U_{\alpha^*}.$$

Hence $[a_N, b_N] \cap K$ has a finite subcover by members of U, namely, the single cover U_{α^*}. This contradiction shows that every open cover of a compact set has a finite subcover.

($\Leftarrow$) Let $K \subseteq \mathbb{R}$ be such that every open cover of K has a finite subcover. We want to prove K is compact (i.e., K is closed and bounded). We first show K is bounded. To see this, observe that the family $U = \{(-n, n)\}_{n=1}^{\infty}$ covers $\mathbb{R}$ and hence covers K. By hypothesis, there exists $N_0 \in \mathbb{N}$ such that $K \subset \bigcup_{n=1}^{N_0} (-n, n) = (-N_0, N_0)$, and so K is bounded. We now show K is closed. We do this by contradiction. Suppose K is not closed. Then there exists at least one sequence $\{x_n\}$ in K such that $x_n \to x^*$ and $x^* \notin K$.

Consider the family $U = \{(-\infty, x^* - \frac{1}{n}) \cup (x^* + \frac{1}{n}, \infty)\}_{n=1}^{\infty}$. This family covers $\mathbb{R}\backslash\{x^*\}$. Hence it covers K. By hypothesis, $\exists N_0 \in \mathbb{N}$ such that

$$(*) \qquad K \subseteq (-\infty, x^* - \frac{1}{N_0}) \cup (x^* + \frac{1}{N_0}, \infty) \equiv C_{N_0} \text{ (say)}.$$

Clearly C_{N_0} does not cover the interval $[x^* - \frac{1}{N_0}, x^* + \frac{1}{N_0}]$. But since $x_n \in K$ and $x_n \to x^*$, some points x_n of K must be in the interval $[x^* - \frac{1}{N_0}, x^* + \frac{1}{N_0}]$, contradicting the inclusion $(*)$. Hence K is closed and so is compact (since we already proved it is bounded). $\quad\square$

EXERCISES 9.1

1. Show that the set of all rational numbers, $\mathbb{Q}$, is neither open nor closed.

2. Give an example to show that an infinite union of closed sets need not be closed.
   Hint: Prove first that any finite set is closed.

3. Prove Corollary 9.2.9.

4. Let $\{x_n\}$ be a convergent sequence and let $x_n \to x^*$. Define $S = \{x_n\} \cup \{x^*\}$. Prove that S is compact.

5. Prove part (iii) of Theorem 9.3.4.

6. Prove that a set $U \subset \mathbb{R}$ is open if and only if U is a union of open intervals.

7. Prove that every nonempty open set $U \subseteq \mathbb{R}$ is a finite or countable union of *disjoint* open intervals. (These disjoint intervals are called *components* of U).

   Hint: For arbitrary $x \in U$, let C_x be the union of all open intervals I such that $x \in I \subset U$. (Here C_x denotes the component of x. Note that such an I exists since U is open and $x \in U$). Show that C_x is an open interval, and that if $C_x \cap C_y \neq \emptyset$ for $x, y \in U$, then $C_x = C_y$.

8. Let F be a closed set and U be an open set. Prove :
   (a) $F - U$ is a closed set.
   (b) $U - F$ is an open set.
   Note: $A - B = \{a - b : a \in A \text{ and } b \in B\}$.

CHAPTER 10

Differentiability

10.1 Introduction

In this Chapter, we re-visit the notion of a limit of a function introduced in Chapter 6. This limit called the **derivative** of the function denotes the rate at which the function changes. It is one of the most important ideas in calculus. Derivatives are used extensively in science, engineering, computer science, economics , and so on, for instance, to calculate velocity and acceleration; to explain the behaviour of machinery; to estimate the drop in fluid levels as fluid is pumped out of a tank; and so on. In this chapter, we study some fundamental theorems of derivatives.

The main results of this chapter are the following theorems.

Theorem 10.4.4 (Rolle's Theorem) *Suppose*
(i) f is continuous on $[\alpha, \beta]$.
(ii) $f(\alpha) = f(\beta)$.
(iii) f' exists on (α, β).

169

Then f has a local maximum or minimum at some $c \in (\alpha, \beta)$, and thus, $f'(c) = 0$.

Theorem 10.5.1 (Mean Value Theorem) *If*
(i) f is continuous on $[a, b]$ and
(ii) f' exists on (a, b).
Then there exists some $c \in (a, b)$ such that $f'(c) = \frac{f(b) - f(a)}{b-a}$.

Theorem 10.5.3 (Cauchy's Mean Value Theorem)
If f and g are continuous on $[a, b]$, $f'(x)$ and $g'(x)$ exist on (a, b), and $g'(x) \neq 0$ on (a, b), then there exists some $c \in (a, b)$ such that

$$\frac{f'(c)}{g'(c)} = \frac{f(b) - f(a)}{g(b) - g(a)}.$$

10.2   The Derivative

Using the idea of the definition of the slope of a function at a point and the notion of limits of functions studied in Chapter 6 (Section 6.2), we can define the **derivative of a real-valued function** f **at a point** $a \in \mathcal{D}(f)$.

Definition 10.2.1 *Let f be a real-valued function. The* **derivative of** f **at** $a \in \mathcal{D}(f)$, *denoted by $f'(a)$, is defined by*

$$f'(a) = \lim_{x \to a} \frac{f(x) - f(a)}{x - a}. \qquad (10.2.1)$$

A function f is called **differentiable at** a *if it has a derivative at a.*

Let $S \subset \mathbb{R}$. A real-valued function f is **differentiable on** S if it is differentiable at s for all $s \in S$. A real-valued function is **differentiable** if it is differentiable on its domain.

Remark 10.2.2 The **difference quotient**, $\frac{f(x) - f(a)}{x-a}$, is not defined at $x = a$, but is defined for all other x where f is defined. The existence of the limit (10.2.1) implies that the function f is defined on some open interval around a, since $f(a)$ must also be defined for (10.2.1) to make sense.

We now prove the following important theorem which says that "a differentiable function is continuous".

Theorem 10.2.3 *If $f'(a)$ exists, then f is continuous at a.*

Proof. **Method I.** By Theorem 6.5.4, it suffices to prove that $\lim\limits_{x \to a} f(x) = f(a)$. This means that f is defined on some deleted interval around a, D_a, and for every sequence $\{x_n\}$ in $D_a, \exists N_1 > 0$, such that $f(x_n) \to f(a) \; \forall \, n \geq N_1$. Suppose this is not true, i.e., suppose $f(x) - f(a)$ does not approaches 0 as $x \to a$, then there exist an $\epsilon > 0$ and a sequence $\{x_n\}_{n=1}^{\infty}$ such that $x_n \to a$ with $|f(x_n) - f(a)| \geq \epsilon$. This implies that

$$\left| \frac{f(x_n) - f(a)}{x_n - a} \right| \geq \frac{\epsilon}{|x_n - a|} \to \infty \text{ as } x_n \to a,$$

contradicting the existence of the limit in (10.2.1), i.e., the existence of $f'(a)$.

Method II. We give here a less rigorous proof based on the use of Theorem 6.2.6 on limits and Theorem 6.5.4 on characterization of continuity.

Let $a \in D(f)$ be arbitrary. It suffices to prove that f is continuous at a. Now, for any $x \in D(f)$, $x \neq a$, we have

$$f(x) = (x - a) . \frac{f(x) - f(a)}{(x - a)} + f(a). \qquad (10.2.2)$$

Since f is differentiable at $x = a$, $f'(a)$ exists and we know that

$$\lim_{x \to a} \frac{f(x) - f(a)}{(x - a)} = f'(a).$$

Now, taking limits as $x \to a$ in (10.2.2), and using Theorem 6.2.6, we obtain that

$$\lim_{x \to a} f(x) = \left[\lim_{x \to a}(x-a).\lim_{x \to a}\left(\frac{f(x)-f(a)}{(x-a)}\right) + f(a)\right]$$
$$= 0.f'(a) + f(a),$$

so that $\lim_{x \to a} f(x) = f(a)$. By Theorem 6.5.4, f is continuous at $x = a$. $\square$

Theorem 10.2.4   (a) *Any constant mapping is differentiable, and its derivative is the zero mapping.*

(b) *The identity function $f(x) = x$ is differentiable, and its derivative is the constant mapping 1.*

Proof. Obvious, and so is omitted. $\square$

We now prove a number of rules for combining differentiable functions to give new differentiable functions.

Theorem 10.2.5 *Let f and g be both differentiable at a. Then,*

(i) *If $h(x) = f(x) + g(x)$, then $h'(a) = f'(a) + g'(a)$.*

(ii) *If $h(x) = f(x) \cdot g(x)$, then $h'(a) = f(a)g'(a) + g(a)f'(a)$.*

(iii) *If $h(x) = \frac{f(x)}{g(x)}$ and $g(a) \neq 0$, then*

$$h'(a) = \frac{[g(a)f'(a) - f(a)g'(a)]}{[g(a)]^2}.$$

Proof.

(i) If $h(x) = f(x) + g(x)$, then

$$
\begin{aligned}
h'(a) \\
&= \lim_{x \to a} \frac{h(x) - h(a)}{x - a} \\
&= \lim_{x \to a} \frac{f(x) + g(x) - (f(a) + g(a))}{x - a} \\
&= \lim_{x \to a} \left[\frac{f(x) - f(a)}{x - a} + \frac{g(x) - g(a)}{x - a} \right] \\
&= \lim_{x \to a} \frac{f(x) - f(a)}{x - a} + \lim_{x \to a} \frac{g(x) - g(a)}{x - a} \\
&= f'(a) + g'(a).
\end{aligned}
$$

Similarly, if $h(x) = f(x) - g(x)$ then $h'(a) = f'(a) - g'(a)$.

(ii) If $h(x) = f(x) \cdot g(x)$ then

$$
\begin{aligned}
h'(a) \\
&= \lim_{x \to a} \frac{h(x) - h(a)}{x - a} \\
&= \lim_{x \to a} \left[\frac{f(x)g(x) - f(a)g(x) + f(a)g(x) - f(a)g(a)}{x - a} \right] \\
&= \lim_{x \to a} \frac{f(x) - f(a)}{x - a} g(x) + \lim_{x \to a} f(a) \frac{g(x) - g(a)}{x - a} \\
&= g(a)f'(a) + f(a)g'(a).
\end{aligned}
$$

(iii) If $h(x) = \frac{f(x)}{g(x)}$ and $g(a) \neq 0$, then

$$
\begin{aligned}
h'(x) \\
&= \lim_{x \to a} \frac{h(x) - h(a)}{x - a} \\
&= \lim_{x \to a} \left[\frac{f(x)g(a) - f(a)g(x)}{(x - a)g(x)g(a)} \right] \\
&= \lim_{x \to a} \left[\frac{f(x)g(x) - f(a)g(x) - f(x)g(x) + f(x)g(a)}{(x - a)g(x)g(a)} \right] \\
&= \lim_{x \to a} \frac{[f(x) - f(a)]g(x)}{(x - a)g(x)g(a)} \\
&\quad - \lim_{x \to a} \frac{[g(x) - g(a)]f(x)}{(x - a)g(x)g(a)} \\
&= \lim_{x \to a} \left[\frac{f(x) - f(a)}{x - a} \right] \frac{1}{g(a)} \\
&\quad - \lim_{x \to a} \left[\frac{g(x) - g(a)}{x - a} \right] \frac{1}{g(a)} \lim_{x \to a} \frac{f(x)}{g(x)} \\
&= f'(a) \cdot \frac{1}{g(a)} - g'(a) \cdot \frac{1}{g(a)} \frac{f(a)}{g(a)} \\
&= \frac{f'(a)g(a) - f(a)g'(a)}{[g(a)]^2},
\end{aligned}
$$

as required. $\square$

Theorem 10.2.6 (The Chain Rule) *Let $h(x) = f(g(x))$. If $g'(a)$ exists and $f'(g(a))$ exists, then*

$$
h'(a) = f'(g(a))g'(a).
$$

Proof. Assume that $f'(g(a))$ and $g'(a)$ exist. Then f is defined on some interval $(g(a) - \epsilon, g(a) + \epsilon)$ around $g(a)$. Since g is continuous at a, then

$$
g(x) \in (g(a) - \epsilon, g(a) + \epsilon) \ \forall \, x \in (a - \delta, a + \delta), \text{ for some } \delta > 0.
$$

This implies $f\big(g(x)\big)$ is defined for all $x \in (a - \delta,\ a + \delta)$. For $u \neq g(a)$ with $u \in \big(g(a) - \epsilon,\ g(a) + \epsilon\big)$, define $e(u)$ by

$$\frac{f(u) - f(g(a))}{u - g(a)} - f'(g(a)) =: e(u) \qquad (*)$$

and let $e(g(a)) = 0$. Then $e(u) \to 0$ as $u \to g(a)$, and so e is continuous at $g(a)$. From $(*)$, we obtain that for all $u \in \big(g(a) - \epsilon,\ g(a) + \epsilon\big)$ (including $u = g(a)$, where we obtain $e(u) = 0$),

$$f(u) - f\big(g(a)\big) = f'\big(g(a)\big)\big(u - g(a)\big) + e(u)\big(u - g(a)\big). \quad (**)$$

Replacing u by $g(x)$ in $(**)$, with $x \in (a - \delta,\ a + \delta)$ so that $g(x) \in \big(g(a) - \epsilon,\ g(a) + \epsilon\big)$, and dividing both sides by $(x - a)$ we obtain that if, $0 < |x - a| < \delta$, then

$$\frac{f\big(g(x)\big) - f\big(g(a)\big)}{x - a} = f'\big(g(a)\big)\frac{[g(x) - g(a)]}{x - a}$$
$$+ e\big(g(x)\big)\frac{[g(x) - g(a)]}{x - a}.$$

As $x \to a$, we obtain from this equation that

$$h'(a) = f'\big(g(a)\big)g'(a) + 0 \cdot g'(a),$$

completing the proof. $\quad \square$

10.3   Example

We shall use the notation $\frac{d}{dx}f(x) = f'(x)$, whenever $f'(x)$ exists. We now present the following example.

Example 10.3.1 For all integers n, $\frac{d}{dx}x^n = nx^{n-1}$.

Solution: For $n = 0$, we have $\frac{d}{dx}x^0 = \frac{d}{dx}(1) = 0 = 0x^{-1}$ and so the result is true for $n = 0$. We first prove the result holds for all **positive** integers. We do this by induction.

For $n = 1$, the result clearly holds (Theorem 10.2.4(b)). So, assume it holds for $n = k$. Then

$$
\begin{aligned}
\frac{d}{dx}x^{k+1} &= \frac{d}{dx}(x.x^k) = (\frac{d}{dx}x)x^k + x\frac{d}{dx}(x^k) \\
&= x^k + x.kx^{k-1}, \quad \text{using the induction hypothesis} \\
&= x^k + kx^k = (1+k)x^{(k+1)-1}
\end{aligned}
$$

which implies that the result holds for $n = k + 1$. By induction, the result holds for all positive integers. For negative integers n, set $n = -m$ where m is a positive integer. Then, if $x \neq 0$, (the result is trivial for $x = 0$),

$$
\begin{aligned}
\frac{d}{dx}x^n &= \frac{d}{dx}x^{-m} = \frac{d}{dx}\left(\frac{1}{x^m}\right) \\
&= \frac{\left[x^m\frac{d}{dx}(1) - 1\frac{d}{dx}x^m\right]}{(x^m)^2}, \quad \text{by Theorem 10.2.5(iii)} \\
&= \frac{[0 - mx^{m-1}]}{x^{2m}}, \quad \text{since } m \text{ is a positive integer} \\
&= -mx^{-m-1} = nx^{n-1},
\end{aligned}
$$

and the result holds.

We have the following proposition on the derivative of an *inverse function.*

Proposition 10.3.2 *Let f be continuous and one-to-one on an open interval I_a containing a. Let $f'(a) = m \neq 0$ and let $f(a) = b$. Then, the derivative of f^{-1} at b, $(f^{-1})'(b)$ is given by $(f^{-1})'(b) = \frac{1}{m}$.*

Proof. A continuous one-to-one function on an interval I is either strictly increasing or strictly decreasing. Without loss of generality, let us assume it is strictly increasing and let f map I_a onto an open interval I_b containing b (see Figure 10.1). We know f^{-1} is continuous. Set $x = f^{-1}(y)$, $f(x) = y$

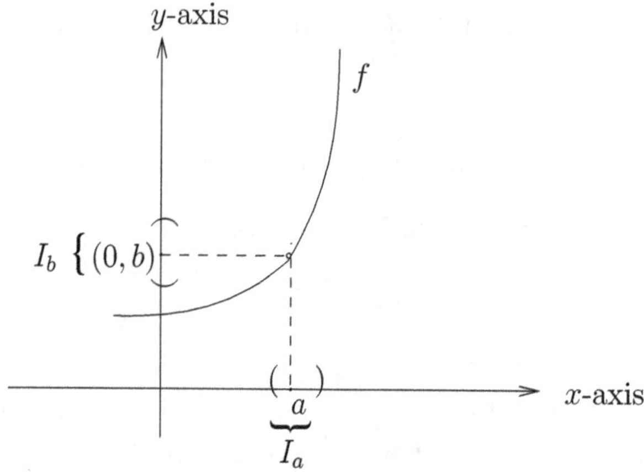

Figure 10.1:

then

$$(f^{-1})'(b) \;=\; \lim_{y \to b} \frac{f^{-1}(y) - f^{-1}(b)}{y - b}$$

$$=\; \lim_{f(x) \to f(a)} \frac{f^{-1}(f(x)) - f^{-1}(f(a))}{f(x) - f(a)}$$

$$=\; \lim_{f(x) \to f(a)} \frac{x - a}{f(x) - f(a)}$$

$$=\; \frac{1}{\displaystyle\lim_{x \to a} \frac{f(x) - f(a)}{x - a}} \;=\; \frac{1}{m}. \quad \square$$

Remark 10.3.3 We note that in the proof of Proposition 10.3.2, as
$y \to b$, $f^{-1}(y) = x \to a$, and so the last limit makes sense. We also note that if $y \neq b$, $f^{-1}(y) \neq f^{-1}(b)$, i.e, $x \neq a$, so that the division is legitimate.

Example 10.3.4 For all positive integers n and for $x > 0$, $\frac{d}{dx} x^{\frac{1}{n}} = \frac{1}{n} x^{\frac{1}{n} - 1}$.

Solution: We know that x^n and $x^{\frac{1}{n}}$ have derivatives at every $x > 0$. Then we consider the identity

$$(x^{\frac{1}{n}})^n = x.$$

Differentiating both sides of this identity, using the chain rule, we obtain that

$$n(x^{\frac{1}{n}})^{n-1}\frac{d}{dx}x^{\frac{1}{n}} = 1$$

so that

$$\frac{d}{dx}x^{\frac{1}{n}} = \frac{1}{n}(x^{\frac{1}{n}})^{-(n-1)} = \frac{1}{n}x^{\frac{1}{n}-1}.$$

10.4 Rolle's Theorem

In this section we prove an important theorem associated with differentiable functions: **Rolle's theorem**. We begin with the following propositions.

Proposition 10.4.1 (a) If $f'(a) > 0$, (see Figure 10.2) then there exists $\delta > 0$ such that,

(i) f is defined on $(a - \delta, a + \delta)$;

(ii) $f(x) > f(a)$ if $a < x < a + \delta$;

(iii) $f(x) < f(a)$ if $a - \delta < x < a$.

(b) Similarly, if $f'(a) < 0$, (see Figure 10.3) , then there exists $\delta > 0$ such that,

(i) f is defined on $(a - \delta, a + \delta)$;

(ii) $f(x) < f(a)$ if $a < x < a + \delta$;

(iii) $f(x) > f(a)$ if $a - \delta < x < a$.

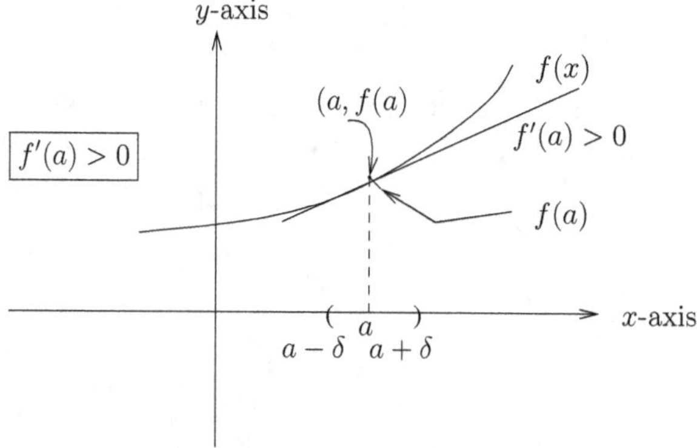

Figure 10.2:

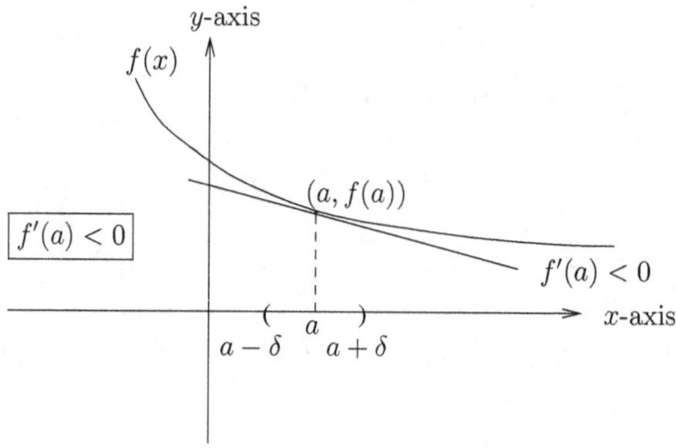

Figure 10.3:

Proof. (a)   Let $f'(a) > 0$. Recall $f'(a) = \lim\limits_{x \to a} \dfrac{f(x) - f(a)}{x - a}$.
This limit implies, given any $\epsilon > 0$, $\exists\, \delta > 0$ such that

$$\left| \frac{f(x) - f(a)}{x - a} - f'(a) \right| < \epsilon \quad if\ 0 < |x - a| < \delta. \qquad (10.4.1)$$

Take $\epsilon = f'(a) > 0$. Then, we obtain that

$$\left| \frac{f(x) - f(a)}{x - a} - f'(a) \right| < f'(a) \quad for\ 0 < |x - a| < \delta.$$

This implies

$$-f'(a) < \frac{f(x) - f(a)}{x - a} - f'(a) < f'(a), \quad 0 < |x - a| < \delta,$$

which implies

$$\frac{f(x) - f(a)}{x - a} > 0, \quad 0 < |x - a| < \delta$$

and so,

$$f(x) > f(a) \quad if\ \ x > a,$$

and

$$f(x) < f(a) \quad if\ \ x < a,$$

completing the proof of part (a).

(b) If $f'(a) < 0$ then $-f'(a) > 0$. Take $\epsilon = -f'(a)$ in inequality (10.4.1) and the result follows. $\square$

An immediate consequence of Proposition 10.4.1 is the following **local** theorem which will be needed in the proof of Rolle's Theorem.

Proposition 10.4.2 *Suppose f is defined on $(a - \delta, a + \delta)$, for some $\delta > 0$. Suppose either*

$$\text{(i) f(a)} \ \le\ \ f(x)\ \forall\ x \in (a - \delta, a + \delta),\ \ or$$
$$\text{(ii) f(a)} \ \ge\ \ f(x)\ \forall\ x \in (a - \delta, a + \delta).$$

Suppose $f'(a)$ exists. Then, $f'(a) = 0$. (See Figure 10.4 and Figure 10.5).

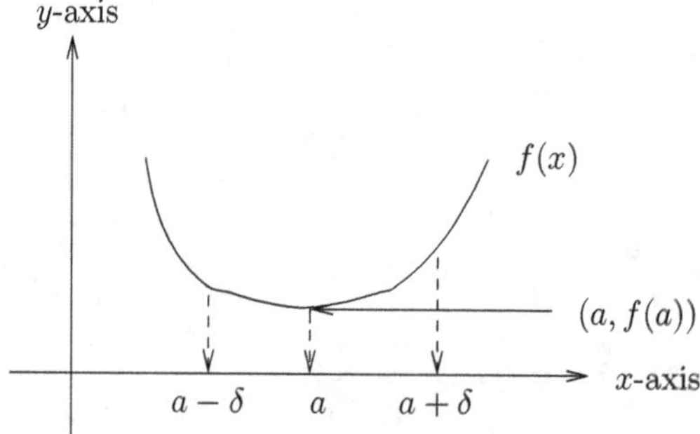

Figure 10.4:

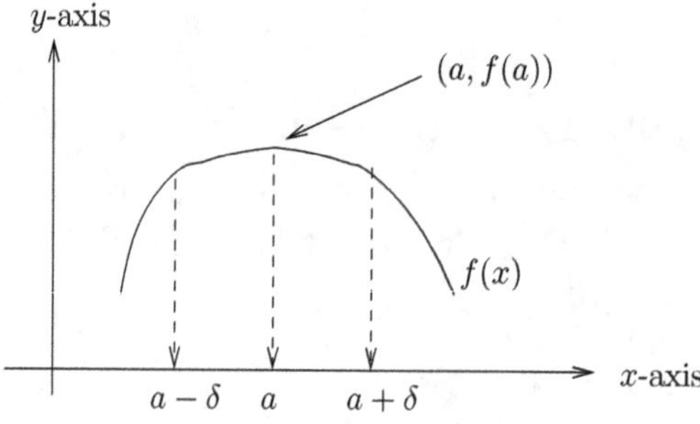

Figure 10.5:

Remark 10.4.3 We remark that in Proposition 10.4.2, the function f may be defined on all of $\mathbb{R}$ and may have higher and lower values than $f(a)$, but if f has a **local** maximum or minimum **at a**, (i.e., if condition (ii) or condition (i) holds, respectively), then $f'(a) = 0$.

The following theorem, which is one of our main theorems of this section is a corollary of Proposition 10.4.2.

Theorem 10.4.4 (Rolle's Theorem) *Suppose*

(i) *f is continuous on $[\alpha, \beta]$;*

(ii) *$f(\alpha) = f(\beta)$;*

(iii) *f' exists on (α, β).*

Then f has a local maximum or minimum at some $c \in (\alpha, \beta)$, and thus, $f'(c) = 0$.

Proof. (see Fig. 10.1). If f is constant on $[\alpha, \beta]$, then $f'(c) = 0 \; \forall \; c \in (\alpha, \beta)$ and there is nothing left to prove. If f is not constant on $[\alpha, \beta]$, then there is either a number $s \in (\alpha, \beta)$ such that $f(s) > f(\alpha)$ or a number $t \in (\alpha, \beta)$ such that $f(t) < f(\alpha)$ (or both). Recall that $f(\alpha) = f(\beta)$. (See Fig. 10.6). Without loss of generality, suppose $f(s) > f(\alpha)$ for

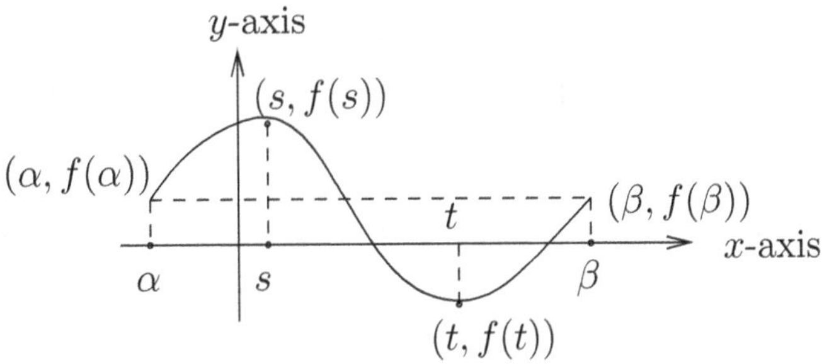

Figure 10.6:

some $s \in (\alpha, \beta)$. Then $f([\alpha, \beta]) = [\inf f(x), \sup f(x)]$, $s \in$

$[\alpha, \beta]$ so that $\sup\limits_{x\in[\alpha,\beta]} f(x) \geq f(s) > f(x)$. Since f is continuous on $[\alpha, \beta]$, (by Theorem 7.4.4) there exists a number $c \in [\alpha, \beta]$ such that $f(c) = \sup_{x\in[\alpha,\beta]} f(x)$. Hence, $f(c) > f(\alpha) = f(\beta)$. Since $f(c) \neq f(\alpha) = f(\beta)$, then c must lie in the open interval (α, β), i.e., $f(c) \geq f(x) \; \forall \; x \in [\alpha, \beta]$. But f is differentiable at c. By Proposition 10.4.2, $f'(c) = 0$.

Now if there is no number s such that $f(s) > f(\alpha)$, then the second alternative must occur. Then, applying similar reasoning we show that f must have a minimum at some c^* in (α, β), so that $f'(c^*) = 0$. This completes the proof. $\quad\square$

10.5   The Mean Value Theorem

The main application of Rolle's theorem is that it is used in the proof of the *Mean Value Theorem*. We explain this theorem.

The **mean value (or average value)** of a function over an interval is generally defined as a certain integral.

For now, we shall take as a definition that the **mean value of the derivative** $f'(x)$ **over the interval** $[a, b]$ **is** $\dfrac{f(b) - f(a)}{b - a}$. Geometrically, the mean value of the derivative over $[a, b]$ **is the constant slope** that would take the function from the point $(a, f(a))$ to the point $(b, f(b))$.

The mean value theorem asserts that the mean value of the derivative on $[a, b]$, i.e., $\frac{f(b)-f(a)}{b-a}$ must be achieved at some point $c \in (a, b)$, i.e., there exists a point $c \in (a, b)$ such that $f'(c) = \frac{f(b)-f(a)}{b-a}$. We state this more formally.

Theorem 10.5.1 (Mean Value Theorem) *If f is continuous on $[a, b]$ and f' exists on (a, b), then there exists some*

$c \in (a, b)$ *such that*

$$f'(c) = \frac{f(b) - f(a)}{b - a}.$$

Proof.   The equation of a line joining the points $(a, f(a))$

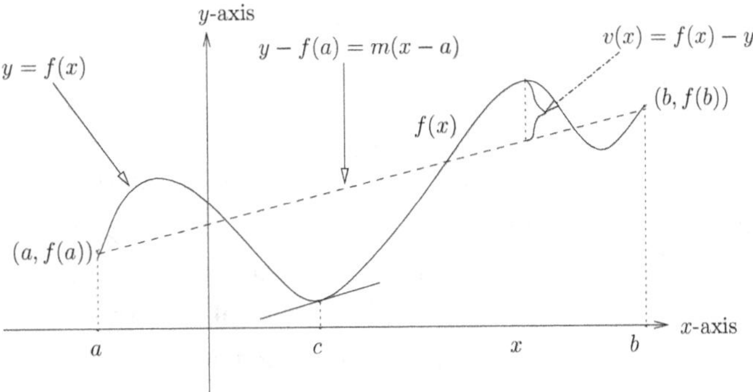

Figure 10.7:

and $(b, f(b))$ is given by $y - f(a) = m(x - a)$, where $m = \frac{f(b) - f(a)}{b - a}$ is the slope. (See Fig. 10.7). So, we write this equation as $y = f(a) + m(x - a)$. The vertical distance between this line and the given function f, denoted by $v(x)$ is given by $v(x) = f(x) - y$ (or $y - f(x)$) which we can write as follows:

$$v(x) - f(x) - \Big(f(a) + m(x - a) \Big).$$

Now,

$$\begin{aligned}
v(a) &= f(a) - [f(a) + m(a - a)] = 0 \\
v(b) &= f(b) - [f(a) + m(b - a)] \\
&= f(b) - f(a) - \frac{[f(b) - f(a)]}{b - a}[b - a] = 0.
\end{aligned}$$

So we have the following conditions:

(i) v is continuous on $[a,b]$, (ii) $v(a) = v(b)$, (iii) v' exists on (a,b).

By Rolle's theorem, v has a local maximum or minimum at some point $c \in (a,b)$, and thus $v'(c) = 0$. But $v'(x) = f'(x) - m$ so that $v'(c) = f'(c) - m$ and $v'(c) = 0 \Rightarrow f'(c) = m$, i.e.,

$$f'(c) = m = \frac{f(b) - f(a)}{b - a}, \text{ for some } c \in (a,b).$$

The proof is complete. $\square$

Remark 10.5.2 Geometrically, the mean value theorem asserts that the slope of the chord joining two points $(a, f(a))$ and $(b, f(b))$ on the graph of a differentiable curve is always less than or equal to the slope of the steepest tangent to the graph at any **intermediate point** (i.e., at some point $c \in (a,b)$).

The following is an important generalization of mean value theorem due to Cauchy.

Theorem 10.5.3 Cauchy's Mean Value Theorem *If f and g are continuous on $[a,b]$, $f'(x)$ and $g'(x)$ exist on (a,b), and $g'(x) \neq 0$ on (a,b), then there exists some $c \in (a,b)$ such that*

$$\frac{f'(c)}{g'(c)} = \frac{f(b) - f(a)}{g(b) - g(a)}.$$

Proof. This proof is similar to the proof of (Theorem 10.5.1). Consider the equation of the line joining the points $(g(a), f(a))$ and $(g(b), f(b))$ given by

$$y - f(a) = m(x - g(a)) \text{ where } m = \frac{f(b) - f(a)}{g(b) - g(a)}.$$

So, $y = f(a) + m(x - g(a))$. Consider the curve $h(t)$ defined parametrically by

$$y_t = f(t), \ x_t = g(t) \text{ where } t \in [a,b].$$

At $x = a, h(a) = (g(a), f(a))$, and at $x = b, h(b) = (g(b), f(b))$. This curve and the line meet at $(g(a), f(a))$ and $(g(b), f(b))$. So, if the vertical distance between them is denoted by $v(t)$, then

$$v(t) = f(t) - [f(a) + m(g(t) - g(a))].$$

Moreover, $v(a) = 0 = v(b)$; v is continuous on $[a, b]$, v' exists on (a, b), and so by Rolle's theorem, v has a local maximum or minimum at some point $c \in (a, b)$. Hence, $v'(c) = 0$ which yields the desired result. $\square$

EXERCISES 10.1

1. Prove that a continuous one-to-one function on an interval I is either strictly increasing or strictly decreasing.

2. If $f(x) = |x|$, show that f has no derivative at $x = 0$.

3. If
$$f(x) = \begin{cases} x, & \text{when } x \text{ is irrational,} \\ 0, & \text{when } x \text{ is rational,} \end{cases}$$
show that f does not possess a derivative anywhere.

4. Show that $f(x) = x \sin(\frac{1}{x})$, $x \neq 0$, $f(0) = 0$ is continuous at $x = 0$ but $f'(0)$ does not exist.

5. If $f(x) = x^2 \sin(\frac{1}{x})$, $x \neq 0$, $f(0) = 0$, show that $f'(0)$ exists and find it.

6. Prove that for $x > 0$, $\sin x < x$ and $\cos x > 1 - \frac{x^2}{2}$.

7. Prove that if $f'(x) = 0$ for $a < x < b$, then f is a constant in $[a, b]$.

8. Verify Rolle's theorem when $f(x) = (x + 1)^m(x - 1)^n$, $-1 \leq x \leq 1$. Show that the result of Rolle's theorem is not true for
   (a) $f(x) = 2x^{-2}$, on $[-1, 1]$ (b) $g(x) = |x|$, on $[-1, 1]$.

9. Find values of $x_0 \in [a, b]$ in the mean value theorem when $f(x) = x^k$ and $k = 1, 2$ and 3.

10. Find $x_0 \in (0, \frac{1}{2})$ when the mean value theorem is applied to
$$f(x) = x(x - 1)(x - 2).$$

11. Prove that, when $0 < \theta < \frac{\pi}{2}$,
    (a) $\frac{2\theta}{\pi} < \sin\theta < \theta$ (b) $1 - \frac{\theta^2}{2} < \cos\theta < 1 - \frac{\theta^2}{2} + \frac{\theta^4}{24}$.

12. Show that $f(x) = e^x(x^2 - 6x + 12) - (x^2 + 6x + 12)$ is an increasing function of x in $(0, \infty)$. Prove that $0 < \frac{1}{e^x - 1} - \frac{1}{x} + \frac{1}{2} < \frac{x}{12}$, when $x > 0$.

EXERCISES 10.2

1. Prove the following results which are always used in applications:

    (i) If $f'(x) \geq 0$ on (a, b), then f is increasing on (a, b).

    (ii) If $f'(x) > 0$ on (a, b), then f is strictly increasing on (a, b).

    (iii) If $f'(x) \leq 0$ on (a, b), then f is decreasing on (a, b).

    (iv) If $f'(x) < 0$ on (a, b), then f is strictly decreasing on (a, b).

    Deduce that if $f'(x) = 0$ on (a, b), then f is a constant on (a, b).

    Hint: Apply the mean value theorem. For the last deduction notice that f is both increasing and decreasing.

2. (a) Prove that if f is continuous on $(a - \delta, a]$ and $f'(x) < m$ on $(a - \delta, a)$, then $f(x) > m(x - a) + f(a)$ on $(a - \delta, a)$.

State the analogous properties for $f'(x) > m$ on $[a, a+\delta)$ for some $\delta > 0$.

(b) Show that if f' is defined on an open interval around a, and $f'(a) = 0$, $f''(a) < 0$, then f has a local maximum at a. (Recall that this is one of your tests for "maximum" in Calculus!).

3. Prove that if f' is defined and bounded on (a, b), then f is uniformly continuous on (a, b).

4. Prove that if f' exists on an open interval containing α and β and $f'(\alpha) < k < f'(\beta)$, then there exists $c \in (\alpha, \beta)$ such that $f'(c) = k$.

(This problem asserts that derivatives have the intermediate value property).

Hint: Show first, by replacing $f(x)$ by $f(x) - kx$ that it is sufficient to prove in the special case where $f'(\alpha) < 0 < f'(\beta)$ that $f'(c) = 0$ for some c. Then show that if $f'(\alpha) < 0$ and $f'(\beta) > 0$, then the minimum of f on $[\alpha, \beta]$ must be strictly less than both $f(\alpha)$ and $f(\beta)$, and thus must occur at some $c \in (\alpha, \beta)$.

10.6   L'Hospital's Rule

The reader is familiar with evaluation of limit of quotients of functions: $\lim\limits_{x \to c} \dfrac{f(x)}{g(x)}$. For example, the evaluation of $\lim\limits_{x \to 3} \dfrac{x^2 - 9}{x - 3}$. In high school, this is generally done as follows:

$$\lim_{x \to 3} \frac{x^2 - 9}{x - 3} = \lim_{x \to 3} \frac{(x - 3)(x + 3)}{x - 3} = \lim_{x \to 3}(x + 3) = 6.$$

In several problems involving limits of quotients, factorization may not be easy or may be even impossible. For example, $\lim_{x \to 0} \frac{1 - \cos x}{x}$. In some other problems, an attempt to evaluate such a limit may lead to a situation where $\lim\limits_{x \to c} f(x) =$

$0 = \lim\limits_{x \to c} g(x)$. In this case the limit of the quotient is called *indeterminate (i.e. cannot be determined)* because different values may be obtained for the limit, depending on the particular f and g. For example, let $f(x) = 5x$ and $g(x) = x$. Here, $\lim\limits_{x \to 0} f(x) = \lim\limits_{x \to 0} 5x = 0$ and $\lim\limits_{x \to 0} g(x) = \lim\limits_{x \to 0} x = 0$. But

$$\lim_{x \to 0} \frac{f(x)}{g(x)} = \lim_{x \to 0} \frac{5x}{x} = 5.$$

Thus, the indeterminate form $\frac{0}{0}$ can lead to any real number as a limit.

In this section, we derive a good technique that is often easier to use than factorizing and cancelling common factors in the quotient. This technique is the so-called *L'Hospital's Rule* which we now establish.

Theorem 10.6.1 *(L'Hospital's Rule for $\frac{0}{0}$ as $x \to c$).*

(i) Let f and g be continuous on $[a, b]$ and differentiable on (a, b).

(ii) Suppose that $c \in [a, b]$ and $f(c) = 0 = g(c)$.

(iii) Suppose $g'(x) \neq 0$ for $x \in D_c \cap (a, b)$ where $D_c = \{x \in [a, b] : 0 < |x - c|\}$.

If

$$\lim_{x \to c} \frac{f'(x)}{g'(x)} = l \in \mathbb{R},$$

then

$$\lim_{x \to c} \frac{f(x)}{g(x)} = l.$$

Proof. We want to prove $\lim\limits_{x \to c} \dfrac{f(x)}{g(x)} = l$. So, we take an arbitrary sequence $\{x_n\} \in D_c$ such that $x_n \to c$. We need to prove that

$$\lim_{n \to \infty} \frac{f(x_n)}{g(x_n)} = l.$$

By Cauchy's Mean Value Theorem, $\forall\, n \in N$, there exists a sequence $\{c_n\}$ such that c_n is between x_n and c and such that

$$\frac{f'(c_n)}{g'(c_n)} = \frac{f(x_n) - f(c)}{g(x_n) - g(c)}. \tag{10.6.1}$$

Since $g'(x) \neq 0$ for all $x \in D_c$, the map $g : D_c \cup \{c\} \to \mathbb{R}$ is $1-1$ and onto (Exercises 10.3, Problem 1). Then, $g(x_n) \neq 0$ for all $n \in \mathbb{N}$. Since $f(c) = g(c) = 0$, we have, from (10.6.1) that

$$\frac{f'(c_n)}{g'(c_n)} = \frac{f(x_n)}{g(x_n)} \quad \forall\, n \in \mathbb{N}. \tag{10.6.2}$$

Furthermore, $x_n \to c$ and c_n is between x_n and c. It follows that $c_n \to c$. But, by the hypothesis,

$$\lim_{x \to c} \frac{f'(x)}{g'(x)} = l.$$

This implies, from the definition of the limit of a function $\left(\text{here our function is } H(x) = \frac{f'(x)}{g'(x)}\right)$ we have, $\lim\limits_{n \to \infty} \dfrac{f'(c_n)}{g'(c_n)} = l.$
Hence, taking limits in (10.6.2), we obtain that

$$\lim_{n \to \infty} \frac{f(x_n)}{g(x_n)} = l.$$

But this is the same as

$$\lim_{x \to c} \frac{f(x)}{g(x)} = l. \quad \square$$

Theorem 10.6.2 *(L'Hospital's Rule for $\frac{\infty}{\infty}$ as $x \to \infty$).*

(i) Let f and g be differentiable on $[b, +\infty)$.

(ii) Suppose $\lim\limits_{x\to\infty} f(x) = \infty = \lim\limits_{x\to\infty} g(x)$ *and* $g(x) \neq 0 \; \forall \; x \in (b, +\infty)$.

(iii) Suppose

$$\lim_{x\to\infty} \frac{f'(x)}{g'(x)} = l \in \mathbb{R},$$

then

$$\lim_{x\to\infty} \frac{f(x)}{g(x)} = l.$$

Proof. We want to prove $\lim\limits_{x\to\infty} \dfrac{f(x)}{g(x)} = l$. So, let $\epsilon > 0$ be given. Since (by (iii)), $\lim\limits_{x\to\infty} \dfrac{f'(x)}{g'(x)} = l$, there exists $b_\epsilon > 0$ such that for all $x > b_\epsilon$

$$\left| \frac{f'(x)}{g'(x)} - l \right| < \frac{\epsilon}{2}.$$

Choose $N_\epsilon > b_\epsilon$. Then for all $x > N_\epsilon$, we have

$$\left| \frac{f'(x)}{g'(x)} - l \right| < \frac{\epsilon}{2}. \tag{10.6.3}$$

Since (by (ii)), $\lim\limits_{x\to\infty} f(x) = \infty = \lim\limits_{x\to\infty} g(x)$, given $0 \in \mathbb{R}$, there exists $N_2 > N_1$ such that $x > N_2$ implies

$$f(x) > 0, \quad g(x) > 0;$$

and there exists $N_3 > N_2$ such that $x > N_3$ implies

$$f(x) > f(N_2) \; , \; g(x) > g(N_2).$$

Now, by Cauchy's Mean Value Theorem, there exists a point $c \in (N_2, x)$ such that

$$\frac{f'(c)}{g'(c)} = \frac{f(x) - f(N_2)}{g(x) - g(N_2)} = \frac{f(x)}{g(x)} \cdot \frac{1 - \frac{f(N_2)}{f(x)}}{1 - \frac{g(N_2)}{g(x)}}.$$

But for $x > N_3$, we have,

$$\frac{f(x)}{g(x)} = \frac{f'(c)}{g'(c)} H(x),$$

where

$$H(x) = \frac{1 - \frac{g(N_2)}{g(x)}}{1 - \frac{f(N_2)}{f(x)}}.$$

Now, from the hypothesis on f and g we have that

$$\lim_{x \to \infty} H(x) = 1.$$

We now estimate as follows: For all $x > N_3$,

$$
\begin{aligned}
\left| \frac{f(x)}{g(x)} - l \right| &= \left| \frac{f'(c)}{g'(c)} H(x) - l \right| \\
&\leq \left| \frac{f'(c)}{g'(c)} H(x) - \frac{f'(c)}{g'(c)} \right| + \left| \frac{f'(c)}{g'(c)} - l \right| \\
&= \left| \frac{f'(c)}{g'(c)} \left(H(x) - 1 \right) + \left| \frac{f'(c)}{g'(c)} - l \right| .
\end{aligned}
$$

Furthermore, since $H(x) \to 1$ as $x \to \infty$, there exists $N_4 > N_3$ such that $x > N_4$ implies

$$|H(x) - 1| < \frac{\epsilon}{2\left(\left| \frac{f'(c)}{g'(c)} \right| + 1 \right)}.$$

Now, the point c depends on x but we always have $c > N_2$ so that by using (10.6.3),

$$\left| \frac{f'(c)}{g'(c)} - l \right| < \frac{\epsilon}{2}.$$

Hence, for all $x > N_4$, we obtain that

$$\left| \frac{f(x)}{g(x)} - l \right| \leq \frac{\epsilon}{2\left(\left| \frac{f'(c)}{g'(c)} \right| + 1 \right)} + \frac{\epsilon}{2} < \epsilon,$$

so that $\displaystyle \lim_{x \to \infty} \frac{f(x)}{g(x)} = l.$ $\square$

EXERCISES 10.3

1. Prove that the map $g : D_c \cup \{c\} \to \mathbb{R}$ used in the proof of Theorem 10.6.1 is $1-1$ and onto.

$\Big($Hint: g is differentiable on $[a, b]$. Suppose $g'(x) \geq 0$ for all $x \in [a, b]$ and that $g' \equiv 0$ on any subinterval of $[a, b]$. Prove that g is strictly increasing on $[a, b]\Big)$.

2. Evaluate the following limits.

    (a) $\lim_{x \to \infty} \frac{\log x}{x}$ (b) $\lim_{x \to 0} \frac{\sin x - x}{x^2}$

    (c) $\lim_{x \to \infty} \left(1 + \frac{1}{x}\right)^x$ (d) $\lim_{x \to 0+} \left(1 + 2x\right)^{\frac{1}{x}}$

    (e) $\lim_{x \to \infty} \frac{x^3}{e^x}$ (f) $\lim_{x \to 0} \frac{e^{3x} - 1}{x}$.

194

CHAPTER **11**

Series of Nonnegative Real Numbers

11.1   Introduction

Having studied the convergence properties of sequences, we now apply this study to **infinite series**. In section 11.2, we define infinite series, give some examples and study some of their basic properties. The rest of the chater is devoted to developing several useful tests for determining whether or not a given series is convergent.

11.2   Definition, Example and Basic Properties

Definition 11.2.1 *A series* $\sum_{i=1}^{\infty} a_i$ *of real numbers is defined as a double sequence* $\{a_n, S_n\}$ *satisfying the following*

195

conditions:

$$S_n = \sum_{i=1}^{n} a_i$$

where

$$a_n = S_n - S_{n-1}.$$

The number a_n is called the **general term** *of the series* $\sum_{i=1}^{\infty} a_i$ *and S_n is called the nth* **partial sum** *of the series.*

Definition 11.2.2 *A series $\sum_{i=1}^{\infty} a_i$ is called* **convergent** *if and only if* **its sequence of partial sums $\{S_n\}$** *is convergent to some number a^*, say. In this case, the number a^* is called the sum of the series and we write:*

$$\sum_{i=1}^{\infty} a_i = a^*.$$

The number $a^* - S_n = \sum_{i=n+1}^{\infty} a_i$ is called **the remainder** of the series or the **tail end** or simply **the tail** of the series. In the sequel, we shall use the later terminology. We shall denote the tail of the series $\sum_{i=1}^{\infty} a_i$ by $R_n = a^* - S_n$.

Definition 11.2.3 *A series $\sum_{i=1}^{\infty} a_i$ is called* **divergent** *if it is not convergent.*

We consider some examples:

Example 11.2.4 (i) The geometric series $\sum\limits_{i=1}^{\infty}\left(\dfrac{2}{3}\right)^{i}$ is convergent to the number 2. In fact, its partial sums are:

$$S_n = \sum_{i=1}^{n}\left(\frac{2}{3}\right)^{i} = \frac{2}{3} + \left(\frac{2}{3}\right)^{2} + \left(\frac{2}{3}\right)^{3} + \cdots + \left(\frac{2}{3}\right)^{n}$$

$$= \frac{2}{3}\left(\frac{1-\left(\frac{2}{3}\right)^{n}}{1-\frac{2}{3}}\right) = 2\left(1-\left(\frac{2}{3}\right)^{n}\right) \to 2 \text{ as } n \to \infty.$$

(ii) Determine whether or not the series $1+\frac{1}{2}+\frac{1}{4}+\frac{1}{8}+\cdots$ converges.

Solution: Here,

$$S_n = 1 + \frac{1}{2} + \left(\frac{1}{2}\right)^{2} + \left(\frac{1}{2}\right)^{3} + \cdots + \left(\frac{1}{2}\right)^{n}$$

$$= 2\left(1-\left(\frac{1}{2}\right)^{n}\right)$$

$$\text{(sum of a geometric progression)}$$

$$\to \; 2 \text{ as } n \to \infty$$

and so the geometric progression converges to the sum 2. The tail R_n is given by $R_n = 2 - S_n = 2(\frac{1}{2})^{n}$.

(iii) Determine whether or not the series $1 + 3 + 5 + \cdots$ converges.

Solution: In this case the series diverges. For,

$$S_n = 1 + 3 + 5 + \cdots + (2n-1)$$

$$= \frac{1}{2}n(2 + 2(n-1))$$

$$\text{(sum of an arithmetic progression)}$$

$$= n^{2}$$

and $S_n \to \infty$ as $n \to \infty$.

(iv) Determine whether or not the series $\frac{1}{2\cdot5} + \frac{1}{5\cdot8} + \frac{1}{8\cdot11} + \cdots$ converges.

Solution: The nth term of the given series is

$$\frac{1}{(3n-1)(3n+2)},$$

so

$$S_n = \sum_{r=1}^{n} \frac{1}{(3r-1)(3r+2)}$$

$$= \frac{1}{3}\sum_{r=1}^{n}\left(\frac{1}{3r-1} - \frac{1}{3r+2}\right)$$

(by partial fractions).

We examine $\sum_{r=1}^{n}\left(\frac{1}{3r-1} - \frac{1}{3r+2}\right)$ more closely. We write out this sum explicitly as follows: Let $T_r = \frac{1}{3r-1} - \frac{1}{3r+2}$. Then,

$$r = 1, \quad T_1 = \frac{1}{2} - \frac{1}{5}$$

$$r = 2, \quad T_2 = \frac{1}{5} - \frac{1}{8}$$

$$r = 3, \quad T_3 = \frac{1}{8} - \frac{1}{11}$$

$$r = 4, \quad T_4 = \frac{1}{11} - \frac{1}{14}$$

$$\vdots$$

$$r = n-1, \quad T_{n-1} = \frac{1}{3n-4} - \frac{1}{3n-1}$$

$$r = n, \quad T_n = \frac{1}{3n-1} - \frac{1}{3n+2}.$$

Summing column-wise, we observe that terms cancel in

an obvious manner by **telescoping**. Hence we obtain,

$$\sum_{r=1}^{n} T_r = \sum_{r=1}^{n} \left(\frac{1}{3r-1} - \frac{1}{3r+2} \right)$$

$$= \frac{1}{2} - \frac{1}{3n+2}.$$

Substituting this in the expression for S_n we obtain that

$$S_n = \frac{1}{3}\left(\frac{1}{2} - \frac{1}{3n+2} \right) \to \frac{1}{6} \text{ as } n \to \infty.$$

Therefore the series $\displaystyle\sum_{r=1}^{n} \frac{1}{(3r-1)(3r+2)}$ converges to $\frac{1}{6}$ and the tail of the series R_n is given by

$$R_n = \frac{1}{6} - S_n = \frac{1}{3}\frac{1}{3n+2}.$$

Remark 11.2.5 The method of summation used in Example 11.2.4(iv) is called **telescoping method** for obvious reasons. The method is particularly suitable in some cases when the general term of a series can be resolved into partial fractions. We give more examples to illustrate this.

Example 11.2.6   (i) Prove that $\sum_{n=1}^{\infty} \frac{n}{(n+1)!}$ converges to 1.

Solution: Here,

$$S_n = \sum_{r=1}^{n} \frac{r}{(r+1)!} = \sum_{r=1}^{n} \left(\frac{1}{r!} - \frac{1}{(r+1)!} \right)$$

Let $T_r = \frac{1}{r!} - \frac{1}{(r+1)!}$, then,

$$
\begin{aligned}
T_1 &= \frac{1}{1} - \frac{1}{2!} \\
T_2 &= \frac{1}{2!} - \frac{1}{3!} \\
&\;\;\vdots \\
T_{n-1} &= \frac{1}{(n-1)!} - \frac{1}{n!} \\
T_n &= \frac{1}{n!} - \frac{1}{(n+1)!}.
\end{aligned}
$$

So,

$$
S_n = 1 - \frac{1}{(n+1)!} \to 1 \text{ as } n \to \infty.
$$

(ii) Consider the series

$$
\sum_{n=2}^{\infty} \frac{n-1}{(n+1)(n+2)(n+3)}.
$$

Resolving into partial fractions we obtain that

$$
\frac{r-1}{(r+1)(r+2)(r+3)} = -\frac{1}{r+1} + \frac{3}{r+2} - \frac{2}{r+3}.
$$

Now let, $T_r = -\frac{1}{r+1} + \frac{3}{r+2} - \frac{2}{r+3}$ so that,

$$r = 2, \ T_2 \ = \ -\frac{1}{3} + \frac{3}{4} - \frac{2}{5}$$

$$r = 3, \ T_3 \ = \ -\frac{1}{4} + \frac{3}{5} - \frac{2}{6}$$

$$r = 4, \ T_4 \ = \ -\frac{1}{5} + \frac{3}{6} - \frac{2}{7}$$

$$r = 5, \ T_5 \ = \ -\frac{1}{6} + \frac{3}{7} - \frac{2}{8}$$

$$\vdots \quad \vdots \qquad \vdots \quad \vdots$$

$$r = n - 2, \ T_{n-2} \ = \ -\frac{1}{n-1} + \frac{3}{n} - \frac{2}{n+1}$$

$$r = n - 1, \ T_{n-1} \ = \ -\frac{1}{n} + \frac{3}{n+1} - \frac{2}{n+2}$$

$$r = n, \ T_n \ = \ -\frac{1}{n+1} + \frac{3}{n+2} - \frac{2}{n+3}.$$

So, summing and observing that the terms cancel by telescoping, we obtain that

$$
\begin{aligned}
S_n \ &= \ \sum_{r=2}^{n} \frac{r-1}{(r+1)(r+2)(r+3)} \\
&= \ -\frac{1}{3} + \frac{3}{4} - \frac{1}{4} - \frac{2}{n+2} + \frac{3}{n+2} - \frac{2}{n+3} \\
&= \ \frac{1}{6} - \frac{n+1}{(n+2)(n+3)}.
\end{aligned}
$$

Hence, $\lim_{n \to \infty} S_n = \frac{1}{6}$, and so the given series converges to $\frac{1}{6}$. Furthermore, the tail end of the series is given by

$$R_n = \frac{1}{6} - S_n = \frac{(n+1)}{(n+2)(n+3)}. \quad \square$$

So far, we have used the definition $S_n = \sum_{i=1}^{n} a_i$. We now use the condition $a_n = S_n - S_{n-1}$ (which is part of the definition of the series $\sum_{i=1}^{\infty} a_i$) and prove the following proposition.

Proposition 11.2.7 *A necessary condition for a series* $\sum_{n=1}^{\infty} a_n$ *to be convergent is that* $\lim_{n\to\infty} a_n = 0$.

Proof. Let $\sum_{n=1}^{\infty} a_n$ be convergent. This means (by definition) that $\{S_n\}_{n=1}^{\infty}$ converges to some number, say a^*, i.e.

$$\lim_{n\to\infty} S_n = a^*. \quad \text{(This also implies } \lim_{n\to\infty} S_{n+1} = a^*\text{)}.$$

But,

$$a_n = S_n - S_{n-1}, \quad \text{(by definition)}.$$

This implies that

$$\lim_{n\to\infty} a_n = \lim_{n\to\infty} S_n - \lim_{n\to\infty} S_{n-1} = a^* - a^* = 0,$$

as required. $\quad \square$

Remark 11.2.8 We emphasize that Proposition 11.2.7 **does not** mean that for a given series $\sum_{n=1}^{\infty} a_n$, if $\lim_{n\to\infty} a_n = 0$ then the series converges. It only says that for any given series to have any chance of converging, limit of $\{a_n\}_{n=1}^{\infty}$ must be zero, i.e., $\lim_{n\to\infty} a_n = 0$ must be true. The contrapositive statement of this then means that if $\lim_{n\to\infty} a_n \neq 0$, then the series automatically **is not** convergent. *Note that this is true for any series* $\sum_{n=1}^{\infty} a_n$, *the* $a_n's$ *need not be non-negative.*

Example 11.2.9 The series

$$\sum_{n=1}^{\infty} \frac{n^2}{n^2 + 4}$$

is **not** convergent because

$$\lim_{n\to\infty} a_n = \lim_{n\to\infty} \frac{n^2}{n^2 + 4} = 1 \neq 0.$$

On the other hand, the series

$$\sum_{n=1}^{\infty} \frac{1}{n+1} \quad \text{has} \quad \lim_{n\to\infty} a_n = \lim_{n\to\infty} \frac{1}{n+1} = 0,$$

but this is **not enough** for us to decide whether or not the series converges.

We must continue the investigation with other methods. In examples 11.2.4 and 11.2.6, we computed the partial sum S_n of the given series, then computed its limit to be able to decide whether or not the given series converges. In many problems, the computation of S_n may be very difficult or even impossible. In many such cases, one can employ some "Tests" to determine whether or not the given series converges.

In many books, there are numerous tests for convergence of series of nonnegative numbers. Our experience is that students tend to get confused with too many of them. In what follows, we shall discuss FIVE TESTS which are certainly adequate for most of the problems that will be encountered at this stage. We list these five tests in the box below and then take them up, one at a time. These tests are for series $\sum a_n$ with $a_n \geq 0$ for all $n \in \mathbb{N}$.

1. The Integral Test:

(i) $a_n \geq 0$,

(ii) $a_n \geq a_{n+1}$ $\forall$ $n \geq b$, some $b \in \mathbb{R}$,

(iii) $\lim a_n = 0$.

Then, $\int_b^\infty f(t)dt$ converges if and only if

$\sum_b^\infty a_n$ converges, where $a_n = f(t)$.

2. The Comparison Test:

$$(a) \text{ If } \ 0 \leq a_n \leq kb_n, \quad k > 0,$$

then,

$$\sum b_n \text{ converges } \Rightarrow \sum a_n \text{ converges.}$$

$$\sum b_n \text{ diverges } \Rightarrow \text{ no conclusion.}$$

$$(b) \text{ If } 0 \leq kb_n \leq a_n, \quad k > 0,$$

then,

$$\sum b_n \text{ converges } \Rightarrow \text{ no conclusion.}$$

$$\sum b_n \text{ diverges } \Rightarrow \sum a_n \text{ diverges.}$$

3. The Limit Comparison Test :

$$
\lim \frac{a_n}{b_n} =
\begin{cases}
l = 0, & \sum b_n \text{ converges} \\
& \Rightarrow \sum a_n \text{ converges.} \\[2mm]
l \in (0, \infty), & \sum a_n, \sum b_n \text{ converge} \\
& \text{or diverge, together .} \\[2mm]
l = \infty, & \sum b_n \text{ diverges} \\
& \Rightarrow \sum a_n \text{diverges.}
\end{cases}
$$

4. The Cauchy's Root Test:

$$
\text{If } \lim_{n \to \infty} \sqrt[n]{a_n} =
\begin{cases}
l < 1, & \sum a_n, \text{ converges.} \\
l > 1, & \sum a_n \text{ diverges.} \\
l = 1, & \text{nothing to conclude.}
\end{cases}
$$

5. The D'Alembert's Ratio Test:

$$
\lim_{n \to \infty} \frac{a_{n+1}}{a_n} =
\begin{cases}
l < 1, & \sum a_n, \text{ converges.} \\
l > 1, & \sum a_n \text{ diverges.} \\
l = 1, & \text{nothing to conclude.}
\end{cases}
$$

We now prove our next proposition which will provide us with a very powerful method of testing a large class of series for convergence.

11.3　The Integral Test

Definition 11.3.1 *An infinite integral $\int_b^\infty f(t)dt$, is said to* **converge** *if*

$$
\mathbb{I}(t) = \int_b^N f(t)dt
$$

tends to a finite limit as $N \to \infty$, otherwise the integral is said to **diverge**.

In the sequel, we shall suppose that a is a function from $[b, \infty)$ to $[0, \infty)$. Then, it is clear that the integral $\int_b^u f(t)dt$ is a monotone increasing function of u, so that the improper (infinite) integral $\int_b^\infty f(t)dt$, converges if and only if it is bounded above (see Theorem 4.3.1). With this setting, we now state our next result.

Theorem 11.3.2 (Integral test) *If f is a non-negative decreasing integrable function such that $f(n) = a_n$ for all $n \in [b, \infty)$, then the series $\sum_{n=b}^{\infty} a_n$ and the integral $\int_b^\infty a(t)dt$, converge or diverge together.*

Proof. As f is a monotone decreasing function, we have

$$f(n) \geq f(t) \geq f(n+1), \text{ whenever } n \leq t \leq n+1.$$

(See Fig. 11.1).
Also, since f is non-negative and integrable,

$$\int_n^{n+1} f(n)dt \geq \int_n^{n+1} f(t)dt \geq \int_n^{n+1} f(n+1)dt,$$

which implies

$$f(n)\Big|_n^{n+1} \geq \int_n^{n+1} f(t)dt \geq f(n+1)\Big|_n^{n+1},$$

or,

$$a_n \geq \int_n^{n+1} f(t)dt \geq a_{n+1}. \tag{i}$$

Let $S_n = a_1 + a_2 + \cdots + a_n$ and $\mathbb{I}_n = \int_1^n f(t)dt$. Putting $n = 1, 2, ..., (n-1)$ successively in (i), we obtain the following set of inequalities:

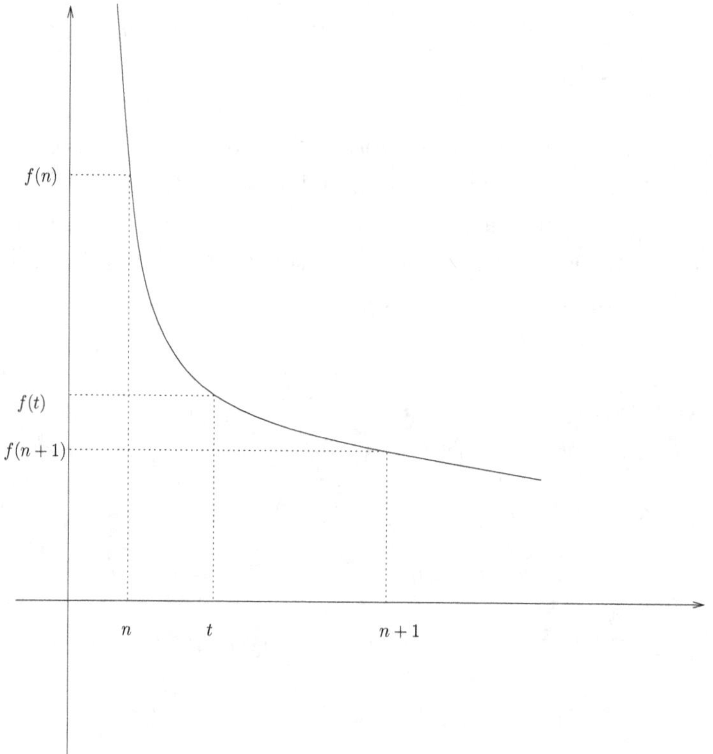

Fig. 11.1

$$a_1 \;\geq\; \int_1^2 f(t)dt \geq a_2$$

$$a_2 \;\geq\; \int_2^3 f(t)dt \geq a_3 \qquad (11.3.1)$$

$$\vdots \qquad \vdots$$

$$a_{n-1} \;\geq\; \int_{n-1}^n f(t)dt \geq a_n.$$

Adding, we obtain,

$$S_n - a_n \geq \mathbb{I}_n \geq S_n - a_1 \implies 0 < a_n \leq S_n - \mathbb{I}_n \leq a_1.$$

Let us consider the sequence $\{S_n - \mathbb{I}_n\}$.

$$(S_n - \mathbb{I}_n) - (S_{n-1} - \mathbb{I}_{n-1}) = S_n - S_{n-1} - (\mathbb{I}_n - \mathbb{I}_{n-1})$$
$$= a_n - \int_{n-1}^{n} f(t)dt$$
$$\leq 0,$$

by replacing n by $n - 1$ on the second inequality of (i). Therefore, the sequence $\{S_n - \mathbb{I}_n\}$ is monotone decreasing and bounded below by 0. Hence the sequence converges and has a limit, say, l. Then,

$$0 \leq \lim_{n \to \infty} (S_n - \mathbb{I}_n) = l,$$

i.e., $\lim S_n = \lim \mathbb{I}_n + l$. Thus, if $\{\mathbb{I}_n\}$ converges, then $\{S_n\}$ converges, i.e., $\sum a_n$ converges. If $\{\mathbb{I}_n\}$ diverges, then $\{S_n\}$ diverges, i.e., $\sum a_n$ diverges. Thus, the series $\sum_{n=1}^{\infty} a_n$ converges or diverges if and only if the integral $\int_{b}^{\infty} f(t)dt$ converges or diverges, respectively. $\square$

Remark 11.3.3 We note from Theorem 11.3.2, that if the series converges with the integral, then the difference between sum of the series and that of the integral is less than or equal to a_1. On the other hand, if divergence takes place, then the limit of $(S_n - \mathbb{I}_n)$ still exists and lies between 0 and a_1.

Example 11.3.4 Show that the series $\sum_{n=1}^{\infty} \dfrac{1}{n^p}$ converges if $p > 1$ and diverges if $p \leq 1$.

Solution: We use the **integral test**. Let $f(t) = 1/(t^p)$, so that for $t \geq 1$, the function f is non-negative, monotone decreasing and integrable. Setting

$$a_n = f(n) = \frac{1}{n^p}, \ \forall \, n \in \mathbb{N},$$

then by the integral test, $\displaystyle\sum_{n=1}^{\infty} a_n$ and $\int_1^{\infty} f(t)dt$ converge or diverge together. But

$$\int_1^N f(t)dt = \int_1^N \frac{1}{t^p}dt = \begin{cases} \frac{N^{1-p}-1}{1-p}, & \text{if } p \neq 1, \\ \log N, & \text{if } p = 1. \end{cases}$$

Therefore,

$$\int_1^{\infty} f(t)dt = \lim_{N \to \infty} \int_1^N f(t)dt = \begin{cases} \frac{-1}{1-p}, & \text{if } p > 1, \\ \infty, & \text{if } 0 < p \leq 1. \end{cases}$$

Thus $\int_1^{\infty} f(t)dt$ converges if $p > 1$ and diverges if $0 < p \leq 1$. Hence the given series converges if $p > 1$ and diverges if $0 < p \leq 1$. But when $p < 0$, the given series diverges, for then the nth term $1/(n^p)$ does not tend to zero as $n \to \infty$. Hence, the series $\displaystyle\sum_{n=1}^{\infty} \frac{1}{n^p}$ converges when $p > 1$ and diverges when $p \leq 1$. $\square$

Corollary 11.3.5 *The series* $\displaystyle\sum_{n=1}^{\infty} \frac{1}{n}$ *is divergent.*

Proof. This follows from Theorem 11.3.2 with $p = 1$. $\square$

Remark 11.3.6 The series $\displaystyle\sum_{n=1}^{\infty} \frac{1}{n}$ is called the **harmonic series**.

We infer from Theorem 11.3.2 that $\{S_n - I_n\}$ is monotone decreasing and bounded below by zero. So, it converges. Now, using Remark 11.2.3 and Remark 11.2.6, we obtain that $\lim(S_n - I_n)$ exists and lies between 0 and a_1 where , $a_1 = 1$, $I_n = \int_1^n \frac{1}{t}dt = \ln t \Big|_1^n = \ln n$, so that

$$\lim_{n \to \infty} \left(1 + \frac{1}{2} + \frac{1}{3} + \cdots + \frac{1}{n} - \log n\right)$$

exists and lies between 0 and 1. This limit is called **Euler's constant**, and is generally denoted by γ. Its value is $0.57721\cdots$. Thus,

$$1 + \frac{1}{2} + \frac{1}{3} + \cdots + \frac{1}{n} - \log n \to \gamma.$$

Example 11.2.7 Show that the series $\sum_{n=2}^{\infty}\left(\frac{1}{n(\log n)^p}\right)$, $p > 0$, converges for $p > 1$ and diverges for $p \le 1$.

Solution: Let $f(t) = 1/\left(t(\log t)^p\right)$, so that for $t \ge 2$, the function f is non-negative and monotone decreasing to 0.

By the integral test, $\sum_{n=2}^{\infty} a_n$ and $\int_2^{\infty} f(t)dt$ converge or diverge together. Now,

$$\int_2^N f(t)dt \; = \int_2^N \frac{1}{t(\log t)^p}dt, \; p > 0,$$

$$= \begin{cases} \frac{(\log N)^{1-p}-(\log 2)^{1-p}}{1-p}, & \text{if } p \ne 1, \\ \log\log N - \log\log 2, & \text{if } p = 1. \end{cases}$$

Therefore,

$$\int_2^{\infty} f(t)dt \; = \lim_{N\to\infty} \int_2^N f(t)dt$$

$$= \begin{cases} \frac{-(\log 2)^{1-p}}{1-p}, & \text{if } p > 1, \\ \infty, & \text{if } 0 < p \le 1. \end{cases}$$

Thus $\int_2^{\infty} f(t)dt$ converges if $p > 1$ and diverges if $0 < p \le 1$. Hence the given series converges if $p > 1$ and diverges if $p \le 1$. $\square$

(iii) Test the convergence of the series

$$1 - \frac{1}{1\cdot 2} + \frac{1}{2} - \frac{1}{2\cdot 3} + \frac{1}{3} - \frac{1}{3\cdot 4} + \cdots$$

Solution: The $2n$th partial sum of the given series is

$$S_{2n} = 1 - \frac{1}{1\cdot 2} + \frac{1}{2} - \frac{1}{2\cdot 3} \tag{11.3.2}$$
$$+ \frac{1}{3} - \frac{1}{3\cdot 4} + \cdots + \frac{1}{n} - \frac{1}{n(n+1)}$$
$$= \frac{2-1}{1\cdot 2} + \frac{3-1}{2\cdot 3} + \frac{4-1}{3\cdot 4} + \cdots + \frac{(n+1)-1}{n(n+1)}$$
$$= \frac{1}{2} + \frac{1}{3} + \frac{1}{4} + \cdots + \frac{1}{n+1}$$
$$- \log(n+1) \to \gamma - 1 \text{ (this follows from Remark 11.3.6)}.$$

Thus $\lim_{n\to\infty} S_{2n} = \infty$. Therefore the given series is not convergent. $\square$

EXERCISES 11.1

1. Prove that $1 + \frac{1}{2} + \frac{1}{3} + \cdots + \frac{1}{2n} - \log 2n \to \gamma$, ($\gamma$ being the Euler's constant). Hence or otherwise, show that

$$1 - \frac{1}{2} + \frac{1}{3} - \frac{1}{4} + \cdots = \log 2 \text{ as } n \to \infty.$$

   Hint: Use Remark 11.3.6, i.e., $1 + \frac{1}{2} + \frac{1}{3} + \cdots + \frac{1}{n} - \log n \to \gamma$.

2. Using the integral test, test the convergence or otherwise of the following series:

$$\text{(i)} \quad \sum_{n=1}^{\infty} \frac{1}{n(n+1)} \qquad \text{(ii)} \quad \sum_{n=1}^{\infty} \frac{1}{n^2+1}$$

$$\text{(iii)} \quad \sum_{n=2}^{\infty} \frac{1}{n(\log n)^p}, p \in \mathbb{R}.$$

   Using (iii), what can you deduce about convergence or divergence of the following series

$$\text{(a)} \quad \sum_{n=2}^{\infty} \frac{1}{n\log n} \qquad \text{(b)} \quad \sum_{n=2}^{\infty} \frac{1}{n(\log n)^{1.01}}$$

$$\text{(c)} \quad \sum_{n=2}^{\infty} \frac{1}{n(\log n)^3} \qquad \text{(d)} \quad \sum_{n=2}^{\infty} \frac{1}{n(\log n)^{(n+1)/n}}.$$

3. Show that $\displaystyle\sum_{n=1}^{\infty} \frac{1}{n^2}$ converges to a sum less than 2.

4. Test the convergence of $\displaystyle\sum_{n=2}^{\infty} \frac{1}{n \log n (\log \log n)^p}$.

Theorem 11.3.7 General Principle of Convergence *The series $\displaystyle\sum_{n=1}^{\infty} a_n$ converges if and only if given any $\epsilon > 0$ there exists a natural number N_0 such that*

$$|a_{n+1} + a_{n+2} + \cdots + a_{n+p}| < \epsilon$$

for every $n \geq N_0$ and every $p \in \mathbb{N}$.

Theorem 11.3.7 gives some basic facts about series. The **convergence** of a series corresponds to the limiting behaviour of the sequence of partial sums. In other words, the convergence character of a series is completely determined in "the tail" of the series. Hence the convergence and indeed, the divergence of a series are not affected by changing a **finite** number of terms. Of course, if a finite number of terms is added to or subtracted from the series, the sum is changed, if the series converges.

Illustration:

(i) $1+\frac{1}{16}+\frac{1}{32}+\cdots$ is the series in Example 11.2.4(ii) with three terms omitted. It still converges (verify); but its sum is no longer 2, in fact it is

$$2 - \left(\frac{1}{2} + \frac{1}{4} + \frac{1}{8}\right) = \frac{9}{8}.$$

(ii) If $\displaystyle\sum_{n=1}^{\infty} a_n$ and $\displaystyle\sum_{n=1}^{\infty} b_n$ are both convergent, then so also is $\displaystyle\sum_{n=1}^{\infty}(a_n + b_n)$. In fact, if the partial sums of $\displaystyle\sum_{n=1}^{\infty} a_n$ and $\displaystyle\sum_{n=1}^{\infty} b_n$ are (s_n) and (t_n) respectively such that as $n \to \infty, s_n \to s$ and $t_n \to t$ then $s_n + t_n \to s + t$ as n $\to \infty$.

(iii) If $\displaystyle\sum_{n=1}^{\infty} a_n$ is convergent and $\displaystyle\sum_{n=1}^{\infty} b_n$ is divergent, then $\displaystyle\sum_{n=1}^{\infty}(a_n \pm b_n)$ is divergent. This follows directly from a consideration of the behaviour of the partial sums of the series as in (ii) above.

(iv) If both $\displaystyle\sum_{n=1}^{\infty} a_n$ and $\displaystyle\sum_{n=1}^{\infty} b_n$ diverge, nothing can be inferred about the behaviour of $\displaystyle\sum_{n=1}^{\infty}(a_n \pm b_n)$.

(v) If $\displaystyle\sum_{n=1}^{\infty} a_n$ is convergent (or divergent) and k is a **non-zero constant** then $\displaystyle\sum_{n=1}^{\infty}(ka_n)$ also converges (or diverges).

EXERCISES 11.2

1. Find the sum of the first n terms of the following series and hence decide whether each series converges or diverges. If the series converges find its sum.

   (a) $\frac{1}{3} + \frac{2}{9} + \frac{4}{27} + \cdots$

   (b) $2 - 4 + 6 - 8 + \cdots$

   (c) $\frac{1}{1\cdot2} + \frac{1}{2\cdot3} + \frac{1}{3\cdot4} + \cdots$

   (d) $\frac{1}{1\cdot2\cdot3} + \frac{1}{2\cdot3\cdot4} + \frac{1}{3\cdot4\cdot5} + \cdots$

   (e) $\log 2 + \log \frac{3}{2} + \log \frac{4}{3} + \cdots$

   (f) $a + \frac{1}{2} + a^2 + \frac{1}{4} + a^3 + \frac{1}{8} + \cdots$

   (g) $\displaystyle\sum_{r=1}^{\infty} \frac{2r + 1}{r^2(r + 1)^2}$

   (h) $\displaystyle\sum_{r=0}^{\infty} \frac{(-1)^r(2r + 3)}{(r + 1)(r + 2)}$

   (i) $\displaystyle\sum_{r=0}^{\infty} \frac{a}{(1 + a)^r}$

   (j) $\displaystyle\sum_{r=1}^{\infty} \frac{a^2}{(1 + a^2)^{r-1}}.$

2. Prove that, if $\{d_n\}$ is increasing and unbounded, then:

   (a) $\displaystyle\sum_{n=1}^{\infty}(d_{n+1} - d_n)$ is divergent;

   (b) $\displaystyle\sum_{n=1}^{\infty}\left(\frac{1}{d_n} - \frac{1}{d_{n+1}}\right)$ is convergent.

3. Prove that if $\displaystyle\sum_{n=1}^{\infty} d_n$ converges and $d_n \neq 0$, then $\displaystyle\sum_{n=1}^{\infty} \frac{1}{d_n}$ diverges.

4. Prove that $\displaystyle\lim_{n\to\infty} \frac{1}{n}\left(1 + \frac{1}{2} + \cdots + \frac{1}{n}\right) = 0.$

11.4   The Comparison Test

Theorem 11.4.1 (Comparison Test)(a) *Suppose, the following inequality holds:*
(i) $0 \leq a_n \leq kb_n$, some constant $k > 0$ and $\forall\, n \geq n_0$
(for some integer n_0).

(ii) $\displaystyle\sum_{n=1}^{\infty} b_n$ converges .

Then $\displaystyle\sum_{n=1}^{\infty} a_n$ converges.

Proof. $S_n = \displaystyle\sum_{k-1}^{n} a_k \leq a_1 + a_2 + ... + a_{N_0} + \displaystyle\sum_{n=N_0+1}^{\infty} b_n$. But $\sum b_n$ converges implies, since the "tail" of the series is finite, there exists $M > 0$ such that $\displaystyle\sum_{N_0+1}^{\infty} b_n < M$. Hence,

$$S_n = \sum_{k-1}^{n} a_k \leq a_1 + a_2 + ... + a_{N_0} + M \leq K, \text{ for some}$$

constant K. Hence, $\{S_n\}$ is a monotone nondecreasing sequence bounded above. Hence, it converges. This means, $\sum a_n$ converges. $\square$

Theorem 11.4.2 (Comparison Test)(b)
Suppose
(i) $a_n \geq kb_n$, for $n \geq n_0$, some $k \in \mathbb{R}$.

(ii) $\displaystyle\sum_{n=1}^{\infty} b_n$ diverges.

Then, $\displaystyle\sum_{n=1}^{\infty} a_n$ diverges.

Proof. We prove by contradiction. Suppose $\sum a_n$ converges. Then, the sequence $\{s_n\}$ of partial sums converges. Hence, it is bounded. Then, if $\{S_n\}$ is the sequence of partial sums of $\sum b_n$, we would have

$$S_n = b_0 + b_1 + ... + b_n \leq b_0 + b_1 + ... + b_{N_0} + \sum_{N_0+1}^{\infty} a_n.$$

Since $\sum a_n$ is assumed to be convergent, the "tail" must be finite so that, there exists a constant $L > 0$ such that $S_n \leq L$ for all $n \geq N_0$. This implies that $\{S_n\}$ is a monotone nondecreasing sequence bounded above by L. Hence it converges, i.e., the series $\sum b_n$ converges. This s a contradiction to (ii). This implies that our supposition that $\sum a_n$ converges is false. Hence $\sum a_n$ diverges. $\square$

Remark 11.4.3 Think of $\displaystyle\sum_{n=1}^{\infty} a_n$ and $\displaystyle\sum_{n=1}^{\infty} b_n$ as infinitely long strings. Think of a convergent series as one that can be put inside a rectangular box (because it is finite) (See Fig. 11 .3).

$$\boxed{\text{Can } \sum b_n \text{ fit in here?}}$$

Fig. 11.3

Now, recall that you are generally given only *one* series $\sum a_n$, say, whose convergence or divergence you want to check. To apply the comparison test, *you have to generate, by yourself, a series $\sum b_n$ whose convergence or divergence* **you know**. This is easy because one can always rely on the $p-$series, $\sum \frac{1}{n^p}$. This $p-$series is always obtained by starting with the nth term of the given series, $\sum a_n$, using some reasonable estimates, to obtain a lower bound or an upper bound, b_n, for a_n. This b_n which is generally of the form $\frac{1}{n^p}$ is the one to use for the direct comparison test. Now, Theorem 11.4.1 says that if $\displaystyle\sum_{n=1}^{\infty} b_n$ can be put inside a rectangular box (i.e., converges), and $b_n \geq a_n$, then $\sum_{n=1}^{\infty} a_n$ can also be put inside the box (i.e., also converges). Similarly Theorem 11.4.2 says that if $\displaystyle\sum_{n=1}^{\infty} b_n$ is too big to be put inside a box (i.e., diverges), and $a_n \geq b_n$, than $\sum_{n=1}^{\infty} a_n$ is, of course, also too big for the box (and so diverges). Note that in the comparison test, only the nth terms of the two series are compared.

11.5   The Limit Comparison Test

Theorem 11.5.1 (Limit Comparison Test)
Suppose $a_n > 0, b_n > 0 \; \forall \; n \geq N_0 \geq 1$.

$$\lim \frac{a_n}{b_n} = \begin{cases} l = 0, & \sum b_n \text{ converges} \Rightarrow \sum a_n \text{ converges.} \\ l \in (0, \infty), & \sum a_n, \sum b_n \text{ converge/diverge,} \\ & \text{together.} \\ l = \infty, & \sum b_n \text{ diverges} \Rightarrow \sum a_n \text{ diverges.} \end{cases}$$

Proof. If $l = 0$, given $\epsilon > 0$, there exists an integer, $n_0 > 0$ such that for all $n \geq n_0$,

$$\left| \frac{a_n}{b_n} - 0 \right| < \epsilon.$$

This implies,

$$a_n < \epsilon b_n \; \forall \; n \geq n_0.$$

By the comparison test, $\sum b_n$ converges implies $\sum a_n$ converges.

Now, since $\lim \frac{a_n}{b_n} = l$, given $\epsilon > 0$, (for $l \in (0, \infty)$, take $\epsilon = \frac{l}{2} > 0$) there exists an integer, $n_0 > 0$ such that for all $n \geq n_0$,

$$\left| \frac{a_n}{b_n} - l \right| < \frac{l}{2}.$$

This implies,

$$\frac{l}{2} b_n < a_n < \frac{3l}{2} b_n \; \forall \; n \geq n_0.$$

Now, if $\sum b_n$ converges, using $a_n < \frac{3l}{2} b_n$, and the comparison test, we obtain that $\sum a_n$ converges.

If, on the other hand, $\sum b_n$ diverges, using $\frac{l}{2}b_n < a_n$, the comparison test gives that $\sum a_n$ diverges.

Finally, if $l = \infty$, then (by Theorem 4.8.5), $\lim \frac{b_n}{a_n} = 0$. Thus, given $\epsilon > 0$, there exists an integer $n_0 > 0$ such that for all $n \geq n_0$,

$$\left| \frac{b_n}{a_n} - 0 \right| < \epsilon.$$

This implies,

$$b_n < \epsilon a_n \ \forall \ n \geq n_0.$$

By the comparison test, $\sum b_n$ diverges implies $\sum a_n$ diverges.
$\square$

Example 11.5.2 Verify the convergence or divergence of the following series:

$$\text{(a)} \sum_{n=1}^{\infty} \frac{n}{n^4 - 3} \quad \text{(b)} \sum_{n=1}^{\infty} \frac{n^2}{n^3 - 3} \quad \text{(c)} \sum_{n=1}^{\infty} \frac{n^2}{\exp(n^2)} \quad \text{(d)} \sum_{n=1}^{\infty} \frac{3^n + 1}{4^n - 1}.$$

Solution:

(a) Here

$$a_n = \frac{n}{n^4 - 3} < \frac{n}{n^4 - \frac{n^4}{2}} = \frac{2}{n^3} \text{ if } n \geq 2.$$

Hence, one is led to compare the given series with the following p series $\sum_{n=1}^{\infty} \frac{1}{n^3}$ which is a convergent series (by Example 11.3.4 part (i)). We then conclude that the given series $\sum_{n=1}^{\infty} \frac{n}{n^4 - 3}$ converges (thanks to Theorem 11.4.1). $\square$

Remark 11.5.3 Usually it is easier to use the **limit** comparison test (Theorem 11.5.1). In many cases, the

b_n is very easily chosen as follows: Take the highest power of n appearing in the numerator and divide by the highest power of n appearing in the denominator. Take the quotient as your b_n. We illustrate. In Example 11.5.2 part (a),

$$b_n = \frac{n}{n^4} = \frac{1}{n^3}.$$

So,

$$\frac{a_n}{b_n} = \frac{n^4}{n^4 - 3} = \frac{1}{1 - \frac{3}{n^4}} \to 1 \text{ as } n \to \infty.$$

$$\implies \sum_{n=1}^{\infty} a_n \text{ converges (by Theorem 11.5.1).}$$

(b) Here $a_n = \frac{n^2}{n^3-3}$ and so we take $b_n = \frac{n^2}{n^3} = \frac{1}{n}$. Then,

$$\frac{a_n}{b_n} = \frac{n^3}{n^3 - 3} \to 1 \text{ as } n \to \infty.$$

By applying Theorem 11.5.1, the given series $\sum_{n=1}^{\infty} a_n$ diverges by comparison with the harmonic series $\sum_{n=1}^{\infty} \frac{1}{n}$.

$\square$

(c) Here,

$$a_n = \frac{n^2}{1 + n^2 + \frac{n^4}{2!} + \cdots} < \frac{n^2}{n^2 + \frac{n^4}{2!} + \cdots}$$

$$= \frac{1}{1 + \frac{n^2}{2!} + \cdots} < \frac{1}{\frac{n^2}{2!}} = \frac{2}{n^2}.$$

Choosing $b_n = \frac{2}{n^2}$, we then obtain that $\sum_{n=1}^{\infty} a_n$ converges.

(d) Here $a_n = \frac{3^n + 1}{4^n - 1}$ and take $b_n = \left(\frac{3}{4}\right)^n$, then

$$\frac{a_n}{b_n} = \frac{3^n + 1}{4^n - 1} \times \frac{4^n}{3^n} = \frac{1 + \left(\frac{1}{3}\right)^n}{1 - \left(\frac{1}{4}\right)^n} \to 1 \text{ as } n \to \infty.$$

Therefore $\sum_{n=1}^{\infty} a_n$ converges by comparison with the convergent

geometric progression $\sum_{n=1}^{\infty} \left(\frac{3}{4}\right)^n$. $\square$

EXERCISES 11.3

1. Using the comparison test decide if the following series converges or diverges:

(a) $1 + \frac{1}{9} + \frac{1}{25} + \frac{1}{49} + \cdots$

(b) $\frac{1}{1\cdot3} + \frac{1}{2\cdot4} + \frac{1}{3\cdot5} + \cdots$

(c) $\frac{1}{3\cdot4} + \frac{2}{5\cdot6} + \frac{3}{7\cdot8} + \cdots$

(d) $\frac{1+2}{2^3} + \frac{1+2+3}{3^3} + \frac{1+2+3+4}{4^3} + \cdots$

(e) $\displaystyle\sum_{n=1}^{\infty} \frac{\sqrt{n}}{2n^2 + 1}$

(f) $\displaystyle\sum_{n=1}^{\infty} \frac{n+1}{3n^2 - 1}$

(g) $\displaystyle\sum_{n=1}^{\infty} \frac{10^n}{n!}$

(h) $\displaystyle\sum_{n=1}^{\infty} \frac{2^n - 1}{5^n - 1}$

(i) $\displaystyle\sum_{n=1}^{\infty} \frac{(n+2)(n+4)}{(n+1)(n+3)(n+5)}$

(j) $\displaystyle\sum_{n=1}^{\infty} \frac{1}{n} \sin \frac{x}{n}$

(k) $\displaystyle\sum_{n=1}^{\infty} \frac{a^{n-1}}{1 + a^n} \quad (a > 0)$

(l) $\displaystyle\sum_{n=1}^{\infty} n^{-\frac{1}{2n}}.$

2. Prove that, if $a_n > 0$ and $\displaystyle\sum_{n=1}^{\infty} a_n$ is convergent, so also are

$$\sum_{n=1}^{\infty} a_n^2, \quad \sum_{n=1}^{\infty} \frac{a_n}{n}, \quad \sum_{n=1}^{\infty} \frac{a_n}{1 + a_n}, \quad \text{and} \quad \sum_{n=1}^{\infty} \frac{a_n}{1 - a_n}, \quad a_n \neq 1.$$

11.6   Cauchy's Root Test

Theorem 11.6.1

$$\limsup_{n\to\infty} \sqrt[n]{a_n} = \begin{cases} l < 1 & \Rightarrow \sum a_n \text{ converges.} \\ l > 1 & \Rightarrow \sum a_n \text{ diverges.} \\ l = 1 & \Rightarrow \text{ nothing to conclude.} \end{cases}$$

Proof. This is left as an exercise for the reader (see Exercises11.4, Problem (6)).

EXERCISES 11.4

Test the following series for convergence:

(1) $\displaystyle\sum_{n=1}^{\infty} \frac{1}{3^n n}$ (2) $\displaystyle\sum_{n=1}^{\infty} \frac{1}{n}\left(\frac{e}{\pi-1}\right)^n$

(3) $\displaystyle\sum_{n=1}^{\infty} \frac{1}{2^{2n+(-1)^n}}$ (4) $\displaystyle\sum_{n=1}^{\infty} n^2 e^{an}$

(5) $\displaystyle\sum_{n=1}^{\infty} \frac{1}{n^{3+(-1)^n}}.$ (6) Prove Cauchy's Root Test.

11.7   D'Alembert's Ratio Test

Theorem 11.7.1

$$\limsup_{n\to\infty} \frac{a_{n+1}}{a_n} = \begin{cases} l < 1 \Rightarrow & \sum a_n \ \textit{converges.} \\ l > 1 & \Rightarrow \sum a_n \ \textit{diverges.} \\ l = 1 & \Rightarrow \ \textit{nothing to conclude.} \end{cases}$$

Proof. (a) Pick $r \in (l, 1)$ and take $\epsilon = r - l > 0$. Then $r = l + \epsilon = \limsup\limits_{n\to\infty} \frac{a_{n+1}}{a_n} + \epsilon$. Therefore, by a property of limit superior (see box **C1** in section 5.4.1), we have that $\exists n_0 \in \mathbb{N}$ such that

$$\frac{a_{n+1}}{a_n} < r \ \forall \ n \geq n_0.$$

This implies, in particular, that

$$a_{n+1} < r a_n \ \forall \ n \geq n_0.$$

This implies,

$$\begin{aligned} a_{N_0+1} &\leq r a_{N_0} \\ a_{N_0+2} &\leq r a_{N_0+1} \leq r^2 a_{N_0} \\ a_{N_0+3} &\leq r^3 a_{N_0} \\ &\ \ \vdots \qquad \vdots \\ a_{N_0+m} &\leq r^m a_{N_0} \end{aligned}$$

Now,

$$\sum_{n=1}^{\infty} a_n = a_1 + a_2 + ... + a_{N_0-1} + a_{N_0} + a_{N_0+1} + \cdots.$$

$$\leq a_1 + a_2 + ... + a_{N_0-1} + a_{N_0} + r a_{N_0} + \cdots.$$

Define

$$b_n = a_1 + a_2 + ... + a_{N_0-1} + a_{N_0} + r a_{N_0} + r^2 a_{N_0} + ...$$

Then,

$$a_n \leq b_n \ \forall \ n \geq n_0. \tag{$*$}$$

Observe that

$$\sum_{n=1}^{\infty} b_n = a_1 + a_2 + ... + a_{N_0-1} + a_{N_0}\left(1 + r + r^2 + ...\right).$$

The geometric series $(1 + r + r^2 + ...)$ converges since $|r| < 1$. Hence, $\sum b_n$ converges. From $(*)$, using the comparison test, $\sum a_n$ converges and this completes the proof.

(ii). If $1 < l < \infty$, then we show that $\lim a_n \neq 0$. To see this, using a property of limit superior (see box **C2** in section 5.4.1), we obtain a subsequence $\{a_{n_j}\}$ of $\{a_n\}$ such that $\lim\limits_{j\to\infty} \dfrac{a_{n_j+1}}{a_{n_j}} = l$. Since $l > 1$, we simply observe that for some index $j_0 \in \mathbb{N}$,

$$\frac{a_{n_j+1}}{a_{n_j}} > 1 \ \forall \ j \geq j_0.$$

This implies that $a_{n_j+1} > a_{n_j} \ \forall \ j \geq j_0$. In particular, for $j \geq j_0$, every term of the sequence $\{a_{n_j}\}$ is greater than or equal to a_{j_0}, and so, a_{n_j} cannot converge to 0. This implies that a_n cannot converge to 0. Hence, $\sum a_n$ is not convergent.

(iii) $\sum \frac{1}{n}$ diverges and $\sum \frac{1}{n^2}$ converges. In each case,

$$\lim \frac{a_{n+1}}{a_n} = 1.$$

So, whenever $\lim \frac{a_{n+1}}{a_n} = 1$, we cannot make any conclusion. Further test is necessary. $\square$

Example 11.7.2 Test the convergence or otherwise of the following series:

(i) $\displaystyle\sum_{n=1}^{\infty} \frac{10^n}{n}$ (ii) $\displaystyle\sum_{n=1}^{\infty} \frac{a^n}{n^2}$, $a > 0$

(iii) $\displaystyle\sum_{n=1}^{\infty} \frac{a^n}{n!}$, $a > 0$ (iv) $\displaystyle\sum_{n=1}^{\infty} \frac{n}{2^n}$

(v) $\displaystyle\sum_{n=1}^{\infty} \frac{\log n}{2^n}$ (vi) $\displaystyle\sum_{n=1}^{\infty} \frac{n^2}{n^3 + 1}$.

Solution

(*i*) $\frac{a_{n+1}}{a_n} = \frac{10n}{n+1} \to 10$ as $n \to \infty$. Hence $\displaystyle\sum_{n=1}^{\infty} a_n$ diverges by the ratio test.

(*ii*) Here $\frac{b_n}{b_{n+1}} = \left(\frac{n+1}{n}\right)^2 \frac{1}{a} \to \frac{1}{a}$ as $n \to \infty$. Then by the ratio test the given series $\displaystyle\sum_{n=1}^{\infty} \frac{a^n}{n^2}$ converges for $0 < a < 1$ and diverges for $a > 1$. For the case when $a = 1$, the series is just the p series with $p = 2$.

(*iii*) $\frac{a_n}{a_{n+1}} = \frac{n+1}{a} \to \infty$ as $n \to \infty$ and the series converges for $a > 0$.

(*iv*) Here $a_n = \frac{n}{2^n} > 0$. Applying the Cauchy's root test,

$$\sqrt[n]{a_n} = \sqrt[n]{\frac{n}{2^n}} = \frac{\sqrt[n]{n}}{2} \to \frac{1}{2} \text{ as } n \to \infty.$$

So, $\displaystyle\sum_{n=1}^{\infty} a_n$ converges.

Note that one could have used the ratio test also to obtain the same result. (Try this).

(v) Here $a_n = \frac{\log n}{2^n}$. So by the root test,

$$\sqrt[n]{\frac{\log n}{2^n}} = \frac{\sqrt[n]{\log n}}{2}.$$

But,

$$0 \le \sqrt[n]{\log n} \le \sqrt[n]{n} \text{ and } \sqrt[n]{n} \to 1 \text{ as } n \to \infty.$$

Hence

$$\frac{\sqrt[n]{\log n}}{2} \to \frac{1}{2} < 1 \text{ as } n \to \infty.$$

Therefore, $\sum_{n=1}^{\infty} \frac{\log n}{2^n}$ converges. $\square$

Alternatively, by the ratio test:

$$\begin{aligned}
\frac{a_{n+1}}{a_n} &= \frac{\log(n+1)}{2^{n+1}} \frac{2^n}{\log n} = \frac{\log(n+1)}{2\log n} \\
&= \frac{\log(n(1+\frac{1}{n}))}{2\log n} = \frac{\log n + \log(1+\frac{1}{n})}{2\log n} \\
&= \frac{1}{2}\left\{1 + \frac{\log(1+\frac{1}{n})}{\log n}\right\} \to \frac{1}{2} \text{ as } n \to \infty.
\end{aligned}$$

$$\Rightarrow \sum_{n=1}^{\infty} \frac{\log n}{2^n} \text{ converges.}$$

(vi) Here $a_n = \frac{n^2}{n^3+1}$. Take $b_n = \frac{n^2}{n^3} = \frac{1}{n}$. Then

$$\lim_{n\to\infty} \frac{a_n}{b_n} = \lim_{n\to\infty} \frac{n^3}{n^3+1} = 1.$$

Since $\sum_{n=1}^{\infty} \frac{1}{n}$ diverges, it follows (limit comparison test) that $\sum_{n=1}^{\infty} \frac{n^2}{n^3+1}$ diverges.

EXERCISES 11.5

1. Discuss the convergence of the following series:

$(i)\quad \displaystyle\sum_{n=1}^{\infty} \frac{3n+1}{n-2}$ $(ii)\quad \displaystyle\sum_{n=2}^{\infty} \frac{1}{n(\ln n)^2}$

$(iii)\quad \displaystyle\sum_{n=1}^{\infty} \frac{n!}{n!+3}$ $(iv)\quad \displaystyle\sum_{n=2}^{\infty} \frac{1}{n(\ln n)^3},$

$(v)\quad \displaystyle\sum_{n=2}^{\infty} \frac{(\ln n)^2}{(\ln n)^2+\ln n},$ $(vi)\quad \displaystyle\sum_{n=2}^{\infty} \frac{(\ln n)^{\frac{5}{4}}}{(\ln n)^{\frac{5}{4}}+\ln n^2}.$

2. By using the Limit Comparison Test, or otherwise, determine which of the following converge and which diverge.

$(i)\quad \displaystyle\sum_{n=2}^{\infty} \frac{1}{(\ln n)^2}$ $(ii)\quad \displaystyle\sum_{n=1}^{\infty} \frac{(\ln n)^4}{n^3}$

$(iii)\quad \displaystyle\sum_{n=1}^{\infty} \frac{(\ln n)^2}{n^2}$ $(iv)\quad \displaystyle\sum_{n=1}^{\infty} \frac{(\ln n)^2}{n^{\frac{3}{4}}}$

$(v)\quad \displaystyle\sum_{n=2}^{\infty} \frac{1}{\sqrt{n}\ \ln n}$ $(vi)\quad \displaystyle\sum_{n=2}^{\infty} \frac{2}{3+\ln n}.$

3. Using the Ratio Test or the Root Test, or otherwise, determine which of the following series converge and which diverge.

$(i)\quad \displaystyle\sum_{n=1}^{\infty} \left(\frac{n-1}{n^2}\right)^n$ $(ii)\quad \displaystyle\sum_{n=2}^{\infty} \frac{n}{(\ln n)^n}$

$(iii)\quad \displaystyle\sum_{n=1}^{\infty} \frac{n^n}{(3^n)^2}$ $(iv)\quad \displaystyle\sum_{n=1}^{\infty} \frac{n\ln n}{3^n}$

$(v)\quad \displaystyle\sum_{n=1}^{\infty} n!e^{-n}$ $(vi)\quad \displaystyle\sum_{n=1}^{\infty} \frac{n^5}{5^n}$

$(vii)\quad \displaystyle\sum_{n=1}^{\infty} \frac{(n!)^n}{(n^n)^3}$ $(vii)\quad \displaystyle\sum_{n=1}^{\infty} e^{-n}(n^2).$

4. Which of the following series converge, and which diverge? Give reasons for your answers.

$$(i) \quad \sum_{n=1}^{\infty} \frac{3}{n\sqrt{n}} \qquad\qquad (ii) \quad \sum_{n=1}^{\infty} \frac{\ln(n+2)}{n+2}$$

$$(iii) \quad \sum_{n=1}^{\infty} \left(\frac{n+2}{n}\right) \qquad (iv) \quad \sum_{n=1}^{\infty} \frac{(n+2)!}{2!n!2^n}$$

$$(v) \quad \sum_{n=1}^{\infty} \left(1 - \frac{1}{2n}\right)^n$$

$(vi) \quad a_1 = 2, \; a_{n+1} = \frac{1+\cos n}{n} a_n$

$(vii) \quad a_1 = \frac{2}{3}, \; a_{n+1} = \frac{3n-2}{2n+3} a_n$

$(viii) \quad a_1 = \frac{1}{2}, \; a_{n+1} = \left(a_n\right)^{\frac{1}{n}}$

$(ix) \quad a_1 = 2, \; a_{n+1} = \frac{n}{n+2} a_n$

$(x) \quad a_1 = \frac{1}{3}, \; a_{n+1} = \left(a_n\right)^{n+1}.$

5. Suppose $\sum_{n=1}^{\infty} a_n$ is a convergent series of nonnegative numbers. Can anything be said about $\sum_{n=1}^{\infty} \frac{1}{n} a_n$? Justify your answer.

6. Suppose that $a_n > 0$ and $b_n > 0$ for all $n \geq N_0$ for some $N_0 \in \mathbb{N}$. Suppose

$(i) \lim \frac{a_n}{b_n} = \infty; \; (ii) \sum_{n=1}^{\infty} a_n$ converges.

Can anything be said about $\sum_{n=1}^{\infty} b_n$? Justify your answer.

7. (a) Prove that if $\sum_{n=1}^{\infty} a_n$ converges, then $\sum_{n=1}^{\infty} a_n^2$ converges.

   (b) For what values of α, if any, does the series

$$\sum_{n=2}^{\infty} \left(\frac{2}{n-1} - \frac{\alpha}{n+1}\right)$$

converge?

8. (a) Show that $\int_2^{\infty} \frac{dx}{x(\ln x)^p}$ converges if $p > 1$. Apply this

to discuss the convergence or divergence of the series

$$\sum_{n=2}^{\infty} \frac{1}{n(ln\ n)^p}.$$

(b) Use part (a) to determine which of the following series converge and which diverge.

$(i)\ \sum_{n=2}^{\infty} \frac{1}{n(ln\ n)};\ (ii)\ \sum_{n=2}^{\infty} \frac{1}{n(ln\ n)^{1.03}};\ (iii)\ \sum_{n=2}^{\infty} \frac{1}{n(ln\ n)^2};$

$(iv)\ \sum_{n=2}^{\infty} \frac{1}{n(ln\ n^2)}.$

Open Question: It is not yet known by anyone whether the series

$$\sum_{n=1}^{\infty} \frac{1}{n^3 sin^2 n}$$

converges or diverges!!

CHAPTER 12

Alternating Series, Absolute and Conditional Convergence, Rearrangement of Series.

12.1 Introduction

In chapter 11, we studied series of nonnegative terms. In this chapter, we consider series that may have negative terms. The simplest series of this type is one whose terms are alternately positive and negative; such a series is called an **alternating series**.

12.2 Alternating Series.

A series in which the terms are alternately positive and negative is an *alternating series*. It is convenient to write such a series as $\sum_{n=1}^{\infty} (-1)^{n-1} a_n$, where $a_n > 0$. Here are some examples.

$$-1 + 2 - 3 + 4 - 5 + 6... + (-1)^n n + ... \qquad (12.2.1)$$

$$1 - \frac{1}{2} + \frac{1}{3} - \frac{1}{4} + \frac{1}{5} - \frac{1}{6}... + \frac{(-1)^{n+1}}{n} + ... \qquad (12.2.2)$$

The series (12.2.2) is called the *alternating harmonic series.*

Theorem 12.2.1 (Alternating Series Test) *Let*

(i) $\lim a_n = 0,$
(ii) $a_n \geq a_{n+1},$
(iii) $a_n > 0,$ *for all* $n \geq N_0,$ *for some* $N_0 \in \mathbb{N}.$

Then, the alternating series
$$\sum_{n=1}^{\infty} (-1)^{n-1} a_n, \ converges.$$

Proof. If n is even, say $n = 2m$, then the sum of the first n terms $S_n \equiv S_{2m}$ is given by

$$\begin{aligned}
S_n \equiv S_{2m} &= (a_1 - a_2) + (a_3 - a_4) + ... + (a_{2m-1} - a_{2m}) \\
&= a_1 - (a_2 - a_3) - (a_4 - a_5) - ... \\
&\quad -(a_{2m-2} - a_{2m-1}) - a_{2m}.
\end{aligned}$$

By hypothesis, $\{a_n\}$ is monotone decreasing, so that each term in parenthesis in the first equality is nonnegative. The first equality then implies that S_{2m} is the sum of m nonnegative terms so that the sum is monotone nondecreasing. Hence $S_{2m+2} \geq S_{2m}$. The second equality shows that $S_{2m} \leq a_1$. Thus, we obtain that the sequence $\{S_{2m}\}$ is monotone nondecreasing and bounded above by a_1, so it converges. Let

$$\lim_{n \to \infty} S_{2m} = s. \qquad (12.2.3)$$

If n is odd, say $n = 2m+1$, then the sum of the first n terms is

$$S_n \equiv S_{2m+1} = S_{2m} + a_{2m+1}.$$

By hypothesis, $a_n \to 0$, as $n \to \infty$ so that

$$\lim_{m \to \infty} a_{2m+1} = 0$$

and, as $m \to \infty$,

$$S_n \equiv S_{2m+1} = S_{2m} + a_{2m+1} \to s. \qquad (12.2.4)$$

From (12.2.3) and (12.2.4) we obtain (exercises 5.3, Problem 12(a)) that

$$\lim_{n \to \infty} S_n = s. \quad \square$$

Corollary 12.2.2 *If* $\displaystyle\sum_{n=1}^{\infty}(-1)^{n-1}a_n, \quad a_n > 0$ *converges to the sum* s, *then* s *lies between* s_n *and* s_{n+1} *for all* n.

We have seen that $|s_{n+p} - s_n| \leq a_{n+1}$. Let $p \to \infty$ holding n fixed; then $|s - s_n| \leq a_{n+1}$. In other words, the error in taking the sum to be s_n is not greater than the modulus of the first term omitted.

Example 12.2.3

1. $1 - \frac{1}{2} + \frac{1}{3} - \frac{1}{4} + \cdots$ converges by the alternating series test. For, we have $\{a_n\} = \{\frac{1}{n}\}$ is a monotone decreasing null sequence.

2. Consider $\displaystyle\sum_{n=1}^{\infty}(-1)^{n+1}\frac{1}{n^2} = 1 - \frac{1}{4} + \frac{1}{9} - \frac{1}{16} + \cdots$ Here $\{a_n\} = \{\frac{1}{n^2}\}$ is monotone decreasing and $\frac{1}{n^2} \to 0$ as $n \to \infty$. Hence the given series converges by the alternating series test.

3. Consider $a_n = \frac{1}{\sqrt{n}+(-1)^{n-1}}$. Then

$$(-1)^n a_n = (-1)^n \left(\frac{\sqrt{n} - (-1)^{n-1}}{n-1}\right) = (-1)^n a_n + b_n.$$

$\sum_{n=1}^{\infty}(-1)^n a_n$ is convergent by the alternating series test

and $\sum_{n=1}^{\infty} b_n$ is divergent (the harmonic series). There-

fore $\sum_{n=1}^{\infty}(-1)^n a_n$ is divergent.

12.3   Convergence of the partial sum of an alternating series.

Fig 12.1 shows the manner in which an alternating series converges when it satisfies the condition of Theorem 12.1.1.

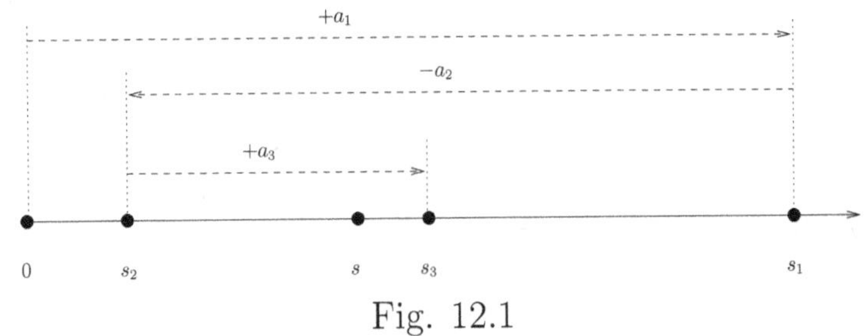

Fig. 12.1

The partial sums keep "jumping" the limit s as they go back and forth on $\mathbb{R}$, generally closing in on s as the terms a_n go to zero. Thus, if we stop at the nth partial sum, we know that the next term, a_{n+1}, will again cause us to "jump" the limit s in the positive or negative direction, depending on the sign carried by a_{n+1}. This then gives us a convenient bound for the *truncated error*. In particular, we have the following theorem.

Theorem 12.3.1 *(The Alternating Series Estimation The-orem). If the alternating series* $\sum_{n=1}^{\infty}(-1)^{n+1} a_n$ *converges, then the truncated error for the nth partial sum is less than* a_{n+1} *and has the same sign as the unused term.*

Example 12.3.2 *(The Alternating Harmonic Series). We have seen that the alternating harmonic series converges. We now want to find a bound for the truncation error after 299 terms.*

The alternating Series Estimation Theorem guarantees that the truncation error after 299 terms is less than $a_{299+1} = \frac{1}{300}$.

Example 12.3.3 *Consider the alternating series*

$$\sum_{n=1}^{\infty} (-1)^{n-1} \frac{1}{2^{n-1}} = 1 - \frac{1}{2} + \frac{1}{4-\frac{1}{8}} + \frac{1}{16} - \frac{1}{32}$$

$$+ \frac{1}{64} - \frac{1}{128} + \frac{1}{256} + \dots \quad (12.3.1)$$

Recall that Theorem 12.3.1 says that if we truncate the series after 6 terms (say), we discard a total that is positive and less than $\frac{1}{64}$. The sum of the first 6 terms is 0.6563 and the sum of the series (a G. P. with common ratio $(-\frac{1}{2})$) is

$$\frac{1}{1-r} = \frac{2}{3}.$$

Then, the difference is $\frac{2}{3} - 0.6563 = 0.0103$ which is less than $(\frac{1}{64}) = 0.02$.

12.4   Absolute and Conditional Convergence

It is known that both $\displaystyle\sum_{n=1}^{\infty} \left(-\frac{1}{2}\right)^{n-1}$ and $\displaystyle\sum_{n=1}^{\infty} \left(\frac{1}{2}\right)^{n-1}$ converge. The former being an alternating series while the latter (which is obtained by replacing the terms of the former by their absolute values) is a geometric series with ratio $r = \frac{1}{2}$. On

the other hand, $\displaystyle\sum_{n=1}^{\infty} \frac{(-1)^{n+1}}{n}$ converges while $\displaystyle\sum_{n=1}^{\infty} \frac{1}{n}$ diverges.
Behaviors like these lead us to the following definition.

Definition 12.4.1 *A series* $\displaystyle\sum_{n=1}^{\infty} a_n$ *is said to* converge absolutely *(or is* absolutely convergent*) if the corresponding series of absolute values,* $\displaystyle\sum_{n=1}^{\infty} |a_n|$ *converges.*
A series that converges but does not converge absolutely is said to converge conditionally *(or is* conditionally convergent*).*

Example 12.4.2

1. The alternating harmonic series

$$1 - \frac{1}{2} + \frac{1}{3} - \frac{1}{4} + \frac{1}{5} - \frac{1}{6} \cdots + \frac{(-1)^{n+1}}{n} + \cdots$$

   converges by the alternating series test but the corresponding series of absolute values (the harmonic series)

$$1 + \frac{1}{2} + \frac{1}{3} + \frac{1}{4} + \frac{1}{5} + \frac{1}{6} \cdots + \frac{1}{n} + \cdots$$

   diverges. Hence the alternating harmonic series

$$\sum_{n=1}^{\infty} \frac{(-1)^{n+1}}{n}$$

   converges conditionally.

2. The geometric series $\displaystyle\sum_{n=0}^{\infty} (-1)^n \frac{1}{2^n}$ converges (by the alternating series test) and the corresponding series of

absolute values, $\displaystyle\sum_{n=0}^{\infty}\frac{1}{2^n}$ (a geometric series with first term 1 and common ratio $\frac{1}{2}$) converges. Hence,

$$\sum_{n=0}^{\infty}(-1)^n\frac{1}{2^n}$$

converges absolutely.

3. $\displaystyle\sum_{n=2}^{\infty}(-1)^n\left(1+\frac{1}{n}\right)^n = \left(\frac{3}{2}\right)^2 + \left(\frac{4}{3}\right)^2 + \dots$ diverges since $\displaystyle\lim_{n\to\infty}\left(1+\frac{1}{n}\right)^n = e \neq 0.$

4. $\displaystyle\sum_{n=1}^{\infty}(-1)^{\frac{n(n+1)}{2}}\frac{1}{3^n} = -\frac{1}{3} - \frac{1}{3^2} + \frac{1}{3^3} - \dots,$ is not an alternating series but the corresponding series of absolute terms $\displaystyle\sum_{n=1}^{\infty}\frac{1}{3^n}$ is a geometric progression with first term $\frac{1}{3}$ and common ratio $\frac{1}{3}$ and so converges (to $\frac{\frac{1}{3}}{1-\frac{1}{3}} = \frac{1}{2}$). Hence $\displaystyle\sum_{n=1}^{\infty}(-1)^{\frac{n(n+1)}{2}}\frac{1}{3^n}$ converges absolutely.

Question: Why do we study *absolutely convergent* series?

Answer: They are important mainly for the following reasons:

(i) We have good tests for convergence of series with positive tests, so we can use them.

(ii) It turns out that a series converges absolutely, it converges. For example, we proved above that $\displaystyle\sum_{n=1}^{\infty}(-1)^{\frac{n(n+1)}{2}}\frac{1}{3^n}$

converges absolutely, we can then conclude that it converges. (Observe that since this is not alternating, we would not have gotten this conclusion by means of the alternating series test). We now prove the fact that an absolutely convergent series converges.

Theorem 12.4.2 *(The Absolute Convergence Test). If* $\sum_{n=1}^{\infty} |a_n|$ *converges then* $\sum_{n=1}^{\infty} a_n$ *converges.*

Proof. For each $n \in \mathbb{N}$,

$$-|a_n| \leq a_n \leq |a_n|$$

so that

$$0 \leq a_n + |a_n| \leq 2|a_n|.$$

Then, if $\sum_{n=1}^{\infty} |a_n|$ converges, $\sum_{n=1}^{\infty} 2|a_n|$ also converges, and by comparison test for series of nonnegative terms, $\sum_{n=1}^{\infty} (a_n + |a_n|)$ converges. But then

$$a_n = (a_n + |a_n|) - |a_n|$$

so that

$$\sum_{n=1}^{\infty} a_n = \sum_{n=1}^{\infty} (a_n + |a_n|) - \sum_{n=1}^{\infty} |a_n|,$$

and the RHS is the differences of two convergent series and is therefore convergent. This implies that $\sum_{n=1}^{\infty} a_n$ converges. $\square$

Example 12.4.3   *1. For the series* $\sum_{n=1}^{\infty} \dfrac{\cos n}{n^2}$, *the corresponding series of absolute value is* $\sum_{n=1}^{\infty} \dfrac{|\cos n|}{n^2}$, *which* *converges by the comparison test with $\sum\limits_{n=1}^{\infty} \dfrac{1}{n^2}$, (since $|cosn| \leq 1$ for every $n \in \mathbb{N}$). Hence, by Theorem 12.4.2, $\sum\limits_{n=1}^{\infty} \dfrac{cosn}{n^2}$, converges.*

2. *Let $p > 0$, then $\{\dfrac{1}{n^p}\}_{n=1}^{\infty}$ is a nonnegative decreasing sequence with limit zero. By the alternating series test, $\sum\limits_{n=1}^{\infty}(-1)^n\dfrac{1}{n^p}$ converges. This is called the alternating p–series, $p > 0$. Recall that the p–series $\sum\limits_{n=1}^{\infty}\dfrac{1}{n^p}$ converges if $p > 1$ and diverges for all other values of p. Hence, for $\sum\limits_{n=1}^{\infty}(-1)^n\dfrac{1}{n^p}$, the corresponding series of absolute values, $\sum\limits_{n=1}^{\infty}\dfrac{1}{n^p}$ converges if $p > 1$. So, for $p > 1$, the series $\sum\limits_{n=1}^{\infty}(-1)^n\dfrac{1}{n^p}$ converges absolutely. For $0 < p \leq 1$, the series converges conditionally.*

12.5 Rearrangement Theorem for Absolutely Convergent Series.

We prove the following theorem.

Theorem 12.5.1 *If $\sum\limits_{n=1}^{\infty} a_n$ converges absolutely, and $b_1, b_2, b_3 \cdots$, is any arrangement of the sequence $\{a_n\}$, then $\sum\limits_{n=1}^{\infty} b_n$ also converges absolutely. Furthermore, $\sum\limits_{n=1}^{\infty} b_n = \sum\limits_{n} a_n.$*

Proof. We first prove that $\sum_{n=1}^{\infty} b_n$ converges. Let $\epsilon > 0$ be given; let $\sum_{n=1}^{\infty} a_n = s$ and let $S_k = \sum_{n=1}^{k} a_n$ be the *nth* partial sum of $\sum_{n=1}^{\infty} a_n$. Since $\sum_{n=1}^{\infty} |a_n|$ converges, its "tail" is as small as we want. Hence, there exists $N_1 \in \mathbb{N}$ such that

$$\sum_{n=N_1}^{\infty} |a_n| < \frac{\epsilon}{2} \text{ and } |S_{N_2} - s| < \frac{\epsilon}{2},$$

for some $N_2 \geq N_1$, the second inequality following since $S_n \to s$. Now, since all the terms a_1, a_2, ..., a_{N_1} appear somewhere in the sequence $\{b_n\}$, there exists $N_3 \geq N_2$ such that for all

$$n \geq N_3, \ \sum_{k=1}^{n} b_k - S_{N_2}$$

is at most a sum of the terms a_m with $m \geq N_1$. Thus, for $n \geq N_3$,

$$\left| \sum_{k=1}^{n} b_k - s \right| \leq \left| \sum_{k=1}^{n} b_k - S_{N_2} \right| + |S_{N_2} - s|$$

$$\leq \sum_{k=N_1}^{\infty} |a_k| + |S_{N_2} - s| < \epsilon.$$

Thus, if $\sum_{n=1}^{\infty} a_n$ converges absolutely, then $\sum_{n=1}^{\infty} b_n$ converges absolutely and $\sum_{n=1}^{\infty} b_n = \sum_{n=1}^{\infty} a_n$. It is now easy to show that because $\sum_{n=1}^{\infty} |a_n|$ converges, $\sum_{n=1}^{\infty} |b_n|$ also converges to $\sum_{n=1}^{\infty} |a_n|$.

Remark 12.5.2 *If we rearrange infinitely many terms of a series that converges conditionally, we can get results that are far different from the sum of the original series.*

EXERCISES 12.1

1. Determine whether the following series converges or diverges:

   (i) $\displaystyle\sum_{n=2}^{\infty} \frac{1}{\log n}$ (ii) $\displaystyle\sum_{n=1}^{\infty} \frac{n^2}{2^n}$

   (iii) $\displaystyle\sum_{n=1}^{\infty} \frac{\log n}{n^3}$ (iv) $\displaystyle\sum_{n=1}^{\infty} \frac{|\sin n|}{n^2 + 1}$

   (v) $\displaystyle\sum_{n=1}^{\infty} \frac{\sqrt{n+1} - \sqrt{n}}{n}$ (vi) $\displaystyle\sum_{n=1}^{\infty} \frac{n!}{n^2}$

   (vii) $\displaystyle\sum_{n=1}^{\infty} \frac{(\log n)^3}{n^2}$ (viii) $\displaystyle\sum_{n=1}^{\infty} \frac{n!}{3^n}$

   (ix) $\displaystyle\sum_{n=1}^{\infty} \frac{\sin(n^2 x)}{n^2}$

   (x) $1 - \frac{1}{\sqrt{2}} + \frac{1}{\sqrt{3}} - \frac{1}{\sqrt{4}} + \cdots$.

2. Determine the convergence or otherwise of the following series:

   (i) $2 - \frac{3}{2} + \frac{4}{3} - \frac{5}{4} + \cdots$ (ii) $\displaystyle\sum_{n=2}^{\infty} \frac{(-1)^n}{\log n}$

   (iii) $\displaystyle\sum_{n=1}^{\infty} \frac{(-1)^n(n+1)}{n^2 + 5n + 6}$ (iv) $\displaystyle\sum_{n=1}^{\infty} \frac{(-1)^n n \pi^n}{e^{2n} + 1}$

   (v) $\displaystyle\sum_{n=1}^{\infty} \frac{(-1)^n}{n + 2 + (-1)^n}$

3. Which of the following alternating series converge and which diverge? Justify your answers:

(i) $\displaystyle\sum_{n=1}^{\infty}(-1)^{n+1}\frac{1}{n^3}$ (ii) $\displaystyle\sum_{n=1}^{\infty}(-1)^{n+1}\left(\frac{n}{5}\right)^n$

(iii) $\displaystyle\sum_{n=1}^{\infty}(-1)^{n+1}\frac{5^n}{n^5}$ (iv) $\displaystyle\sum_{n=2}^{\infty}(-1)^{n+1}\frac{1}{\log n}$

(v) $\displaystyle\sum_{n=1}^{\infty}(-1)^{n+1}\frac{\log n}{n}$ (vi) $\displaystyle\sum_{n=2}^{\infty}(-1)^{n+1}\frac{\log n}{\log n^3}$

(vii) $\displaystyle\sum_{n=1}^{\infty}(-1)^{n}\ln\left(1+\frac{2}{n}\right)$ (viii) $\displaystyle\sum_{n=1}^{\infty}(-1)^{n}\frac{\sqrt{n}+3}{n+2}$

(ix) $\displaystyle\sum_{n=1}^{\infty}(-1)^{n+1}\frac{3\sqrt{n}+2}{\sqrt{n}+2}$

4. Which of the following series converge absolutely, which converge conditionally and which diverge? Justify your answers:

(i) $\displaystyle\sum_{n=1}^{\infty}(-1)^{n+1}(0.2)^n$ (ii) $\displaystyle\sum_{n=1}^{\infty}(-1)^{n+1}\frac{(0.2)^n}{n}$

(iii) $\displaystyle\sum_{n=1}^{\infty}\frac{(-1)^n}{3+\sqrt{n}}$ (iv) $\displaystyle\sum_{n=1}^{\infty}(-1)^{n+1}\frac{n!}{3^n}$

(v) $\displaystyle\sum_{n=2}^{\infty}(-1)^{n}\frac{1}{\log n^2}$ (vi) $\displaystyle\sum_{n=1}^{\infty}(-1)^{n+1}\frac{n^2+3}{n^2+1}$

(vii) $\displaystyle\sum_{n=1}^{\infty}(-1)^{n}\frac{\log n}{n-\log n}$ (viii) $\displaystyle\sum_{n=1}^{\infty}\frac{\sqrt{n+1}-\sqrt{n}}{(-1)^n}$

(ix) $\displaystyle\sum_{n=1}^{\infty}\frac{(-1)^n}{\sqrt{n}+\sqrt{n+2}}$ (x) $\displaystyle\sum_{n=1}^{\infty}\frac{(-1)^n(n!)^2 5^n}{(2n+1)!}$

(xi) $\displaystyle\sum_{n=1}^{\infty}(-1)^{n}\frac{(2n)!}{2^n n! n}$.

5. By considering the series $\displaystyle\sum_{n=1}^{\infty}\frac{(-1)^n}{\sqrt{n}}$ and

$\displaystyle\sum_{n=1}^{\infty}\frac{(-1)^n}{\sqrt{n}+(-1)^n\log n}$, show that one of the series $\displaystyle\sum_{n=1}^{\infty}a_n,$

$\sum\limits_{n=1}^{\infty} b_n$ may be convergent and the other divergent even though $\frac{a_n}{b_n} \to 1$ as $n \to \infty$, when all the terms are not of the same sign.

6. Prove that a series is absolutely convergent if the series of positive terms and the series of negative terms are both convergent.

7. Prove that, if $\sum\limits_{n=1}^{\infty} a_n$ is conditionally convergent then the series of positive terms and the series of negative terms separately are both divergent.

8. Show that if $\sum\limits_{n=1}^{\infty} a_n$ diverges, then $\sum\limits_{n=1}^{\infty} |a_n|$ diverges.

9. Show that if $\sum\limits_{n=1}^{\infty} a_n$ converges absolutely, then

$$\left| \sum_{n=1}^{\infty} a_n \right| \leq \sum_{n=1}^{\infty} |a_n|.$$

10. Show that if $\sum\limits_{n=1}^{\infty} a_n$ and $\sum\limits_{n=1}^{\infty} b_n$ both converge absolutely, then so does

$$(a)\ \sum_{n=1}^{\infty} (a_n + b_n);\ (b)\ \sum_{n=1}^{\infty} (a_n - b_n);\ (c)\ \sum_{n=1}^{\infty} c a_n,$$

for any $c \in \mathbb{R}$.

11. Prove or give a counter example: $\displaystyle\sum_{n=1}^{\infty} a_n$ converges,

$\displaystyle\sum_{n=1}^{\infty} b_n$ converges implies $\displaystyle\sum_{n=1}^{\infty} a_n b_n$ converges.

12. Determine whether each of the following series converges conditionally, converges absolutely, or diverges. Justify your answer.

(i) $\displaystyle\sum_{n=1}^{\infty} \frac{(-3)^n}{n^2}$ (ii) $\displaystyle\sum_{n=1}^{\infty} \frac{(-3)^n}{2^n}$

(iii) $\displaystyle\sum_{n=2}^{\infty} \frac{(-1)^n}{\log n}$ (iv) $\displaystyle\sum_{n=2}^{\infty} \frac{(-1)^n}{n^2+1}$

(v) $\displaystyle\sum_{n=1}^{\infty} \frac{\sin n\pi}{\sqrt{n}}$ (vi) $\displaystyle\sum_{n=2}^{\infty} \frac{(-1)^n \log n}{n}$

13. Let $a_n = \frac{1}{\sqrt{n}} + \frac{(-1)^{n-1}}{n}$.
Show that,
(a) $a_n > 0 \ \forall \ n \geq 1$,
(b) $\lim a_n = 0$,
(c) $\sum (-1)^{n+1} a_n$ diverges.
Why does this not contradict Theorem 12.2.1.?

MISCELLANEOUS EXERCISES

1. (a) Carefully define what it means to say that an infinite series $\sum\limits_{n=1}^{\infty} a_n$ is convergent.

   (b) Decide for what values of x in the given intervals the following series are convergent.

   $$\sum_{n=1}^{\infty} \frac{(-1)^n x^n}{n[ln(x+1)]^2}, \quad (-3 < x < 17).$$

   $$\sum_{n=1}^{\infty} \frac{(-x)^n}{\sqrt{x}} \quad (-2 < x < 2).$$

2. Prove that $ln2 = \sum\limits_{k=1}^{\infty} \frac{(-1)^{k+1}}{k}$.

3. Let $\{a_n\}$ be a monotone decreasing sequence of positive real numbers converging to 0. Prove that $\sum\limits_{n=1}^{\infty} (-1)^n a_n$ converges.

4. Prove or give a counterexample:

   If $\sum\limits_{k=1}^{\infty} a_n < \infty$, and each $a_n \geq 0$, then $\lim na_n = 0$.

5. (a) Formulate in $\epsilon - \delta$ terms, the statement that f is *not* uniform continuous on $[0, 1]$.

   (b) Using first principles, prove that $g(x) = \sqrt{x}$ is uniformly continuous on $[0, 1]$. (If a theorem is used, it must be proved).

6. Consider the series defined by

   $$\sum \frac{1}{n^{\alpha}(\ln n)^{\beta}}, \quad n \geq 2,$$

   where α and β are real numbers. Prove that
   (a)   the series converges for $\alpha > 1$;
   (b)   the series diverges for $\alpha < 1$.

7. Prove that the series

$$\sum_{n=2}^{\infty} \frac{1}{n(\ln n)^{\beta}}$$

converges for $\beta > 1$ and diverges for $\beta \leq 1$.

8. Let $\{S_n\}$ be a sequence with general term given by

$$S_n = 1 + \frac{1}{2} + \cdots + \frac{1}{n} - \ln n.$$

Prove that the sequence $\{S_n\}$ is convergent.
(Hint: Consider the series $\sum a_n$ where $a_n = S_n - S_{n-1}$. The limit is called the Euler constant, generally denoted by γ, where $\gamma \approx 0.5772...$.

9. Study the convergence of the series $\sum a_n$ in each of the following cases:
   (a) $a_n = (1 - \frac{1}{\sqrt{n}})^n$
   (b) $a_n = \frac{n!}{n^n}$
   (c) $a_n = ne^{-n^2}$.

10. Consider the series $\sum a_n$ where

$$a_n = \sqrt{1 + \frac{(-1)^n}{n^{\beta}}} - 1, \quad n \geq 1, \quad \beta > 0.$$

   (a)   For what values of β is the series convergent?
   (b)   For values of β is the series <u>absolutely</u> convergent?

11. Prove that if $\{a_n\}$ is monotone decreasing to 0 and $\sum_{n=1}^{\infty} a_n$ converges, then $\lim_{n\to\infty} na_n = 0$.

   (b) Prove or disprove : if $a_n \geq 0$ for each n and $\sum_{n=1}^{\infty} a_n$ converges, then, $\lim_{n\to\infty} na_n = 0$.

   (c) Prove or disprove: if $\{a_n\}$ is monotone decreasing to 0 and $\lim_{n\to\infty} na_n = 0$, then $\sum_{n=1}^{\infty} a_n$ converges.

12. (a) Is $f(x) = \dfrac{sin x}{x}$ uniformly continuous on $0 < x < \pi$?

(b) For what positive values of α and β is

$$\sum_{n=2}^{\infty} \frac{(-1)^n (lnn)^\alpha}{n^\beta}$$

convergent?

13. Investigate the convergence of the series

$$\sum_{n=1}^{\infty} \frac{4^n n! n!}{(2n)!}.$$

14. For which real x does $\sum_{n=1}^{\infty} n^x x^n$ converge (justify your answer)?

15. Let

$$f(x) = \begin{cases} \dfrac{x}{2} + x^2 sin\left(\dfrac{1}{x}\right), & x \neq 0, \\ 0, & x = 0. \end{cases}$$

(a) Does the derivative $f'(x)$ exist everywhere ? Explain.

(b) Is there an open interval containing $x = 0$ in which $f(x)$ is increasing? justify your answer.

16. Let

$$a_n = \begin{cases} \dfrac{n}{2^n}, & n \text{ odd}, \\ 2^{-n}, & n \text{ even}. \end{cases}$$

Does $\sum_{n=1}^{\infty} a_n$ converge ? Justify your answer.

17. Suppose that $\{\rho_n\}$, $\{\sigma_n\}$ are two sequences of nonnegative numbers such that for some real number $N_0 \geq 1$, the following recursion inequality holds:

$$\rho_{n+1} \leq \rho_n + \sigma_n \ \forall \ n \geq N_0.$$

Prove that,
(a) if $\sum \sigma < \infty$, then $\lim \rho_n$ exists.
(b) if $\sum \sigma_n < \infty$ and ρ_n has a subsequence converging to zero, then

$$\lim \rho_n = 0.$$

18. Let $\{a_n\}$ be a sequence of nonnegative real numbers such that

$$a_{n+1} \leq (1 - \alpha_n)a_n + \alpha_n\beta_n, \quad n + 1, 2, 3, ...,$$

where $\{\alpha_n\} \subset [0,1], \{\beta_n\} \subset [0,1]$ and $\sum \alpha_n = \infty$, $\lim \beta_n = 0$. Prove that $a_n \to 0$ as $n \to \infty$.

19. Let $\{\lambda_n\}$ and $\{\gamma_n\}$ be two sequences of nonnegative numbers and $\{\alpha_n\}$ be a sequence of positive numbers satisfying the conditions $\sum_{n=1}^{\infty} \alpha_n = \infty$ and $\frac{\gamma_n}{\alpha_n} \to 0$ as $n \to \infty$. Let the recursive inequality

$$\lambda_{n+1} \leq \lambda_n - \alpha_n\psi(\lambda_n) + \gamma_n, \quad n = 1, 2, 3, ...,$$

be given where $\psi : [0, \infty) \to [0, \infty)$ is a strictly increasing continuous function such that it is positive on $(0, \infty)$ and $\psi(0) = 0$. Prove that $\lambda_n \to 0$ as $n \to \infty$.

20. Let $\{\lambda_n\}$ and $\{b_n\}$ be sequences of nonnegative numbers and
$\{\alpha_n\} \subseteq (0, 1)$ a sequence satisfying the conditions that $\{\lambda_n\}$ is bounded,
$\sum_{n=1}^{\infty} \alpha_n = \infty$ and $b_n \to 0$ as $n \to \infty$. Let the recursive inequality

$$\lambda_{n+1}^2 \leq \lambda_n^2 - 2\alpha_n\psi(\lambda_{n+1}) + 2\alpha_n\beta_n\lambda_{n+1}, \quad n = 1, 2, 3, ...,$$

be given where $\psi : [0, \infty) \to [0, \infty)$ is a strictly increasing continuous function such that it is positive on $(0, \infty)$ and $\psi(0) = 0$. Prove that $\lambda_n \to 0$ as $n \to \infty$.

Part II
The Riemann Integral

CHAPTER **13**

The Riemann Integral

13.1   Introduction

You are certainly familiar with the ordinary integral of calculus $\int_a^b f(x)dx$. This integral is designed to make sense from limits of sums of the form

$$\sum_{i=1}^{n} f(x_i)\Delta x_i.$$

Sums of this form have many important interpretations in physical sciences and engineering. One such interpretation is that of *area between the function f and the x−axis*. In this chapter, we shall use this interpretation to introduce a definition of the integral, $\int_a^b f(x)dx$, which is familiar from calculus and lends itself best to an interpretation as area.

We begin in the next section with some definitions and examples that will lead us to a definition of this integral.

13.2   Definitions and examples

We begin with the following concepts.

Definition 13.2.1 A partition P of the closed bounded interval $[a, b]$ is a finite set of points $P = \{x_0, x_1, ..., x_n\}$ of $[a, b]$ labelled so that $a = x_0 < x_1 < x_2 < ... < x_n = b$.

Definition 13.2.2 (Upper and Lower Darboux sums) . Let $f : [a, b] \to \mathbb{R}$ be a fixed *bounded* real-valued function defined on the interval $[a, b]$ (recall that this implies, in particular, that "$\sup f(x)$" and "$\inf f(x)$" exist for every $x \in [a, b]$). Let P be any partition of $[a, b]$ and let

$$M_i = \sup\{f(x) : x_{i-1} \leq x < x_i\},$$

$$m_i = \inf\{f(x) : x_{i-1} \leq x < x_i\}.$$

The *Upper and Lower Darboux sums* are defined by

$$U(f, P) = \sum_{i=1}^{n} M_i(x_i - x_{i-1}),$$

$$L(f, P) = \sum_{i=1}^{n} m_i(x_i - x_{i-1}),$$

respectively (see Fig. 13.1).

Remark 13.2.3 If $f(x) \geq 0$ for all $x \in [a, b]$, the upper sum $U(f, P)$ can be interpreted as the total area of a finite number of rectangles that *cover* the area under f (Fig 13.2(a)), and the lower sum $L(f, P)$ as the total area of a finite number of rectangles *under* the graph of f (see e.g., Fig. 13.2(b)).

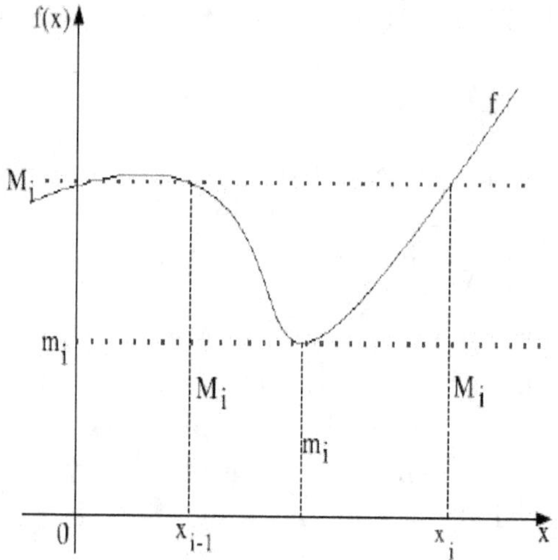

Fig. 13.1

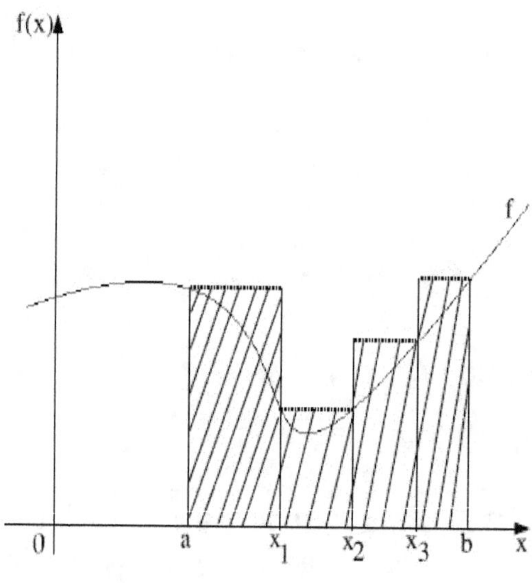

Upper Darboux Sum
Fig. 13.2(a)

We observe that m_i and M_i are "infs" and "sups" over the so-called half-open intervals, $[x_{i-1}, x_i)$. We have not used the closed and bounded interval $[x_{i-1}, x_i]$. This is to ensure

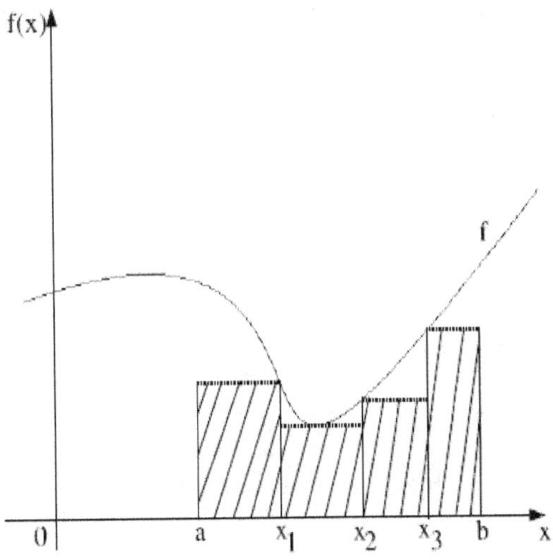

Lower Darboux Sum
Fig. 13.2(b)

that we partition the closed and bounded interval $[a, b]$ into
disjoint sets, since this is the approach generally used in the
study of another very important integral called the *Lebesque
integral* which is a topic for future studies.

Remark 13.2.4   (a) If $m \leq f(x) \leq M$ for all $x \in [a, b]$,
then $m \leq m_i \leq M_i \leq M$.

(b) From definition 13.2.2, one can easily see that, for any
partition P,
$$L(f, P) \leq U(f, P).$$

Before we define the Riemann integral, let us say a little
more about partitions of the interval $[a, b]$. We begin with
the following definition.

Definition 13.2.5 A partition Q is said to be finer than a
partition P (or is called a refinement of P) on the interval
$[a, b]$ if P and Q are partitions of $[a, b]$ and $P \subset Q$. This is
denoted by $P < Q$ or $Q > P$. In other words, Q is finer than
P if Q is a proper *superset* of P.

It is a fact that if we add one point to any given partition, then the new upper Darboux sum becomes less than the original one while the new lower Darboux sum becomes greater than the original one. More generally, if we replace a partition P by a finer partition Q, then the upper Darboux sum diminishes and the lower Darboux sum increases. We illustrate with the following example.

Example 13.2.6 Let $f(x) = x^3$ and $[a, b] = [0, 5]$, $P = \{0, 1, 2, 3, 5\}$, $Q = \{0, 1, 2, 3, 4, 5\}$. Then clearly f is bounded on $[0, 5]$. In fact, $0 \le f(x) \le 125$ $\quad \forall \quad x \in [0, 5]$. Since $P \subsetneq Q$, Q is finer than P. For the partition P we have (see Fig. 13.3(a)):

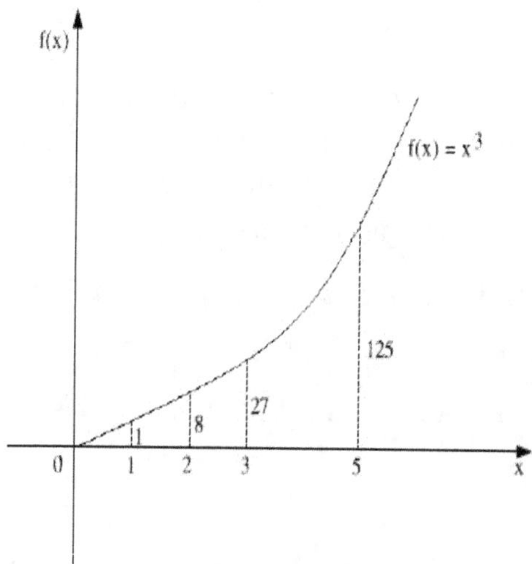

Fig. 13.3(a)

$m_i = 0, 1, 8, 27$ for $i = 1, 2, 3, 4$, respectively.

$M_i = 1, 8, 27, 125$ for $i = 1, 2, 3, 4$, respectively.

So, from (Fig. 13.3(a),)

$$U(f, P) \;=\; \sum_{i=1}^{4} M_i(x_i - x_{i-1}) = M_1(x_1 - x_0)$$
$$+ \; M_2(x_2 - x_1) + M_3(x_3 - x_2) + M_4(x_4 - x_3)$$
$$= 1 \times 1 + 8 \times 1 + 27 \times 1 + 125 \times 2 = 286.$$

$$L(f, P) \;=\; \sum_{i=1}^{4} m_i(x_i - x_{i-1}) = m_1(x_1 - x_0)$$
$$+ m_2(x_2 - x_1) + m_3(x_3 - x_2) + m_4(x_4 - x_3)$$
$$= 0 \times 1 + 1 \times 1 + 8 \times 1 + 27 \times 2 = 63.$$

For the finer partition Q, we have:

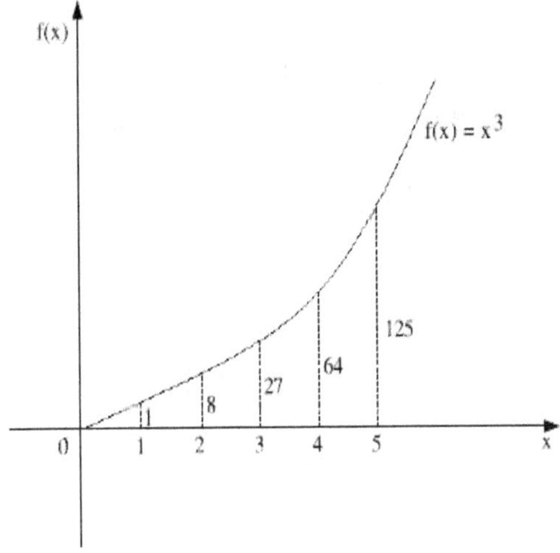

Fig. 13.3(b)

$m_i = 0, 1, 8, 27, 64$ for $i = 1, 2, 3, 4, 5$, respectively.

$M_i = 1, 8, 27, 64, 125$ for $i = 1, 2, 3, 4, 5$, respectively.

So, from (Fig.13.3(b)),

$$U(f,Q) = 1\times1+8\times1+27\times1+64\times1+125\times1 = 225,$$

$$L(f,Q) = 0\times1+1\times1+8\times1+27\times1+1\times64 = 100.$$

One can see that, in this example, the upper sum decreased from 286 to 225 while the lower sum increased from 63 to 100.

We now give a formal proof of this fact.

Proposition 13.2.7 *Let*

$$P = \{x_0, x_1, ..., x_n\}$$

and

$$Q = \{x_0, x^*, x_1, ..., x_n\}$$

be two partitions of the interval $[a, b]$ where Q contains only one point x^* more than P. Then, for $f : [a, b] \longrightarrow \mathbb{R}$ bounded, we have the following inequalities:

(a) $U(f,Q) \leq U(f,P)$, i.e., the upper sum diminishes.

(b) $L(f,Q) \geq L(f,P)$, i.e., the lower sum increases.

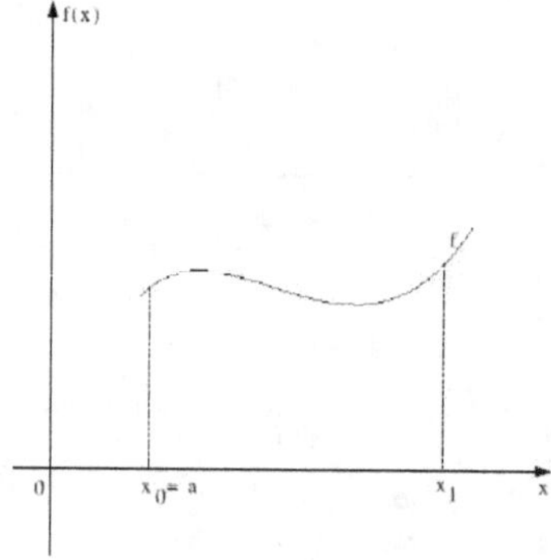

Fig. 13.4(a)

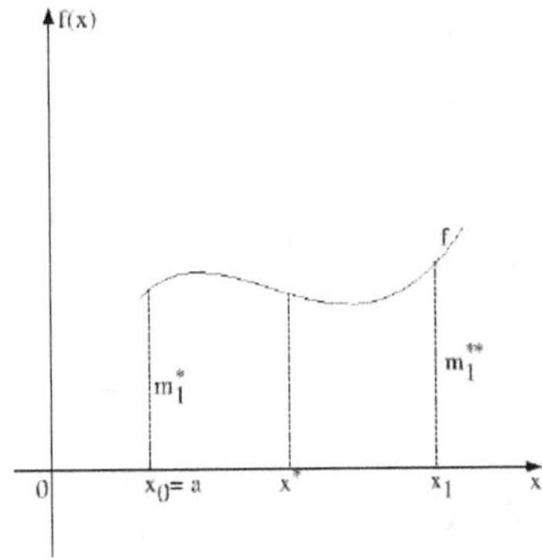

Fig. 13.4(b)

Proof. We give a proof of part (b) only. The proof of part (a) is similar. Let

$$m_1^* = \inf\{f(x) : x_0 \leq x < x^*\}.$$

$$m_1^{**} = \inf\{f(x) : x^* \leq x < x_1\}.$$

Recall that $m_1 = \inf\{f(x) : x_0 \leq x < x_1\}$. Then, $m_1^* \geq m_1$ and $m_1^{**} \geq m_1$ (since m_1^* and m_1^{**} are "infs" over smaller sets). Hence, on the interval $[x_0, x_1)$ we have:

$$m_1^*(x^* - x_0) + m_1^{**}(x_1 - x^*) \geq m_1(x_1 - x_0),$$

and the other terms of $L(f, Q)$ are the same as those of $L(f, P)$. Hence $L(f, Q) \geq L(f, P)$, verifying (b). $\square$

We now prove the following useful proposition.

Proposition 13.2.8 *Let $f : [a, b] \longrightarrow \mathbb{R}$ be bounded. If P and Q are partitions of $[a, b]$ and Q is a refinement of P, then*

$$L(f, P) \leq L(f, Q) \leq U(f, Q) \leq U(f, P).$$

Proof. Without loss of generality, we assume that Q has exactly one point x^* more than P. Let $x_{i-1} \leq x^* < x_i$. We prove first that $U(f, Q) \leq U(f, P)$. Let

$$M_i^* = \sup\{f(x) : x_{i-1} \leq x < x^*\}.$$

$$M_i^{**} = \sup\{f(x) : x^* \leq x < x_i\}.$$

Recall that $M_i = \sup\{f(x) : x_{i-1} \leq x < x_i\}$. Then, $M_i^* \leq M_i$ and $M^{**} \leq M_i$. So, we obtain that, since $x_i - x_{i-1} > 0$, $x^* - x_{i-1} > 0$, and $x_i - x^* > 0$, we have:

$$
\begin{aligned}
U(f, P) - U(f, Q) &= M_i(x_i - x_{i-1}) - M_i^*(x^* - x_{i-1}) \\
&\quad - M_i^{**}(x_i - x^*) \\
&\geq M_i(x_i - x_{i-1}) \\
&\quad - M_i(x^* - x_{i-1}) - M_i(x_i - x^*) = 0,
\end{aligned}
$$

so that $U(f, P) \geq U(f, Q)$. We already proved that $L(f, P) \leq L(f, Q)$, (Proposition 13.2.7). $\square$

Remark 13.2.9 It follows from Proposition 13.2.8 that *every* upper Darboux sum *with any partition* is greater than or equal to *any* lower Darboux sum with any partition. Furthermore, it is clear (from Proposition 13.2.8) that as a given partition is refined, the lower sum increases to give a better approximation of the area under the graph of f, while the upper sum decreases to do the same.

Let A denote the area of the region under a *nonnegative* bounded function f defined on the interval $[a, b]$. It is clear that $L(f, P) \leq A \leq U(f, Q)$ for *any* partitions P and Q of $[a, b]$ (Remark 13.2.9). As we take refinements of P, $L(f, P)$ increases (Proposition 13.2.8) and is bounded above by A (Fig. 13.2(b)). Hence "$\sup L(f, P)$" over all possible partitions P exists. Similarly, by taking refinements of Q, the upper sum $U(f, Q)$ decreases and is bounded below by area

A, Fig. 13.2(a). So, "$\inf U(f, Q)$" over all possible partitions Q exists. Consequently, we have the following inequality

$$\sup_{P} L(f, P) \leq A \leq \inf_{Q} U(f, Q).$$

Definition 13.2.10 Let $f : [a, b] \longrightarrow \mathbb{R}$ be a *bounded* function. Then f is called *Riemann integrable* if

$$\sup_{P} L(f, P) = \inf_{Q} U(f, Q)$$

where P and Q are any partitions and, $U(f, Q)$ and $L(f, P)$ have their usual meanings. In this case we write

$$\int_{a}^{b} f(x)dx = A = \sup_{P} L(f, P) = \inf_{Q} U(f, Q).$$

Remark 13.2.11 The variable x in the notation $\int_{a}^{b} f(x)dx$ is *a dummy,* and can be replaced by any other letter except f or d. Thus, we can write $\int_{a}^{b} f = \int_{a}^{b} f(x)dx = \int_{a}^{b} f(s)ds = \int_{a}^{b} f(t)dt$, and so on. Also, in definition 13.2.10, it was convenient to picture the area under *a nonnegative function f* so that $L(f, P)$ and $U(f, Q)$ represent areas of rectangles *inside* and *above* the region under f, respectively. However, one observes that none of the above inequalities depends on f being nonnegative. All that is needed to define the Riemann integral is that f be bounded on $[a, b]$. So, from now on, we shall assume only this.

Example 13.2.12 Let $f : [0, 1] \longrightarrow \mathbb{R}$ be defined by

$$f(x) = \begin{cases} 1, & \text{if } x \text{ is rational.} \\ 0, & \text{if } x \text{ is irrational.} \end{cases}$$

We show that f is *not* Riemann integrable.
Observe first that f is bounded on $[0, 1]$. In particular, $0 \leq f(x) \leq 1$ for all $x \in [0, 1]$. Since each subinterval $[x_{i-1}, x_i)$ contains both rational and irrational numbers, we have (using $x_0 = 0$ and $x_n = 1$):

$$m_i = 0 \text{ for all } i = 1, 2, ..., n.$$

$$M_i = 1 \text{ for all } i = 1, 2, ..., n.$$

Thus,

$$L(f, P) = \sum_{i=1}^{n} m_i(x_i - x_{i-1}) = 0;$$

$$U(f, P) = \sum_{i=1}^{n} M_i(x_i - x_{i-1}) = \sum_{i=1}^{n}(x_i - x_{i-1}) = x_n - x_0 = 1 - 0 = 1.$$

Hence,

$$0 = \sup_{P} L(f, P) \neq 1 = \inf_{P} U(f, P),$$

and f is *not* Riemann integrable.

Remark 13.2.13 Example 13.2.12 shows that there are *bounded* functions that are *not* Riemann integrable. So, we are faced with the problem of determining when the *Riemann integral* of a given *bounded* function exists. The answer is contained in our next proposition which will also serve as a constant *tool* for proving Riemann integrability.

Proposition 13.2.14 *A bounded function $f : [a, b] \to \mathbb{R}$ is Riemann integrable if and only if for arbitrary $\epsilon > 0$, there exists a partition P_ϵ of $[a, b]$ such that*

$$0 \leq U(f, P_\epsilon) - L(f, P_\epsilon) < \epsilon. \tag{13.2.1}$$

Proof. ($\Rightarrow$) Assume f is Riemann integrable (i.e., $\inf_{P} U(f, P) = \sup_{Q} L(f, Q)$) for arbitrary partitions of P and Q of $[a, b]$. We want to prove condition (13.2.1) holds. Let

$$\inf_{P} U(f, P) = \sup_{Q} L(f, Q) = \alpha, \text{ say.}$$

From the definition of "sup" "inf" and, we obtain that, given $\epsilon > 0$, $\exists$ partitions P_ϵ^1 and Q_ϵ^1 such that

$$\alpha - \frac{\epsilon}{2} < L(f, Q_\epsilon^1) \leq \alpha, \qquad (13.2.2)$$

$$\alpha \leq U(f, P_\epsilon^1) < \alpha + \frac{\epsilon}{2}. \qquad (13.2.3)$$

Define $P_\epsilon = P_\epsilon^1 \cup Q_\epsilon^1$. Then P_ϵ is a refinement of the partitions P_ϵ^1 and Q_ϵ^1. Hence, we have (using Proposition 13.2.8):

$$L(f, Q_\epsilon^1) \leq L(f, P_\epsilon) \leq U(f, P_\epsilon) \leq U(f, P_\epsilon^1) \qquad (13.2.4)$$

Using inequalities (13.2.2), (13.2.3) and (13.2.4), we obtain that

$$\begin{aligned}
0 \leq U(f, P_\epsilon) - L(f, P_\epsilon) \;&\leq\; U(f, P_\epsilon^1) - L(f, Q_\epsilon^1) \\
&<\; \alpha + \frac{\epsilon}{2} - \left(\alpha - \frac{\epsilon}{2}\right) = \epsilon,
\end{aligned}$$

verifying inequality (13.2.1).

($\Leftarrow$) Assume that condition (13.2.1) holds. We want to prove that f is Riemann integrable (i.e., $\inf_P U(f, P) = \sup_Q L(f, Q)$ where the "inf" and "sup" are taken over arbitrary partitions P and Q of $[a, b]$). But, for the partition P_ϵ, in condition (13.2.1), we know that

$$\inf_P U(f, P) \leq U(f, P_\epsilon) \text{ and } \sup_Q U(f, Q) \geq L(f, P_\epsilon).$$

Hence, we have that

$$\begin{aligned}
0 \;\leq\; &\inf_P U(f, P) - \sup_Q L(f, Q) \\
&\leq U(f, P_\epsilon) - L(f, P_\epsilon) < \epsilon \text{ (by condition (13.2.1))}.
\end{aligned}$$

This implies, for arbitrary $\epsilon > 0$, that

$$0 \leq \inf_P U(f, P) - \sup_Q L(f, Q) < \epsilon.$$

This further implies, since $\epsilon > 0$ is arbitrary, that

$$\inf_{P} U(f, P) = \sup_{Q} L(f, Q),$$

and so f is Riemann integrable. $\square$

For the rest of this book, we shall understand the term *integrable* to mean *Riemann integrability*.

We now illustrate Proposition 13.2.14 by using it to show that the function defined by $f(x) = x^2$ is integrable on $[0, 1]$ and that $\int_0^1 x^2 dx = \frac{1}{3}$.

Example 13.2.15 *The function defined by $f(x) = x^2$ is integrable on $[0, 1]$, and*

$$\int_0^1 x^2 dx = \frac{1}{3}.$$

Solution. For each $n \in \mathbb{N}$, consider the partition

$$P_n = \left\{ 0, \frac{1}{n}, \frac{2}{n}, \frac{3}{n}, ..., \frac{n-1}{n}, 1 \right\},$$

in which $(x_i - x_{i-1}) = \frac{1}{n}$ for each $i = 1, 2, ..., n$. Observe that $f(x) = x^2$ is bounded and is *an increasing function* on $[0, 1]$. Hence, on any subinterval $[\frac{i-1}{n}, \frac{i}{n})$ we have

$$m_i = \inf\{f(x) : x \in [\tfrac{i-1}{n}, \tfrac{i}{n})\} = f(\tfrac{i-1}{n}) = (\tfrac{i-1}{n})^2,$$

$$M_i = \sup\{f(x) : x \in [\tfrac{i-1}{n}, \tfrac{i}{n})\} = f(\tfrac{i}{n}) \le (\tfrac{i}{n})^2.$$

Hence,

$$L(f, P_n) = \sum_{i=1}^{n} \left(\frac{i-1}{n}\right)^2 \left(\frac{1}{n}\right) = \frac{1}{n^3}[1^2 + 2^2 + ... + (n-1)^2],$$

and

$$U(f, P_n) \leq \sum_{i=1}^{n} \left(\frac{i}{n}\right)^2 \left(\frac{1}{n}\right) = \frac{1}{n^3}[1^2 + 2^2 + \ldots + n^2],$$

so that

$$0 \leq U(f, P_n) - L(f, P_n) \leq \frac{1}{n} < \epsilon, \quad \text{if } n > \frac{1}{\epsilon}.$$

Thus, given any $\epsilon > 0$, choose $n > \frac{1}{\epsilon}$. Then $\exists$ a partition P_ϵ such that

$$0 \leq U(f, P_\epsilon) - L(f, P_\epsilon) < \epsilon,$$

provided $x_i - x_{i-1} < \epsilon \, \forall \, i = 1, 2, \ldots, n$. Hence, by Proposition 13.2.14, f is integrable.

Now, to find the value of $\int_0^1 x^2 dx$, we proceed as follows:

$$L(f, P_n) \leq \int_0^1 x^2 dx \leq U\left(f, P_n\right).$$

Thus,

$$\frac{1}{n^3}\left[1^2 + 2^2 + \ldots + (n-1)^2\right] \leq \int_0^1 x^2 dx \leq \frac{1}{n^3}\left[1^2 + 2^2 + \ldots + n^2\right].$$

This implies

$$\frac{1}{3}\left(\frac{n-1}{n}\right)\left(\frac{2n-1}{2n}\right) \leq \int_0^1 x^2 dx \leq \frac{1}{3}\left(\frac{n+1}{n}\right)\left(\frac{2n+1}{2n}\right),$$

so that as $n \to \infty$, (using Sandwich theorem) we obtain that $\int_0^1 x^2 dx = \frac{1}{3}$.

EXERCISES 13.1

1. Show that the constant function $f(x) = k$ for all $x \in [a, b]$ is integrable and that $\int_a^b k dx = k(b - a)$.

2. Prove that the function defined by $f(x) = x$ is integrable on the interval $[a, b]$ and that $\int_a^b x\,dx = \frac{1}{2}(b^2 - a^2)$.

SUMMARY

We summarize the key results of this chapter for ease of remembering.

S1. A bounded function $f : [a, b] \to \mathbb{R}$ is Riemann integrable if and only if for arbitrary $\epsilon > 0$, there exists a partition P_ϵ of $[a, b]$ such that

$$0 \leq U(f, P_\epsilon) - L(f, P_\epsilon) < \epsilon. \tag{13.2.5}$$

S2. An example of a *bounded* real-valued function $f : [a, b] \to \mathbb{R}$ that is *not* Riemann integrable is given by

$$f(x) = \begin{cases} 1, & \text{if } x \text{ is rational;} \\ 0, & \text{if } x \text{ is irrational.} \end{cases}$$

264

CHAPTER **14**

Basic Properties of Riemann Integral

In this chapter, we use the definition of the Reimann integral
to establish some basic properties of the integral.

14.1   Two basic theorems

Theorem 14.1.1   (a) *Any constant function* $f : [a, b] \to$
$\mathbb{R}$ *defined by*

$$f(x) = c, \text{ where c is a constant,}$$

is integrable on $[a, b]$, *and*

$$\int_a^b c \, dx = (b - a) \, c.$$

(b) *Any monotonically nonincreasing (or nondecreasing)
function* $f : [a, b] \to \mathbb{R}$ *is integrable on* $[a, b]$.

(c) *Any continuous function* $f : [a, b] \to \mathbb{R}$ *is integrable on*
$[a, b]$.

Proof.

(a) This is Problem 1, Exercises 13.1.

(b) Let f be a nonincreasing function on $[a, b]$.
Let

$$P = \{a = x_0 < x_1 < x_2 < ... < x_i < ... < x_n = b\}$$

be an arbitrary partition of $[a, b]$. Since f is nonincreasing,

$$M_i = \sup\{f(x) : x_{i-1} \le x < x_i\} = f(x_{i-1}),$$

$$m_i = \inf\{f(x) : x_{i-1} \le x < x_i\} \ge f(x_i).$$

Therefore,

$$U(f, P) = \sum_{i=1}^{n} M_i\,(x_i - x_{i-1}) = \sum_{i=1}^{n} f(x_{i-1})\,(x_i - x_{i-1}),$$

$$L(f, P) = \sum_{i=1}^{n} m_i\,(x_i - x_{i-1}) \ge \sum_{i=1}^{n} f(x_i)\,(x_i - x_{i-1}).$$

Now,

$$U(f, P) - L(f, P)$$

$$\le \sum_{i=1}^{n} (f(x_{i-1}) - f(x_i))\,(x_i - x_{i-1})$$

$$\le \max_{1 \le i \le n}(x_i - x_{i-1})\,(f(x_0) - f(x_n))$$

$$= \max_{1 \le i \le n}(x_i - x_{i-1})\,(f(a) - f(b)).$$

Observe that $f(a) - f(b) \ge 0$. Hence, given any $\epsilon > 0$, if we choose P_ϵ for which $\max_{1 \le i \le n}(x_i - x_{i-1}) < \frac{\epsilon}{1+(f(a)-f(b))}$, then

$$U(f, P_\epsilon) - L(f, P_\epsilon) < \epsilon.$$

Hence, f is integrable. The proof for nondecreasing f is similar and is left as an easy exercise.

(c) Let $f : [a, b] \to \mathbb{R}$ be continuous. Then f is *uniformly* continuous on $[a, b]$. Hence, given $\epsilon > 0$, there exists $\delta = \delta(\epsilon) > 0$ such that for all x, $y \in [a, b]$ with $|x - y| \leq \delta$, we have $|f(x) - f(y)| < \frac{\epsilon}{1+(b-a)}$.
Let

$$P = \{a = x_0 < x_1 < x_2 < ... < x_i < ... < x_n = b\}$$

be any partition of $[a, b]$. Then,

$$U(f, P) = \sum_{i=1}^{n} M_i \, (x_i - x_{i-1}),$$

$$L(f, P) = \sum_{i=1}^{n} m_i \, (x_i - x_{i-1}),$$

where M_i and m_i have their usual meanings. Hence,

$$\begin{aligned}
U(f, P) - L(f, P) &= \sum_{i=1}^{n} (M_i - m_i)) \, (x_i - x_{i-1}) \\
&\leq \max_{1 \leq i \leq n} (M_i - m_i) \sum_{i=1}^{n} (x_i - x_{i-1}) \\
&= \max_{1 \leq i \leq n} (M_i - m_i)(b - a).
\end{aligned}$$

So, given $\epsilon > 0$, choose a partition P_ϵ such that $\max\limits_{1 \leq i \leq n} (x_i - x_{i-1}) < \delta$. Then

$$\max_{x, y \in [x_{i-1}, x_i]} \left| f(x) - f(y) \right| < \frac{\epsilon}{1 + (b - a)}, \quad i = 1 \cdots, n.$$

In particular, $\max\limits_{1 \leq i \leq n} |M_i - m_i| < \frac{\epsilon}{1+(b-a)}$. Hence, $U(f, P) - L(f, P) < \epsilon$, and so f is integrable on $[a, b]$. $\quad \square$

Theorem 14.1.2 *If f and g are two integrable functions on $[a, b]$ and $k \in \mathbb{R}$, then,* (*i*) $(k\,f)$ *is integrable on* $[a,b]$ *and*

$$\int_a^b (k\,f(x))\ dx = k\ \int_a^b f(x)\ dx.$$

(*ii*) $(f+g)$ *is integrable on* $[a,b]$, *and*

$$\int_a^b (f(x)+g(x))\ dx = \int_a^b f(x)\ dx + \int_a^b g(x)\ dx.$$

(*iii*) *If* $a < c < b$, *then* f *is integrable on* $[a,c]$ *and* f *is integrable on* $[c,b]$. *We also have*

$$\int_a^b f(x)dx = \int_a^c f(x)dx + \int_c^b f(x)dx.$$

(*iv*) *If* $f(x) \le g(x)$ *for all* x *in* $[a,b]$, *then*

$$\int_a^b f(x)dx \le \int_a^b g(x)dx.$$

(*v*) $|f|$ *is integrable on* $[a,b]$ *and*

$$\left|\int_a^b |f(x)|dx\right| \le \int_a^b |f(x)|dx.$$

(*vi*) f^2 *and* fg *are integrable on* $[a,b]$.

Proof.
(*i*) Let

$$P = \{a = x_0 < x_1 < x_2 < ... < x_i < ... < x_n = b\}$$

be an arbitrary partition of $[a,b]$. Let

$$M_i = \sup\{f(x) : x_{i-1} \le x < x_i\},$$

$$m_i = \inf\{f(x) : x_{i-1} \le x < x_i\}.$$

Let

$$M_i^* = \sup\left\{(k\,f)(x) : x_{i-1} \le x < x_i\right\},$$

$$m_i^* = \inf\left\{(k\,f)(x) : x_{i-1} \le x < x_i\right\}.$$

Then,

$$
\begin{aligned}
U(k\,f, P) \\
= \sum_{i=1}^{n} M_i^*(x_i - x_{i-1}) \qquad\qquad &(14.1.1)\\
= \sum_{i=1}^{n} \sup\left\{(k\,f)(x) : x_{i-1} \le x < x_i\right\}(x_i - x_{i-1})\\
= k \sum_{i=1}^{n} \sup\left\{f(x) : x_{i-1} \le x < x_i\right\}(x_i - x_{i-1})\\
= k \sum_{i=1}^{n} M_i\,(x_i - x_{i-1}) = k\,U(f, P).
\end{aligned}
$$

Similarly, $L(k\,f, P) = k\,L(f, P)$. Since f is integrable, given any $\epsilon > 0$, there exists a partition P_ϵ such that $U(f, P_\epsilon) - L(f, P_\epsilon) < \frac{\epsilon}{|k|+1}$. Using the above computations, we obtain that

$$
\begin{aligned}
U(k\,f, P_\epsilon) - L(k\,f, P_\epsilon) &= k\,(U(f, P_\epsilon) - L(f, P_\epsilon))\\
&< \frac{|k|\,\epsilon}{|k|+1}\\
&< \epsilon.
\end{aligned}
$$

Hence, $(k\,f)$ is integrable on $[a, b]$. Moreover,

$$
\begin{aligned}
\int_a^b (k\,f)(x)\,dx &= \sup_P L(k\,f, P)\\
&= k \sup_P L(f, P) = k \int_a^b f(x)\,dx.
\end{aligned}
$$

(ii) Let $P = \{a = x_0 < x_1 < ... < x_i < ... < x_n = b\}$ be an arbitrary partition of $[a, b]$. Let

$$M_i^f = \sup \{f(x) : x_{i-1} \leq x < x_i\},$$

$$m_i^f = \inf \{f(x) : x_{i-1} \leq x < x_i\},$$

$$M_i^g = \sup \{g(x) : x_{i-1} \leq x < x_i\},$$

$$m_i^g = \inf \{g(x) : x_{i-1} \leq x < x_i\}.$$

Let

$$M_i = \sup \{f(x) + g(x) : x_{i-1} \leq x < x_i\}$$

$$m_i = \inf \{f(x) + g(x) : x_{i-1} \leq x < x_i\}.$$

Since f and g are integrable, given any $\epsilon > 0$, there exist partitions P_ϵ^f and P_ϵ^g of $[a, b]$ such that

$$U(f, P_\epsilon^f) - L(f, P_\epsilon^f) < \frac{\epsilon}{2}, \qquad (14.1.2)$$

$$U(g, P_\epsilon^g) - L(g, P_\epsilon^g) < \frac{\epsilon}{2}. \qquad (14.1.3)$$

But, for any partition P of $[a, b]$, using properties of "inf" and "sup" we obtain that

$$
\begin{aligned}
U(f + g, P) &= \sum_{i=1}^{n} M_i (x_i - x_{i-1}) \\
&\leq \sum_{i=1}^{n} (M_i^f + M_i^g)(x_i - x_{i-1}) \\
&= U(f, P) + U(g, P). \qquad (14.1.4)
\end{aligned}
$$

Similarly

$$L(f + g, P) \geq L(f, P) + L(g, P). \qquad (14.1.5)$$

Let $P_\epsilon = P_\epsilon^f \cup P_\epsilon^g$. Then P_ϵ is a refinement of both P_ϵ^f and P_ϵ^g. Thus, from inequalities (14.1.2) and (14.1.3), and Proposition 13.2.8

$$\begin{aligned}
0 \leq\ & U(f+g, P_\epsilon) - L(f+g, P_\epsilon) \\
\leq\ & U(f, P_\epsilon^f) + U(g, P_\epsilon^g) - L(f, P_\epsilon^f) - L(g, P_\epsilon^g) \\
<\ & \epsilon.
\end{aligned}$$

Since $\epsilon > 0$ is arbitrary, $(f+g)$ is integrable. To compute $\int_a^b (f+g)$ we use the inequalities (14.1.4) and (14.1.5). From

$$\begin{aligned}
L(f, P_\epsilon) + L(g, P_\epsilon) \leq\ & L(f+g, P_\epsilon) \\
\leq\ & U(f+g, P_\epsilon) \\
\leq\ & U(f, P_\epsilon) + U(g, P_\epsilon),
\end{aligned}$$

we obtain that, for any partition P,

$$\begin{aligned}
\int_a^b (f+g) =\ & \inf_P U(f+g, P) \\
\leq\ & U(f+g, P_\epsilon) \\
\leq\ & U(f, P_\epsilon) + U(g, P_\epsilon) \\
<\ & L(f, P_\epsilon) + \frac{\epsilon}{2} + L(g, P_\epsilon) + \frac{\epsilon}{2} \\
\leq\ & \sup L(f, P) + \sup L(g, P) + \epsilon \\
=\ & \int_a^b f + \int_a^b g + \epsilon.
\end{aligned}$$

Since $\epsilon > 0$ is arbitrary, we obtain that

$$\int_a^b (f+g) \leq \int_a^b f + \int_a^b g.$$

Now, replacing f and g by $(-f)$ and $(-g)$ in this inequality, respectively, and using part (i) we obtain that

$$\int_a^b (f+g) \geq \int_a^b f + \int_a^b g,$$

so that

$$\int_a^b (f+g) = \int_a^b f + \int_a^b g,$$

as required.

(iii) Let $a < c < b$ and $\epsilon > 0$, then there exists a partition P_ϵ of $[a,b]$ such that $U(f, P_\epsilon) - L(f, P_\epsilon) < \epsilon$ since f is integrable on $[a,b]$. Define P'_ϵ as $P'_\epsilon := P_\epsilon \cup \{c\}$, then P'_ϵ is a partition of $[a,b]$ which is a refinement of P'_ϵ. Therefore,

$$U(f, P'_\epsilon) \leq U(f, P_\epsilon), \quad \text{and} \quad L(f, P_\epsilon) \leq L(f, P'_\epsilon).$$

Thus

$$U(f, P'_\epsilon) - L(f, P'_\epsilon) \leq U(f, P_\epsilon) - L(f, P_\epsilon) < \epsilon.$$

That is, $U(f, P'_\epsilon) - L(f, P'_\epsilon) < \epsilon$. Now if we let P''_ϵ be the set containing all points of $P'\epsilon$ less than or equal to c, then P''_ϵ is a partition of $[a,c]$ and it follows from definition that

$$U(P''_\epsilon, f) - L(f, P''_\epsilon) \leq U(f, P'_\epsilon) - L(f, P'_\epsilon) < \epsilon.$$

Thus f is integrable on $[a,c]$. By similar arguments we also have that f is integrable on $[c,b]$. For the concluding part, let P_1 and P_2 be partitions of $[a,c]$ and $[c,b]$, respectively. If $Q := P_1 \cup P_2$, then Q is a partition of $[a,b]$ by direct computation we obtain

$$U(f, Q) = U(f, P_1) + U(f, P_2).$$

This implies

$$\inf_P U(f, P) \leq U(f, P_1) + U(f, P_2),$$

where "inf" is taken over all partitions P of $[a,b]$. Also taking "inf" over P_1 and P_2 we get

$$\inf_P U(f, P) \leq \inf_{P_1} U(f, P_1) + \inf_{P_2} U(f, P_2).$$

Therefore, using integrability of f on $[a, b]$, $[a, c]$ and $[c, b]$), we have

$$\int_a^b f(x)dx \leq \int_a^c f(x)dx + \int_c^b f(x)dx. \qquad (14.1.6)$$

Similarly, $L(f, Q) = L(f, P_1) + L(f, P_2)$. This implies

$$L(f, P_1) + L(f, P_2) \leq \sup_P L(f, P),$$

where "sup" is taken over all partitions P of $[a, b]$. Also taking "sup" over P_1 and P_2 we get

$$\sup_{P_1} U(f, P_1) + \sup_{P_2} U(f, P_2) \leq \sup_P U(f, P), \qquad (14.1.7)$$

that is, by integrability of f on $[a, b]$, $[a, c]$ and $[c, b]$,

$$\int_a^c f(x)dx + \int_c^b f(x)dx \leq \int_a^b f(x)dx, \qquad (14.1.8)$$

Hence (14.1.6) and (14.1.8) give

$$\int_a^b f(x)dx = \int_a^c f(x)dx + \int_c^b f(x)dx.$$

(iv) For any partition

$$P = \{a = x_0, x_1, x_3, \cdots, x_n = b\}$$

of $[a, b]$, let $I_i := [x_{i-1}, x_i)$, $i = 1, 2, 3, \cdots, n - 1$ and let $I_n := [x_{n-1}, x_n]$. Define

$$M_i^f := \sup_{x \in I_i} f(x), \quad M_i^g := \sup_{x \in I_i} g(x).$$

Since for each $x \in I_i$, $f(x) \leq g(x)$, we have

$$M_i^f \leq M_i^g \text{ and } m_i^f \leq m_i^g \text{ for } i = 1, 2, 3, \cdots, n.$$

This implies

$$M_i^f(x_i - x_{i-1}) \le M_i^g(x_i - x_{i-1}), \quad i = 1, 2, 3, \cdots, n.$$

Therefore,

$$\sum_{i=1}^{n} M_i^f(x_i - x_{i-1}) \le \sum_{i=1}^{n} M_i^g(x_i - x_{i-1}),$$

that is

$$U(f, P) \le U(g, P).$$

Taking "inf" over all partitions P, we have

$$\inf_P U(f, P) \le \inf_P U(g, P).$$

Therefore, by integrability of f and g on $[a, b]$, we get

$$\int_a^b f(x)dx \le \int_a^b g(x)dx.$$

(v) For any partition

$$P = \{a = x_0, x_1, x_3, \cdots, x_n = b\}$$

of $[a, b]$, let $I_i := [x_{i-1}, x_i)$, $i = 1, 2, 3, \cdots, n - 1$ and let $I_n := [x_{n-1}, x_n]$. Define

$$M_i := \sup_{x \in I_i} f(x), \quad m_i := \inf_{x \in I_i} f(x),$$

$$M_i' := \sup_{x \in I_i} |f(x)|, \quad m_i' := \inf_{x \in I_i} |f(x)|.$$

Then for each $x, y \in I_i$,

$$f(x) - f(y) \le M_i - m_i \text{ for } i = 1, 2, 3, \cdots, n.$$

This implies that for $i = 1, 2, 3, \cdots, n$,

$$|f(x)| - |f(y)| \le |f(x) - f(y)| \le M_i - m_i.$$

Taking "sup" over x and y in I_i, we obtain

$$M_i' - m_i' \leq M_i - m_i, \quad i = 1, 2, 3, \cdots, n.$$

Therefore, for any partition P of $[a, b]$,

$$U(|f|, P) - L(|f|, P) \leq U(f, P) - L(f, P). \quad (14.1.9)$$

Now let $\epsilon > 0$. Then by integrability of f on $[a, b]$, there exists a partition P_ϵ of $[a, b]$ such that

$$U(f, P_\epsilon) - L(f, P_\epsilon) < \epsilon.$$

Therefore, using (14.1.9) we have

$$U(|f|, P_\epsilon) - L(|f|, P_\epsilon) < \epsilon.$$

Hence $|f|$ is integrable on $[a, b]$. For the remaining part, we know

$$-|f(x)| \leq f(x) \leq |f(x)|, \quad \forall x \in [a, b].$$

It follows from (ii) and (iv), therefore, that

$$-\int_a^b |f(x)|dx \leq \int_a^b f(x)dx \leq \int_a^b |f(x)|dx.$$

This is equivalent to

$$\left| \int_a^b |f(x)|dx \right| \leq \int_a^b |f(x)|dx.$$

This concludes proof of (v).

(vi) Since f is bounded (as an integrable function), there exists $K > 0$ such that $|f(x)| \leq K$ for all $x \in [a, b]$. For any partition

$$P = \{a = x_0, x_1, x_3, \cdots, x_n = b\}$$

of $[a, b]$, let

$$I_i := [x_{i-1}, x_i), \quad i = 1, 2, 3, \cdots, n-1$$

and let

$$I_n := [x_{n-1}, x_n].$$

Define

$$M_i := \sup_{x \in I_i}(f(x))^2, \quad m_i := \inf_{x \in I_i}(f(x))^2,$$

$$M_i' := \sup_{x \in I_i}|f(x)|, \quad m_i' := \inf_{x \in I_i}|f(x)|.$$

Then for each $x, y \in I_i$,

$$
\begin{aligned}
(f(x))^2 - (f(y))^2 &= (|f(x)| + |f(y)|)(|f(x)| - |f(y)|) \\
&\leq 2K(|f(x)| - |f(y)|) \\
&\leq 2K(M_i' - m_i') \text{ for } i = 1, 2, 3, \cdots, n.
\end{aligned}
$$

This implies

$$(f(x))^2 - (f(y))^2 \leq 2K(M_i - m_i), \text{ for } i = 1, 2, 3, \cdots, n.$$

Taking "sup" over x and y in I_i, we obtain

$$M_i - m_i \leq 2K(M_i' - m_i'), \quad i = 1, 2, 3, \cdots, n.$$

Therefore, for any partition P of $[a, b]$,

$$U(f^2, P) - L(f^2, P) \leq 2K(U(|f|, P) - L(|f|, P)). \tag{14.1.10}$$

Now let $\epsilon > 0$. Since $|f|$ is integrable (from (v) above), there exists a partition P_ϵ of $[a, b]$ such that

$$U(p, |f|) - L(p, |f|) < \frac{\epsilon}{2K}.$$

From this and (14.1.10) we get

$$U(f^2, P_\epsilon) - L(f^2, P_\epsilon) \leq 2KU(|f|, P_\epsilon) - L(|f|, P_\epsilon) < \epsilon.$$

Hence f^2 is integrable. To show fg is integrable given f and g are integrable, we use (i), (ii), the first part (of (vi)) and the identity

$$fg = \frac{1}{4}((f+g)^2 - (f-g)^2).$$

This concludes the proof. $\square$

EXERCISES 14.1

1. Let $f : [a, b] \to \mathbb{R}$ be a nondecreasing function. Prove that f is integrable on $[a, b]$.

14.2   Fundamental theorem of calculus

The fundamental of calculus has two forms, basically stated in (a) and (b) below. Recall what you learned in high school that: "if a function is well behaved", then

(a) The derivative of the integral of a function is the original function.

(b) The integral of the derivative of a function is again the same function, up to an additive constant
i.e., differentiation is the opposite of integration and vice-versa.

We illustrate statements (a) and (b).

For (a), if, for example, $f : [a, b] \to \mathbb{R}$ is integrable (here f is our original function) and we define

$$F(x) = \int_a^x f(t)dt \ \forall \ x \in [a, b],$$

so that F is the integral of f. Then, statement (a) asserts that the derivative of F is the original function f, i.e.,

$$F'(x) = \frac{d}{dx}\left(\int_a^x f(t)dt\right) = f(x) \ \forall \ x \in [a,b].$$

This is one of the fundamental theorems of calculus.

Example 14.2.1 We know that $t \to t^2$ is integrable over any closed and bounded interval. Let

$$F(x) = \int_0^x t^2 dt.$$

The Fundamental Theorem of Calculus, part (a), asserts that

$$F'(x) = x^2.$$

Of course, we could have evaluated directly to obtain $F(x) = \frac{1}{3}t^3\big|_0^x = \frac{1}{3}x^3$ so that $F'(x) = x^2$, the same result.

Part (b). If $f : [a,b] \to \mathbb{R}$ is differentiable and we define

$$G(x) = \frac{df}{dx},$$

the statement of part (b) asserts that the integral of G is the original function f, i.e.,

$$\int G(x)dx \equiv \int \left(\frac{df}{dx}\right)dx = f(x).$$

We illustrate with the following example.

Example 14.2.2 Let $f : [a,b] \to \mathbb{R}$ be defined by $f(x) = x^2 + 3x + 1$. Then, $f'(x) = 2x + 3$.

Part (b) asserts that if we integrate $f'(x)$, we obtain our original function f. But we know from high school that

$$\int_a^x f'(x)dx = \int_a^x (2t+3)dt = x^2 + 3x - (a^2 + 3a).$$

Under the additional condition that $f(a) = a^2 + 3a + 1 = 0$, we obtain

$$\int_a^x f'(x)dx = x^2 + 3x + 1 \equiv f(x).$$

Remark 14.2.3 Each part of the conditions (a) and (b) tells us that *differentiation and integration are inverse operations.* Historically, the operation of integration was developed in the process of finding the area under a curve; and the operation of differentiation was developed to find the slope of a curve at any point on the curve.

Consequently, the operations of integration and differentiation were developed to solve seemingly unrelated problems. The proof of the fact that, under suitable conditions, one is the inverse of the other was one of the important contributions of Newton and Leibnitz.

In our discussion of the Riemann integral, we defined $\int_a^b f$ only when $a < b$. We now extend this condition and let

$$\int_a^b f = -\int_b^a f;$$

and,

$$\int_a^a f = 0.$$

With these extensions, we now state and prove the *two parts* of the Fundamental Theorem of Calculus.

Theorem 14.2.4 (The Fundamental Theorem of Calculus, (a)). *Let*

$$f : [a, b] \to \mathbb{R}$$

be integrable on $[a, b]$. *For each* $x \in [a, b]$, *let*

$$F(x) = \int_a^x f(t)dt.$$

Then,
(i) F is uniformly continuous on $[a, b]$.
*(ii) If f is continuous at $c \in (a, b)$, then F is differentiable
at c and*

$$F'(c) = f(c).$$

Proof (i) Since f is Riemann integrable, it is bounded (we defined Riemann integrals for bounded functions). So, there exists a constant $M > 0$ such that $|f(t)| \leq M \ \forall \ t \in [a, b]$. Furthermore,

$$\left| F(y) - F(x) \right| = \left| \int_y^x f(t)dt \right| \leq \max_{a \leq t \leq b} |f(t)| \int_x^y dt \leq M|y - x|.$$

Now, given any $\epsilon > 0$, choose $\delta = \frac{\epsilon}{M+1}$, so that if $|x - y| < \delta$, then,

$$\left| F(y) - F(x) \right| < M\delta = \frac{M\epsilon}{M + 1} < \epsilon.$$

Hence, F is uniformly continuous on $[a, b]$.
(ii) Let f be continuous at $x = c \in [a, b]$. Then, given any $\epsilon > 0$, there exists $\delta = \delta(\epsilon) > 0$ such that

$$t \in (a, b), \ |t - c| < \delta \Rightarrow |f(t) - f(c)| < \epsilon.$$

Since $f(c)$ is constant, we may write

$$f(c) = \frac{1}{x - c} \int_c^x f(c)dt, \ \ x \neq c.$$

Thus, for any $x \in (a, b)$ with $0 < |x - c| < \delta$, we have,

$$\begin{aligned}
\left| \frac{|F(x) - F(c)|}{x - c} - f(c) \right| &= \left| \frac{1}{x - c} \int_c^x [f(t) - f(c)]dt \right| \\
&\leq \frac{1}{|x - c|} \int_c^x |f(t) - f(c)|dt \\
&< \frac{1}{|x - c|} \int_c^x \epsilon dx; \\
&\quad \text{since } |t - c| < \delta \\
&< \frac{1}{|x - c|} \epsilon |x - c| = \epsilon.
\end{aligned}$$

Since $\epsilon > 0$ is arbitrary, we conclude that

$$F'(c) = \lim_{x \to c} \frac{F(x) - F(c)}{x - c} = f(c). \quad \Box$$

Remark 14.2.5 *(i) We first observe that only integrability of f (which implies the boundedness of f) is required for the F to be uniformly continuous on $[a, b]$.*

(ii) If f is continuous at $x = c \in (a, b)$, (which then implies it is integrable), then F becomes differentiable at $x = c$ with $F'(c) = f(c)$.

Observe that the main use we made of the fact that f is continuous at $x = c$ is to obtain the estimate:

$$t \in (a, b), |t - c| < \delta \Rightarrow |f(t) - f(c)| < \epsilon.$$

We now prove the second part of the Fundamental Theorem of Calculus.

Theorem 14.2.6 (The Fundamental Theorem of Calculus, (b)). *If*

(i) f is differentiable on $[a, b]$, and,

(ii) f' is integrable on $[a, b]$, then,

$$\int_a^b f'(t)dt = f(b) - f(a).$$

Proof Since f is differentiable on $[a, b]$, we have that $f'(t)$ exists for any $t \in [a, b]$. Let $P = \{x_0, x_1, x_3, ..., x_n\}$ be any partition of $[a, b]$. By applying the Mean Value Theorem to each sub-interval $[x_{i-1}, x_i]$ we obtain points $t_i \in (x_{i-1}, x_i)$ such that

$$f(x_i) - f(x_{i-1}) = f'(t_i)(x_i - x_{i-1}).$$

Thus, we have,

$$f(b) - f(a) = \sum_{i=1}^{n}[f(x_i) - f(x_{i-1})] = \sum_{i} f'(t_i)(x_i - x_{i-1}).$$

Since $m_i^{f'} \leq f'(t_i) \leq M_i^{f'}$ for all i, we obtain that

$$L(f', P) \leq f(b) - f(a) \leq U(f', P).$$

Since this inequality holds for each partition P, we also have

$$\sup_{P} L(f', P) \leq f(b) - f(a) \leq \inf_{P} U(f', P).$$

Since f' is integrable on $[a, b]$ we have,

$$\sup_{P} L(f', P) = \inf_{P} U(f') = \int_{a}^{b} f'(t)dt,$$

so that

$$\int_{a}^{b} f'(t)dt = f(b) - f(a). \qquad \square$$

14.3   Integration by parts Formula

We now justify our usual integration by parts formula.

Corollary 14.3.1 (Integration by parts). *Suppose f and g are differentiable on $[a, b]$ and f' and g' are integrable on $[a, b]$. Then,*

$$\int_{a}^{b} (fg') = \left[fg\right]_{a}^{b} - \int_{a}^{b} f'g.$$

Proof. Let $h = fg$ so that $h' = fg' + f'g$. Now, f and g are differentiable $\Rightarrow f$ and g are continuous (justify that fg' and $f'g$ are integrable). Hence h' is integrable on $[a, b]$. Then, the fundamental theorem of calculus yields that $\int_a^b h' = h(b) - h(a)$, i.e.,

$$\int_a^b fg' + \int_a^b f'g \;=\; h(b) - h(a)$$

$$= f(b)g(b) - f(a)g(a) = \left[fg\right]_a^b$$

so that, solving for $\int_a^b fg'$ we obtain that

$$\int_a^b (fg') = \left[fg\right]_a^b - \int_a^b f'g,$$

completing proof of the corollary.

$\square$

14.4   Integration by substitution

The following theorems are needed in order to evaluate some integrals. In fact, they give the justification for using the popular technique of integration by substitution used in calculus.

Theorem 14.4.1 (Integration by substitution (a)) *Let* $f : [a, b] \to \mathbb{R}$, $g : J :\to \mathbb{R}$ *be two real-valued functions such that J is an interval containing $f([a, b])$. Suppose f is differentiable, f' is integrable and g is continuous. Then*

$$\int_a^b g(f(t))f'(t)dt = \int_{f(a)}^{f(b)} g(t))dt.$$

Proof.   Define

$$G : J \to \mathbb{R} \text{ by } G(t) = \int_{f(a)}^t g(s)ds$$

and define

$$F : [a, b] \to \mathbb{R} \text{ by } F(t) = G \circ f(t).$$

Since g is continuous, then by theorems 14.2.4 and 14.2.6 (Fundamental Theorems of Calculus (a) and (b)), G is differentiable with $G' = g$. Therefore, F is differentiable and by using chain rule we have

$$F'(t) = G'(f(t))f'(t) = g(f(t))f'(t).$$

Also integrability of F' follows from the continuity of $g \circ f$ and integrability of f'. Therefore, using theorem 14.2.6 (Fundamental Theorems of Calculus (b)) again, we have

$$\int_{f(a)}^{f(b)} g(f(t))f'(t)dt = \int_{f(a)}^{f(b)} G'(t)dt$$
$$= G(f(b)) - G(f(a))$$
$$= \int_{f(a)}^{f(b)} g(t))dt.$$

Example 14.4.2 *Evaluate the integral $\int_0^2 \sqrt{4 - x^2}dx$.*

Solution. If we define

$$f : \left[0, \frac{\pi}{2}\right] \to \mathbb{R} \text{ by } f(x) = 2\sin x$$

and

$$g : [0, 2] \to \mathbb{R} \text{ by } g(x) = \sqrt{4 - x^2},$$

then we have f is differentiable, f' and g are continuous. Also since f is increasing, $f([0, \frac{\pi}{2}]) = [0, 2]$. So by theorem 14.4.1, we have

$$\int_0^2 \sqrt{4 - t^2}dt = \int_{f(0)}^{f(\frac{\pi}{2})} g(t))dt = \int_0^{\frac{\pi}{2}} g(f(t))f'(t)dt.$$

Now

$$\int_0^{\frac{\pi}{2}} g(f(t))f'(t)dt = \int_0^{\frac{\pi}{2}} 2\sqrt{1 - \sin^2 t}\, 2\cos t\, dt = 4\int_0^{\frac{\pi}{2}} \cos^2 t\, dt.$$

Since $\cos^2 t = \dfrac{1}{2}(1 + \cos 2t)$, we have

$$4\int_0^{\frac{\pi}{2}} \cos^2 t\, dt = 4\int_0^{\frac{\pi}{2}} \frac{1}{2}(1 + \cos 2t)dt = \pi.$$

Theorem 14.4.3 (Integration by substitution (b)) *Let*

$$f : [a, b] \to \mathbb{R}, \quad g : J :\to \mathbb{R}$$

be two real-valued functions such that J is an interval containing $f([a, b])$. Suppose f is differentiable, f' and g are continuous. Suppose further that $f'(t) \neq 0$ for all $t \in [a, b]$. Then

$$\int_a^b g(f(t))dt = \int_{f(a)}^{f(b)} g(u)(f^{-1})'(u)du.$$

Proof. We observe that since $f'(t) \neq 0$, $\forall t \in [a, b]$, by theorem 10.3.2, f^{-1} exists on $f([a, b])$. Also f^{-1} is continuous. Furthermore, the continuity of f' implies continuity of $(f^{-1})'$. Now define

$$F : [a, b] \to \mathbb{R} \text{ by } F(t) = \int_a^t g(f(s))ds$$

and define

$$G : f([a, b]) \to \mathbb{R} \text{ by } G(u) = F \circ f^{-1}(u).$$

Using continuity of g and f, we get using theorem 14.2.4 (Fundamental Theorem of Calculus(a)), that F is differentiable with $F'(t) = g(f(t))\ \forall t \in [a, b]$. Hence, by differentiability of f^{-1}, G is diffrentiable with

$$\begin{aligned} G'(u) &= G'(f^{-1}(u))(f^{-1})'(u) \\ &= g(f(f^{-1}(u)))(f^{-1})'(u) \end{aligned}$$

for all $u \in f([a, b])$. By definition of G,

$$G(f(b)) = F(f^{-1}(f(b))) = F(b) = \int_a^b g(f(s))ds. \quad (14.4.1)$$

On the other hand, we obtain using theorem 14.2.6 (Fundamental Theorem of Calculus(b)), that

$$G(f(b)) = \int_{f(a)}^{f(b)} G'(u)du - G(f(a))$$

$$= \int_{f(a)}^{f(b)} g(u)(f^{-1})'(u). \quad (14.4.2)$$

The result follows from (14.4.1) and (14.4.2).

Example 14.4.4 *Evaluate the integral* $\displaystyle\int_1^9 \frac{dt}{2 + \sqrt{t}}.$

Solution. Define

$$f : [1, 9] \to \mathbb{R} \text{ by } f(x) = \sqrt{x}$$

and

$$g : [1, 3] \to \mathbb{R} \text{ by } g(x) = \frac{1}{2 + x}.$$

Then, we have f is differentiable, f' is continuous, $f'(x) = \frac{1}{2\sqrt{x}} > 0 \; \forall \; x \in [1, 9]$ and g are continuous. Also , $f([1, 9]) \subseteq [1, 3]$. So by theorem 14.4.3, we have

$$\int_1^9 \frac{dt}{2 + \sqrt{t}} = \int_1^9 g(f(t))dt$$

$$= \int_{f(1)}^{f(9)} g(u)(f^{-1})'(u)du$$

$$= \int_1^3 \frac{2u}{2 + u}du$$

$$= 2\int_1^3 \left(1 - \frac{2}{2 + u}\right)du. \quad (14.4.3)$$

Integral (14.4.3) can easily be evaluated.

CHAPTER **15**

Sequences of real-valued functions

15.1 Pointwise convergence

15.1.1 Introduction and definition

In this chapter, we shall define a kind of convergence of a sequence of real-valued functions defined on a subset D of $\mathbb{R}$ - *pointwise* convergence. Pointwise convergence is the natural extension of the convergence of sequences and series of real numbers, but it lacks many important desirable properties. A stronger notion of convergence called *uniform convergence* will be defined in section 15.3 and will be shown to possess these properties. We begin with the following definition.

Definition 15.1.1 *Let* $\{f_n\}$ *be a sequence of real-valued functions* $f_n : D \subset \mathbb{R} \to \mathbb{R}$ *defined on a subset* D *of* $\mathbb{R}$. *Then,* $\{f_n\}$ *is said to converge*

$$\boxed{\textit{pointwise on } D \textit{ to } f : D \subset \mathbb{R} \to \mathbb{R}}$$

if and only if

$$\boxed{\forall \; \epsilon > 0, \; \textbf{and given } x \in D,}$$

$\exists N = N(\epsilon, x) \in \mathbb{N}$ *such that*

$$|f_n(x) - f(x)| < \epsilon \quad \forall \; n \geq N.$$

Observe that N depends on both x and ϵ. If we keep $\epsilon > 0$ fixed and choose consecutively various values of x, the N will also vary, according to the x we choose.

In studying *sequences of real numbers*, in order to fix ideas, it is customary to list a few elements of a given sequence and then to use our knowledge of the real numbers to guess what the limit is (when there is likelyhood that the sequence converges). For example, $\{\frac{1}{n}\}_{n=1}^{\infty}$ is listed as $1, \frac{1}{2}, \frac{1}{3}, \ldots$ and one easily guesses that as $n \to \infty$, the sequence converges to 0. For *sequences of functions*, it is sometimes useful to sketch, when this is possible, on the same diagram, the first few elements of a given sequence. In this section, we sketch a few terms in some examples. We begin with the following example.

Example 15.1.2 For $n \in \mathbb{N}$, define $f_n : [0, 1] \longrightarrow [0, 1]$ by

$$f_n(x) = x^n \; \forall x \in [0, 1].$$

Then, for $x = 0$, $f_n(0) = 0 \; \forall n$. Also, $f_n(1) = 1 \forall \; n \geq 1$.
Claim.
(i) $f_n(0) \to 0$, as $n \to \infty$.
(ii) $f_n(1) \to 1$, as $n \to \infty$.
(iii) $f_n(x) \to 0 \; \forall \; x \in (0, 1)$ as $n \to \infty$.

Proof of Claim.
(i) Let $\epsilon > 0$ be given and $x = 0$. Then,

$$|f_n(0) - 0| = 0 < \epsilon,$$

for *any* $n \geq 1$. So, we can choose $N = N(\epsilon, 0) = 1$. Hence, $\{f_n\}$ converges to f, where $f(x) = 0 \ \forall \, x \in [0, 1]$.

(*ii*) Let $\epsilon > 0$ be given and $x = 1$. Then,

$$|f_n(1) - 1| = 0 < \epsilon,$$

for *any* $n \geq 1$. So, we can choose $N = N(\epsilon, 1) = 1$. Hence, $\{f_n\}$ converges to f, where $f(x) = 1 \, \forall \, x \in [0, 1]$.

(*iii*) Let $\epsilon > 0$ be given and $x \in (0, 1)$. Observe that $x \in (0, 1) \Rightarrow |x| < 1 \Rightarrow \frac{1}{|x|} > 1$ (since $x \neq 0$. Let $\frac{1}{|x|} = 1 + p_x$ for some $p_x > 0$. Then,

$$\frac{1}{|x|^n} = (1 + p_x)^n > 1 + np_x > np_x \ \forall \ n > 1,$$

i.e., $0 \leq np_x|x|^n < 1$ for all integers $n > 1$, so that

$$0 \leq |x|^n < \frac{1}{np_x}, n > 1, x \neq 0.$$

But this inequality also holds for $x = 0$. Hence, it holds for all x such that $|x| < 1$.

We now compute as follows:

$$|f_n(x) - 0| = |x|^n < \frac{1}{np_x} < \epsilon,$$

if $n > \frac{1}{p_x \epsilon}$. Thus, given $\epsilon > 0$, and $x \in (0, 1)$ we can choose $N = N(x, \epsilon) = 1 + [\frac{1}{p_x \epsilon}]$, where $[\cdot]$ denotes the *greatest integer function*. Then, for all $n \geq N$, we have $|f_n(x) - 0| < \epsilon$, and so $\{f_n\}$ converges to f given by $f(x) = 0$ for all $x \in (0, 1)$. Hence $\{f_n\}$ converges *pointwise* to the function $f : [0, 1] \longrightarrow \mathbb{R}$ defined by

$$f(x) = \begin{cases} 1, & x = 1, \\ 0, & 0 \leq x < 1. \end{cases}$$

The first three terms of the sequence $\{f_n(x)\}_{n=1}^{\infty}$ are sketched in Fig. 15.1.

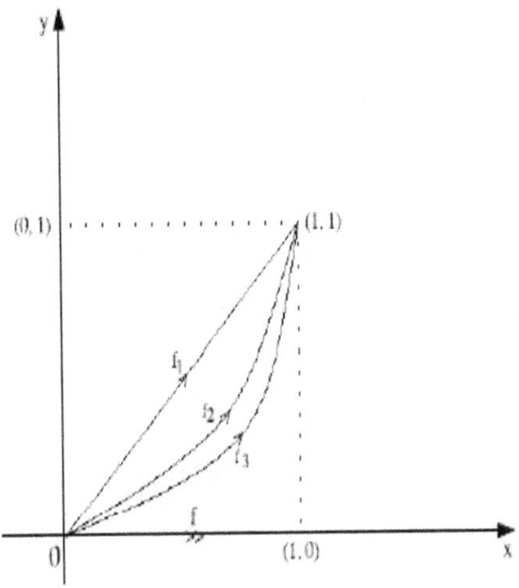

Fig. 15.1

Example 15.1.3 For $n \in \mathbb{N}$, define $f_n : [-1, 1] \longrightarrow [0, 1]$ by

$$f_n(x) = \begin{cases} 0, & -1 \leq x \leq 0, \\ nx, & 0 \leq x \leq \frac{1}{n}, \\ 1, & \frac{1}{n} \leq x \leq 1. \end{cases}$$

The first three elements of the sequence $\{f_n\}_{n=1}^{\infty}$ are sketched in Fig. 15.2(a); and the nth and $(m)^{\text{th}}$ elements with $m > n$ are sketched in Fig. 15.2(b).

It is now not difficult to *guess* that as $n \to \infty$, the sequence $\{f_n\}$ converges pointwise to a function f defined by

$$f(x) = \begin{cases} 0, & -1 \leq x \leq 0, \\ 1, & 0 < x \leq 1. \end{cases}$$

The function f is sketched in Fig. 15.3.

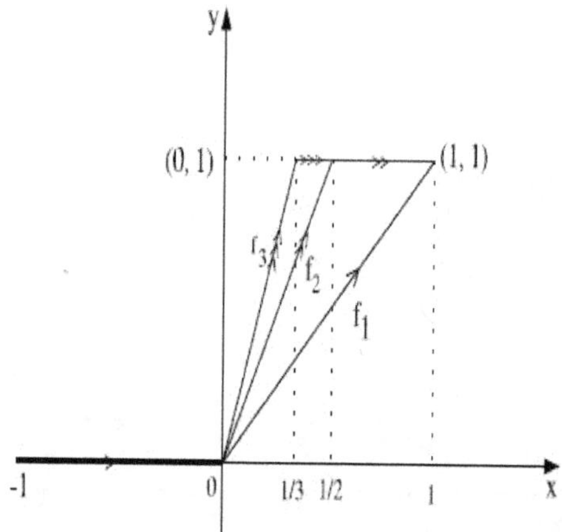

Fig. 15.2(a)

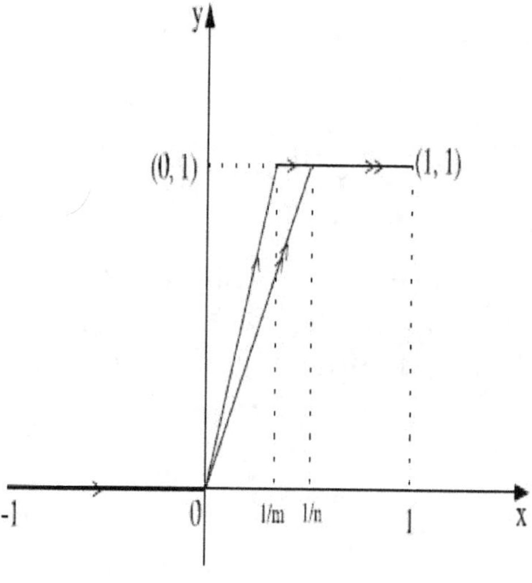

Fig. 15.2(b)

More formally, if $-1 \leq x \leq 0$, then $f_n(x) = 0 \ \forall \ n \geq 1$ so
$f_n(x) \to 0$ as $n \to \infty$. For $0 < x \leq 1$, there exists $n_x \in \mathbb{N}$

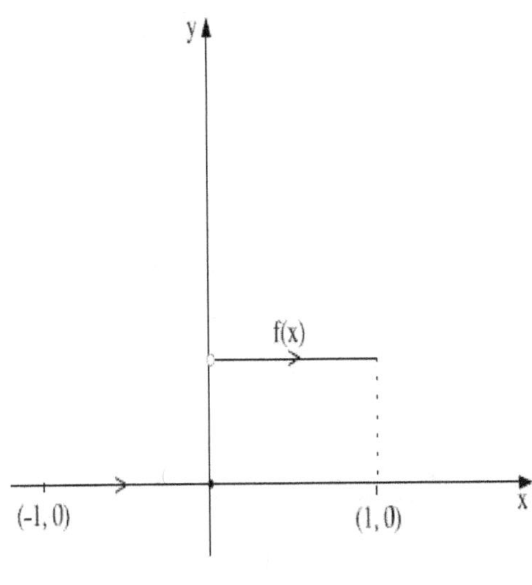

Fig. 15.3

such that $\frac{1}{n} \leq x \; \forall n \geq n_x$. Hence, $f_n(x) = 1 \forall \; n \geq n_x$ and so $f_n(x) \to 1$ as $n \to \infty$. Therefore, $\{f_n\}$ converges *pointwise* to the function f defined above.

Example 15.1.4 For each $n \in \mathbb{N}$, let the nth term, f_n, of a sequence of functions be the one sketched in Fig. 15.4.

(*i*) Sketch the first 3 terms of $\{f_n\}$.

(*ii*) Write down the explicit formula for f_n.

(*iii*) *Guess* the pointwise limit of f_n as $n \to \infty$.

Solution. (*i*) This is left as an easy exercise for the reader. (*ii*) Clearly f_n maps $[0, 4]$ into $[0, 1]$. Moreover, $f_n(x) = 0$ for all $0 \leq x \leq 2$. Now, for the line segment A to B, we observe that the coordinates of B are $(2 + \frac{2}{n}, 1)$. So, the slope m of AB is given by $m = \frac{n}{2}$. Hence, the equation of the line joining AB is given by

$$y - 0 = \frac{n}{2}(x - 2) \text{ or } y = \frac{n}{2}(x - 2).$$

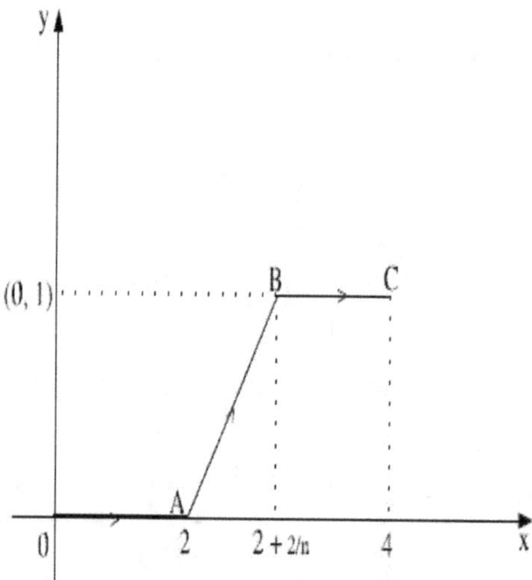

Fig. 15.4

Hence, we can now define f_n explicitly as follows:

$$f_n(x) = \begin{cases} 0, & \text{if } 0 \le x \le 2, \\ \frac{n}{2}(x-2), & \text{if } 2 \le x \le 2 + \frac{2}{n}, \\ 1, & \text{if } 2 + \frac{2}{n} \le x \le 4. \end{cases}$$

(iii) To guess the pointwise limit of $\{f_n\}$, we observe that as $n \to \infty$, the interval $2 \le x \le 2 + \frac{2}{n}$ "shrinks" to $x = 2$. Thus, as the interval shrinks to $x = 2$, $f_n(x) = \frac{n}{2}(x-2) \to 0$ as $n \to \infty$. Also, on the interval $2 + \frac{2}{n} \le x \le 4$, we observe that $f_n(x) \equiv 1$ and so $f_n(x) \to 1$ as $n \to \infty$ on this interval. Hence, we guess that

$$\lim_{n \to \infty} f_n(x) = \begin{cases} 0, & \text{if } 0 \le x \le 2, \\ 1, & \text{if } 2 < x \le 4. \end{cases}$$

15.2   Questions of interest

Our main interest in sequences of real-valued functions is the following: If $\{f_n\}$ converges to f, we would like the limit function f to enjoy some of the properties of the individual functions, f_n. For example, let $\{f_n\}$ converge *pointwise* to f. Then, the following questions are of interest.

Q1. If f_n is continuous for each n, is f necessarily continuous?

Q2. If f_n is integrable for each n, is f necessarily integrable?

Q3. If f_n is differentiable for each n, is f necessarily differentiable?

Q4. If f_n is differentiable for each n and f is also differentiable, does $\{f_n'\}$ converge to f'.

Q5. If f_n is integrable for each n and f is integrable , can we "pass limit over integral"? i.e., is the following always true?

$$\lim \int_D f_n(x)dx = \int_D \lim f_n(x)dx \left(= \int_D f(x)dx \right).$$

There are several other questions of interest. We shall encounter some of them in what follows. Meanwhile, we give examples to show that the answer to *all* of the above five questions is "NO", *if f_n converges only pointwise to f.*

Example 15.2.1 For each n, let $f_n : [0,1] \longrightarrow [0,1]$ be defined by

$$f_n(x) = x^n \ \forall \ x \in [0,1].$$

We already saw in Example 15.1.2 that $\{f_n\}$ converges pointwise to f, where

$$f(x) = \begin{cases} 1, & x = 1, \\ 0, & 0 \le x < 1. \end{cases}$$

(see Fig.15.5).

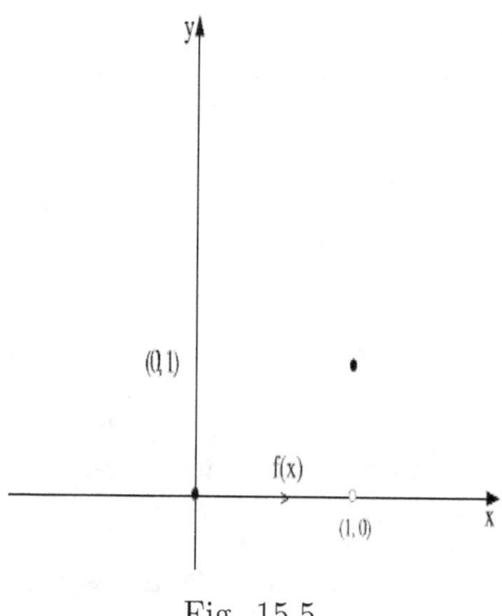

Fig. 15.5

Clearly, f_n is continuous on $[0,1]$ for each n but the limit function f is *not* continuous at $x = 1$. This example provides a negative answer to Q1.

Example 15.2.2 Let $\mathbb{Q} = \{r_n\}_{n=1}^{\infty}$ be an enumeration of the rationals in $[0,1]$. Recall that $\mathbb{Q}$ is countable. For each $n \in \mathbb{N}$, define

$$f_n(x) = \begin{cases} 1, & \text{if } x \in \{r_1, r_2, r_3, \cdots, r_n\}, \\ 0, & \text{if } x \notin \{r_1, r_2, r_3, \cdots, r_n\}. \end{cases}$$

Then we show that $\{f_n\}$ (see Fig. 15.6) is a sequence of integrable functions on $[0,1]$ which converges to a function that is not integrable on $[0,1]$. We first show that f_n is integrable on $[0,1]$ for each $n \in \mathbb{N}$. Indeed, let $n \in \mathbb{N}$. Let $\epsilon > 0$. Take $K \in \mathbb{N}$ such that $\frac{1}{K} < \epsilon$. Let $N := K + n$ and let $P_\epsilon := \{0 = x_0, x_1, x_2, \cdots, x_n = 1\}$ be a partition of $[0,1]$ such that $x_i = \frac{i}{N^2}, i = 0, 1, 2, \cdots, N^2$, that is $P_\epsilon := \{0, \frac{1}{N^2}, \frac{2}{N^2}, \frac{3}{N^2}, \cdots, 1\}$. Setting

$$M_i = \sup\{f_n(x) : x_{i-1} \leq x < x_i\}$$

and

$$m_i = \inf\{f_n(x) : x_{i-1} \leq x < x_i\}, \quad i = 1, 2, 3 \cdots, n,$$

we have, by the definition of f_n that $m_i = 0$ for each $i = 1, 2, 3 \cdots, n$. Let $J := \{i \in \{1, 2, 3, \cdots, N^2\} : r_k \in [x_{i-1}, x_i)$ for some $k \in \{1, 2, 3 \cdots, n\}\}$. Then the number of elements of the set J cannot exceed n and $M_i = 1$ for each $i \in J$. Therefore,

$$\begin{aligned}
U(f_n, P_\epsilon) - L(f_n, P_\epsilon) &= \sum_{i=1}^{N^2} (M_i - m_i)(x_i - x_{i-1}) \\
&= \sum_{i \in J} M_i(x_i - x_{i-1}) \\
&\leq \sum_{i \in J} 1 \cdot \frac{1}{N^2} \leq \frac{n}{N^2} < \frac{1}{N} < \epsilon.
\end{aligned}$$

Hence f_n is integrable on $[0, 1]$. Next we show that $f_n \to f$ as $n \to \infty$ ponitwise where f (see Fig. 15.7) is defined by

$$f(x) = \begin{cases} 1, & \text{if } x \text{ is rational.} \\ 0, & \text{if } x \text{ is irrational.} \end{cases}$$

Clearly, for each $x \in [0, 1] \cap \mathbb{Q}^c$, $f_n(x) = 0$ for all $n \in \mathbb{N}$. Therefore, $f_n(x) \to f(x)$ as $n \to \infty$ for each $x \in [0, 1] \cap \mathbb{Q}^c$. Let $x \in [0, 1] \cap \mathbb{Q}$. Then, there exists $n_x \in \mathbb{N}$ such that $r_{n_x} = x$ and $x \in \{r_1, r_2, r_3, \cdots r_n\}$ for each $n \geq n_x$. Thus, $f_n(x) = 1$ for each $n \geq n_x$. Hence $f_n(x) \to f(x)$ as $n \to \infty$ for each $x \in [0, 1] \cap \mathbb{Q}$. So we have $f_n(x) \to f(x)$ as $n \to \infty$ for each $x \in [0, 1]$. But we saw in Example 13.2.12 that the function f is not integrable on $[0, 1]$. Therefore we have provided a negative answer to Q2.

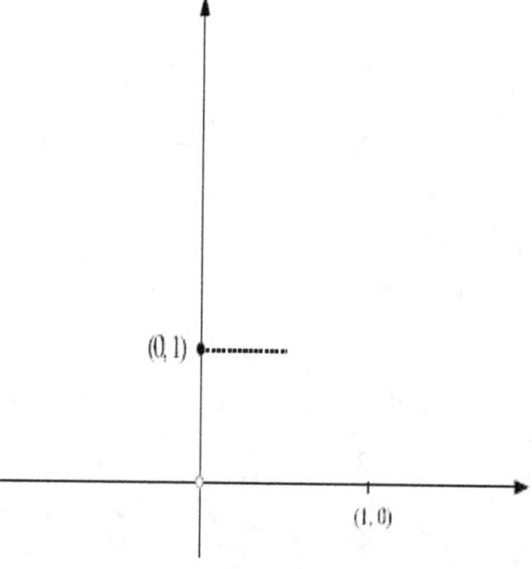

Fig. 15.6

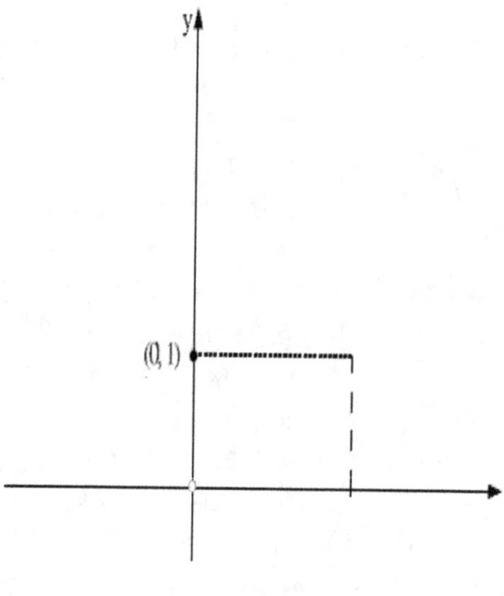

Fig. 15.7

Example 15.2.3 We know that the function $f : [-1, 1] \to$
$\mathbb{R}$ defined by $f(x) = |x|$ is not differentiable at $x = 0$. The
function f is sketched in Fig.15.8(a). The idea here is to
construct a sequence of differentiable functions that will con-

verge pointwise to f where $f(x) = |x|$. Fig.15.8(b) shows one natural way to obtain such a sequence.

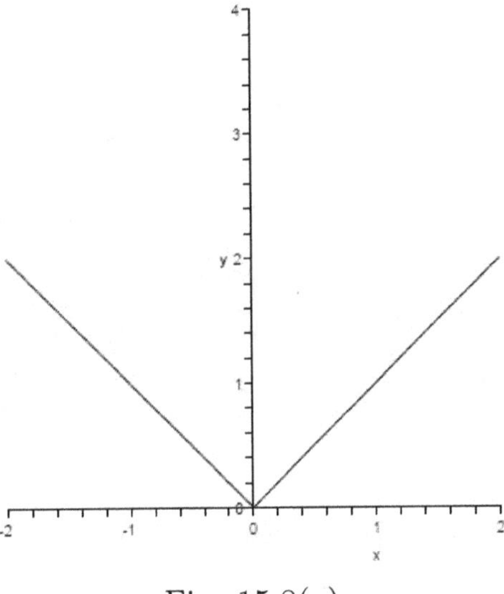

Fig. 15.8(a)

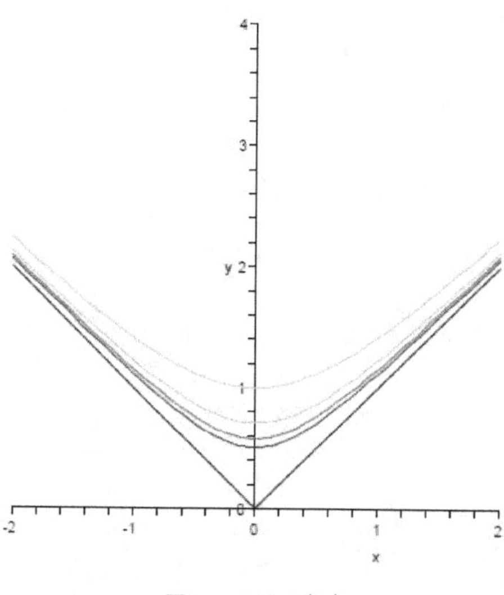

Fig. 15.8(b)

This sequence is defined by

$$f_n(x) = \sqrt{x^2 + \frac{1}{n}}, \ x \in [-1, 1], n \geq 1.$$

(Recall that $x^2 = |x|^2 \ \forall \ x \in \mathbb{R}$).
We now show that $\{f_n\}$ converges pointwise to f defined
by $f(x) = |x| \ \forall \ x \in [-1, 1]$. Let $\epsilon > 0$ be given and let
$x \in [-1, 1]$. Then,

$$|f_n(x) - f(x)| \ \leq \ \left| \sqrt{x^2 + \frac{1}{n}} - |x| \right| \leq \frac{1}{n\left(\sqrt{x^2 + \frac{1}{n}}\right)}$$

$$\leq \ \frac{1}{\sqrt{n}} < \epsilon,$$

provided $n > \epsilon^{-2}$. Hence, given $\epsilon > 0$, choose $N = N(\epsilon) =
1 + [\epsilon^{-2}]$, where $[\epsilon]$ denotes the greatest integer function.
Then, $|f_n(x) - f(x)| < \epsilon \ \forall \ n \geq N$ and $\forall x \in [-1, 1]$. Hence,
$f_n \to f$ as $n \to \infty$. Clearly, $f_n'(x) = \frac{x}{\sqrt{x^2 + \frac{1}{n}}}$, so that f_n is
differentiable for each integer $n \geq 1$ but the limit function

f is *not* differentiable at $x = 0 \in [-1, 1]$. This example provides a negative answer to Q3.

Example 15.2.4 For $n \in \mathbb{N}$ and $x \in [0, 2\pi]$, define

$$f_n(x) = \frac{\sin nx}{\sqrt{n}}.$$

Then, $f_n'(x) = \sqrt{n} \cos nx$. Furthermore,

$$|f_n(x) - 0| = \left| \frac{\sin nx}{\sqrt{n}} \right| \leq \frac{1}{\sqrt{n}} \to 0 \text{ as } n \to \infty.$$

Hence, $\{f_n\}$ converges pointwise to $f \equiv 0$ (i.e., $f(x) = 0$ $\forall\, x \in [0, 2\pi]$). Also, for each $n \in \mathbb{N}$,

$$f_n'(0) = \sqrt{n} \to \infty \text{ as } n \to \infty.$$

Hence, the sequence $\{f_n\}$ is differentiable, converges pointwise to 0, f_n' exists for each $n \in \mathbb{N}$, but $\{f_n'\}$ does not even have a limit if $x = 0$. This example provides a negative answer to $Q4$.

Example 15.2.5 For $n \geq 2$, let $\{f_n\}$ be the sequence whose n^{th} term is sketched in Fig. 15.9

We can write the explicit formula for $f_n(x)$ by using the standard equation of a straight line.

$$\text{On } OA: \quad y - 0 = \frac{2n - 0}{\frac{1}{2n} - 0}(x - 0) = 4n^2 x.$$

$$\text{On } AB: \quad y - 0 = \frac{2n - 0}{\frac{1}{2n} - \frac{1}{n}}\left(x - \frac{1}{n}\right) = -4n^2\left(x - \frac{1}{n}\right)$$

$$\text{On } BC: \quad y = 0 \text{ for all } x.$$

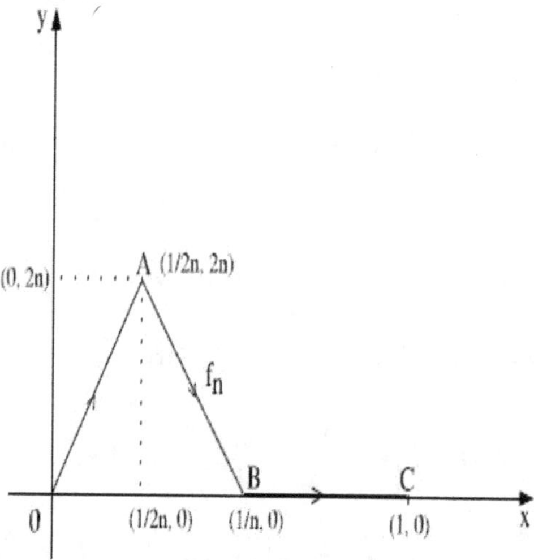

Fig. 15.9

So, we obtain that

$$
f_n(x) = \begin{cases} 4n^2\, x, & \text{if } 0 \le x \le \frac{1}{2n}, \\ -4n^2\left(x - \frac{1}{n}\right), & \text{if } \frac{1}{2n} \le x \le \frac{1}{n}, \\ 0, & \text{if } \frac{1}{n} \le x \le 1. \end{cases}
$$

Given any $x \in (0, 1]$, let $N = \left[\frac{1}{x}\right]$. Then for $n > N$, we have
$\frac{1}{n} < \frac{1}{N} = x$, so that $f_n(x) = 0$. Furthermore, if $x = 0$, then
$f_n(0) = 0$ so that $f_n \to f \equiv 0$, pointwise as $n \to \infty$, i.e., the
limit function f satisfies $f(x) = 0$ for all $x \in [0, 1]$. Clearly
f_n is continuous for each n, so f_n is integrable for each n.
However,
$\int_0^1 f_n(x)\, dx =$ area under the graph of Fig. 15.9 and the $x-$
axis
$=$ area of $\triangle OAB = 1$.
So, $\lim\limits_{n \to \infty} \int_0^1 f_n(x)\, dx = 1$.
However,

$$
\int_0^1 \lim_{n \to \infty} f_n(x)\, dx = \int_0^1 0\, dx = 0.
$$

Hence,

$$\lim_{n\to\infty} \int_0^1 f_n(x)\, dx \neq \int_0^1 \lim_{n\to\infty} f_n(x)\, dx.$$

This completes the example, and provides a negative answer to $Q5$.

Remark 15.2.6 Let $\{f_n\}$ be a sequence of continuous functions which converges pointwise to some f on a set D. Let $\{x_m\}$ be a sequence in D such that $x_m \to x^*$ for some $x^* \in D$. Then, since $\{f_n\}$ converges pointwise (i.e., at each $x \in D$) to f we have,

$$f(x_m) = \lim_{n\to\infty} f_n(x_m) \text{ for each } m \in \mathbb{N}.$$

Since f_n is continuous on D and $x_m \to x^*$, we have

$$f_n(x^*) = \lim_{m\to\infty} f_n(x_m).$$

The condition that the limit function f be continuous can then be written as follows:

$$\lim_{m\to\infty}\lim_{n\to\infty} f_n(x_m) = \lim_{n\to\infty}\lim_{m\to\infty} f_n(x_m). \qquad (15.2.1)$$

This brings us to another question of interest.

Q6. Can the order of the limit process always be interchanged? In particular, is equality (15.2.1) always true?

Remark 15.2.7 Examples 15.2.1, 15.2.2, 15.2.3, 15.2.4 and 15.2.5 show that *pointwise convergence* is a failure with regard to Q1 to Q5.

We shall also see later that equality (15.2.1) does not always hold under *pointwise* convergence. It turns out that there is another mode of convergence under which $Q1$, $Q2$, $Q5$ and Q6 have affirmative answers and Q3 has an affirmative answer *under some additional conditions*. This mode of convergence is called *uniform convergence*. We introduce it next.

15.3 Uniform convergence

15.3.1 Definition and two useful theorems

Definition 15.3.1 Let $\{f_n\}$ be a sequence of real-valued functions defined on a *subset D* of $\mathbb{R}$. Then $\{f_n\}$ is said to

$$\boxed{converge\ uniformly\ on\ D}$$

if given $\epsilon > 0$, $\exists\, N = N(\epsilon) \in \mathbb{N}$ such that

$$|f_n(x) - f(x)| < \epsilon \boxed{\forall\ x \in D}, \ \forall\ n \geq N.$$

Remark 15.3.2 What is the main difference between *pointwise* and *uniform* convergence? This can be seen as follows: If $\{f_n\}$ converges pointwise to f on D, then $\forall\ \epsilon > 0$, **and for each** $x \in D$, there exists a number $N(\epsilon, x) \in \mathbb{N}$, *depending on ϵ* **and** x such that $|f_n(x) - f(x)| < \epsilon\ \forall\ n \geq N(\epsilon, x)$. But, if $\{f_n\}$ converges uniformly to f on D, then it is possible to find, for each $\epsilon > 0$, *one* number $N = N(\epsilon) \in \mathbb{N}$, **depending only on** ϵ, that will work for *all $x \in D$*.

Geometrically, uniform convergence means that given $\epsilon > 0$, *eventually* (i.e., $\exists\, N = N(\epsilon) \in \mathbb{N}$ such that $\forall\ n \geq N(\epsilon)$), the entire graph of f_n and f will lie within the strip bounded above by $f + \epsilon$ and below by $f - \epsilon$ (see Fig. 15.10).

Before we give more examples of sequences of real-valued functions, we give now a useful criterion for testing if a given *sequence of real-valued functions* converges *uniformly*. We begin with the following definition and theorem.

Definition 15.3.3 A sequence $\{f_n\}$ of real-valued functions is called *uniformly Cauchy* on a set D provided that, for any given $\epsilon > 0$, $\exists\, N = N(\epsilon) \in \mathbb{N}$ such that

$$|f_n(x) - f_m(x)| < \epsilon\, \forall\ x \in D, \ \forall\ n, m \geq N(\epsilon).$$

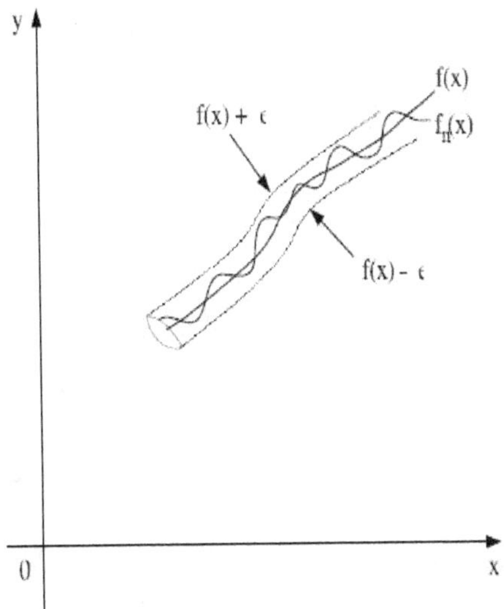

Fig. 15.10

Theorem 15.3.4 *(Uniform Cauchy Criterion). Let* $\{f_n\}$
be a sequence of real-valued functions defined on a subset D
of $\mathbb{R}$*. Then, there exists a function* f *such that* $\{f_n\}$ *con-*
verges uniformly to f *on* D *if and only if the following con-*
dition is satisfied:

$$\text{given } \epsilon > 0, \ \exists\, N = N(\epsilon) \in \mathbb{N}$$

such that

$$|f_n(x) - f_m(x)| < \epsilon, \ \forall\ x \in D, \ \forall\ n, m \geq N.$$

Proof. $(\Rightarrow)$ Suppose $\exists f$ such that $f_n \to f$ uniformly on D.
Then, $\forall\ \epsilon > 0, \ \exists\, N = N(\epsilon) \in \mathbb{N}$ such that

$$|f_n(x) - f(x)| < \frac{\epsilon}{2}, \ \forall\ x \in D, \ \forall\ n \geq N.$$

Let $m \geq N$. Then

$$|f_m(x) - f(x)| < \frac{\epsilon}{2}, \forall\ x \in D, \forall\ m \geq N.$$

So, $\forall\ \epsilon > 0$, $\exists N = N(\epsilon) \in \mathbb{N}$ such that

$$|f_n(x) - f_m(x)| \leq |f_n(x) - f(x)| + |f(x) - f_m(x)| < \epsilon$$

$\forall\ x \in D$, $\forall\ n, m \geq N$, as required.

($\Leftarrow$) Suppose the uniform Cauchy criterion is satisfied. This implies, $\forall\ x \in D$, $\{f_n(x)\}$ is a Cauchy sequence in $\mathbb{R}$. Completeness of $\mathbb{R}$ implies $\{f_n(x)\}$ converges. We may define

$$f(x) = \lim_{n \to \infty} f_n(x) \, \forall\, x \in D.$$

Hence, $\{f_n(x)\}$ converges pointwise to f on D.

Claim. This convergence is also uniform. For, given $\epsilon > 0$, (since uniform Cauchy criterion is satified) $\exists\, N = N(\epsilon) \in \mathbb{N}$ such that $\forall\ n, m \geq N$,

$$|f_n(x) - f_m(x)| < \frac{\epsilon}{2} \,\forall\, x \in D.$$

Fix n and let $m \to \infty$. Then, since $f_m(x) \to f(x)$ as $m \to \infty$, we obtain (since n is fixed, limit is taken with respect to m, the absolute value function is continuous) that $\exists N = N(\epsilon) \in \mathbb{N}$ such that

$$|f_n(x) - f(x)| < \frac{\epsilon}{2} < \epsilon \,\forall\, x \in D, \,\forall\, n \geq N.$$

Hence $\{f_n\}$ converges uniformly to f. $\square$

In some problems, one may know that a given sequence of rea-valued functions converges pointwise (or one may be able to guess the pointwise limit) and may want to find out if the convergence is uniform. In such a situation, the following theorem may be handy.

Theorem 15.3.5 *Suppose $\{f_n\}$ is a sequence of real-valued functions defined on a subset D of $\mathbb{R}$. Then $\{f_n\}$ converges uniformly to a function f on D if and only if*

$$\lim_{n \to \infty} \beta_n = 0,$$

where

$$\beta_n = \sup_{x \in D} |f_n(x) - f(x)|.$$

Proof. ($\Rightarrow$) Let $\{f_n\}$ be a sequence of rea-valued functions which converges uniformly to f on D. This means, $\forall\, \epsilon > 0$, $\exists\, N = N(\epsilon) \in \mathbb{N}$ such that

$$|f_n(x) - f(x)| < \epsilon \,\forall\, x \in D, \,\forall\, n \geq N.$$

Observe that $\epsilon > 0$ is an upper bound for the set

$$S = \{|f_n(x) - f(x)|, \ x \in D, \ n \geq N\}.$$

Hence, "sup" of S exists, and $\sup_{x \in D} |f_n(x) - f(x)| < \epsilon$, i.e., $\beta_n < \epsilon$, $\forall\, n \geq N$ and so $\lim_{n \to \infty} \beta_n = 0$.

($\Leftarrow$) Let $\beta_n = \sup_{x \in D} |f_n(x) - f(x)| \to 0$ as $n \to \infty$. Then, $\forall\, \epsilon > 0$, $\exists\, N \in \mathbb{N}$ such that

$$|f_n(x) - f(x)| \leq \sup_{x \in D} |f_n(x) - f(x)| < \epsilon, \,\forall\, x \in D, \,\forall\, n > N.$$

This proof is complete. $\square$

15.4   Some examples

We now give more examples.

Example 15.4.1 *For $n \in \mathbb{N}$, define $f_n : [0, 1] \to \mathbb{R}$ by*

$$f_n(x) = \frac{x}{3 + nx} \,\forall\, x \in [0, 1], \,\forall\, n \geq 1.$$

Show that $\{f_n\}$ converges uniformly on $[0, 1]$.

Solution. (Method 1. Use of Uniform Cauchy Criterion) Let $m > n$, $m, n \in \mathbb{N}$ and let $\epsilon > 0$ be given. Choose $N = N(\epsilon) \in \mathbb{N}$ such that $N > \frac{2}{\epsilon}$. Then, $\forall\, n > N$,

$$
\begin{aligned}
|f_n(x) - f_m(x)| &= \left| \frac{x^2(m-n)}{(3+nx)(3+mx)} \right| \\
&\leq \left| \frac{m-n}{mn} \right| \\
&\leq \frac{1}{n} + \frac{1}{m} \\
&< \frac{2}{n} < \frac{2}{N} < \epsilon.
\end{aligned}
$$

By uniform Cauchy criterion, $\{f_n\}$ converges uniformly on $[0,1]$.

(Method 2. Use of Theorem 15.3.5). By this method, we need to know the pointwise limit of $\{f_n\}$. From $f_n(x) = \frac{x}{3+nx}$, if x is fixed and $n \to \infty$, one guesses that $f_n(x) \to 0$ pointwise as $n \to \infty$. This is, in fact, true. For, if $x \in [0,1]$,

$$
|f_n(x) - 0| = \left| \frac{x}{3+nx} \right| \leq \frac{1}{3+nx} \to 0, \text{ as } n \to \infty.
$$

We now prove that this convergence is uniform. With the notation of Theorem 15.3.5,

$$
\beta_n = \sup_{x\in[0,1]} \left| \frac{x}{3+nx} \right| = \sup_{x\in[0,1]} \frac{x}{3+nx}.
$$

We use elementary calculus. Set $g_n(x) = \frac{x}{3+nx}$. $g_n'(x) = \frac{3}{(3+nx)^2} > 0$. Hence g_n is a nondecreasing function of x, so maximum value of g_n on $[0,1]$ is $g_n(1) = \frac{1}{3+n}$. Hence $\beta_n = \sup_{x\in[0,1]} \left| \frac{x}{3+nx} \right| = \frac{1}{3+n}$, and so,

$$
\lim_{n\to\infty} \beta_n = \lim_{n\to\infty} \frac{1}{3+n} = 0.
$$

By Theorem 15.3.5, the convergence is uniform.

Example 15.4.2 Let $f_n(x) = \frac{x^2}{x^2+n}$ for $x \in [0, \infty)$.

(*i*) Show that $f(x) = \lim\limits_{n \to \infty} f_n(x) = 0 \; \forall \; x \in [0, \infty)$.

(*ii*) Show that the convergence is *not* uniform on $[0, \infty)$.

(*iii*) Show that the convergence is uniform on $[0, a)$, $a \in \mathbb{R}$.

Solution. (*i*) $|f_n(x) - f(x)| = \left| \frac{x^2}{x^2+n} - 0 \right| < \frac{x^2}{n}$. Given $\epsilon > 0$, choose $N = N(\epsilon) \in \mathbb{N}$ such that $N > \frac{x}{\sqrt{\epsilon}} \; \forall \; x \in [0, \infty)$. Then $\forall \; n > N$, we have $\frac{1}{n} < \frac{1}{N}$ so that $|f_n(x) - f(x)| < \frac{x^2}{N} < \epsilon$. Hence $\{f_n(x)\}$ converges pointwise to $f(x) \equiv 0 \; \forall \; x \in [0, \infty)$.

(*ii*) It suffices to show that

$$\lim_{n \to \infty} \beta_n \neq 0$$

where

$$\beta_n = \sup_{x \in [0,\infty)} |f_n(x) - 0|.$$

But

$$\sup_{x \in [0,\infty)} |f_n(x) - 0| = \sup_{x \in [0,\infty)} \left| \frac{x^2}{x^2+n} \right| = \sup_{x \in [0,\infty)} \frac{x^2}{x^2+n}.$$

We appeal to elementary calculus and set $g_n(x) = \frac{x^2}{x^2+n}$. We then have $g_n'(x) = \frac{2nx}{(x^2+n)^2} \geq 0$ so that $g_n(x)$ is nondecreasing. Consequently,

$$\beta_n = \sup_{x \in [0,\infty)} \frac{x^2}{x^2+n} = \lim_{x \to \infty} \frac{x^2}{x^2+n} = 1,$$

i.e., $\beta_n \equiv 1 \; \forall \; n \geq 1$, so that $\lim\limits_{n \to \infty} \beta_n = 1 \neq 0$. Hence, convergence is *not* uniform on $[0, \infty)$.

(iii) On $[0, a)$, $\beta_n = \sup\limits_{x \in [0,a)} \frac{x^2}{x^2+n} = \frac{a^2}{a^2+n}$, since $\{\frac{x^2}{x^2+n}\}$ is a nondecreasing function of x. Hence,

$$\lim_{n \to \infty} \beta_n = \lim_{n \to \infty} \frac{a^2}{a^2 + n} = 0.$$

By Theorem 15.3.5, convergence is uniform. This completes the example.

Example 15.4.3 Let $f_n(x) = \frac{x^n}{2+x}$ for $x \in [0, 4]$.

(i) Find the set $D \subseteq [0, 4]$ for which $f(x) = \lim\limits_{n \to \infty} f_n(x)$ is defined as a real-valued function.

(ii) Show that if $0 < a < 1$, the convergence is uniform on $[0, a]$.

(iii) Show that the convergence is not uniform on $[0, 1]$.

Solution. (i) Observe that if $x = 1$, then $f_n(1) = \frac{1}{3}$ and so $\lim\limits_{n \to \infty} f_n(1)$ exists and equals $\frac{1}{3}$. If $0 \leq x < 1$, then $\lim\limits_{n \to \infty} f_n(x) = 0$. If $x > 1$, $\lim\limits_{n \to \infty} f_n(x) = +\infty$. So the set $D = [0, 1]$.

(ii) If $0 < a < 1$,

$$\beta_n = \sup_{x \in [0,a]} |f_n(x) - f(x)| = \sup_{x \in [0,a]} \frac{x^n}{2 + x}$$

where we have used the fact that if $x \in (0, 1)$, then $f_n(x) \to f(x) \equiv 0$, $\forall\, x \in (0, 1)$. Again, set $g_n(x) = \frac{x^n}{2+x}$ and observe that $g_n'(x) = \frac{2nx^{n-1}+(n-1)x^n}{(2+x)^2} \geq 0$ so that $g_n(x)$ is a nondecreasing function. Hence, $\sup\limits_{x \in [0,a]} \frac{x^n}{2+x} = \frac{a^n}{2+a} = \beta_n$, so that since $0 < a < 1$, $\lim\limits_{n \to \infty} \beta_n = 0$. Hence, convergence is uniform on $[0, a]$.

(iii) On $[0, 1]$, $\beta_n = \sup\limits_{x \in [0,1]} \frac{x^n}{2+x} = \frac{1}{3}$ and so $\lim\limits_{n \to \infty} \beta_n = \frac{1}{3}$. In this case, convergence is *not* uniform.

15.5 Questions of interest

We now return to the questions of interest we studied under *pointwise* convergence of sequences. Our main interest here is the following. If $\{f_n\}$ converges *uniformly* to f, we would like the limit function f to enjoy some of the properties of the individual functions, f_n. For example, let $\{f_n\}$ converge *uniformly* to f. Then, the following questions are of interest.

Q1. If f_n is continuous for each n, is f necessarily continuous?

Q2. If f_n is integrable for each n, is f necessarily integrable?

Q3. If f_n is differentiable for each n, is f necessarily differentiable?

Q4. If f_n is differentiable for each n and f is also differentiable, does $\{f_n'\}$ converge to f'.

Q5. If f_n is integrable for each n, and $f_n \to f$ uniformly, can we "pass limit over integral"? i.e., is the following always true?

$$\lim \int_D f_n(x)dx = \int_D \lim f_n(x)dx \left(= \int_D f(x)dx \right).$$

We saw in section 15.2 that the answer to *all* these questions is *NO* if the convergence is only pointwise. We shall now prove here that the answers to Q1, Q2 and Q5 are *YES if the convergence is uniform*. The answer is still NO for Q3

and Q4 (i.e., for the two questions involving differentiability). We begin with the following theorem.

Theorem 15.5.1 *Let $\{f_n\}$ be a sequence of real-valued continuous functions on a set D in $\mathbb{R}$. If $f_n \to f$ uniformly on
D, then f is continuous on D.*

Proof. We want to prove that f is continuous on D. So,
let $x_0 \in D$ be arbitrary. Then, it suffices to prove that given
$\epsilon > 0$, there exists $\delta = \delta(\epsilon) > 0$ such that

$$|x - x_0| < \delta \Rightarrow |f(x) - f(x_0)| < \epsilon.$$

Since $f_n \to f$ *uniformly* on D, there exists $N = N(\epsilon) \in \mathbb{N}$
such that

$$|f_n(x) - f(x)| < \frac{\epsilon}{3} \ \forall\, n \geq N, \ \forall\, x \in D.$$

Because of the *uniform convergence*, this inequality holds for
any $x \in D$. In particular, it holds for $x = x_0$. So we have:

$$|f_n(x_0) - f(x_0)| < \frac{\epsilon}{3} \ \forall\, n \geq N.$$

In particular, these inequalities hold for $n = N + 1$. Hence,
we have,

$$|f_{N+1}(x) - f(x)| \leq \frac{\epsilon}{3} \ \forall\, x \in D,$$

and

$$|f_{N+1}(x_0) - f(x_0)| \leq \frac{\epsilon}{3}.$$

We now use the fact that $\{f_n\}$ is continuous for each $n \in \mathbb{N}$.
In particular, f_{N+1} is continuous at x_0. So, with $\epsilon > 0$ given,
$\exists\, \delta = \delta(\epsilon) > 0$ such that

$$|f_{N+1}(x) - f_{N+1}(x_0)| < \frac{\epsilon}{3} \ \text{whenever} \ |x - x_0| < \delta.$$

Hence,

$$
\begin{aligned}
|f(x) - f(x_0)| \;\leq\; & |f(x) - f_{N+1}(x)| + |f_{N+1}(x) - f_{N+1}(x_0)| \\
& + |f_{N+1}(x_0) - f(x_0)| \\
<\; & \frac{\epsilon}{3} + \frac{\epsilon}{3} + \frac{\epsilon}{3} = \epsilon, \quad \text{whenever } |x - x_0| < \delta.
\end{aligned}
$$

Hence f is continuous at x_0. Since x_0 is arbitrary, we have f is continuous on D.

Remark 15.5.2 Theorem 15.5.1 is useful, in some cases, in showing that a given sequence of continuous functions *does not* converge *uniformly*. The theorem asserts the following: (i) $\{f_n\}$ is a sequence of continuous functions; $f_n \to f$ uniformly $\Longrightarrow$ f is continuous. The contrapositive statements to this theorem (i.e., another way of stating the same theorem) is the following: (i^*) $\{f_n\}$ is a sequence of continuous functions; $f_n \to f$ (pointwise), then, f not continuous $\Longrightarrow$ convergence is *not* uniform.

Example 15.5.3 Consider Example 15.2.1 given as follows: For $n \in \mathbb{N}$, $f_n : [0, 1] \to [0, 1]$ is defined by $f_n(x) = x^n \ \forall \ x \in [0, 1]$.
Clearly, f_n is continuous on $[a, b]$. We saw that $f_n \to f$ pointwise where

$$
f(x) = \begin{cases} 0, & 0 \leq x < 1 \\ 1, & x = 1. \end{cases}
$$

Since f is not continuous at $x = 1$, it follows that this convergence is *not* uniform.

The next theorem shows that uniform convergence allows us to "pass limit over integral", i.e., to interchange the order of limit processes. Recall that differentiation and integration are defined in terms of limits.

Theorem 15.5.4 *Let $\{f_n\}$ be a sequence of real-valued integrable functions on $[a, b]$. Let $f_n \to f$ uniformly on $[a, b]$. Then, f is integrable on $[a, b]$ and*

$$\lim_{n \to \infty} \int_a^b f_n(x)\, dx = \int_a^b f(x)\, dx.$$

Proof. We first prove that f is integrable. Let $\epsilon > 0$. Then by definition, there exists $N = N(\epsilon) \in \mathbb{N}$ such that

$$|f_n(x) - f(x)| \leq \frac{\epsilon}{2(1 + b - a)} \quad \forall x \in [a, b],\ \forall n \geq N.$$

That is,

$$f_n(x) - \epsilon' \leq f(x) \leq f_n(x)\epsilon' \quad \forall x \in [a, b],\ \forall n \geq N,$$

where $\epsilon' = \dfrac{\epsilon}{2(1 + b - a)}$. In particular,

$$f_N(x) - \epsilon' \leq f(x) \leq f_N(x) + \epsilon' \quad \forall x \in [a, b]. \qquad (15.5.1)$$

Since f_N is integrable over $[a, b]$ and $\epsilon' > 0$, there exists a partition P of $[a, b]$ such that

$$U(f_N, P) - L(f_N, P) < \epsilon'. \qquad (15.5.2)$$

Using inequalities (15.5.1), we have

$$L(f_N, P) - \epsilon'(b - a) \leq L(f, P) \leq U(f, P) \leq U(f_N, P) + \epsilon'(b - a).$$

This and (15.5.2) imply that

$$\begin{aligned}
U(f, P) - L(f, P) &\leq U(f_N, P) - L(f_N, P) + 2(b - a)\epsilon' \\
&= \frac{2(b - a)\epsilon}{2(1 + b - a)} < \epsilon.
\end{aligned}$$

Thus, f is integrable. Next we show that,

$$\lim_{n\to\infty}\int_a^b f_n(x)\,dx = \int_a^b f(x)\,dx.$$

$$\left|\int_a^b f_n(x)\,dx - \int_a^b f(x)\,dx\right| = \left|\int_a^b [f_n(x)-f(x)]\,dx\right|$$
$$\le \int_a^b |f_n(x)-f(x)|\,dx.$$

But, $f_n \to f$ uniformly $\implies$ given $\epsilon > 0$, $\exists\, N \in \mathbb{N}$ such that

$$|f_n(x)-f(x)| < \frac{\epsilon}{b-a} \quad \forall\, x \in [a,b], \ \ \forall\, n \ge N.$$

Hence, $\forall\, n \ge N$, we have

$$\left|\int_a^b f_n(x)\,dx - \int_a^b f(x)\,dx\right| \le \int_a^b \frac{\epsilon}{b-a}\,dx = \epsilon.$$

So,

$$\lim_{n\to\infty}\int_a^b f_n(x)\,dx = \int_a^b f(x)\,dx.$$

This completes the proof. $\square$

Remark 15.5.5 We observe that the sequence $\{f_n\}$ in Theorem 15.5.4 is assumed to be only integrable, no continuity is assumed. Of course, the assumptions of integrability implies the sequence is bounded. If the sequence $\{f_n\}$ is assumed to be continuous on $[a,b]$, and $f_n \to f$ uniformly, then f is continuous (Theorem 15.5.1) and so is integrable (Theorem 14.1.1 (c)). Thus, the following is an immediate corollary of Theorem 14.5.4.

Corollary 15.5.6 *Let $\{f_n\}$ be a sequence of continuous functions on $[a,b]$. If $f_n \to f$ uniformly on $[a,b]$, then,*

(a) f is integrable on $[a,b]$.

(b) $\lim\limits_{n\to\infty} \int_a^b f_n(x)\,dx = \int_a^b f(x)\,dx$.

Example 15.5.7 Let $f_n(x) = \frac{n^2 x}{1+n^2 x}$ for $x \in [0,1]$.

(a) Show that $\{f_n\}$ converges pointwise on $[0,1]$.

(b) Is the convergence uniform?

Solution: (a) Observe that if $x = 0$, then $f_n(0) = 0$ so that $f_n(0) \to 0$ as $n \to \infty$. For $x \in (0,1]$, given any $\epsilon > 0$, choose $N = N(\epsilon, x) > \frac{1}{\sqrt{\epsilon x}}$. Then for all $n \geq N$,

$$|f_n(x) - 1| = \frac{1}{1+n^2 x} \leq \frac{1}{N^2 x} < \epsilon.$$

Hence $f_n(x) \to 1 \ \forall \ x \in (0,1]$. Since $f_n(0) \to 0$ as $n \to \infty$, it follows that the sequence $\{f_n\}$ converges pointwise to f as $n \to \infty$, $\forall x \in [0,1]$, where f is defined as follows:

$$f(x) = \begin{cases} 0, & if\ x = 0 \\ 1, & if\ x \in (0,1]. \end{cases}$$

(b) Since f is not continuous at 0, and $\{f_n\}$ is a sequence of continuous functions, it follows that the convergence is not uniform (By Remark 15.5.2).

Example 15.5.8 Let $f_n(x) = \frac{2n+\sin nx}{3n+\sin^2 nx}$ for $x \in \mathbb{R}$.

(a) Show that $\{f_n\}$ converges uniformly on $\mathbb{R}$.

(b) Compute $\lim\limits_{n\to\infty} \int_0^{3\pi} f_n(x)\,dx$.

Solution: (a) *Method* 1 (By means of uniform Cauchy criterion).

So, we compute as follows: Let $m > n$. Then,

$$\begin{aligned} |f_n(x) - f_m(x)| &= \left| \frac{2n + \sin nx}{3n + \sin^2 nx} - \frac{2m + \sin mx}{3m + \sin^2 mx} \right| \\ &\leq \left| \frac{5(n+m) + 2|\sin nx \sin mx|}{(3m + \sin^2 mx)(3n + \sin^2 nx)} \right| \\ &\leq \frac{5\left(\frac{1}{n} + \frac{1}{m}\right) + \frac{2}{mn}}{9} \to 0 \text{ as } m,\ n \to \infty. \end{aligned}$$

By the uniform Cauchy condition, $\{f_n\}$ converges uniformly on $\mathbb{R}$.

Method 2 (By means of Theorem 15.3.5).
We guess that $\{f_n(x)\}$ converges to $2/3$, and now justify this guess as follows:

$$
\begin{aligned}
\left| f_n(x) - \frac{2}{3} \right| &= \left| \frac{2n + \sin nx}{3n + \sin^2 nx} - \frac{2}{3} \right| \\
&= \left| \frac{3\,\sin nx - 2\,\sin^2 nx}{3(3n + \sin^2 nx)} \right| \\
&\le \frac{5}{3(3n + \sin^2 nx)} \\
&\le \frac{5}{9n} \to 0
\end{aligned}
$$

as $n \to \infty$. Finally, it is easy to see that

$$
0 \le \beta_n = \sup_{x \in \mathbb{R}} \left| f_n(x) - \frac{2}{3} \right| \le \frac{5}{9\,n} \to 0
$$

as $n \to \infty$. Hence, $\lim_{n \to \infty} f_n(x) = \frac{2}{3}$.

(*b*) Since convergence is uniform, we can pass limit over integration. So, we obtain,

$$
\lim_{n \to \infty} \int_0^{3\pi} f_n(x)\, dx = \int_0^{3\pi} \lim_{n \to \infty} f_n(x)\, dx = \int_0^{3\pi} \frac{2}{3}\, dx = 2\pi.
$$

Remark 15.5.9 In Chapter 15, Example 15.2.4 we considered the following sequence: For $n \in \mathbb{N}$ and $x \in [0, 2\pi]$, f_n is defined by

$$
f_n(x) = \frac{\sin nx}{\sqrt{n}}.
$$

We showed that $\{f_n\}$ converges pointwise to f where $f(x) = 0$ for all $x \in [0, 2\pi]$. We show in the next example that actually $\{f_n\}$ converges *uniformly* to f. Moreover, $\{f_n'\}$ *does not* converge to f'.

Example 15.5.10 For each $n \in \mathbb{N}$, and $x \in [0, 2\pi]$, let f_n be defined by

$$f_n(x) = \frac{\sin nx}{\sqrt{n}}.$$

Then,

(a) $f_n \to f$ uniformly on $[0, 2\pi]$, where $f(x) = 0 \; \forall x \in [0, 2\pi]$.

(b) f_n' does not converge to f' as $n \to \infty$.

Solution (a) We compute as follows:

$$0 \leq \beta_n = \sup_{x \in [0, 2\pi]} |f_n(x) - f(x)| = \sup_{x \in [0, 2\pi]} \left| \frac{\sin nx}{\sqrt{n}} \right| \leq \frac{1}{\sqrt{n}}.$$

So $\lim_{n \to \infty} \beta_n = 0$, and hence $\{f_n\}$ converges *uniformly* to $f \equiv 0$, on $[0, 2\pi]$.

(b) $f_n'(x) = \sqrt{n} \, \cos nx$. Furthermore,

$$f_n'(0) = \sqrt{n} \to +\infty \text{ as } n \to \infty.$$

Hence, $\{f_n'\}$ is not even convergent on $[0, 2\pi]$. This completes the example.

Remark 15.5.11 We have seen in Example 15.5.10 that *uniform* convergence of a sequence of functions $\{f_n\}$ to a function f *is not sufficient* in itself to allow us to conclude that $f_n' \to f'$. It turns out that an additional condition is required for this conclusion to be drawn. This additional condition is the following:

The sequence of derivatives $\{f_n'\}$ is required to converge uniformly.

In fact we prove the following theorem.

Theorem 15.5.12 *Let* $\{f_n\}$ *be a sequence of real-valued functions defined on an open interval* (a, b). *Assume:*

(i) f_n *is differentiable for each* n;

(ii) $\{f_n(x_0)\}$ *converges for some* $x_0 \in (a, b)$;

(iii) $\{f'_n\}$ *converges uniformly on* (a, b).

Then,

(a) $\{f_n\}$ *converges* **uniformly** *on* (a, b) *to a function* f;

(b) f *is differentiable;*

(c) $f'_n \to f'$ **uniformly** *on* (a, b).

Proof Let $\epsilon > 0$ be given. By condition *(iii)*, $\exists\, N \in \mathbb{N}$ such that

$$|f'_n(x) - f'_m(x)| < \frac{\epsilon}{1 + 2(b - a)} \ \forall\ x \in (a, b),\ \forall n,\ m \geq N.$$

$$(a^*)$$

By condition *(ii)*, $\{f_n(x_0)\}$ is Cauchy. Hence, we may assume, without loss of generality, that for all $m,\ n \geq N$

$$|f_n(x_0) - f_m(x_0)| < \frac{\epsilon}{2}.$$

To prove **(a)**, it suffices to prove $|f_n(x) - f_m(x)| < \epsilon\ \forall m,\ n \geq N\ \forall\ x \in (a, b)$. We use the Mean Value Theorem applied to $(f_n - f_m)$ on any interval $[x_0, x]$ or $[x, x_0]$ to get, for all $m,\ n \geq N$, for some $\xi \in [x_0, x]$ or $[x, x_0]$,

$$|(f_n - f_m)(x) - (f_n - f_m)(x_0)| = |(f_n - f_m)'(\xi)|.|x - x_0|.$$

$$(b^*)$$

Thus, using (a^*) and (b^*), we obtain that for all $m, n \geq N$,

$$|(f_n - f_m)(x) - (f_n - f_m)(x_0))| \ = \ |f'_n(\xi) - f'_m(\xi)|.|x - x_0|$$
$$< \ \frac{\epsilon}{2}.$$

The last inequality implies that

$$|f_n(x) - f_m(x)| \; < \; \frac{\epsilon}{2} + |f_n(x_0) - f_m(x_0)|$$

$$< \; \frac{\epsilon}{2} + \frac{\epsilon}{2} = \epsilon, \;\; \forall\, m,\, n \geq N.$$

Hence, by the uniform Cauchy creterion, $\{f_n\}$ converges uniformly on (a, b) to some function f. This completes the proof of part (a).

Observe that each f_n is continuous (since it is differentiable) and $f_n \to f$ uniformly, so f is continuous.

(b) and **(c)** We now show f is differentiable and that $f_n' \to f'$ uniformly on (a, b). Let x^* be an arbitrary but fixed number in (a, b). Define

$$g_n(x) = \begin{cases} \frac{f_n(x) - f_n(x^*)}{x - x^*} & \text{if } x \neq x^* \\ f_n'(x^*) & \text{if } x = x^*. \end{cases}$$

Claim 1. For each n, g_n is a continuous function of x on (a, b). Given the function f we define a new function g by

$$g(x) = \frac{f(x) - f(x^*)}{x - x^*}, \; x \neq x^*.$$

Claim 2. $g_n(x) \to g(x)$ for all $x \neq x^*$.

We now show that the sequence $\{g_n(x)\}$ which depends on x^*, converges uniformly for $x \neq x^*$. For this, we again apply the Mean Value Theorem to $(f_n - f_m)$ on $[x^*, x]$ or $[x, x^*]$ to get

$$|(f_n - f_m)(x) - (f_n - f_m)(x^*)| = |(f_n - f_m)'(\xi)| \cdot |x - x^*|,$$

for some $\xi \in [x^*, x]$ or $[x, x^*]$. This implies, $\forall\, n,\, m \geq N$,

$$\frac{|f_n(x) - f_m(x) - \{f_n(x^*) - f_m(x^*)\}|}{|x - x^*|} = |(f_n - f_m)'(\xi)|,$$

$x \neq x^*$. This implies tha for all $x \in (a,b)$ and for all $n, m \geq N$,

$$|g_n(x) - g_m(x)| = |f'_n(\xi) - f'_m(\xi)| < \epsilon.$$

Thus, by the uniform Cauchy creterion, $\{g_n\}$ converges uniformly on (a,b).

Now, since $\{g_n\}$ is a sequence of continuous functions on (a,b) and converges uniformly on (a,b), then the following equality holds:

$$\lim_{x \to x^*} \lim_{n \to \infty} g_n(x) = \lim_{n \to \infty} \lim_{x \to x^*} g_n(x),$$

i.e.,

$$\lim_{x \to x^*} g(x) = \lim_{n \to \infty} f'_n(x),$$

or $f'(x^*) = \lim_{n \to \infty} f'_n(x^*)$. Since $x^* \in (a,b)$ is arbitrary, this shows that f is differentiable and that $f'_n(x) \to f'(x) \ \forall \ x$. This convergence is uniform by hypothesis. This completes the proof. $\square$

Remark 15.5.13 If we assume that f'_n is continuous on (a,b) for each n, Theorem 15.5.12 becomes much easier to prove. In fact, we give a proof of the following theorem (which is easier than the proof of Theorem 15.5.12).

Theorem 15.5.14 *Let $\{f_n\}$ be a sequence of real-valued functions on $[a,b]$. Suppose:*

(i) f_n is differentiable for each n; on (a,b);

(ii) $\{f_n\}$ converges to some f; on $[a,b]$

(iii) $\{f'_n\}$ converges uniformly on (a,b);

(iv) f'_n is continuous on (a,b) for each n.

Then,

(a) $\{f_n\}$ converges uniformly on $[a,b]$ to f;

(b) *f is differentiable; on* (a, b)

(c) $f'_n \to f'$ *uniformly on* (a, b).

Proof By condition (iii), define $g(x) = \lim_n f'_n(x)$ for each $x \in (a, b)$, so that $\{f'_n\}$ converges uniformly to g on (a, b). Since, by condition (iv), f'_n is continuous for each n, we can apply Theorem 15.5.4 (passing limit) to obtain that

$$\int_a^x g(t)\, dt = \lim_{n \to \infty} \int_a^x f'_n(t)\, dt, \quad \text{where } x \in (a, b).$$

By the Fundamental Theorem of Calculus,

$$\int_a^x f'_n(t)\, dt = f_n(x) - f_n(a).$$

Furthermore, $\lim_{n \to \infty} f_n(x) = f(x)$, where, we obtain that

$$\int_a^x g(t)\, dt = f(x) - f(a),$$

so that

$$f(x) = f(a) + \int_a^x g(t)\, dt, \quad \text{for all } x \in (a, b).$$

Furthermore, since f'_n is continuous for each n, and $\{f'_n\}$ converges uniformly to g on (a, b), it follows that g is continuous on (a, b). Thus, by the Fundamental Theorem of Calculus, f is differentiable on (a, b) and $f'(x) = g(x) = \lim_{n \to \infty} f'_n(x)$ for all $x \in (a, b)$. (Note that the derivative of $f(a)$ is zero since $f(a)$ is a constant). This completes the proof. $\square$

EXERCISES 15.1

1. For each integer $n \geq 1$, let $f_n(x) = \frac{5}{5+x^n}$ on $[0, 1]$.

(a) Prove that $\{f_n\}$ converges pointwise on $[0, 1]$.

(b) Is the convergence uniform? Justify your answer.

15.6   Further Questions of Interest

We know that if $\{f_n\}$ is a sequence of real-valued continuous functions defined on $[a, b]$ which converges *pointwise* to a real-valued function f defined on $[a, b]$, then f need not be continuous (see example 15.2.1).

One question of interest here is the following: Suppose $\{f_n\}$ is a sequence of real-valued continuous functions defined on $[a, b]$ which converges *pointwise* to a real-valued function f on $[a, b]$. Suppose the limit function is continuous.

Q7. Does this imply that this convergence is uniform?

Example 15.2.5 tells us that the answer to $Q7$ is *No*. (Justify this and convince yourself).

This brings us to the question of interest of this section.

Let $f_n : [a, b] \to \mathbb{R}, \ \ n = 1, 2, 3, \cdots$, be a sequence of *continuous* functions $\{f_n\}$ which converges *pointwise* to a function $f : [a, b] \to \mathbb{R}$ and suppose that f is *continuous*.

Q8. What additional condition on $\{f_n\}$ will guarantee that this convergence is uniform?

Before we give an answer to this question, we make the following important observation. The domain of the sequence $\{f_n\}$ and the domain of f in the above setting is $[a, b]$ which, as we know, is a *compact* subset of of $\mathbb{R}$.

With this in mind, we state the following theorem called *Dini's Theorem* which provides an answer to $Q8$.

Theorem 15.6.1 (Dini's Theorem) *Let $\{f_n\}$ be decreasing sequence of continuous real-valued functions that con-*

verges pointwise to a continuous function f on a compact subset S of $\mathbb{R}$, then $f_n \to f$ uniformly on S.

Proof. *Method 1.* We use the following characterization of compact sets in $\mathbb{R}$ (in fact in any metric space). A subset S of $\mathbb{R}$ (or any metric space) is compact if and only if any family $\{S_\alpha\}_{\alpha \in \Lambda}$ of closed subsets of S with finite intersection property, (that is $\cap_{\alpha \in J} S_\alpha \neq \emptyset$ for any finite subset J of Λ), has a nonempty intersection, i.e., $\cap_{\alpha \in \Lambda} S_\alpha \neq \emptyset$.

Recall that we want to prove that $f_n \to f$ uniformly on S. Now, given any $\epsilon > 0$, for each $n \in \mathbb{N}$ define

$$B_n := \{x \in S : |f_n(x) - f(x)| \geq \epsilon\}.$$

(i) Prove that B_n is a closed subset of S and so is compact. (Hint: use the continuity of f_n and f).

(ii) Since the sequence $\{f_n\}$ is monotone decreasing, justify the inclusion

$$B_{n+1} \subseteq B_n, \quad \forall n \in \mathbb{N}.$$

(iii) Show that

$$\bigcap_{n=1}^{\infty} B_n = \emptyset.$$

(iv) Use the characterization of compactness to conclude that there exists $N = N(\epsilon) \in \mathbb{N}$ such that $B_n = \emptyset$ for all $n \geq N$. Then conclude that

$$|f_n(x) - f(x)| < \epsilon, \quad \forall x \in S, n \geq N.$$

Method 2. Define $h_n := f_n - f$, $\forall n \in \mathbb{N}$. Then we have, from the monotonicity of $\{f_n\}$, that

$$0 \leq h_{n+1}(s) \leq h_n(s), \quad \forall s \in S, \ n \in \mathbb{N}$$

and $h_n \to 0$ as $n \to \infty$ pointwise on S. Let $\epsilon > 0$. Then, for each $s \in S, \exists\ N_s \in \mathbb{N}$ (since $h_n \to 0$) such that

$$0 \le h_{N_s}(s) < \epsilon.$$

Since h_{N_s} is continuous, we have

$$h_{N_s}(b) < \epsilon\ \ \forall\ b \in (s - r_s, s + r_s) \cap S, \quad \text{for some } r_s > 0.$$

By compactness of S, a finite number of such sets cover S, i.e.,

$$S \subset S \cap \bigcap_{k=1}^{n} (s - r_{s_k}, s + r_{s_k})$$

for some $\{s_1, s_2, s_3, \cdots s_n\} \subset S$. Take $M := \{N_{s_1}, N_{s_2}, N_{s_3}, \cdots, N_{s_n}\}$. Then $0 \le h_M(s) < \epsilon\ \forall s \in S$. Since $h_{n+1} \le h_n$, for each $n \in \mathbb{N}$, we have

$$0 \le h_n(s) < \epsilon\ \ \forall s \in S,\ \forall n \ge M.$$

That is,

$$|f_n(s) - f(s)| < \epsilon\ \ \forall s \in S,\ \forall n \ge M,$$

since $0 \le h_n = |h_n|$.
This completes the proof using *Method 2*.

(i) Where is the continuity of f used in this proof?

(ii) Is the conclusion of the theorem true if f is not continuous?

EXERCISES 15.2

1. Find an example of a sequence $\{f_n\}$ of continuous functions $f_n : [a, b] \to \mathbb{R}$ that converges pointwise to a continuous function $f : [a, b] \to \mathbb{R}$, but such that the convergence is not uniform. (This shows that the monotonicity in Dini's theorem is essential).

2. Find an example of a sequence $\{f_n\}$ of continuous functions $f_n : (a, b) \to \mathbb{R}$ that converges pointwise to a continuous function $f : (a, b) \to \mathbb{R}$, and such that $\{f_n(x)\}$ is decreasing for each $x \in (a, b)$, but such that the convergence is not uniform. (This shows that the domain of $\{f_n\}$ and f in Dini's theorem must be $[a, b]$, i.e., the domain must be compact).

15.7 Stone-Weierstrass approximation

In this section we state an importatnt theorem whose proof is not given.

Theorem 15.7.1 *Let $f : [a, b] \to \mathbb{R}$ be a continuous real-valued function. Then there exists a sequence of polynomials $\{p_n\}$ which conveges uniformly to f.*

Proof. . See W. Rudin *Principles of Mathematical Analysis.* McGraw-Hill 1976.

CHAPTER 15. SEQUENCES OF REAL-VALUED FUNCTIONS

<h1>CHAPTER 16</h1>

Series of real-valued functions; Power series

Section 16.1 of this chapter contains the following *two* very important theorems.

Theorem 16.1.3 (Weierstrass M-Test). *Suppose that* $\{f_n\}_{n\geq 1}$ *is a sequence of real-valued functions defined on a subset* $D \subseteq \mathbb{R}$ *and* $\{M_n\}_{n\geq 1}$ *is a sequence of nonnegative numbers such that for some* $N_0 \in \mathbb{N}$,

$$|f_n(x)| \leq M_n \ \text{ for all } x \in D, \text{ for all } n \geq N_0.$$

If the series $\displaystyle\sum_{n=0}^{\infty} M_n$ *converges, then* $\displaystyle\sum_{n=0}^{\infty} f_n$ *converges uniformly.*

This theorem gives a powerful tool for establishing the *uniform* convergence of a **series** of real-valued functions.

Theorem 16.1.8 Let $\{f_n\}_{n\geq 1}$ be a sequence of real-valued functions on $[a, b]$. Assume that there exists a function $f :$ $[a, b] \to \mathbb{R}$ such that the series $\sum\limits_{n=0}^{\infty} f_n$ converges **uniformly** to f on $[a, b]$. Then,

(a) If each f_n is continuous on $[a, b]$, then $f = \sum\limits_{n=0}^{\infty} f_n$ is continuous on $[a, b]$.

(b) If each f_n is integrable on $[a, b]$, then f is integrable on $[a, b]$ and,

$$\int_a^b f(x)\, dx = \int_a^b \left(\sum_{n=0}^{\infty} f_n(x) \right) dx = \sum_{n=0}^{\infty} \int_a^b f_n(x)\, dx.$$

$$(16.0.1)$$

(c) If,
(i) each f_n is differentiable on (a, b);
(ii) f_n' is continuous on (a, b) and ;
(iii) the series $\sum\limits_{n=1}^{\infty} f_n'(x)$ **converges uniformly** on (a, b),
then, f is differentiable on (a, b) and

$$f'(x) = \sum_{n=1}^{\infty} f_n'(x) = f_1'(x) + f_2'(x) + \cdots.$$

$$(16.0.2)$$

This theorem asserts that **if** an infinite series converges *uniformly* on $[a, b]$ to f, then it can be integrated term-by-term to obtain the integral of f. If in addition, $\sum\limits_{n=1}^{\infty} f_n'(x)$ converges **uniformly** on (a, b), then it can be differentiated term-by-term to obtain the derivative of f.

16.1   General series of functions

16.1.1   Definition and a fundamental theorem

Recall (see Definition 11.2.1) that a series $\sum\limits_{n=1}^{\infty} a_n$ of real numbers is defined as a double sequence $\{a_n, s_n\}_{n\geq 1}$ satisfying the following conditions:

$$s_n = \sum_{i=1}^{n} a_i \quad \text{where,} \quad a_n = s_n - s_{n-1},$$

and the series $\sum\limits_{n=1}^{\infty} a_n$ is called **convergent** if and only if its **sequence** $\{s_n\}_{n\geq 1}$ of partial sums is convergent.

We handle series of real-valued **functions** in a way that is analogous to series of real numbers.

Definition 16.1.1 *Suppose $\{f_n\}_{n\geq 1}$ is a sequence of real-valued functions defined on a set $D \subseteq \mathbb{R}$. The series $\sum\limits_{n=1}^{\infty} f_n$ is said to **converge pointwise** (respectively, **uniformly**) on D if and only if the **sequence** $\{s_n\}_{n\geq 1}$ of partial sums given by*

$$s_n(x) = \sum_{i=1}^{n} f_i(x)$$

converges pointwise (respectively, uniformly) on D.

Remark 16.1.2 *From the above definitions, it is evident that in order to prove theorems concerning the convergence of a **series** of real-valued functions, it suffices to consider the **sequence** $\{s_n\}_{n\geq 1}$ of partial sums of the series. To illustrate this, we derive a very useful test for establishing the **uniform** convergence of a series of real-valued functions.*

Theorem 16.1.3 (Weierstrass M-Test) *Suppose that $\{f_n\}_{n\geq 1}$ is a sequence of real-valued functions defined on a subset $D \subseteq \mathbb{R}$ and $\{M_n\}_{n\geq 1}$ is a sequence of nonnegative numbers such that for some $N_0 \in \mathbb{N}$,*

$$|f_n(x)| \leq M_n \quad \text{for all } x \in D, \ \text{for all } n \geq N_0.$$

If the series $\displaystyle\sum_{n=1}^{\infty} M_n$ converges, then $\displaystyle\sum_{n=1}^{\infty} f_n$ converges uniformly on D.

Proof.

We consider the sequence $\{s_n\}_{n\geq 1}$ of partial sums given by

$$s_n(x) = \sum_{i=1}^{n} f_i(x),$$

for $n = 1, 2, \ldots$ It suffices to show that $\{s_n\}_{n\geq 1}$ converges *uniformly* on D. To do this, we must show that $\{s_n\}_{n\geq 1}$ satisfies the *uniform Cauchy criterion* (see Theorem 15.3.4). Now, since the series $\displaystyle\sum_{n=1}^{\infty} M_n$ converges, its sequence $\{t_n\}_{n\geq 1}$ of partial sums converges, where

$$t_n := \sum_{i=1}^{n} M_i.$$

Being convergent, this implies that $\{t_n\}$ is a Cauchy sequence. Hence, given any $\epsilon > 0$, there exists an integer $N = N(\epsilon) > 0$ such that if $n > m > N$, then $|t_n - t_m| < \epsilon$. Equivalently, we have

$$|t_n - t_m| = \left| \sum_{i=1}^{n} M_i - \sum_{i=1}^{m} M_i \right| = M_{m+1} + M_{m+2} + \cdots + M_n < \epsilon$$

for all $n > m > N$. (Observe that the absolute-value bars have been dropped because the M_i's are nonnegative.) Thus, for $n > m > N$, we have, **for all** $x \in D$:

$$\begin{aligned}
|s_n(x) - s_m(x)| &= \left| \sum_{i=1}^{n} f_i(x) - \sum_{i=1}^{m} f_i(x) \right| \\
&= |f_{m+1}(x) + f_{m+2}(x) + \cdots + f_n(x)| \\
&\leq |f_{m+1}(x)| + |f_{m+2}(x)| + \cdots + |f_n(x)| \\
&\leq M_{m+1} + M_{m+2} + \cdots + M_n \\
&\quad \text{by hypothesis} \\
&< \epsilon.
\end{aligned}$$

By the Uniform Cauchy Criterion, $\{s_n\}_{n\geq 1}$ converges uniformly on D. Hence, $\sum_{n=1}^{\infty} f_n$ converges uniformly on D. This completes the proof. $\square$

16.1.2   Some examples

Determine whether or not the given **series** of real-valued functions converges *uniformly* on the indicated set. Justify your answer.

Example 16.1.4 $\displaystyle\sum_{n=1}^{\infty} \frac{x^{3n}}{(n + 2x)^2}, \qquad x \in [0, 1].$

Solution. Define $f_n : [0, 1] \to \mathbb{R}$ by

$$f_n(x) = \frac{x^{3n}}{(n + 2x)^2}.$$

Since $0 \leq x \leq 1$, we have,

$$|f_n(x)| = \left| \frac{x^{3n}}{(n + 2x)^2} \right| = \frac{x^{3n}}{(n + 2x)^2} \leq \frac{1}{n^2} =: M_n.$$

Since $\displaystyle\sum_{n=1}^{\infty} M_n = \sum_{n=1}^{\infty} \frac{1}{n^2} < \infty$, by Weierstrass M-Test, the given series converges uniformly on the set $[0, 1]$.

Example 16.1.5 $\displaystyle\sum_{n=1}^{\infty}\frac{x^2}{3+n^2x^2}, \qquad x \in \mathbb{R}.$

Solution. Define $f_n : \mathbb{R} \to \mathbb{R}$ by

$$f_n(x) = \frac{x^2}{3+n^2x^2}.$$

For any real number x, we have,

$$|f_n(x)| = \frac{x^2}{3+n^2x^2} \le \frac{1}{n^2} =: M_n.$$

Since $\displaystyle\sum_{n=1}^{\infty} M_n = \sum_{n=1}^{\infty}\frac{1}{n^2} < \infty$, by Weierstrass M-Test, the given series converges uniformly on $\mathbb{R}$.

Example 16.1.6 $\displaystyle\sum_{n=1}^{\infty}\frac{3}{5+n^2x^2}, \qquad x \ge 1.$

Solution. Define $f_n : [1,\infty) \to \mathbb{R}$ by

$$f_n(x) = \frac{3}{5+n^2x^2}.$$

For any number $x \ge 1$, we have,

$$|f_n(x)| = \frac{3}{5+n^2x^2} \le \frac{3}{n^2x^2} \le \frac{3}{n^2} =: M_n.$$

Since $\displaystyle\sum_{n=1}^{\infty} M_n = 3\sum_{n=1}^{\infty}\frac{1}{n^2} < \infty$, by Weierstrass M-Test, the given series converges uniformly on the set $[1,\infty)$.

Example 16.1.7 *Consider the series* $\displaystyle\sum_{n=0}^{\infty} f_n$ *where*

$$f_n(x) = \frac{x^n}{n!} \ \forall \ x \in \mathbb{R}.$$

It is known that the series $\displaystyle\sum_{n=0}^{\infty} f_n$ converges pointwise on $\mathbb{R}$.

(a) Show that the convergence is not uniform on $\mathbb{R}$.

(b) Show that the convergence is uniform on $[-a, a]$ for any $a > 0$.

Solution.

(a) Suffices to show that the sequence of partial sums does not satisfy the uniform Cauchy criterion. For this, take $\epsilon = 1$. Then, given any $n \in \mathbb{N}$, let $x_n = n$. Then,

$$|s_n(x_n) - s_{n-1}(x_n)| = |f_n(x_n)| = \frac{n^n}{n!} \geq 1 = \epsilon.$$

Hence, the series is not uniformly convergent on $\mathbb{R}$.

(b) For $a > 0$, define $M_n := \frac{a^n}{n!}$. Then, for any $x \in [-a, a]$, we have,

$$|f_n(x)| = \left|\frac{x^n}{n!}\right| \leq \frac{a^n}{n!} = M_n.$$

Then, using the ratio test, $\displaystyle\sum_{n=1}^{\infty} M_n$ converges. By the Weierstrass M-test, the result follows.

16.1.3 Term-by-term differentiation and integration

Suppose that we have a sequence $\{f_n\}$ of real-valued functions defined on **a closed and bounded interval** $[a, b]$. If the series $\sum f_n$ converges **uniformly** to some function f, then we want to know sufficient conditions for f_n that will guarantee nice properties for f. In particular, when will f be continuous, integrable, and differentiable if f_n has these properties for each n? The answers are provided in the following theorem.

Theorem 16.1.8 *Let $\{f_n\}_{n\geq 1}$ be a sequence of real-valued functions on $[a,b]$. Assume that there exists a function $f : [a,b] \to \mathbb{R}$ such that the series $\sum\limits_{n=0}^{\infty} f_n$ converges* **uniformly** *to f on $[a,b]$. Then,*

(a) If each f_n is continuous on $[a,b]$, then $f = \sum\limits_{n=0}^{\infty} f_n$ is continuous on $[a,b]$.

(b) If each f_n is integrable on $[a,b]$, then f is integrable on $[a,b]$ and,

$$\int_a^b f(x)\,dx = \int_a^b \left(\sum_{n=0}^{\infty} f_n(x)\right)dx = \sum_{n=0}^{\infty}\int_a^b f_n(x)\,dx.$$

$$(16.1.1)$$

(c) If,
(i) each f_n is differentiable on (a,b);
(ii) f_n' is continuous on (a,b) and ;

(iii) the series $\sum\limits_{n=1}^{\infty} f_n'(x)$ **converges uniformly** *on (a,b), then, f is differentiable on (a,b) and*

$$f'(x) = \sum_{n=1}^{\infty} f_n'(x) = f_1'(x) + f_2'(x) + \cdots.$$

$$(16.1.2)$$

Proof. Consider the sequence of partial sums $\{s_n\}_{n\geq 1}$ defined by

$$s_n(x) = \sum_{i=1}^{n} f_i(x).$$

(a) If each f_n is continuous on $[a,b]$ then, $s_n = \sum\limits_{i=0}^{n} f_i$ being a *finite* sum of continuous functions is continuous on $[a,b]$.

Now, by assumption, s_n converges *uniformly* to f; hence, by Theorem 15.5.1, the uniform limit f is continuous on $[a, b]$.

(b) If each f_n is integrable on $[a, b]$ then, $s_n = \sum_{i=0}^{n} f_i$ being a *finite* sum of integrable functions is integrable on $[a, b]$. Moreover,

$$\int_a^b s_n(x)\,dx = \int_a^b \sum_{i=0}^{n} f_i(x)\,dx = \sum_{i=0}^{n} \int_a^b f_i(x)\,dx. \quad (16.1.3)$$

Now, by assumption, $\{s_n\}$ converges *uniformly* to f; hence, by Theorem 15.5.4, the uniform limit f is integrable and we can "pass limit over integral", so we have that,

$$\int_a^b \left(\sum_{n=0}^{\infty} f_n(x) \right) dx \;\equiv\; \int_a^b f(x)\,dx$$

$$= \int_a^b \lim_{n\to\infty} s_n(x)\,dx$$

$$= \lim_{n\to\infty} \int_a^b s_n(x)\,dx$$

$$= \lim_{n\to\infty} \sum_{i=0}^{n} \int_a^b f_i(x)\,dx, \quad \text{using } (16.1.3)$$

$$= \sum_{n=0}^{\infty} \int_a^b f_n(x). \quad (16.1.4)$$

(c) If each f_n is differentiable on (a, b) then, $s_n = \sum_{i=0}^{n} f_i$ being a *finite* sum of differentiable functions is differentiable on (a, b). Moreover,

$$\frac{d}{dx} s_n(x) = \frac{d}{dx} \left(\sum_{i=0}^{n} f_i(x) \right) = \sum_{i=0}^{n} \frac{d}{dx} f_i(x). \quad (16.1.5)$$

Now, by assumption, $\{s_n'\}$ converges uniformly on (a, b). Hence, by Theorem 15.5.12(b), the uniform limit f is differentiable and by Theorem 15.5.12(c), $\{s_n'\}$ converges uniformly to f' on (a, b), that is, on (a, b) we have

$$\frac{d}{dx}\left(\sum_{n=0}^{\infty} f_n(x)\right) \equiv f'(x) = \lim_{n\to\infty} s_n'(x)$$

$$= \lim_{n\to\infty} \sum_{i=0}^{n} \frac{d}{dx} f_i(x)$$

$$= \sum_{n=0}^{\infty} \frac{d}{dx} f_n(x), \qquad (16.1.6)$$

using equation (16.1.5). This completes the proof. $\square$

Remark 16.1.9 *We re-iterate that **if** the series $\sum f_n$ converges **uniformly** on $[a, b]$, then it can be integrated term-by-term (equation (16.1.4)) and if, in addition, f_n' exists, is continuous on (a, b) and $\sum_{n=1}^{\infty} f_n'(x)$ converges uniformly on (a, b), then it can be differentiated term-by-term (equation (16.1.6)).*
Equation (16.1.4) may be remembered as an interchange *result because the **integral** and the **infinite sum** are swapped (provided that the convergence is uniform:*

$$\int_a^b \sum_{n=1}^{\infty} f_n(x) \equiv \int_a^b f(x)\,dx = \sum_{n=1}^{\infty} \int_a^b f_n(x)\,dx.$$

Similarly, the differential and the infinite sum are swapped (equation (16.1.6)) (under the conditions of Theorem (16.1.8)) in the following sense:

$$\frac{d}{dx} \sum_{n=0}^{\infty} f_n(x) = \frac{d}{dx} f(x) = \sum_{n=0}^{\infty} \frac{d}{dx} f_n(x).$$

Example 16.1.10 *Consider the series $\sum_{n=0}^{\infty} (-1)^n t^n$.*

This is, in fact, a geometric series $\sum\limits_{n=0}^{\infty}(-t)^n$ with first term 1 and common ratio $(-t)$. Suppose that $0 < s < 1$. For $t \in [-s, s] \subset (-1, 1)$ we obtain that $\sum\limits_{n=0}^{\infty}(-t)^n$ converges to $f(t) = \frac{1}{t+1}$. Furthermore, we have

$$|(-t)^n| \le s^n,$$

and clearly $\sum\limits_{n=0}^{\infty} s^n$ converges. Hence, by the Weierstrass M-Test, $\sum\limits_{n=0}^{\infty}(-t)^n$ converges *uniformly* on any interval $[-s, s]$, where $0 < s < 1$. Then, if $x \in (-1, 1)$, we can integrate the series term-by-term from 0 to x to obtain

$$\int_0^x \frac{dt}{1+t} = \int_0^x f(t)dt = \sum_{n=0}^{\infty}(-1)^n \int_0^x t^n dt = \sum_0^{\infty}(-1)^n \frac{x^{n+1}}{n+1}.$$

But from Calculus, this equation yields, for any $x \in (-1, 1)$, that

$$ln\,(1+x) = \sum_{n=0}^{\infty}(-1)^n \frac{x^{n+1}}{n+1}.$$

We shall return to this important example in the next section. We now conclude this section with the following remarks.

Remark 16.1.11 *Theorem 16.1.8 asserts that **if** a given series converges **uniformly** on $[a, b]$, then (under the hypotheses of the theorem) it can be differentiated and integrated term-by-term.*

Consequently, given an infinite series, in order to decide *whether or not term-by-term integration or differentiation is legitimate, one needs to check whether or not the series converges uniformly on some interval $[a, b]$. The Weierstrass $M-$ Test is very useful for doing this in many cases. However, there is a special type of infinite series which appears in numerous applications for which we can pre-determine its uniform convergence on a certain part of its domain of definition. This type of series is called **power series** and will be the main topic of our next section.*

EXERCISES 16.1

1. Determine whether or not the given series of real-valued functions converges uniformly on the indicated set. Justify your answer.

2. $\displaystyle\sum_{n=1}^{\infty} n^{-x}$ for $x > \sqrt{3}$.

3. $\displaystyle\sum_{n=1}^{\infty} \frac{x^3}{n^2}$ for $x \in [0, 3]$.

4. $\displaystyle\sum_{n=1}^{\infty} \frac{3}{3 + n^2 x^2}$ for $x \in (0, 1]$.

5. $\displaystyle\sum_{n=1}^{\infty} \frac{1}{1 + x^n}$ for $x \in [0, 1]$.

6. For each n, define $f_n : \mathbb{R} \to \mathbb{R}$ by

$$f_n(x) = \frac{x^2}{(1 + x^2)^n}.$$

338

Consider the function $f : \mathbb{R} \to \mathbb{R}$ defined by

$$f(x) = \sum_{n=0}^{\infty} f_n(x) = \sum_{n=0}^{\infty} \frac{x^2}{(1+x^2)^n}.$$

7. Show that $f(x) = 1 + x^2$ for $x \neq 0$.

8. Does the series converge uniformly on $\mathbb{R}$? Does it converge uniformly on $[-1, 1]$? Justify your answers.

9. Show that the following series is uniformly convergent on $\mathbb{R}$:

$$\sum_{n=1}^{\infty} (-1)^{n+1} \frac{1}{n + x^4},$$

but that it is not absolutely convergent for any $x \in \mathbb{R}$.

10. Show that the following series is uniformly convergent on every bounded interval $D \subseteq \mathbb{R}$:

$$\sum_{n=1}^{\infty} (-1)^{n+1} \frac{n + x^4}{n^2},$$

but that it is not absolutely convergent for any $x \in \mathbb{R}$.

11. Let $0 < c < 1$. Show that the series

$$\sum_{n=0}^{\infty} x^n$$

converges uniformly on $[-c, c]$ but that it does not converge uniformly on $(-1, 1)$.

12. Let $f_n(x) = \frac{x^4}{(1+x^4)^n}$ for $x \in \mathbb{R}$. Consider the function f defined by

$$f(x) = \sum_{n=0}^{\infty} f_n(x) \equiv \sum_{n=0}^{\infty} \frac{x^4}{(1+x^4)^n}.$$

(a) Use the geometric series to show that $f(x) = 1 + x^4$ for $x \neq 0$.

(b) Does the series converge uniformly on $\mathbb{R}$? Justify your answer.

(c) Does the series converge uniformly on $[-1, 1]$? Justify your answer.

13. Consider the series $\displaystyle\sum_{n=1}^{\infty} \frac{(-1)^{n+1}}{2n + x^2}$.

(a) Is the series uniformly convergent on $\mathbb{R}$? Justify.

(b) Is it absolutely convergent for any $x \in \mathbb{R}$? Justify.

14. Consider the series $\displaystyle\sum_{n=1}^{\infty} (-1)^{n+1} \frac{(x)^2 + 3n}{2n^2}$ in $\mathbb{R}$.

(a) Show that the series converges uniformly on any bounded subset of $\mathbb{R}$.

(b) Show that the series is not absolutely convergent.

15. Consider the geometric series

$$\frac{1}{1-x} = 1 + x + x^2 + x^3 + \ldots + x^n + \ldots.$$

(a) Show that the series converges uniformly on $\lfloor -a, a \rfloor$ where $a \in (-1, 1)$.

(b) Integrate the series term-by-term from $-x$ to x for $x \in (-1, 1)$.

(c) Using (b), obtain a series for $\log_e \left(\frac{1+x}{1-x}\right)$.

16.2   Power Series

This section contains the following *three* important funt theorems and *one* very important corollary.

Theorem 16.2.5 (Radius of Convergence Theorem)
*If $\sum\limits_{n=0}^{\infty} a_n x^n$ is a power series, then there is a **unique** R, $0 \le R \le \infty$, called its radius of convergence such that*

(a) $\sum\limits_{n=0}^{\infty} a_n x^n$ converges whenever $|x| < R$ i.e., $\forall\ x : -R < x < R$;

(b) $\sum\limits_{n=0}^{\infty} a_n x^n$ diverges whenever

$$|x| > R.$$

Moreover, R is given by the formula:

$$R = \frac{1}{\limsup\limits_{n\to\infty} \sqrt[n]{|a_n|}}.$$

Theorem 16.2.13 *Let R be the radius of convergence of the power series $\sum\limits_{n=0}^{\infty} a_n x^n$, where $0 < R \le \infty$. If $0 < r < R$, then the power series converges **uniformly** on $[-r, r]$.*

Theorem 16.2.17 (Convergence at endpoints) *Let $\sum\limits_{n=0}^{\infty} a_n x^n$ be a power series with a finite radius of convergence R.*
(a) If the series converges at $x = R$, (an endpoint), then it converges uniformly on the interval $[0, R]$.
(b) If the series converges at $x = -R$, (an endpoint), then it converges uniformly on $[-R, 0]$.

Corollary 16.2.18(Continuity at endpoints) *Let the power series* $f(x) = \sum_{n=0}^{\infty} a_n x^n$ *have a radius of convergence* R, $0 < R < \infty$.

(a) *If the series converges at* $x = R$, *then* f *is continuous at* $x = R$.

(b) *If the series converges at* $x = -R$, *then* f *is continuous at* $x = -R$.

16.2.1   Introduction

So far, we have studied sequences and series of arbitrary real-valued functions. In this section, we consider an important series of real-valued functions of a special kind called **power series** which appears in many important areas of mathematical sciences.

16.2.2   Definition and examples

We now begin our study of power series. We begin with the following definition.

Definition 16.2.1 Let $\{a_n\}_{n=0}^{\infty}$ be a sequence of real numbers. The series

$$\sum_{n=0}^{\infty} a_n x^n = a_0 + a_1 x + a_2 x^2 + ... + ...,$$

is called a *power series*. The number a_n is called the nth *coefficient* of the power series.

Remark 16.2.2 In Definition 16.2.1 the coefficients a_n are constants and x is a real variable. For example, the geometric series $\sum_{n=0}^{\infty} x^n$ is a power series whose coefficients a_n are 1.

Furthermore, if $x = 0$ in definition 16.2.1, the power series trivially converges to a_0. This leads to the following question.

Question 16.2.3 *For what values of the variables x is a given power series convergent?*

Example 16.2.4 Consider the power series $\sum_{n=0}^{\infty} x^n$. In this case, $a_n \equiv 1$ for all positive integers n. This is a geometric series and we know from high school that it converges for all values of x such that $|x| < 1$.

Regarding question 16.2.3, it turns out that the answer to the question is easily resolved in the following fundamental theorem.

Theorem 16.2.5 *[Radius of Convergence Theorem]. If $\sum_{n=0}^{\infty} a_n x^n$ is a power series, then there is a* **unique** *R, $0 \leq R \leq \infty$, called its radius of convergence such that*

(a) $\sum_{n=0}^{\infty} a_n x^n$ converges whenever $|x| < R$ i.e., $\forall\ x : -R < x < R$;

(b) $\sum_{n=0}^{\infty} a_n x^n$ diverges whenever

$$|x| > R.$$

Moreover, R is given by the formula:

$$R = \frac{1}{\limsup_{n \to \infty} \sqrt[n]{|a_n|}}.$$

Proof. Apply the *root test* to the series $\sum_{n=0}^{\infty} a_n x^n$. This yields

$$\limsup_{n \to \infty} \sqrt[n]{|a_n x^n|} = |x| \limsup_{n \to \infty} \sqrt[n]{|a_n|} = |x| \cdot \frac{1}{R}$$

and we immediately obtain conclusions (a) and (b). This completes the proof. $\square$

Remark 16.2.6 For a given radius R, $0 \leq R \leq \infty$, there is a power series with R as its radius of convergence. For example,

(i) If $R = 0$, the series $\sum_{n=0}^{\infty} n^n x^n$ has radius of convergence R;

(ii) If $0 < a < \infty$, the series $\sum_{n=0}^{\infty} \left(\frac{x}{a}\right)^n$ has radius of convergence $R = a$; and

(iii) If $R = \infty$, the series $\sum_{n=0}^{\infty} \frac{1}{n!} x^n$ has radius of convergence R.

Remark 16.2.7 The following statements are conventional.

(1) If $R = \infty$, then the series $\sum_{n=0}^{\infty} a_n x^n$ is said to converge **absolutely** *for* **all** *values of x.*

(2) If $R = 0$, then the series $\sum_{n=0}^{\infty} a_n x^n$ converges only for $x = 0$.

Remark 16.2.8 Theorem 16.2.5 does not say anything about the convergence or divergence of $\sum_{n=0}^{\infty} a_n x^n when |x| = R$. It is always necessary in this case to check the convergence or otherwise of the series by substituting x=+R and x=-R in the given series. We shall illustrate with some examples.

It is clear that, from Theorem 16.2.5, the set $S \subseteq \mathbb{R}$ for which the power series $\sum_{n=0}^{\infty} a_n x^n$ *converges* will be either $\{0\}$, $\mathbb{R}$, or *a bounded interval centred at* 0.

The set S is called the interval of convergence .

It is conventional to adapt the following idea.

(i) $\{0\}$ is an interval of convergence of zero radius.

(ii) $\mathbb{R}$ is an interval of convergence of infinite radius.

We now derive a *ratio criterion for determining the radius of a power series* $\sum\limits_{n=0}^{\infty} a_n x^n$.

Theorem 16.2.9 *[Ratio Criterion]. Let R be the radius of convergence of the power series* $\sum\limits_{n=0}^{\infty} a_n x^n$. *Then*

$$R = \frac{1}{\lim\limits_{n\to\infty}\left|\frac{a_{n+1}}{a_n}\right|},$$

provided the limit exists.

Proof.   The proof follows from the following inequality: if $\{a_n\}$ is a sequence of positive numbers, then (see Problem 8, Exercises 16.2 where a proof is sketched)

$$\liminf_{n\to\infty}\frac{a_{n+1}}{a_n} \leq \liminf_{n\to\infty}\left(a_n\right)^{\frac{1}{n}} \leq \limsup_{n\to\infty}\left(a_n\right)^{\frac{1}{n}} \leq \limsup_{n\to\infty}\frac{a_{n+1}}{a_n}.$$

From this inequality, it follows that whenever the root test determines convergence or divergence, the ratio test does too. The proof now follows from Theorem 16.2.5.   □

We now give some examples.

Example 16.2.10 *For each of the following series, find*

(a) the radius of convergence.

(b) the interval of convergence.

(i) $\sum\limits_{n=1}^{\infty} \frac{(-3)^{-n}}{n} x^n.$

$$(ii) \quad \sum_{n=1}^{\infty} \frac{(x-3)^n}{3^n}.$$

$$(iii) \quad \sum_{n=1}^{\infty} \frac{2^{3n}}{n}(x-4)^{2n}.$$

Solution.

(i) $a_n = \frac{(-3)^{-n}}{n}$. So, $\left|\frac{a_{n+1}}{a_n}\right| = \frac{n}{3(n+1)}$ and $\lim\limits_{n\to\infty}\left|\frac{a_{n+1}}{a_n}\right| = \frac{1}{3}$. Therefore, $R = \frac{1}{\lim\limits_{n\to\infty}\left|\frac{a_{n+1}}{a_n}\right|} = 3$.

Hence, the series converges for x such that $-3 < x < 3$. Next, we consider what happens when $x = -3$ and when $x = 3$. If $x = -3$, *the series* becomes $\sum\limits_{n=1}^{\infty}\frac{(-3)^{-n}(-3)^n}{n} = \sum\limits_{n=1}^{\infty}\frac{1}{n}$, which is the harmonic series and so diverges. If $x = 3$, the series becomes $\sum\limits_{n=1}^{\infty}\frac{(-3)^{-n}3^n}{n} = \sum\limits_{n=1}^{\infty}(-1)^n\frac{1}{n}$, which converges (by the alternating series test). Hence, the interval of convergence is $(-3, 3]$.

(ii) For this, we first observe that $\sum\limits_{n=1}^{\infty}\frac{(x-3)^n}{3^n}$ is *not* exactly in the form $\sum\limits_{n=1}^{\infty}a_n x^n$. So, we make a suitable substitution. Let $\boxed{X = x - 3}$. Then the series becomes $\sum\limits_{n=1}^{\infty}\frac{X^n}{3^n}$ with $a_n = \frac{1}{3^n}$. Now, $\lim\limits_{n\to\infty}\left|\frac{a_{n+1}}{a_n}\right| = \frac{1}{3}$ so that $R = 3$. Hence, the series $\sum\limits_{n=1}^{\infty}\frac{X^n}{3^n}$ converges for

$$-3 < X < 3.$$

We now check the end points $X = -3$ and $X = +3$.

Case 1. $X = -3$, then the series becomes $\sum_{n=1}^{\infty}(-1)^n$ which clearly diverges (why?).

Case 2. $X = 3$, then the series becomes $\sum_{n=1}^{\infty} 1 = +\infty$ and so diverges. Hence, the interval of convergence is

$$-3 < X < 3,$$

i.e., using $X = x - 3$,

$$-3 < x - 3 < 3,$$

or,

$$0 < x < 6.$$

(iii) For $\sum_{n=1}^{\infty} \dfrac{2^{3n}}{n}(x - 4)^{2n}$, we have to put it in the form $\sum_{n=1}^{\infty} a_n x^n$. We first make the substitution $\boxed{X = x - 4}$ to get:

$$\sum_{n=1}^{\infty} \frac{2^{3n}}{n} X^{2n}.$$

This series is *yet not in the form* $\sum_{n=1}^{\infty} a_n x^n$. So, we make the following *additional substitution* $\boxed{y = X^2}$ to get

$$\sum_{n=1}^{\infty} \frac{2^{3n}}{n}(x - 4)^{2n} = \sum_{n=1}^{\infty} \frac{2^{3n}}{n} y^n$$

which is now in the form $\sum_{n=1}^{\infty} a_n x^n$ with $a_n = \frac{2^{3n}}{n}$, $x = y$.
Now,

$$\lim_{n\to\infty}\left|\frac{a_{n+1}}{a_n}\right| = \lim_{n\to\infty}\left|8\frac{n}{n+1}\right| = 8.$$ Hence, the radius of convergence of $\sum_{n=1}^{\infty}\frac{2^{3n}}{n}y^n$ is $\frac{1}{8}$. Consequently, the series converges for

$$-\frac{1}{8} < y < \frac{1}{8}.$$

For the interval of convergence, we consider the end-points.

Case 1: $y = \frac{-1}{8}$ is not possible since $y = X^2$. So, we consider,

Case 2: For $y = \frac{1}{8}$, the series $\sum_{n=1}^{\infty}\frac{2^{3n}}{n}y^n$ becomes $\sum_{n=1}^{\infty}\frac{1}{n}$, which diverges.

Hence, the interval of convergence is

$$y < \frac{1}{8},$$

i.e.,

$$X^2 < \frac{1}{8}.$$

But,

$$X^2 < \frac{1}{8} \Rightarrow \left(X - \frac{\sqrt{2}}{4}\right)\left(X + \frac{\sqrt{2}}{4}\right) < 0,$$

i.e.,

$$-\frac{\sqrt{2}}{4} < X < \frac{\sqrt{2}}{4}$$

or, using $X = x - 2$,

$$-\frac{\sqrt{2}}{4} < x - 4 < \frac{\sqrt{2}}{4}$$

i.e.,

$$4 - \frac{\sqrt{2}}{4} < x < 4 + \frac{\sqrt{2}}{4}.$$

Example 16.2.11 *Find the interval of convergence of the series*

$$\sum_{n=1}^{\infty} \frac{x^n}{n!}, \quad x \in \mathbb{R}.$$

The given series is a power series called the *exponential series.* We first show that it converges *pointwise* on $\mathbb{R}$. Applying the Ratio Test, with $a_n = \frac{1}{n!}$, we have

$$R = \lim_{n \to +\infty} \left| \frac{a_n}{a_{n+1}} \right| = \lim_{n \to +\infty} \left| \frac{(n+1)!}{n!} \right| = \lim_{n \to +\infty} (n+1) = +\infty,$$

which shows that the radius of convergence is $+\infty$. Thus, the **interval** of convergence of the given power series is $\mathbb{R}$.

However, this convergence is *not uniform* on $\mathbb{R}$. One way to show this is to produce *at least one* $\epsilon > 0$ for which the sequence of partial sums $\{s_n\}_{n \geq 1}$ does not satisfy the uniform Cauchy criterion (Theorem 15.3.4) **for some** $x \in \mathbb{R}$. We proceed as follows:

Step 1. Take $m = (n-1)$. Then

$$
\begin{aligned}
|s_n(x) - s_m(x)| &= |s_n(x) - s_{n-1}(x)| \\
&= \left| \sum_{i=1}^{n} \frac{x^i}{i!} - \sum_{i=1}^{n-1} \frac{x^i}{i!} \right| \\
&= \frac{|x|^n}{n!}.
\end{aligned}
$$

Step 2. Choose a suitable x such that *a lower bound* for $\frac{|x|^n}{n!}$ can easily be found. This will help us to choose $\epsilon > 0$ that will contradict Theorem 15.3.4 For example, if we choose $x = n$, we obtain

$$|s_n(n) - s_m(n)| = \frac{n^n}{n!} \geq 1.$$

Hence, if we choose $\epsilon = \frac{1}{2}$ and $x = n$, the Uniform Cauchy Criterion does not hold and so $\{s_n\}_{n \geq 1}$ does not converge uniformly on $\mathbb{R}$; therefore the series $\sum_{n=1}^{\infty} \frac{x^n}{n!}$ does not converge uniformly on $\mathbb{R}$.

This procedure (the uniform Cauchy criterion) can also be used to show that if R is a fixed positive number, then the given series is uniformly convergent on $[-R, R]$, justify. This example emphasizes that **uniformity of convergence depends on the domain**.

Example 16.2.12 *Consider the series* $\sum_{n=1}^{\infty} \frac{x^2}{n^2},$ $x \geq 3.$

If $x = a$ where $a \geq 3$ then

$$\sum_{n=1}^{\infty} \frac{x^2}{n^2} = a^2 \sum_{n=1}^{+\infty} \frac{1}{n^2} < +\infty,$$

and so the series converges pointwise (why?). We claim that this convergence is *not uniform* on $[3, +\infty)$. As in the previous example, we need to produce an $\epsilon > 0$ **and** an $x \in [3, +\infty)$ such that the uniform Cauchy criterion is violated.

Step 1. Take $m = (n - 1)$. Then

$$|s_n(x) - s_m(x)| = |s_n(x) - s_{n-1}(x)| = \frac{x^2}{n^2}.$$

Step 2. We need to choose $x \in [3, +\infty)$ so that *a lower bound* for $\frac{x^2}{n^2}$ can easily be found. It suffices to choose $x = 3n$. Observe that $3n$ is always in $[3, +\infty)$. With this choice, we have

$$|s_n(3n) - s_m(3n)| = \frac{9n^2}{n^2} = 9.$$

Hence, if we choose $\epsilon = 8$ (or any positive number less that 9) and $x = 3n \in [3, +\infty)$, the uniform Cauchy criterion does not hold. Hence, $\{s_n\}_{n \geq 1}$ does not converge uniformly on $[3, +\infty)$ and so the series $\sum_{n=1}^{\infty} \dfrac{x^2}{n^2}$ *does not converge uniformly* on $[3, +\infty)$.

16.2.3 Uniform convergence of power series.

We have seen that every power series $\sum_{n=0}^{\infty} a_n x^n$ has a radius of convergence R, where $0 \leq R \leq +\infty$. Furthermore, we showed that the series converges absolutely for $|x| < R$ and diverges for $|x| > R$. In this section we establish condition for the **uniform convergence** of **power series** .

Theorem 16.2.13 *Let R be the radius of convergence of the power series* $\sum_{n=0}^{\infty} a_n x^n$, *where $0 < R \leq \infty$. If $0 < r < R$, then the power series converges* **uniformly** *on $[-r, r]$.*

Proof. **Method 1.** Choose α such that $r < \alpha < R$. For n sufficiently large, $\sqrt[n]{|a_n|} < \frac{1}{\alpha}$ since $\alpha < R$. Thus, if $|x| \leq r$, then

$$|a_n x^n| \leq \left(\frac{r}{\alpha}\right)^n.$$

But $r < \alpha \Rightarrow \frac{r}{\alpha} < 1$ so that $\sum_{n=0}^{\infty} \left(\frac{r}{\alpha}\right)^n < \infty$. By Weierstrass M-test, $\sum_{n=0}^{\infty} a_n x^n$ converges **uniformly**.

Method 2 If $x \in [-r, r]$, then $|a_n x^n| \leq |a_n| r^n$. Since $0 < r < R$, and R is the radius of convergence of $\sum_{n=0}^{\infty} a_n x^n$, the series $\sum |a_n| r^n$ converges. Thus, by the Weierstrass

$M-$Test, $\sum a_n x^n$ converges uniformly on $[-r, r]$. $\square$

Remark 16.2.14 *Combining Theorem 16.2.13 and Theorem 16.1.8 (c), we obtain that a power series may be differentiated term-by-term on any compact interval* **in the interior of its interval of convergence.**

Theorem 16.2.15 *Let R be the radius of convergence of the power series* $\sum_{n=0}^{\infty} a_n x^n$, *where $0 < R < \infty$. Then,*

(a) the series can be differentiated term-by-term on $[-r, r]$, where $0 < r < R$; i.e., if

$$f(x) = \sum_{n=0}^{\infty} a_n x^n,$$

then, on $[-r, r]$,

$$f'(x) = \sum_{n=1}^{\infty} n a_n x^{n-1} \ \forall \ x \in [-r, r], \ 0 < r < R.$$

Furthermore,

(b) $\sum_{n=0}^{\infty} a_n x^n$ *and* $\sum_{n=1}^{\infty} n a_n x^{n-1}$ *have the same radius of convergence.*

Proof. (a) By Theorem 16.2.13, the series $\sum_{n=0}^{\infty} a_n x^n$ converges *uniformly* on $[-r, r]$ for any r such that $0 < r < R$. By Remark 16.2.14, $f(x) = \sum_{n=0}^{\infty} a_n x^n$ can be differentiated term by term for all $x \in [-r, r]$, establishing (a).

(b) Since $R > 0$, it follows from the definition of radius of convergence that $\{|a_n|^{\frac{1}{n}}\}$ is bounded. Since $\lim n^{\frac{1}{n}} = 1$, we have (see Problem 7, Exercises 16.2) that:

$$\lim sup \, |a_n|^{\frac{1}{n}} = \lim sup \, |na_n|^{\frac{1}{n}},$$

so that $\sum_{n=0}^{\infty} a_n x^n$ and $\sum_{n=1}^{\infty} na_n x^{n-1}$ have the same radius of convergence, $R > 0$. Hence, by part (a), the differentiated series $\sum_{n=1}^{\infty} na_n x^{n-1}$ converges *uniformly* on $[-r, r]$ for any r such that $0 < r < R$. By Theorem 16.1.8 (c),

$$f'(x) = \sum_{n=1}^{\infty} na_n x^{n-1} = \sum_{n=0}^{\infty} (n+1)a_{n+1} x^n$$

for all $x \in [-r, r]$. Since this holds for arbitrary r such that $0 < r < R$, the differentiated series converges to f' on $(-R, R)$, i.e.,

$$f(x) = \sum_{n=0}^{\infty} a_n x^n \Rightarrow f'(x) = \sum_{n=1}^{\infty} na_n x^{n-1}.$$

This completes the proof. $\square$

Furthermore, we have the following theorem.

Theorem 16.2.16 *A power series with radius of convergence R, $0 < R < \infty$, can be integrated term-by-term on $[-r, r]$, where $0 < r < R$,*

i.e., if $f(x) = \sum_{n=0}^{\infty} a_n x^n$ and $|x| < R$ we have:

$$\int_0^x f(t)dt = \int_0^x \sum_{n=0}^{\infty} a_n t^n \, dt$$

$$= \sum_{n=0}^{\infty} \int_0^x a_n t^n \, dt = \sum_{n=0}^{\infty} \frac{a_n}{n+1} x^{(n+1)}.$$

Furthermore,

$$\sum_{n=0}^{\infty} a_n x^n$$

and

$$\sum_{n=0}^{\infty} \frac{a_n}{n+1} x^{(n+1)}$$

have the same radius of convergence.

Proof.   We compute the radius of convergence of the integral series.   Observe first that $\sum_{n=0}^{\infty} \frac{a_n}{n+1} x^{(n+1)} \equiv \sum_{n=1}^{\infty} \frac{a_{n-1}}{n} x^n$.   So, (see Problem 9, Exercises 6.1)

$$\limsup_{n\to\infty} \sqrt[n]{\left|\frac{a_{n-1}}{n}\right|} = \limsup_{n\to\infty} \left(|a_{n-1}|^{\frac{1}{n-1}}\right)^{\frac{n-1}{n}} \left(\frac{1}{n}\right)^{\frac{1}{n}}.$$

Since $\lim_{n\to\infty} \frac{n-1}{n} = 1$ and $\lim_{n\to\infty} n^{-\frac{1}{n}} = 1$, we see that the integral series has the same radius of convergence R as the original series. Thus, the integral series converges uniformly on any interval $[-r, r] \subset (-R, R)$. By Theorem 16.1.8(b), term-by-term integration is valid for any $x \in [-r, r]$. $\square$

16.2.4   Uniform convergence at endpoints

Theorem 16.2.13 shows that a power series converges *uni formly* on any compact interval *in the interior* of its interval of convergence.   If the interval of convergence includes an endpoint, a result of Niels Abel (1802 - 1829) shows that the power series converges *uniformly* on any compact interval that includes this endpoint.

Theorem 16.2.17 *[Convergence at endpoints] Let* $\sum_{n=0}^{\infty} a_n x^n$ *be a power series with a finite radius of convergence R.*

(a) *If the series converges at $x = R$, (an endpoint), then it converges uniformly on the interval $[0, R]$.*

(b) *If the series converges at $x = -R$, (an endpoint), then it converges uniformly on $[-R, 0]$.*

Proof.   Without loss of generality we take $R = 1$. Our technique is to prove that the Uniform Cauchy Criterion is satisfied for the partial sum $s_n(x) = \sum_{i=1}^{n} a_i x^i$, i.e., given any $\epsilon > 0$, we find an integer $N = N(\epsilon)$ such that

$$|s_m(x) - s_{m+k}(x)| = |a_m x^m + a_{m+1} x^{m+1} + ... + a_{m+k} x^{m+k}| < \epsilon,$$

for all $x \in [0, 1]$ and for all $m > N, k = 0, 1, ...$. Now, since the series converges at $x = 1$, there exists an integer $N > 0$ such that

$$|a_m + a_{m+1} + ... + a_{m+k}| < \epsilon, \ \forall \ m > N, k = 0, 1, ...$$

Fix $m > N$ and for each $i \geq 0$, let

$$s_i = a_m + a_{m+1} + ... + a_{m+i}.$$

Then, $|s_i| < \epsilon \ \forall \ i \geq 0$. So,

$$
\begin{aligned}
a_m x^m \ &+ \ a_{m+1} x^{m+1} + ... + a_{m+k} x^{m+k} \\
&= \ s_0(x^m - x^{m+1}) + s_1(x^{m+1} - x^{m+2}) \\
&\quad +... + s_{k-1}(x^{m+k-1} - x^{m+k}) + s_k x^{m+k} \\
&= \ s_0 x^m + (s_1 - s_0)x^{m+1} \\
&\quad +... + s_{k-1}(x^{m+k-1} - x^{m+k}) + s_k x^{m+k} \\
&= \ x^m(1 - x)\left[s_0 + s_1 x + ... + s_{k-1}x^{k-1}\right] + s_k x^{m+k}.
\end{aligned}
$$

Hence, for all $x \in [0, 1)$, we have

$$
\begin{aligned}
|a_m x^m &+ a_{m+1} x^{m+1} + \ldots + a_{m+k} x^{m+k}| \\
&\leq x^m (1 - x) \left[\epsilon + \epsilon x + \ldots + \epsilon x^{k-1} \right] + \epsilon x^{m+k} \\
&\leq x^m (1 - x) \left[1 + x + x^2 + \ldots + x^{k-1} \right] \epsilon + \epsilon x^{m+k} \\
&= \epsilon x^m (1 - x^k) + \epsilon x^{m+k} = \epsilon x^m < \epsilon.
\end{aligned}
$$

This inequality also holds when $x = 1$ since $|s_k| < \epsilon$. Hence, the series converges *uniformly* on $[0, 1]$. $\square$

Corollary 16.2.18 (Continuity at endpoints) *Let the power series* $f(x) = \displaystyle\sum_{n=0}^{\infty} a_n x^n$ *have a radius of convergence* R, $0 < R < \infty$.

(a) *If the series converges at* $x = R$, *then* f *is continuous at* $x = R$.

(b) *If the series converges at* $x = -R$, *then* f *is continuous at* $x = -R$.

Proof. Problem 9, Exercises 16.2

We conclude our study of power series with the following important example.

Example 16.2.19 *In Example 16.1.10, we proved that*

$$
f(x) = \ln (1 + x) = \sum_{n=0}^{\infty} (-1)^n \frac{x^{n+1}}{n+1}, \quad x \in (-1, 1).
$$

We now consider the endpoints.

At $x = 1$, the series becomes $\displaystyle\sum_{n=0}^{\infty} \frac{(-1)^n}{n+1}$ which is the alternating harmonic series which is convergent. By Corollary 16.2.18, f is continuous at $x = 1$. Hence, as $x \to 1, f(x) \to f(1)$, i.e.,

$$\lim_{x \to 1} \log\,(1+x) = \lim_{x \to 1} f(x) = f(1) = \sum_{n=0}^{\infty} \frac{(-1)^n}{n+1},$$

which yields

$$\log\,(2) = \sum_{n=0}^{\infty} \frac{(-1)^n}{n+1}.$$

EXERCISES 16.2

1. Find the radius of convergence of the following power series.

   (a) $\sum n^p x^n$, $p > 0$. (b) $\sum \frac{x^n}{n!}$. (c) $\sum n! x^n$.
   (d) $\sum q^{n^2} x^n$ if $|q| < 1$. (e) $\sum x^{n!}$.

2. If the radius of convergence of $\displaystyle\sum_{n=0}^{\infty} a_n x^n$ is R, what is the radius of convergence of $\displaystyle\sum_{n=0}^{\infty} a_n x^{2n}$? (Ans: $\sqrt{R}$).

3. If the radius of convergence of $\displaystyle\sum_{n=0}^{\infty} a_n x^n$ is 5, what is the radius of convergence of $\displaystyle\sum_{n=0}^{\infty} (a_n)^2 x^{5n}$? (Ans: $(25)^{\frac{1}{5}}$).

4. Given that R is the radius of convergence of $\displaystyle\sum_{n=0}^{\infty} a_n x^n$, what is the radius of convergence of $\displaystyle\sum_{n=0}^{\infty} a_n x^{n!}$?

5. Suppose that $f(x) = \sum_{n=0}^{\infty} a_n x^n$ for $x \in (-R, R)$, where $R > 0$ is the radius of convergence of the series. Prove:

   (i) for each $n \in \mathbb{N}$, the rth derivative $f^{(r)}$ of f exists on $(-R, R)$;

   (ii) $f^{(r)}(x) = \sum_{n=r}^{\infty} \frac{n!}{(n-r)!} a_n x^{n-r}$.

   (iii) $f^{(r)}(0) = r! a_r$.

6. If $\sum_{n=0}^{\infty} a_n x^n = \sum_{n=0}^{\infty} b_n x^n$ for all $x \in (-R, R)$, where $R > 0$ is the radius of convergence of each series, prove that $a_n = b_n$ for all $n \in \mathbb{N} \cup \{0\}$.

7. Suppose that $\{a_n\}$ converges to $a > 0$ and $\{b_n\}$ is a bounded sequence in $\mathbb{R}$. Prove that

$$\limsup a_n b_n = a. \limsup b_n.$$

(Hint: Let $b = \limsup b_n$ and $\beta = \limsup a_n b_n$. Suffices now to prove $\beta = ab$. There exists a subsequence $\{b_{n_k}\}$ of $\{b_n\}$ such that $b_{n_k} \to b$ as $k \to \infty$. Consequently, $a_{n_k} \to a$ as $k \to \infty$ (why?), so that $a_{n_k} b_{n_k} \to ab$ as $k \to \infty$. Thus,

$$ab < \limsup a_n b_n = \beta.$$

Similarly, let $\{a_{n_k} b_{n_k}\}$ be a subsequence of $a_n b_n$ such that $a_{n_k} b_{n_k} \to \beta$. Then, since $\beta > 0$, show that

$$\lim_{k \to \infty} b_{n_k} = \frac{\beta}{a},$$

so that $\beta \leq ab$. Since also $ab \leq \beta$, conclude that $\beta = ab$).

8. Prove that if $\{a_n\}$ is a sequence of positive numbers, then

$$\liminf_{n\to\infty} \frac{a_{n+1}}{a_n} \leq \liminf_{n\to\infty} \left(a_n\right)^{\frac{1}{n}}$$

$$\leq \limsup_{n\to\infty} \left(a_n\right)^{\frac{1}{n}}$$

$$\leq \limsup_{n\to\infty} \frac{a_{n+1}}{a_n}. \qquad (16.2.1)$$

From this inequality, conclude that whenever the root test determines convergence or divergence, the ratio test does too. (Hint:To prove the last part of inequality (16.2.1), let $\beta = limsup \frac{a_{n+1}}{a_n}$. If $\beta = \infty$, the result follows trivially. If $\beta < \infty$, for arbitrary $\epsilon > 0$, there exists $N \in \mathbb{N}$ such that $\frac{a_{n+1}}{a_n} < \beta + \epsilon \ \forall n \geq N$. This implies, for all $n \geq N$, we have $a_n < a_{n-1}(\beta + \epsilon)$; $a_{n-1} < a_{n-2}(\beta + \epsilon)$;...; $a_{N+1} < a_N(\beta + \epsilon)$. Combining these $(n-N)$ inequalities, we obtain that $a_n < (\beta+\epsilon)^n k$ for some constant $k > 0$. Now take the nth root of both sides.)

9. Prove Corollary 16.2.18.

360

CHAPTER **17**

Equicontinuity

17.1   Introduction

Recall the Bolzano Weierstrass Theorem: Every bounded sequence in $\mathbb{R}$ has a convergent subsequence. Let us now denote by $C[a, b]$ the collection of all continuous functions $f : [a, b] \to \mathbb{R}$. Let the distance $d(f, g)$ between arbitrary f and g in $C[a, b]$ be denoted by

$$d(f, g) = \sup_{a \leq x \leq b} |f(x) - g(x)|.$$

We are now interested in the following question.

Question. *Does every bounded sequence in $C[a, b]$ have (with respect to this distance) a convergent subsequence?*

In other words, do we have the analogue of Bolzano Weierstrass theorem in $C[a, b]$? The answer to this question is "NO", as can be seen from the following example.

Example 17.1.1 Let $f_n : [0, 1] \to \mathbb{R}$ be defined by $f_n(x) = x^n$. Clearly, f_n is continuous for each n. So, $f_n \in C[0, 1]$. Furthermore, $|f_n(x)| \leq 1 \; \forall \; x \in [0, 1]$, so $\{f_n\}$ is bounded. We claim $\{f_n\}$ has no convergent subsequence in $C[0, 1]$. Assume, for contradiction, that it has. Then, $\{f_{n_k}\}$ converges to some $f \in C[0, 1]$. But $f(x) = \lim_{k \to \infty} f_{n_k}(x) = \lim_{n \to \infty} f_n(x)$. Thus, (recall Example 15.1.2) $f(x) = 1, if x = 1$, and $f(x) = 0$, if $x \in [0, 1)$, a contradiction, since f is *not* continuous.

The question now is: What condition(s) shall be imposed on $\{f_n\} \subset C[a, b]$ to guarantee that it has a convergent subsequence? The condition necessary for this is called *equicontinuity* which we now define.

17.2   Arzela-Ascoli Theorem

Definition 17.2.1 *A sequence of continuous real-valued functions $f_n : [a, b] \to \mathbb{R}$ (i.e., $f_n \in C[a, b]$) is called equicontinuous if, given $\epsilon > 0$, $\exists \delta = \delta(\epsilon) > 0$ such that*

$$|s - t| < \delta \Rightarrow |f_n(s) - f_n(t)| < \epsilon \; \forall n \geq 1.$$

Equicontinuity actually implies that the functions f_n are equally (*cqui*) continuous. The δ depends on the given ϵ, but does not depend on the particular f_n picked. Geometrically, equicontinuity implies that the graphs of all the f_n's look alike.

The definition of equicontinuity works as well for subsets of $C[a, b]$ that are not necessarily sequences.

A subset K of $C[a, b]$ is said to be equicontinuous if given $\epsilon > 0, \exists \delta = \delta(\epsilon) > 0$ such that

$$|s - t| < \delta \Rightarrow |f(s) - f(t)| < \epsilon \forall f \in K.$$

The important point to note is that δ does not depend on the particular $f \in K$ chosen. It is valid for **all** $f \in K$, simultaneously.

The basic theorem about equicontinuity is the Arzela-Ascoli Theorem which we now prove.

Theorem 17.2.2 (Arzela-Ascoli Theorem) *Any uniformly bounded equicontinuous sequence $\{f_n\}$ in $C[a,b]$ has a **uniformly** convergent subsequence.*

Proof. $[a,b]$ has a countable dense subset

$$D = \{x_1, x_2, x_3, ...\}.$$

In particular, one can take $D = Q \cap [a,b]$. Uniform boundedness of $\{f_n\}$ implies there exists $M > 0$ such that

$$|f_n(x)| \leq M \ \forall \, x \in [a,b], \forall \, n \geq 1.$$

Hence, $\{f_n(x_1)\}$ is a bounded sequence in $\mathbb{R}$. By Bolzano Weierstrass theorem, $\{f_n(x_1)\}$ has a subsequence, which we shall denote by $\{f_{1,k}(x_1)\}$, which converges to a limit, say ω_1 in $\mathbb{R}$, i.e.,

$$\lim_{k \to \infty} f_{1,k}(x_1) = \omega_1.$$

Consider now the subsequence $\{f_{1,k}\}$ of $\{f_n\}$ evaluated at x_2 in D. It is a bounded sequence in $\mathbb{R}$. Again, by the Bolzano Weierstrass theorem, it has a subsequence $\{f_{2,k}\}$ such that $\{f_{2,k}(x_2)\}$ converges to a point , say ω_2 in $\mathbb{R}$, i.e.,

$$\lim_{k \to \infty} f_{2,k}(x_2) = \omega_2.$$

Note that this subsequence evaluated at x_1, i.e., $\{f_{2,k}(x_1)\}$ still converges to ω_1. Continuing in this way, we obtain a nested family of subsequences $f_{m,k}$ such that

1. $\{f_{m,k}\}$ is a subsequence of $\{f_{m-1,k}\}$;

2. $i \leq m \Rightarrow f_{m,k}(x_i) \to \omega_i$ as $k \to \infty$.

Now, choose $k_m \geq m$ large enough that if $i \leq m$, and $k_m \leq k$, then,

$$|f_{m,k}(x_i) - \omega_i| < \frac{1}{m}.$$

The superdiagonal subsequence $h_m(x) = f_{m,k_m}(x)$ converges to a limit at each point $x \in D$.

Claim. $h_m(x)$ converges at other points $x \in [a,b]$ and the convergence is uniform.

It suffices to show that $\{h_m\}_{n=1}^{\infty}$ is a Cauchy sequence in $C[a,b]$. Let $\epsilon > 0$ be given. Equicontinuity gives a $\delta > 0$ such that for all $s, t \in [a,b]$,

$$|s - t| < \delta \Rightarrow |h_m(s) - h_m(t)| < \frac{\epsilon}{3}. \tag{17.2.1}$$

Since D is dense in $[a,b]$ and $[a,b]$ is compact, we can choose an integer N_0 sufficiently large such that for each $x \in [a,b]$, there is a δ-neighbourhood of **some** x_i with $i \leq N_0$ which contains x (see, Problem 4, Exercises 17.1). Finally, since $\{x_1, x_2, ..., x_{N_0}\}$ is a finite set and $h_m(x_i)$ converges for each x_i, there exists an integer N such that

$$|h_m(x_i) - h_n(x_i)| < \frac{\epsilon}{3}, \ \forall \ n, m \geq N, \forall i \leq N_0. \tag{17.2.2}$$

If $n, m \geq N$, and $x \in [a,b]$, choose x_i with $|x_i - x| < \delta$ and $i \leq N_0$. Then,

$$
\begin{aligned}
|h_m(x) - h_n(x)| &\leq |h_m(x) - h_m(x_i)| + |h_m(x_i) - h_n(x_i)| \\
&\quad + |h_n(x_i) - h_n(x)| \\
&< \frac{\epsilon}{3} + \frac{\epsilon}{3} + \frac{\epsilon}{3} = \epsilon.
\end{aligned}
$$

Hence, $\{h_n\}$ is Cauchy in $C[a,b]$, and so converges in $C[a,b]$ (which implies it converges uniformly). The proof is complete. $\square$

17.3   Some important corollaries

The following consequences of the Arzela-Ascoli Theorem are very important in applications.

Theorem 17.3.1 (Arzela-Ascoli Propagation Theorem)
Let $\{f_n\}$ be an equicontinuous sequence of real-valued functions defined on a dense subset D of $[a, b]$. Suppose that the limit $\lim\limits_{n\to\infty} f_n(x) = f(x)$ exists for each $x \in D$. Then, $\{f_n\}$ converges uniformly to f on $[a, b]$.

Proof.   This has been given in the $\frac{\epsilon}{3}$ part of theorem 17.2.2.

Remark 17.3.2 *Theorem 17.3.1 asserts that pointwise con-*vergence **of an equicontinuous sequence** *of functions* **on a dense subset of the domain** *propagates to uniform con-vergence on the whole domain.*

The following corollary of Theorem 17.2.2 is, perhaps, the most important, from the point of view of applications.

Corollary 17.3.3 *Let $f_n : [a, b] \to \mathbb{R}$ be a sequence of dif-ferentiable functions such that (i) The derivatives f_n' are uni-formly bounded, (ii) for some x_0, $f_n(x_0)$ is bounded. Then, the sequence $\{f_n\}$ has a subsequence that converges uniformly on $[a, b]$.*

Proof.   Since $\{f_n'\}$ is uniformly bounded, there exists $M > 0$ such that

$$|f_n'(x)| \leq M \ \forall\, x \in [a, b], \ \forall\, n \geq 1.$$

By Mean Value Theorem,

$$|s - t| < \delta \Rightarrow |f_n(s) - f_n(t)| = |f_n'(\psi)| . |s - t| \leq M\delta,$$

for some ψ between s and t. Thus, given $\epsilon > 0$, choose $\delta = \frac{\epsilon}{M+1}$. Then, $\{f_n\}$ is equicontinuous. Since $\{f_n(x_0)\}$ is bounded, there exists $\delta > 0$ such that

$$|f_n(x_0)| < \rho \; \forall \, n \geq 1.$$

So, we have,

$$\begin{aligned} |f_n(x)| &\leq |f_n(x) - f_n(x_0)| + |f_n(x_0)| \\ &\leq M|x - x_0| + \rho \leq M(b - a) + \rho \; \forall \, n \geq 1. \end{aligned}$$

By Arzela-Ascoli Theorem, $\{f_n\}$ has a subsequence that converges uniformly on $[a, b]$. This completes the proof. $\quad\square$

Theorem 17.3.4 *A sequence of solutions to a continuous ordinary differential equatons in $\mathbb{R}^n$ has a subsequence that converges to a limit, and the limit is also a solution of the ordinary differential equation.*

Theorem 17.3.5 *A subset $K \subset C[a, b]$ is compact if and only if it is closed, bounded and equicontinuous.*

Proof. Assume K is compact. Then K is closed and is totally bounded (i.e., given $\epsilon > 0$, there exists a finite covering of K by neighbourhoods $U_{\frac{\epsilon}{3}}(f_j), j = 1, 2, \cdots, n$, for some $n \in \mathbb{N}$, in $C[a, b]$ that have radius $\frac{\epsilon}{3}$). Each f_j is uniformly continuous (why?) so, there exists $\delta > 0$ such that

$$|s - t| < \delta \Rightarrow |f_j(s) - f_j(t)| < \frac{\epsilon}{3} \qquad \forall j.$$

If $f \in K$, then $f \in U_{\frac{\epsilon}{3}}(f_j)$ for some j. Therefore, $|s - t| < \delta$ implies

$$\begin{aligned} |f(s) - f(t)| &\leq |f(s) - f_j(s)| + |f_j(s) - f_j(t)| \\ &\quad + |f_j(t) - f(t)| \\ &< \frac{\epsilon}{3} + \frac{\epsilon}{3} + \frac{\epsilon}{3} = \epsilon. \end{aligned}$$

Thus K is equicontinuous.

Conversely, assume that K is closed bounded and equicontinuous. If $\{f_n\}$ is a sequence in K, then , by Arzela-Ascoli theorem, $\{f_n\}$ has a convergent subsequence $\{f_{n_k}\}$ whose limit lies in K since K is closed. Hence K is compact. The proof is complete. $\square$

EXERCISES 17.1

1. Prove that a compact subset of a metric space is closed.

2. Prove Theorem 17.3.4.

3. Prove that a metric space is compact if and only if it is complete and totally bounded (Hint: Arzela-Ascoli theorem).

4. If (X, ρ) is a compact metric space and D is dense in X, prove that for any $\delta > 0$, there is a finite subset $\{x_1, x_2, x_3, ..., x_k\} \subset D$ which is $\delta-$dense set in X, in the sense that each $x \in X$ lies within distance δ of at least one of the points $x_i, i = 1, 2, ..., k$.

5. Prove that if a sequence of continuous real-valued functions $\{f_n\}$ converges **uniformly** on a compact set K, then the sequence is equicontinuous on K.

368

CHAPTER **18**

Miscellaneous Examples and Exercises

18.1 Miscellaneous examples

Recall the **Limit Comparison Test.** Suppose that $a_n > 0$ and $b_n > 0$ for all $n \geq N_0$ (for some positive integer N_0).

1. If $\lim\limits_{n\to\infty} \frac{a_n}{b_n} = k$, $0 < k < \infty$, then $\sum a_n$ and $\sum b_n$ both converge (diverge), i.e., if one converges (diverges) so does the other.

2. If $\lim\limits_{n\to\infty} \frac{a_n}{b_n} = 0$ and $\sum b_n$ converges, then $\sum a_n$ converges.

3. If $\lim\limits_{n\to\infty} \frac{a_n}{b_n} = \infty$ and $\sum b_n$ diverges, then $\sum a_n$ diverges.

Proof. (1) Let $\epsilon > 0$ be arbitrary. Since $\frac{a_n}{b_n} \to k$, $\exists \, N_\epsilon$ such that for all $n \geq N_\epsilon$,

$$\left| \frac{a_n}{b_n} - k \right| < \epsilon.$$

Take $\epsilon = \frac{k}{2} > 0$. Then, there exists $N_k \in \mathbb{N}$ such that for all $n \geq N_k$

$$\left| \frac{a_n}{b_n} - k \right| < \frac{k}{2}.$$

Thus, for all $n \geq N_k$,

$$-\frac{k}{2} < \frac{a_n}{b_n} - k < \frac{k}{2}$$

or

$$\frac{k}{2} < \frac{a_n}{b_n} < \frac{3}{2}k$$

or

$$\frac{k}{2}b_n < a_n < \left(\frac{3}{2}k\right)b_n.$$

Now, if $\sum b_n$ converges, we have $\sum \frac{3}{2}kb_n = \frac{3}{2}k \sum b_n$ converges, and by the comparison test, we have $\sum a_n$ converges.

If $\sum b_n$ diverges then $\sum \frac{k}{2}b_n = \frac{k}{2} \sum b_n$ diverges. Again, by the comparison test, $\sum a_n$ diverges.

(2) Given $\epsilon > 0 \; \exists \, N_\epsilon$ such that $\frac{a_n}{b_n} \leq \epsilon \; \forall \, n \geq N_\epsilon$. Thus, $a_n \leq \epsilon b_n$. If $\sum b_n < \infty$ then $\sum a_n < \infty$.

(3) $\lim\limits_{n\to\infty} \frac{a_n}{b_n} = +\infty$ implies that given any $\delta \in \mathbb{R}$ there exists n_δ such that for all $n \geq n_\delta$, $\dfrac{a_n}{b_n} > \delta$. Thus $\delta b_n < a_n$ for all $n \geq n_\delta$. Therefore, $\sum b_n = \infty$, and hence $\sum a_n = \infty$.

Example 18.1.1 *Consider the series* $\displaystyle\sum_{n=2}^{\infty} \frac{1}{n^\alpha (\ln n)^\beta}$, *where α and β are real numbers.*

(i) Show that the series $\displaystyle\sum_{n=2}^{\infty} a_n$ *converges for $\alpha > 1$.*

(ii) Show that the series diverges for $\alpha < 1$.

(iii) If $\alpha = 1$, show that the series $\sum\limits_{n=2}^{\infty} a_n$ converges for $\beta > 1$, and diverges for $\beta \le 1$.

Solution. (i) We shall use the Limit Comparison Test. Let $a_n = \frac{1}{n^{\alpha}(\ln n)^{\beta}}$. Define $b_n = \frac{1}{n^{(\alpha+1)/2}}$. Observe that $\alpha > 1 \Rightarrow \frac{\alpha+1}{2} > 1$. Hence, for $\alpha > 1$, $\sum b_n$ converges. Moreover,

$$\lim_{n\to\infty} \frac{a_n}{b_n} = \lim_{n\to\infty} \frac{1}{n^{\frac{1}{2}(\alpha-1)}(\ln n)^{\beta}} = 0.$$

Hence, by the Limit Comparison Test,

$$\sum_{n=2}^{\infty} a_n = \sum_{n=2}^{\infty} \frac{1}{n^{\alpha}(\ln n)^{\beta}} < \infty.$$

(ii) If $\alpha < 1$, using the b_n defined above, we have that

$$\lim_{n\to\infty} \frac{a_n}{b_n} = \lim_{n\to\infty} \frac{1}{n^{\frac{1}{2}(\alpha-1)}(\ln n)^{\beta}} = \infty.$$

In this case, for $\alpha < 1$, $\frac{\alpha+1}{2} < 1$ and so $\sum b_n = \sum \frac{1}{n^{(\alpha+1)/2}}$ diverges. By the Limit Comparison Test, $\sum a_n$ diverges.

(iii) If $\alpha = 1$ and $\beta \ge 0$, we consider the function

$$f(x) = \frac{1}{x(\ln x)^{\beta}}.$$

Verify that f is decreasing, positive and continuous on $[2, \infty)$ and so we apply the Integral Test:

$$\int_2^{\infty} \frac{1}{x(\ln x)^{\beta}} dx = \int_{\ln 2}^{\infty} \frac{dx}{x^{\beta}} \text{ (by substitution)}.$$

Clearly, the integral converges if $\beta > 1$ and diverges if $\beta \le 1$. Consequently, the series $\sum \frac{1}{n(\ln n)^{\beta}}$ converges if $\beta > 1$ and diverges if $\beta \le 1$.

Example 18.1.2 *Discuss the convergence or divergence of the following series:*

(a) $\sum \left(1 - \frac{1}{\sqrt{n}}\right)^n$;

(b) $\sum \frac{n!}{n^n}$;

(c) $\sum n \exp(-n^2)$.

Solution. (a) For $n \geq 1$, set $a_n = \left(1 - \frac{1}{\sqrt{n}}\right)^n$ and take log of both sides to obtain that

$$a_n = \left(1 - \frac{1}{\sqrt{n}}\right)^n = \exp n \ln\left(1 - \frac{1}{\sqrt{n}}\right).$$

Recall that $\ln(1-x) = -x - \frac{1}{2}x^2 - \frac{1}{3}x^3 - \ldots$, so that

$$a_n = \exp(-\sqrt{n})\left[\exp\left(-\frac{1}{2} + o\left(\frac{1}{\sqrt{n}}\right)\right)\right].$$

If we now consider the series $\sum b_n = \sum \exp(-\sqrt{n})$, then

$$\lim_{n \to \infty} \frac{a_n}{b_n} = \exp\left(-\frac{1}{2}\right).$$

Furthermore, there exists a natural number N_0 such that for all $n \geq N_0$, $n^2 \exp(-\sqrt{n}) < 1$. Consequently,

$$\sum_{n=N_0}^{\infty} \exp(-\sqrt{n}) < \sum_{n=N_0}^{\infty} \frac{1}{n^2} < \infty.$$

So, by the Limit Comparison Test, we have that $\sum a_n \equiv \sum\left(1 - \frac{1}{\sqrt{n}}\right)^n$ converges.

(b) Let $a_n = \frac{n!}{n^n}$. Then $\frac{a_{n+1}}{a_n} = \left(\frac{n}{n+1}\right)^n$. Take the log of both sides to base e to obtain

$$\frac{a_{n+1}}{a_n} = \exp\left[-n \ln\left(1 + \frac{1}{n}\right)\right].$$

Now, using the expansion,

$$\ln(1+x) = x - \frac{x^2}{2} + \frac{x^3}{3} - \frac{x^4}{4} + \dots,$$

we obtain that

$$\ln\left(1 + \frac{1}{n}\right) = \frac{1}{n} - \frac{1}{2n^2} + o\left(\frac{1}{n^3}\right).$$

Thus we have, $\lim\limits_{n\to\infty} \frac{a_{n+1}}{a_n} = \exp(-1) < 1$. Hence, by the ratio test, $\sum \frac{n!}{n^n}$ converges.

(c) Let $a_n = ne^{-n^2}$. By ratio test,

$$\begin{aligned}
\lim_{n\to\infty} \frac{a_{n+1}}{a_n} &= \lim_{n\to\infty} \frac{(n+1)\exp(-(n+1)^2)}{n\exp(-n^2)} \\
&= \lim_{n\to\infty} \exp(-(n+1)^2 + n^2) \\
&= \lim_{n\to\infty} \exp(-(2n+1)) \\
&= \lim_{n\to\infty} e^{-2n}e^{-1} = 0 < 1,
\end{aligned}$$

and so $\sum xe^{-n^2}$ converges.

Example 18.1.3 *If $\sum a_n x^n$ has a radius of convergence 5, find the radius of convergence of the series $\sum (a_n)^2 x^{5n}$.*

Solution. Radius of convergence of $\sum a_n x^n = 5$ implies that $\limsup\limits_{n\to\infty} |a_n|^{\frac{1}{n}} = \frac{1}{5}$. Let $\sum\limits_{n=0}^{\infty} (a_n)^2 x^{5n} \equiv \sum\limits_{m=0}^{\infty} b_m y^m$. Then $y^m = x^{5n}$ where

$$b_m = \begin{cases} a_n^2 & \text{if } m = 5n, \\ 0 & \text{if } m \neq 5n. \end{cases}$$

Let the radius of convergence of $\sum_{n=0}^{\infty} (a_n)^2 x^{5n}$ be R. Then,

$$
\begin{aligned}
\frac{1}{R} &= \limsup_{n \to \infty} |b_m|^{\frac{1}{m}} \\
&= \limsup_{n \to \infty} |a_n^2|^{\frac{1}{5n}} \ (\text{since } m = 5n) \\
&= \limsup_{n \to \infty} (|a_n|^{\frac{1}{n}})^{\frac{2}{5}} \\
&= \left[\limsup_{n \to \infty} (|a_n|^{\frac{1}{n}}) \right]^{\frac{2}{5}}, \ (\text{ since } f(x) = x^{2/5} \text{ is continuous}) \\
&= \left(\frac{1}{5}\right)^{\frac{2}{5}} = \left(\frac{1}{25}\right)^{1/5}.
\end{aligned}
$$

18.2 Miscellaneous Exercises

1. Prove that a real-valued monotone function on the real line can have only countably many discontinuities.

2. Let $\{f_n\}$ be a sequence of real-valued functions on $[0, 1]$ and let M be a real number such that:
   (i) for each n, f_n is continuous;
   (ii) for each $x \in [0, 1]$ and for each n, $f_n(x) \leq f_{n+1}(x) \leq M$.
   Prove that the sequence $\{f_n\}_{n=1}^{\infty}$ converges pointwise on $[0, 1]$ to a function f which is *lower semicontinuous* (that is for all $\{x_n\} \subset [0, 1]$ and for all $x \in [0, 1]$, $x_n \to x \Rightarrow \liminf_{n \to \infty}(x_n) \leq f(x)$) on $[0, 1]$.

3. Let $g(x) = \displaystyle\sum_{n=1}^{\infty} \frac{x^n}{n(n + 1)}$. State why it is that $\displaystyle\lim_{x \to 1^-} g(x)$ exists and find this limit.

4. Let $\{f_n\}$ be a sequence defined by

$$f_n(x) = \begin{cases} 1, & \text{if } n \leq x \leq n + 1, \\ 0, & \text{otherwise.} \end{cases}$$

Prove:
   (i) $f_n \to f \equiv 0$ as $n \to \infty$
   (ii) $\displaystyle\liminf_{n \to \infty} \int f_n(x)dx \neq \int f(x)dx.$

5. Let $\{f_n\}$ be defined as follows

$$f_n(x) = \begin{cases} 1, & \text{if } x \geq n, \\ 0, & \text{if } x < n. \end{cases}$$

Prove:
   (i) $\{f_n\}$ is monotone decreasing and nonnegative.
   (ii) $f_n \to f \equiv 0$, pointwise as $n \to \infty$.
   (iii) $\displaystyle\lim_{n \to \infty} \int_n^{\infty} f_n(x)dx \neq \int_n^{\infty} f(x)dx.$

6. If $\{f_n\}$ is a sequence of real-valued continuous functions defined on $[0, 1]$ and if

$$\lim_{n \to \infty} f_n(x) = f(x) \text{ exists for each } x \in [0, 1],$$

then the following statements are not necessarily true:
(a)   the limit function is continuous.

(b) $\lim\limits_{n \to \infty} \int_0^1 f_n(x)dx = \int_0^1 f(x)dx.$

There is, however, a nontrivial additional condition which makes both (a) and (b) true.
(i)   Name such a condition defining your terms carefully.
(ii)   Prove either (a) or (b) assuming the condition is true.
(iii)   Find counterexamples to show that neither (a) nor (b) is necessarily true if this condition is violated.

7. If radius of convergence of $\sum\limits_{n=0}^{\infty} a_n z^n$ is 5, then find the radius of convergence of $\sum\limits_{n=0}^{\infty} a_n^2 z^{5n}$ and prove it.

8. Find the interval of convergence of the following power series:

(a) $\sum\limits_{n=1}^{\infty} \dfrac{x^n}{n^3 3^n},$ (b) $\sum\limits_{n=1}^{\infty} \dfrac{n^n x^n}{n!},$

(c) Prove that if $x_n \to x$ as $n \to \infty$, then

$$\lim_{n \to \infty} \frac{x_1 + x_2 + \cdots + x_n}{n} = x.$$

9. Let $\{f_n\}$ be an *equicontinuous* sequence of real-valued functions defined on $[0, 1]$. Suppose $\lim\limits_{n \to \infty} f_n(x) = f(x)$ exists for each $x \in [0, 1]$. Prove that $f_n \to f$ uniformly on $[0, 1]$.

10. Let $G(x) = \displaystyle\int_{\alpha(x)}^{\beta(x)} g(x,t)dt.$

    (a)   Place conditions on α, β and g so that $G'(x)$ exists, for $0 < x < 1$.

    (b)   Give the formula for computing $G'(x)$ and prove its correctness.

11. Let $a_n > 0$, $a_{n+1} < a_n$, $a_n \to 0$. Define
$$x_1 \quad = a_1$$
$$x_{n+1} \quad = x_n + (-1)^n a_{n+1}.$$
Show that $\{x_n\}$ is Cauchy.

12. Find all x's such that

    (a) $\displaystyle\sum_{n=1}^{\infty} (a_n)^2 x^n$ converges, and

    (b) $\displaystyle\sum_{n=10}^{\infty} \frac{x^n}{n \log n}$ converges.

13. Let f be a function on $[0,1]$ into $\mathbb{R}$. Suppose that if $x \in [0,1]$, then there exists K_x such that $|f(x) - f(y)| \le K_x|x - y|$ for all $y \in [0,1]$. Prove or disprove: There is a constant K such that

$$|f(x) - f(y)| \le K|x - y| \ \forall \ x, y \in [0,1].$$

14. Suppose that for each positive integer n, f_n is a continuous function on $\mathbb{R}$ to $\mathbb{R}$. Show that if for some subset K of $\mathbb{R}$ the sequence $\{f_n\}_{n=0}^{\infty}$ is uniformly convergent on K then $\{f_n\}_{n=1}^{\infty}$ is equicontinuous on K.

15. Suppose that each of f and g is a real-valued function whose domain includes 0 and that $f(0) = g(0) = 0$. Provide additional hypothesis on f and g so that L'Hospital's rule can be used to compute $\displaystyle\lim_{x \to 0} \frac{f(x)}{g(x)}$.
Prove your statement of L'Hospital's rule.

16. A sequence of real numbers $\{b_n\}_{n=1}^{\infty}$ is said to be of *bounded variation* if and only if $\sum_{n=1}^{\infty} |b_n - b_{n-1}|$ exists. Show that if the sequence of real numbers $\{a_n\}_{n=1}^{\infty}$ has the property that $\left\{ \sum_{n=1}^{p} a_n \right\}_{p=1}^{\infty}$ is bounded, $\{b_n\}_{n=1}^{\infty}$ is of bounded variation and $\lim_{n\to\infty} b_n = 0$, then $\sum_{n=1}^{\infty} a_n b_n$ exists.

17. Prove that $\ln 2 = \sum_{k=1}^{\infty} \frac{(-1)^{k+1}}{k}$.

18. Show that $\sum_{n=1}^{\infty} x^n(1 - x)$ converges pointwise on $[0, 1]$ but not uniformly, but that $\sum_{n=1}^{\infty} (-1)^n x^n(1 - x)$ converges uniformly on $[0, 1]$. Does this violate a theorem on absolute convergence?

19. If $f_n \to f$ uniformly on $[0, 1]$ and each f_n is continuous on $[0, 1]$, prove that f is continuous on $[0, 1]$.

20. Let $\{a_n\}_{n=1}^{\infty}$ be a monotone decreasing sequence of positive real numbers converging to 0. Prove that $\sum_{n=1}^{\infty} (-1)^n a_n$ converges.

21. Suppose the power series $\sum_{n=0}^{\infty} a_n x^n$ has radius of convergence 3. Find the radius of convergence of $\sum_{n=0}^{\infty} (a_n)^2 x^{5n}$ and justify your answer.

22. Given that $f_n(x) = \sin\sqrt{x + 4n^2\pi^2}$, $x \geq 0$, prove that:
    (i)   the family $\{f_n\}_{n=1}^{\infty}$ is equicontinuous on $[0, +\infty)$.
    (ii) $f_n \to 0$ pointwise on $[0, +\infty)$.
    Is the convergence uniform on $[0, +\infty)$? Justify your answer.

23. For which real numbers x does $\displaystyle\sum_{n=1}^{\infty} n^n x^n$ converge? Justify your answer.

24. Prove or give a counterexample: If $\displaystyle\sum_{n=1}^{\infty} a_n = 1$ and each $a_n \geq 0$, then $\displaystyle\lim_{n\to\infty} na_n = 0$.

25. Determine which sequences converge *uniformly*. Establish your answer.
    (a) $f_n(x) = \dfrac{\sin(nx)}{n}$, $x \in [0, \infty)$.
    (b) $s_n(x) = \displaystyle\sum_{k=0}^{n} \dfrac{e^{-kx}}{1 + kx}$, $x \in [1, 2]$.
    (c) $f_n(x) = nxe^{-nx}$, $x \in [0, 1]$.

26. (*Abel's Theorem*) :   If $\displaystyle\sum_{n=0}^{\infty} a_n x^n$ converges in $(-1, 1]$, then

$$\lim_{x\to 1^-} \sum_{n=0}^{\infty} a_n x^n = \sum_{n=0}^{\infty} a_n.$$

Use this to show that $\log 2 = \displaystyle\sum_{n=1}^{\infty} \dfrac{(-1)^{n+1}}{n}$.

(Note: You are not asked to prove Abel's Theorem).

27. (*a*) Prove that if $a_n \downarrow 0$ and $\displaystyle\sum_{n=1}^{\infty} a_n$ converges, then

$$\lim_{n\to\infty} na_n = 0.$$

(b) Prove or disprove: if $a_n \geq 0$ and $\displaystyle\sum_{n=1}^{\infty} a_n$ converges, then $\displaystyle\lim_{n\to\infty} na_n = 0$.

(c) Prove or disprove: if $a_n \downarrow 0$ and $\displaystyle\lim_{n\to\infty} na_n = 0$, then $\displaystyle\sum_{n=1}^{\infty} a_n$ converges.

28. If

$$g(x) = \sum_{n=1}^{\infty} \frac{x^n}{n(n+1)},$$

state why it is that $\displaystyle\lim_{x\to 1^-} g(x)$ exists, and *find this limit.*

29. Show that if $f(x) = \displaystyle\sum_{n=0}^{\infty} a_n x^n$ converges for $x = 50$, then $f(x)$ is uniformly continuous on $[0, 10]$.

30. Let $f(x) = \left(\displaystyle\int_0^x e^{-t^2}\, dt \right)^2$, $\quad g(x) = \displaystyle\int_0^1 \frac{e^{-x^2(t^2+1)}}{t^2+1}\, dt.$
  (a)   Show that $f + g$ is a constant function.
  (b)   What is this constant?
  (c)   Show that $\displaystyle\lim_{x\to\infty} \int_0^x e^{-t^2}\, dt = \frac{\sqrt{\pi}}{2}.$

31. Let $\{f_n\}$ be a sequence of functions continuous on $(0, 1)$, and let $\displaystyle\sum_{n=0}^{\infty} f_n(x)$ converge uniformly on compact subsets of $(0, 1)$ to $f(x)$. Show that f is continuous on $(0, 1)$.

32. (a) If $f(x)$ has derivatives of all orders in a neighbourhood of $x = a$, write the Taylor series expansion for $f(x)$ about $x = a$.
  (b) Write the series expansion for e^x, $\sin x$ and $\cos x$ about $x = 0$.
  (c) Prove that $e^{ix} = \cos x + i \sin x$.

33. Prove or disprove: The sequence $f_n(x) = x^n$ converges uniformly on $[0, 1]$.

34. Let f be a continuous real-valued function on $[0, 1]$ and

$$F(x) = \max\{f(t) : 0 \le t \le x\}.$$

Show that $F(x)$ is also continuous on $[0, 1]$.

35. Let $f : [0, 1] \to [-1, 1]$ be arbitrary and define $g(x) = \sup_{a \le t \le x} |f(t)|$.

Must g be Riemann integrable?

If not, give a counterexample. In either case, explain your answer.

36. (a) Let $f(x) = \sin(\frac{1}{x})$, $x \ne 0$; $f(0) = 0$. Does $\int_0^1 f(x)dx$ exist in the sense of Riemann? Explain.

(b) Show that if $f \in C[0, 1]$ and $\int_0^1 x^n f(x)dx = 0 \ \forall \ n = 1, 2, \cdots$, then f is the zero function, i.e., $f(x) = 0 \ \forall \ x \in [0, 1]$.

37. A function $f : \mathbb{R} \to \mathbb{R}$ is such that $f(x + y) = f(x) + f(y)$ for all $x, y \in \mathbb{R}$. If f is continuous at $x = 0$, show that f is continuous on $\mathbb{R}$.

38. For integer $n \ge 1$, let the function f_n be Riemann integrable on the interval $[a, b]$. If f_n converges uniformly to a function f on $[a, b]$, prove that f is Riemann integrable on $[a, b]$.

39. Does $\lim_{n \to \infty} \sum_{k=n}^{n^2} \frac{1}{k}$ exist? Explain your reasoning.

40. A function defined on a closed and bounded interval $[a, b]$ satisfies a Lipschitz condition of order $\alpha > 0$ if and only if $|f(x) - f(y)| \le k|x - y|^\alpha$ for some positive constant k. Show that if $\alpha > 1$, then f is constant.

41. Let f be a nonnegative continuous function on $[a, b]$. Let $M = \max\{f(x) : x \in [a, b]\}$. Show that

$$\lim_{n \to \infty} \left[\int_a^b f^n(x)dx \right]^{\frac{1}{n}} = M.$$

42. For what positive values of p and q does

$$\sum_{n=2}^{\infty} (-1)^n \frac{(\ln n)^p}{n^q}$$

converge?

43. (a) Carefully define what it means to say that an infinite series $\sum_{n=1}^{\infty} a_n$ is convergent.

(b) Decide for values of x in the given intervals the following series are convergent:

    (i) $\displaystyle\sum_{n=1}^{\infty} \frac{(-1)^n x^n}{n[\log(n+1)]^2}$ $(-3 < x < 17)$,

    (ii) $\displaystyle\sum_{n=1}^{\infty} \frac{(-x)^n}{\sqrt{n}}$ $(-2 < x < 2)$.

44. Evaluate $\displaystyle\int_0^{\pi} \left\{ \int_{y^2}^{\pi} \frac{y \sin x}{x} dx \right\} dy.$
Justify your answer.

45. If $\{f_n\}$ is a sequence of continuous real-valued functions defined on $[0, 1]$ and let f be a continuous real-valued function on $[0, 1[$. If $f_n(x) \nearrow f(x)$ (i.e., $f_n(x)$ is monotone increasing to $f(x)$ as $n \to \infty$ for each $x \in [0, 1]$), prove that $f_n(x) \to f(x)$ as $n \to \infty$ uniformly on $[0, 1]$.

46. Let

$$f(x) = \begin{cases} x, & \text{if } x \text{ is irrational} \\ p \sin \frac{1}{q}, & \text{if } x = \frac{p}{q} \text{ in lowest terms.} \end{cases}$$

At what points is f continuous?

47. For $n \geq 1$, let f_n be Riemann integrable on $[a, b]$ and let $f_n \to f$ uniformly on $[a, b]$. Prove that f is Riemann integrable and that

$$\lim_{n \to \infty} \int_a^b f_n(x)dx = \int_a^b f(x)dx.$$

48. For what values of α does $\displaystyle\int_0^\infty x^\alpha \cos x^2 dx$ converge?

49. Let $f : [a, b] \to \mathbb{R}$ be continuous. Prove that

$$\max\{|f(x)| : a \leq x \leq b\}$$

exists.

50. State and prove a theorem which concludes that

$$\frac{d}{dx}\left(\sum_1^\infty f_n(x)\right) = \sum_1^\infty \frac{d}{dx} f_n(x).$$

51. (a) Find explicitly real numbers $a_0, a_1, \ldots$ such that

$$g(x) = \sum_{n=0}^\infty a_n x^n$$

is the Taylor-Maclaurin series of $\sqrt{1-x}$.
(b) Find every x for which $g(x)$ converges.
(c) On what sets does $g(x)$ converge uniformly?
(d) Repeat questions (a), (b) and (c) for $\log(1+x)$.

52. (a) Let $\{a_n\}$ be a sequence. Define

$$\liminf_{n \to \infty} a_n; \qquad \limsup_{n \to \infty} a_n.$$

(b) Consider the sequence defined by

$$a_n = \left(\sqrt{n+1} - \sqrt{n}\right) - (-1)^n\left(1 + \frac{1}{n}\right).$$

What are its $\liminf$ and its $\limsup$?
Does this sequence have a limit?   Justify.

53. Is $f(x) = \frac{1}{x}$ uniformly continuous on $(0, \infty)$?　Justify your answer.

54. Let $\{a_n\}$ be a sequence of real numbers.
    (a)　Define "a^* is a cluster point of $\{a_n\}$".
    (b)　Define $\liminf\limits_{n \to \infty} a_n$;　$\limsup\limits_{n \to \infty} a_n$.
    (c)　Show that $\liminf\limits_{n \to \infty} a_n$ is the smallest cluster point of $\{a_n\}$.
    (d)　Define

$$(i) \quad \sum_{n=1}^{\infty} a_n \text{ converges};$$

$$(ii) \quad \sum_{n=1}^{\infty} a_n \text{ converges absolutely}.$$

    (e)　Suppose $\displaystyle\sum_{n=1}^{\infty} a_n$ converges, show that

$$\limsup_{n \to \infty} |a_n|^{\frac{1}{n}} \leq 1.$$

55. Show that if the series $\displaystyle\sum_{n=0}^{\infty} a_n x^n$ converges when $x = 50$ then it converges for all x, $0 \leq x \leq 25$, and defines a uniformly continuous function in this interval.
    Can you improve the statement of the above conclusion?

Suggested Reading

1. W. Rudin　　*Principles of Mathematical Analysis;* McGraw-Hill 1976

2. J.C. Burkill and H. Burkill,　*A Second Course in Mathematical Analysis;* Cambridge University Press 2002.

3. A.F. Beardon　*Limits, a new approach to real analysis;* Springer 1997.

4. W.A. Sutherland   *Introduction to Metric and Topological Space;* Clarendon 1975.

5. A.J. White   *Real Analysis, An Introduction;* Addison-Wesley 1968.

6. C.E. Chidume   *An Introduction to Metric Spaces;* International Center for Theoretical Physics, Trieste 2006.

Index